Global Industrial Relations

Divided into two distinct, but linked, sections, *Global Industrial Relations* begins by exploring regional characteristics and variations in industrial relations systems around the globe before examining the following contemporary developments:

- international trends in unionisation
- international collective bargaining
- industrial relations conflict
- the juridification of industrial relations
- the impact of multinationals and globalisation on industrial relations.

Providing an overview of the industrial relations systems of nine regions, ranging from North America to India, and an in-depth assessment of key aspects of global industrial relations in the twenty-first century, this text breaks new ground. In bringing together contributions from leading academics in the field, it makes invaluable reading for academics, students, and practitioners alike.

Michael J. Morley is Assistant Dean (Research) and Director of the Graduate Centre of Business at the University of Limerick, Ireland.

Patrick Gunnigle is Professor of Business Studies at the University of Limerick, Ireland, where he is also Director of the Employment Relations Research Unit.

David G. Collings is a lecturer in Human Resource Management and Organisational Behaviour at the Sheffield University Management School, University of Sheffield, UK.

Routledge Global Human Resource Management Series

Edited by Randall S. Schuler, Susan E. Jackson, Paul Sparrow and Michael Poole

Routledge Global Human Resource Management is an important new series that examines human resources in its global context. This series is organised into three strands: Content and issues in global human resource management (HRM); Specific HR functions in a global context; and comparative HRM. Authored by some of the world's leading authorities on HRM, each book in the series aims to give readers comprehensive, in-depth and accessible texts that combine essential theory and best practice. Topics covered include cross-border alliances, global leadership, global legal systems, HRM in Asia, Africa and the Americas, industrial relations, and global staffing.

Managing Human Resources in Cross-border Alliances
Randall S. Schuler, Susan E. Jackson and Yadong Luo

Managing Human Resources in Africa
Edited by Ken N. Kamoche, Yaw A. Debrah, Frank M. Horwitz and Gerry Nkombo Muuka

Globalizing Human Resource Management
Paul Sparrow, Chris Brewster and Hilary Harris

Managing Human Resources in Asia-Pacific
Edited by Pawan S. Budhwar

International Human Resources Management second edition
Policy and practice for the global enterprise
Dennis R. Briscoe and Randall S. Schuler

Managing Human Resources in Latin America
An agenda for international leaders
Edited by Marta M. Elvira and Anabella Davila

Global Staffing
Edited by Hugh Scullion and David G. Collings

Managing Human Resources in the Middle East
Edited by Pawan S. Budhwar and Kamel Mellahi

Managing Human Resources in Europe
A thematic approach
Edited by Henrik Holt Larsen and Wolfgang Mayrhofer

Managing Global Legal Systems
International employment regulation and competitive advantage
Gary W. Florkowski

Global Industrial Relations
Edited by Michael J. Morley, Patrick Gunnigle and David G. Collings

Global Industrial Relations

Edited by
Michael J. Morley, Patrick Gunnigle
and David G. Collings

LONDON AND NEW YORK

First published 2006
by Routledge
2 Park Square, Milton Park, Abingdon, Oxon OX14 4RN

Simultaneously published in the USA and Canada
by Routledge
270 Madison Ave, New York, NY 10016

Routledge is an imprint of the Taylor & Francis Group

© 2006 Edited by Michael J. Morley, Patrick Gunnigle and David G. Collings

Typeset in Times New Roman and Franklin Gothic by GreenGate Publishing Services
Printed and bound in Great Britain by TJ International Ltd, Padstow, Cornwall

British Library Cataloguing in Publication Data
A catalogue record for this book is available from the British Library

Library of Congress Cataloging in Publication Data
Global industrial relations / edited by Michael J. Morley, Patrick Gunnigle and David G. Collings.
    p. cm.
    Includes bibliographical references and index.
    ISBN 0-415-32946-9 (hbk) – ISBN 0-415-32947-7 (pbk) 1. Industrial relations – Cross-cultural studies. 2. Globalization – Economic aspects. 3. Comparative industrial relations. I. Morley, Michael. II. Gunnigle, Patrick. III. Collings, David G.
HD6971.G615 2006
331–dc22

2005030214

ISBN10: 0-415-32946-9 (hbk)
ISBN10: 0-415-32947-7 (pbk)

ISBN13: 978-0-415-32946-0 (hbk)
ISBN13: 978-0-415-32947-7 (pbk)

Contents

Illustrations

Figures

Tables

Contributors

Michael J. Morley is Assistant Dean (Research) and Director of the Graduate Centre of Business at the University of Limerick. He has co-authored/edited some fifteen books including *International Human Resource Management and International Assignments*, co-edited with Noreen Heraty and David Collings (Palgrave Macmillan, 2006), *Human Resource Management in Europe: Evidence of Convergence*, co-edited with Chris Brewster and Wolfgang Mayrhofer (Butterworth–Heinemann, 2004) and *New Challenges for European Human Resource Management*, also with Brewster and Mayrhofer (Palgrave Macmillan, 2000). His refereed journal articles have appeared in international sources such as the *International Journal of Human Resource Management*, *Human Resource Management Journal*, *Industrial Relations Journal*, and *Human Resource Management Review*. He is Consulting Editor of the *Journal of Managerial Psychology* and is a member of the editorial board of several other international journals.

Patrick Gunnigle is Professor of Business Studies at the University of Limerick, where he is also Director of the Employment Relations Research Unit. A graduate of University College Dublin and Cranfield University, he has authored or co-authored fourteen books and well over one hundred refereed journal papers and book chapters. A former Fulbright Scholar and a Fellow of the Chartered Institute of Personnel and Development (FCIPD), his main research interests are in the areas of multinational corporations and human resource management (HRM), trade union membership and recognition and employer strategies in industrial relations. He previously worked as a senior executive in the Semi-State sector in Ireland and lectured for some years in the US and Zambia.

David G. Collings is a lecturer in Human Resource Management and Organisational Behaviour at the Sheffield University Management School, University of Sheffield, UK. He is also a visiting Research Fellow in the Strathclyde International Business Unit, Strathclyde Business School, Glasgow, Scotland. His research interests focus on management issues in multinational corporations with a particular focus on staffing and industrial relations issues and he has published a number of book chapters and journal articles in these areas.

Vidu Badigannavar holds an MSc and PhD in industrial relations from the London School of Economics, UK. His main research interests are in the areas of labour–management partnership, international employment relations and strategic HRM. He has published in leading journals such as the *International Journal of Human Resource Management* and the *British Journal of Industrial Relations*. Prior to joining academia, Vidu has worked as a HR professional in the IT industry and later as a policy researcher with an international trade union federation. He now works at Birmingham Business School, University of Birmingham.

Roger Blanpain is Professor at the Law School, University of Tilburg and Professor at the School of Economics of the University of Limburg. He holds a PhD from the University of Leuven, Belgium. He is a former President of the International Industrial Relations Association (1986–89) and of the International Society for Labour Law and Social Security (2000–2003). He is the Editor in Chief of the *International Encyclopaedia for Labour Law and Industrial Relations* and General Editor of the *International Encyclopaedia of Laws*.

Richard N. Block is Professor in the School of Labour and Industrial Relations at Michigan State University in the United States. He is the author of numerous journal articles, book chapters, and books on issues in labour and employment law, the relationship between law and practice and industrial relations, industrial relations and competitiveness, industrial relations and structural economic change, worker rights, and international labour standards. He is labour arbitrator and a member of the National Academy of Arbitrators. His most recent books are *Labor Standards in the United States and Canada* and *Bargaining for Competitiveness: Law, Research, and Case Studies*, both published by the W.E. Upjohn Institute for Employment Research. Professor Block received his Ph.D. in Industrial and Labor Relations from Cornell University in 1977.

Amnon Caspi is Professor of Human Resources, Industrial Relations and Management and academic head of Zefat College at Bar llan University, Israel. He holds a PhD from Michigan State University in the USA. He is active in both academia and industry, as a consultant, manager and director, in Israel and internationally. He is the author of numerous books and articles in both academic and professional publications.

William N. Cooke is a Professor and Director of the Douglas A. Fraser Center for Workplace Issues at Wayne State University in Detroit, USA. He is also Director of the Labor–Management Relations Center in the Executive Education Center at the University of Michigan. Listed in *Who's Who in Economics, 1999–2000* (Elgar Pub., 2003), Bill has published widely on the global investment and labor relations strategies of multinationals and on transnational activities of unions. He is editor of *Multinational Companies and Global Human Resource Strategies* (Greenwood Pub., 2003).

Alex Covarrubias earned a PhD degree from the New York School of Industrial and Labor Relations at Cornell University, USA. He is a researcher of the College of Sonora in Northern Mexico and chair of the Research Center in Advanced Engineering. He has published extensively on flexible production systems and labour relations issues in Mexico and Brazil. His current research focuses on the Latin American auto-industry and the labour and political culture of qualified workers.

Anamaria M. Cristescu-Martin holds an MSc in Mechanical Engineering and an MBA from Strathclyde Graduate Business School, UK. She works freelance.

Keith D. Ewing is Professor of Public Law at King's College London, UK. He has previously held academic posts at Edinburgh and Cambridge Universities and has also held a number of visiting appointments in Australia and Canada. His current research interests are in labour law and constitutional reform, with special reference to the relationship between social rights and constitutional law.

Benjamin Fraser (BA, RMIT; LLB, La Trobe) is an Associate Lecturer in Human Resource Management and Employee Relations at La Trobe University, Melbourne, Australia. His professional background includes the practice of industrial relations law at both corporate and consulting levels.

Carola Frege is Reader in Industrial Relations at the London School of Economics. She has published widely on comparative industrial relations with a focus on industrial democracy and in particular has examined transformations of workers institutions such as trade unions and works councils in various countries.

Colin Gill is University Senior Lecturer in Industrial Relations in the Institute for Manufacturing, University of Cambridge, UK. He has published numerous articles on industrial relations issues in the European Union. He is a former Editor of the journal *New Technology, Work and Employment* and a former Consultant Editor of the *European Industrial Relations Observatory*. He was awarded the Shingo Prize for research excellence in lean manufacturing in 2004 along with two of his colleagues for their research work on lean manufacturing and job stress.

Raymond Harbridge (LLD Victoria) is the Dean of the Faculty of Law and Management at La Trobe University, Melbourne, Australia. He has written extensively about labour market reform, union membership and collective bargaining in New Zealand and Australia.

Frank M. Horwitz is Director/Dean and Professor in Business Administration, at the Graduate School of Business, University of Cape Town, South Africa, specialising in human resource management and industrial relations. He obtained his PhD from the University of the Witwatersrand. He has been visiting Professor at the Rotterdam School of Management (RSM) Erasmus University in the Netherlands and Nanyang Business School in Singapore. He has authored and co-authored four books including *Managing Human Resources in Africa* (Routledge), *Employment Equity and Affirmative Action: An International Comparison* (M. E. Sharpe). He has over ninety refereed articles in journals such as *Human Resource Management*, the *International Journal of Human Resource Management (IJHRM)*, *International Journal of Manpower and Industrial Relations Journal (IRJ)*. He is on the editorial boards of the *IJHRM*, and other leading international journals.

Ruth Kastiel holds an MA in labour studies from Tel-Aviv University in Israel. She is currently the industrial relations course co-ordinator at the Department of Management and Economics at the Open University of Israel. She has published a number of articles on Israeli industrial relations and is a member of a number of professional and academic associations there.

Dong-One Kim is Professor of employment relations at Korea University, Seoul, Korea. He holds a PhD degree from the University of Wisconsin-Madison. His research interests include high performance work organisations, workplace innovations, and Asian industrial relations. He authored two books in English, *Gainsharing and Goalsharing* and *Employment Relations and HRM in South Korea*. He has also published dozens of research articles in academic journals such as the *Industrial and Labor Relations Review*, *Industrial Relations*, and *European Sociological Review*.

Héctor Lucena earned a PhD from Glasgow University, 1986. He is Head of the Doctoral Programme on Social Sciences, Labour Studies, at the University of Carabobo, Valencia, Venezuela. He has published extensively on Labour Relations and Work Organisation in Venezuela and other Latin American countries. His current research focuses on labour policies, workers' participation and new labour regulatory framework.

Roderick Martin is Professor of Management at the Central European University Business School, Budapest. Until 2006 he was Professor of Organisational Behaviour at the University of Southampton, Visiting Research Associate at Templeton College, University of Oxford, UK, and Visiting Academic at Griffith University and Monash University, in Australia. He has authored 10 books in business management, organisational behaviour, industrial relations and industrial sociology, including *Transforming Management in Central and Eastern Europe* (Oxford University Press, 1999), *Bargaining Power* (Oxford University Press, 1992, 2002) and *New Technology and Industrial Relations in Fleet Street* (Oxford University Press, 1981), and has published over 60 research papers in international journals. He is particularly interested in comparative research involving Central and Eastern Europe (CEE), and he was responsible for developing the large-scale

East–West Research Initiative – a pioneering programme that involved several then-budding CEE researchers, financed by the Economic and Social Research Council (ESRC) between 1988 and 1995. His current research, *The Effects of Financial Institutions and Investor Behaviour on Management Practice*, was funded by the Department of Trade and Industry (DTI), UK, and is part of his continuing interest in the sociological and comparative approach to organisational behaviour as a counterweight to the economic rational choice models dominating organisational studies, especially in the USA. Oxford University Press will publish the book in 2007.

Michelle O'Sullivan is a lecturer in industrial relations in the Department of Personnel and Employment Relations at the University of Limerick, Ireland. She is a graduate of the B.A. (Public Administration) and the PhD programme at the university and is a former Government of Ireland Research Scholar. Her research interests include institutional protection for workers, migrant labour and collective labour law.

Jacques Rojot is Professor of Management and Industrial Relations, Director of the Doctoral Programme and Co-Director of the CIFFOP Centre at the University of Paris 2. He has served, or is presently serving as, a consultant to the OECD, the European Union and the Foundation for the Improvement of Living and Working Conditions of the European Union in Dublin as well as to several corporations and is a scientific adviser to the French Institute of the Enterprise and the French Ministry of Research. He has published widely in French and foreign journals, is the French foreign correspondent of the US National Academy of Arbitrators, has been a visiting Professor in several universities internationally, sits on the editorial boards of academic journals and the management board of professional societies, nationally and internationally, is the Editor of the *Revue de Gestion des Ressources Humaines* (Paris).

Joseph Wallace is a Senior Lecturer in Industrial Relations and Head of the Department of Personnel and Employment Relations at the University of Limerick, Ireland. He teaches Irish and comparative industrial relations and has taught European Industrial Relations at Michigan State University, USA, as a visiting professor. His research interests include collective bargaining and flexibility, strikes and industrial disputes, employment protection, and employment pacts. He is co-author of the main Irish textbook *Industrial Relations in Ireland* (2004) published by Gill & Macmillan.

Pat Walsh is now the Vice-Chancellor of Victoria University of Wellington, New Zealand. In a former life he was Professor of Industrial Relations and Human Resource Management and Director of the Industrial Relations Centre, also at Victoria University. He has published widely on union and employer strategies, collective bargaining and public sector employment relations.

Foreword

Global Human Resource Management is a series of books edited and authored by some of the best and most well-known researchers in the field of human resource management. This series is aimed at offering students and practitioners accessible, co-ordinated and comprehensive books in global HRM. To be used individually or together, these books cover the main bases of comparative and international HRM. Taking an expert look at an increasingly important and complex area of global business, this is a groundbreaking new series that answers a real need for serious textbooks on global HRM.

Several books in this series, **Global Human Resource Management**, are devoted to human resource management policies and practices in multi-national enterprises. For example, some books focus on specific areas of global HRM policies and practices, such as global leadership development, global staffing and global labour relations. Other books address special topics that arise in multinational enterprises across the globe, such as managing HR in cross-border alliances, developing strategies and structures, and managing legal systems for multi-national enterprises. In addition to books on various HRM topics in multi-national enterprises, several other books in the series adopt a global and within region comparative approach to understanding global human resource management. These books on comparative human resource management can adopt two major approaches. One approach is to describe the HRM policies and practices found at the local level in selected countries in several regions of the world. This approach utilises a common framework that makes it easier for the reader to systematically understand the rationale for the existence of various human resource management activities in different countries and easier to compare these activities across countries within a region. The second approach is to describe the HRM issues and topics that are most relevant to the companies in the countries of the region.

This book, *Global Industrial Relations*, edited by Michael J. Morley, Patrick Gunnigle and David G. Collings, combines both approaches. The editors do an excellent job of previewing their entire book in the introduction and setting the stage for the fifteen chapters. In the first part of their book they have outstanding national experts contributing chapters that describe industrial relations systems in specific countries and/or regions of the world. These chapters cover similar topics and issues and thus offer the reader the ability to make cross-regional and cross-country comparisons and contrasts in industrial relations systems. In the second part of their book, there are several chapters by outstanding experts in various topics of industrial relations that cross country and regional lines. These chapters cover topics ranging from international trends in unionism to multinationals, globalisation and industrial relations.

This Routledge series, **Global Human Resource Management**, is intended to serve the growing market of global scholars and professionals who are seeking a deeper and broader understanding of the role and importance of human resource management in companies as they operate throughout the world. With this in mind, all books in the series provide a thorough review of existing research and numerous examples of companies around the world. Mini-company stories and examples are found throughout the chapters. In addition, many of the books in the series include at least one detailed case description that serves as convenient practical illustrations of topics discussed in the book.

Because a significant number of scholars and professionals throughout the world are involved in researching and practising the topics examined in this series of books, the authorship of the books and the experiences of companies cited in the books reflect a vast global representation. The authors in the series bring with them exceptional knowledge of the human resource management topics they address, and in many cases the authors have been the pioneers for their topics. So we feel fortunate to have the involvement of such a distinguished group of academics in this series.

The publisher and editor have also played a major role in making this series possible. Routledge has provided its global production, marketing and reputation to make this series feasible and affordable to academics and practitioners throughout the world. In addition, Routledge has provided its own highly qualified professionals to make this series a reality. In particular we want to indicate our deep appreciation for the work of our series editor, Francesca Heslop. She has been very supportive of the series from the very beginning and has been invaluable in providing the needed support and encouragement to us and to the many authors in the series. She, along with her staff including Emma Joyes, Victoria Lincoln, Jacqueline Curthoys, Lindsie Court, and Adam Gilbert, have helped make the process of completing this series an enjoyable one. For everything they have done, we thank them all.

Randall S. Schuler, *Rutgers University and GSBA Zurich*

Paul Sparrow, *Manchester University*

Susan E. Jackson, *Rutgers University and GSBA Zurich*

Michael Poole, *Cardiff University*

Introduction

**MICHAEL J. MORLEY, PATRICK GUNNIGLE AND
DAVID G. COLLINGS**

Introduction

While on the one hand, scholars are drawing attention to the diminishing popularity of industrial relations as an academic subject, on the other one cannot but be struck by the on-going prevalence afforded labour management issues in public discourse and contemporary social science literature, with discussions on the current nature of the employment relationship appearing almost omnipresent as a consequence of the reach of globalisation (Cooke 2003; Hanami 2002; Jacoby 1995; Locke *et al.* 1995; Belanger *et al.* 1994). As D'Art and Turner (2002: 1) note in their introduction to their volume on *Industrial Relations in the New Economy*:

> ... the idea that the global economy is on the eve of, or actually engaged in, a process of fundamental and radical change is pervasive. All areas of social, economic and political life are expected to undergo a revolutionary transformation constituting a total break with the old order.

Against this backdrop of an increasing pace of internationalisation and the changing forms of globalisation, there is growing support for the argument that many relevant insights into organisation processes and systems in a global era will come from studying it in an international and comparative context (Brewster *et al.* 2004; Evans *et al.* 2002; Strauss 1998; Poole 1993). Budhwar and Sparrow (2002) suggest that the increased level of globalisation and internationalisation of business, the growth of new markets (such as in Eastern Europe, China, India, South East Asia, and Latin America), growth of new international business blocks and an increased level of competition among firms at both national and international level have resulted in an increase in comparative studies. Similarly Morley and Collings (2004) point to an increasing interest in international and comparative studies in a broadening range of countries. This, they suggest, can be explained in part by the changing contours of foreign direct investment (FDI) location decisions in the global economy. While traditionally FDI flows have been concentrated in developed countries, recent years have heralded a shift in investment locations toward new destinations such as the new European Union member countries, particularly in Central and Eastern European (CEE), along with countries such as India and China, all of which have been identified as 'hot spots' for inward FDI in the period 2004-2007 by the UNCTAD (2004) (see also Lane 2000).

Specifically within the industrial relations domain, Frege (2005: 179) notes that 'industrial relations research faces various pressures of internationalisation' not least as a consequence of global economic forces which increasingly shape the subject of the discipline, though her analysis of journal publications reveals that while there is a growing internationalisation, much industrial relations research 'continues to be strongly embedded in nationally specific research traditions and cultures'. This book advances a comparative and international industrial relations analysis in order to explore both regional variations and contemporary international industrial relations developments. Taking global regional blocks as a unit of analysis, a point which we return to later in this introduction, the chapters in Part I explore regional variations in industrial relations systems and practices. Through unearthing historical developments and contextual exigencies, the chapters draw attention to commonalities and contrasts in evidence in the regions explored. In addition, this analysis also points to elements of continuity and change in evidence in the contemporary landscape of industrial relations in these regions, primarily as a result of historical, cultural, political, economic and social processes. Part II focuses on current developments and explores five key themes of ongoing significance in international industrial relations, namely international trends in unionisation, international labour standards, international collective bargaining, international strike trends, the juridification of industrial relations and the influence of multinationals on industrial relations.

In this introductory section, following some perfunctory remarks on the context for change in industrial relations, we turn to the convergence and divergence debate which has been a significant strand of the international and comparative literature for decades. Convergence arguments suggest that while differences in management systems have arisen as a result of the geographical isolation of businesses, the consequent development of differing beliefs and value orientations of national cultures are being superseded by the logic of technology and markets which require the adoption of universally applicable policies, approaches and management techniques (Gooderham *et al.* 2004). By contrast, proponents of the divergence thesis argue that industrial relations systems, far from being economically or technologically derived, reflect national institutional contexts which do not respond readily to the imperatives of technology or the market. Thus, for instance, Guest and Hoque (1996: 50) note that 'even in an increasingly global economy, we find persistent variations in the approaches to the management of human resources'. Following this debate, we highlight the value of a regional perspective and set out the rationale for the approach adopted. Finally we summarily outline the contributions to the book.

The context for change in industrial relations

Traditional definitions of industrial relations stress the rules governing the employment relationship in the workplace as the core focus of the subject. Dunlop (1958), for example, defines industrial relations as the study of employment rules and their variation over time. This definition set a broad and integrated agenda for the study of industrial relations which dominated industrial relations research for several decades and, most notably, offered a particular base for comparative studies (Shalev 1980). According to Dunlop, management, unions and government agencies establish a network of rules to govern the workplace and the work community. This network consists of procedures for establishing the rules along with procedures for determining their application to particular situations. In a unionised environment, collective bargaining between trade unions and management is a recognised procedure for establishing rules governing the employment relationship, and the resulting collective agreement establishes the application of the rules to particular situations. Substantive rules are the output from the collective bargaining process, ones which Dunlop divided into three categories: the rules governing compensation in all its forms; the duties and performance expected from workers; and those rules defining the rights and duties of workers regarding promotions, lay-offs and the deployment of workers to particular positions or jobs (Turner and Morley 1995).

Since substantive rules are viewed as a function of the procedural process, Dunlop (1958: 13) argues that the establishment of procedures is the 'centre of attention in an industrial relations system'. The central task of industrial relations scholars, therefore, was to explain why a particular set of rules were established and how these rules were administered. The actual content of these rules varies across firms and industries as a consequence chiefly of their market and technological contexts.

Over time, the rules alter as a result of changes in the external environment in areas such as the business cycle, technology, the distribution of power in the wider society, employer–labour strategies, and government agencies. In short, the study of industrial relations is concerned with who makes the rules governing worker–management relations in the workplace, the nature of those rules, and how they are administered and regulated. Variations in how the rules are made – who makes them and the content of the rules – is deemed to be a central concern of industrial relations scholars in distinguishing different approaches between firms, industries and national industrial relations systems. This emphasis on rule-making as the central feature of industrial relations represents one of the most distinctive and enduring features of industrial relations research and debate. It finds expression in Flanders' (1965: 4) definition of industrial relations as 'a study of the institutions of job regulation'. While various criticisms have been levelled at Flander's definition, the essential focus remains the making and administering of the rules that regulate the employment relationship. Turner and Morely (1995) argue that the various workplace industrial relations surveys, a significant body of research conducted in Britain and elsewhere, reflect this conventional focus on procedural and substantive workplace rules (Turner and Morley 1995).

As a result of the emphasis on the procedural nature of industrial relations and, to a lesser extent, substantive outputs, little attention has been directed at the actual process of industrial relations, that is, the nature of the relationship between the parties to the labour process as a result of the rule-making activities. As Roche (1986) observed, Dunlop's system is geared literally to the study of rules alone and ignores or overlooks other social processes in an organisation, such as the balance of power between the unions and management, the issue of control in the workplace, and the levels of trust between the parties. A cogent and long-standing criticism of this approach, in particular the emphasis on procedural rules, is that it is more concerned with a descriptive approach in explaining how unions and management work within given rules and institutions than with seeking to explain why employment relations develop as they do (Margerison 1969; Briges and Villemez 1994). Such descriptive analysis, notes Marsh (1969: 261), is now 'not the most highly praised academic technique, though it was that used by the Webbs (Webb and Webb 1897) whose Industrial Democracy became such a landmark in the industrial relations field'.

Economic developments, especially since the 1970s, provide an important context for understanding the contemporary nature of industrial relations (Turner and Morley 1995). First, macroeconomic forces that determine wage and price changes are increasingly affected by expanding global competition in product markets; second, the structure of financial markets – the market for corporate control and access to capital – is increasingly emphasising short term returns to capital over long term development, particularly in the US and the UK (Lazonick and O'Sullivan 2000), but now spreading even to countries like Germany, which have different ownership patterns (O'Sullivan 2003); finally, technological change, primarily production function influences, has changed the optimum scale and nature of production (Mitchell and Saidi 1991). The interrelationship between technological developments and increased competition is viewed by some academic commentators as rendering traditional mass production systems and their supporting institutions redundant (Piore and Sabel 1984; Marshall 1992) – though it is worth pointing out that there are instances where they survive substantially unchanged. Although changes in technology such as the development of information technology and robotics generally provided the possibility of new ways of working, Marshall (1992) argues that it was competition which made new arrangements essential for the economic survival of firms. Along with the twin forces of competition and technology (and partly as a result), consumer demand for high quality customised products increased, fragmenting the traditional mass markets for standardised products. While the standardised mass production system was production driven, the competitive environment is largely consumer driven. The altered economic conditions of recent decades, Marshall claims, did not just change the magnitude of the requirements for economic success but also altered the necessary structures and policies. These new structures and policies centred on developing three key factors at firm level: product quality, productivity and labour flexibility.

These developments heralded a new industrial revolution and a major restructuring of capitalism. The economic viability of firms depends on their ability to restructure to withstand increased global competition and the fragmentation of mass markets. Piore and Sabel (1984) noted that in the 1970s and 1980s both firms and national economies that were capable of offering more diverse and customised products generally fared better than more traditional producers of standardised mass products. Firms that are flexible enough to engage in small-batch or customised production can command higher profit margins and are less vulnerable in their market position. Alternatively, traditional producers of standardised mass products faced greater competition from low cost economies in developing countries particularly in the area of labour costs. Labour intensive industries are especially vulnerable to this type of competition. Significantly, the arguments set out here on pressures for change should not be confined to the (shrinking) production sector. Very similar developments can be adduced in the service sector too while pressures on the public sector are forcing substantial change there. As Ackers and Wilkinson (2003: 3) note there is a need to:

> … grapple with the new changes surrounding the contemporary employment relationship, especially the dramatic changes in the character of the labour force from male, unionised manufacturing to female, non-union services.

Convergence, divergence and international industrial relations

Against the backdrop of the changes outlined above, one of the most significant issues in comparative and international industrial relations studies relates to patterns of convergence or ongoing and enduring divergence evident from this line of enquiry. Referred to as the interrelation of the global with the local (Beukema and Carrillo 2004), this is a substantial if rather dichotomous debate with many contributors suggesting that the national context, and the institutionalisation that flows from it, is all important while others contend that labour management practices are less subject to the constraints of context. Commonly framed as the 'convergence' versus 'divergence' debate, this has been an ongoing strand of the literature for several decades. Gooderham *et al.* (2004), in particular, draw attention to the fact that early post-war thinking was, for the most part convergent. They cite Galbraith who contended that, given the decision to have modern industry, modern man's 'area of decision is, in fact, exceedingly small' (1967: 336). Much of what happens is inevitable and the same so that 'the imperatives of organisation, technology and planning operate similarly, and as we have seen, to a broadly similar result, on all societies' (1967: 336).

In a similar vein Kerr *et al.* in the 1960s argued that there was a logic to industrialism which would lead to greater convergence, with, in particular, technological and economic forces bringing about greater similarities in industrial relations systems and it is to Clark Kerr and his colleagues that Poole (1993) attributes the first 'general theory of international industrial relations'. This debate on the transformation of the industrial relations systems of different countries in response to the internationalisation of markets, technological innovations and increased workforce diversity has been the focus of much research in industrial relations in the last decade (Locke *et al.*1995). However, an issue of considerable debate is the fact that the response to these pressures is not the same in every country. Rather, according to Locke *et al.* (1995: 158) 'employment relations are shaped in systematic and predictable ways by institutions which filter these external pressures and the strategies of the key actors. Patterns of adjustment in countries that have a history of strong centralised industrial relations institutions tend to follow an incremental, negotiated pattern and aim to achieve results that balance the interests of different social groups and economics interests'. In other countries, they argue that the 'adjustment has tended to be unilateral with unions and their traditional institutional supports and political allies put on the defensive'. As Poole suggests:

> The search to resolve or to accommodate conflicts which arise in the conduct of work and in the distribution of the fruits of labour is universal. But varied strategic choices set within heterogeneous cultures and ideologies, political and economic conditions, industrial relations institutions and power distributions have occasioned a rich array of global outcomes.
>
> (Poole 1986: 3)

It is clear that the last decade witnessed large scale change in the social, political, legal and economic climate of many countries, resulting in changes in the nature of the relationship between governments, employers and trade unions and while the consensus emerging from the analysis of the possible ramifications for industrial relations appears to suggest that there is something new in industrial relations, there continues to be considerable disagreement over the nature and extent of the current transformation. Thus in Europe, as in the United States, the 1980s saw major challenges to the established institutions of industrial relations (Hyman 1994). The social and economic environment became increasingly hostile to unionism and to many traditional union practices and policies (Blanchflower and Freeman 1992) and many of the gains made by the labour movement were reversed in the 1980s (Baglioni 1990). It has been argued that that there has been an explosive divergence in industrial relations with different strands of development moving away from each other in different directions, rather than an implosive convergence towards one central best practice (Streeck 1988). Other commentaries have focused on the increased adoption of Human Resource Management (HRM) approaches which, following US usage, are seen as anti-union (Hegewisch *et al.* 1997). Gooderham *et al.* refer to the emergence of US HRM as a new model of management, less compatible with unionisation than the old and purposefully designed to remove the rigidities intrinsic in the mass production system and lay the ground for the use of more flexible production techniques. They suggest that:

> In short, the emergence of US HRM may be viewed as an attempt by US firms to cope with the disappearance of large and stable markets by moving beyond mass standardised production to flexible production by synthesising the elements required for co-operation and self-regulation. At the same time US HRM is attempting to counteract the inheritance of a lack of trust and co-operation between workers and managers, and the effects of short-term systems of cost-benefit calculation.
>
> (2004: 20)

Since the term emerged in the mid-1980s, the HRM label has become the most influential term referring to the activities of management in the employment relationship (Boxall and Purcell 2003). Writing his Guest Editorial to his special issue of *Human Resource Management Review* on 'What Can HR Learn from IR?', Kaufman in a call for greater dialogue and cross-fertilisation of ideas among scholars in both the IR and HR fields notes that:

> It is my strong impression that researchers in HR and IR are too often like the proverbial ships passing in the night – sailing much the same seas but unaware of each other's presence – and that the advancement of knowledge would be materially promoted by greater interaction among people in the two fields.
>
> (2001: 338)

However, in the broader literature the distinction between the fields of study of HRM and industrial relations has been heightened, primarily because of their perceived incompatibility. The focus of HRM on managerial capacity and prerogative and on the establishment of individual relations at the expense of conventional collectivism, along with its general unwillingness to acknowledge the existence of distinct interests within the workplace, has created a picture of simple common interest among managers and the managed, an interest supposedly centred solely on the organisation's success in the marketplace (Blyton and Turnbull 1993; Storey and Sisson 1993). There is an assumption in much of the literature that HRM policies are in some way linked to attempts to replace traditional collective industrial relations bargaining over work issues and to diminishing opportunities for trade unions to exercise their functions. This is the conclusion of Storey's (1992) broad study of the impact of HRM in the UK; and of Kochan *et al.* (1986) and Fiorito *et al.* (1987) in the US. A leading British trade union official writes of 'the experience of many unionists that human resource management is associated with derecognition and a systematic attempt to undermine the union role' (Monks 1994: 45).

The changes alluded to above that have occurred internationally have had the effect of reactivating the debate about convergence. Described as an old debate (Locke *et al.* 1995: 159), it argues that the effects of increasing internationalisation in general, will eventually give rise to an increasing similarity of industrial relations. At organisation level this manifests itself in 'a common logic of industrialism' or a common set of management requirements which are resulting in a convergence of managerial techniques, regardless of cultural or national differences (McGaughey and DeCieri 1999). The logic of this argument is that the impact of national origin on management practices will progressively decline as globalisation leads to the adoption of more generic, standardised practices. Due *et al.* (1991: 88) suggest that it is reasonable to postulate the existence of trends towards convergence, especially in European industrial relations and in the industrial systems prevailing in the individual member states, primarily because there are 'new' actors in European industrial relations: 'Actors have arrived who, via their actions and status, consciously strive to create convergence in industrial relations across the boundaries of member states ... we now have actors who, far from being intent solely on promoting national interests, act solely on the basis of supranational considerations. ... an actor oriented analysis which pays due attention to EC co-operation will inevitably concentrate on convergence trends deriving from the supranational character of the actors.' This convergence, they argue will emerge in parallel to the convergence trends implicit in technology transfer, market developments and other forms of co-operation.

Divergence theorists, however, refuse to subscribe to this notion of convergence. They argue, on the contrary, that national, and in some cases regional, institutional contexts are slow to change, partly because they derive from deep-seated beliefs and value systems and partly because significant redistributions of power are involved (Gooderham *et al.* 2004). In illuminating the debate on the continuing divergence of cross-national practices, we can point to a number of significant studies. For instance, Gunnigle *et al.*'s (2002) study found a clear variation between HRM practice in firms of different national origin (see also Gooderham *et al.* 1998). In a similar vein Harzing and Sorge (2003) found that while internationalisation strategy was more closely related to industry and size than other variables, the country of origin of firms was significant in explaining differences in control mechanisms utilised by firms. Thus there was continued divergence in control mechanisms utilised in firms of different national origin and they argue that on balance divergence remains in place. Geppert and his colleagues also pointed to differences in the change management strategies pursued by organisations of different nationalities (Geppert *et al.* 2003). Thus, on balance, the literature suggests that many practices continue to be characterised by diversity across national borders (Brewster *et al.* 2004; Harzing and Sorge 2003) and despite some shifts that have occurred, it is widely recognised that industrial relations differs significantly from country to country and that the extent and nature of change varies considerably. A variety of reasons have been advanced for the differences that exist: referring to country size (Poole 1986); cultural factors (Hofstede 2001); economic concentration (Stephans 1990) or directly to political factors (Przeworski and Spague 1986). More recently the emerging 'varieties of capitalism' (Hall and Soskice 2002) or 'national business systems' (Whitley 1999) literatures have in a coherent way pointed to the significance of the institutions of the business systems within which firms are established in explaining divergence between firms of different nationalities. Excellent papers by Visser (1992) and Bean and Holden (1992) have tested levels of unionisation as one variable in industrial relations and found that full explanation requires attention to an extensive complex of factors. Visser found that although union membership is subject to variation, countries tend not to change relative to one another, so that the rank ordering of countries' membership levels tend to stay the same. Brewster *et al.* (1994: 6) point to the fact that industrial relations is contextually bound, existing within a cultural, social, structural and most importantly of all, a political web. Or, as one assessment put it, 'critical variables such as culture, ideology and the degree of centralisation of collective bargaining institutions restrict the responses of individual actors to similar changes in their external environments' (Locke *et al.* 1995: 139).

The value of a regional perspective

Organisations are socially embedded in their external environment and affected by external forces that require them to adapt their structures and behaviours to deal with these forces (Berger and Luckmann 1967). Briges and Villemez (1994) argue that because employment in many societies typically involves the establishment of a social tie between an individual and an organisation, the form this relationship takes is unavoidably influenced by the organisational context in which it occurs, while Jackson and Schuler (1995) draw attention to the available empirical evidence which shows the likely impact of variations in prevailing environmental conditions on the approaches adopted by the organisation. In international and comparative studies which have strong tradition in the field of industrial relations (Whitfield *et al.* 1999), 'regionality is an important contexualising variable … which enriches the study of employment relationships by situating the relationship in a complex external environment which shapes that relationship' (Fastenau and Pullin 1996). An important question in the context of the current volume is: what is the value of an analysis based on global regions? 'Diversity, rather than uniformity', notes Poole (1986: 3), 'characterises the industrial relations of nations and the central thrust of the approach is to assess the impact of a number of environmental conditions on divergencies in industrial relations phenomena amongst countries.' Several highly regarded volumes already exist on comparative employment relations focused on understanding in what ways and why practices differ across countries. Rather than seeking to replicate that effort once again, we have on this occasion chosen to focus on regional blocks. While undoubtedly this has resulted in the trading off of a large amount of depth for breadth, with the consequence that certain details on industrial relations systems and their implications are not addressed, it has occasioned the inclusion of countries in our analysis that often rarely receive a mention in the landscape of comparative and international industrial relations. Such a focus, Strauss (1998: 273) suggests, is important in order that we might eschew our ethnocentric tendencies and begin to acquaint industrial relations scholars with developments 'in parts of the world normally ignored'.

Strauss also draws attention to the important distinction between 'splitters', who focus on explaining differences among countries, and 'lumpers', who concern themselves with discovering similarities. In light of the level of analysis pursued in the chapters in Part I of the book, we as an editorial team might be viewed as the ultimate lumpers, naively assuming that there is some type of coherence and integrity in regional types, where in many instances none exists. We prefer to see it more as a modest attempt to broaden the international and comparative industrial relations dialogue and do so in a way that gives local authors the opportunity to give expression to traditions and transitions in industrial relations systems and issues that they regard as important for the international reader.

Part I: Regional Variations in Industrial Relations

Part I on regional variations in industrial relations is truncated into nine chapters.

In chapter 1 Richard Block tackles the industrial relations system in the United States and Canada. Characterising them as 'siblings', he draws attention to some of the commonalities in origin, along with some of the core differences that now characterise the industrial relations landscape of these neighbouring countries. Adopting a systems perspective, he describes the main actors – the state, unions and employers, the nature and extent of collective bargaining coverage and patterns of industrial conflict in the countries. The National Labor Relations Act 1935 as the root source of legislative provision is discussed and the basic tenets of the approach, namely employee choice, majoritarianism, decentralisation, exclusive representation, bargaining power, written legally enforceable collective agreements and administration by a specialist agency, are each examined. Block sets out the organising structure of the US and Canadian union movements and outlines the roles attributed to each level in this structure. He then turns to collective bargaining in both countries, drawing attention to definitional aspects and variations between the countries on what the parties are obligated to bargain on. Finally, he explores the meaning and content of industrial conflict and highlights the downward trend in strikes in both countries since the 1980s.

Against the backdrop of diverse economic, political and socio-cultural processes, Héctor Lucena and Alex Covarrubias in Chapter 2 focus on industrial relations in Latin America. Exploring the more developed countries in the region, the authors note that there has been an evolution in the industrial relations landscape of the region since the abandonment of import substitution as a model of development and the pursuit of a more open neo-liberal approach. Once again the authors spend time exploring the role of the main actors, namely the state, the union movement and employers. In particular attention is drawn to the altering relationship between the state and the labour movement and the laying of the foundations for Latin American corporatism. The fortunes of the labour movement, in particular, and in common with developments around the globe, the falling density levels are set down. The role of the union movement in democratising the region is also introduced. From an industrial development perspective, the authors note the privatisation programme and its impact on collective agreements, the significance of foreign direct investment into the region, the significant casualisation of labour markets, the co-existence of different models of industrial production with varying levels of labour protection and the significance, if underlying difficulty, attached to the development of fair and appropriate economic relations between the region and the US.

In Chapter 3, Colin Gill introduces industrial relations in Western Europe. He traces several common developments that have shaped the evolution of industrial relations in this part of the globe including structural transformations bringing about the shift from manufacturing to services, the single market of the EU, its stubborn unemployment problem occasioning an increasing emphasis on 'employability' rather than workers' rights, a flexibilisation agenda in response to recession and a tilt in the balance of power between unions and management. By way of context for understanding key developments in Western Europe, Gill introduces the European preferred Social Model and its variants in evidence in different countries in the region. He explores the varying fortunes of the trade union movement in terms of membership and density. Trade union responses such as mergers, altered recruitment strategies and organising on a European wide basis rather than a national one are also set down. Varying approaches to, and extent of coverage in, collective bargaining are also touched upon. Gill then switches his attention to the emergence of human resource management in Europe arguing that it has taken, of necessity, a different more 'social democratic' form in Europe than in the US. The evident tension between the drive towards increased individualism inherent in HRM and the necessity for 'partnership' as a central plank of the European preferred approach is highlighted. Europe's experiments with employee participation, both indirect and direct, are also explored. Finally, Gill turns his attention to discussing the influence of the European Union on the industrial relations landscape of Western Europe.

Chapter 4 moves to examine developments in industrial relations in Central and Eastern Europe. Here Roderick Martin and Anamaria Cristescu-Martin concentrate on developments in the seven countries of Bulgaria, Czech Republic, Hungary, Poland, Romania, Slovakia and Slovenia since 1989. They note that while the institutional uniformity in the period between the end of the Second World War and 1989 disappeared, the institutional provision remained broadly similar. The chapter focuses on the emerging industrial relations systems of these nation states in Central and Eastern Europe against a backdrop of social, political and economic transition since 1989 and more recent EU accession. The authors explore sources of industrial relations system integration – namely the state, social partnership structures, national level industrial relations institutions and shared core values – arguing that the level of integration both within the industrial relations system and between the system and its environment is low. This, they suggest, is particularly the case in the countries of Central and Eastern Europe where the pressures for coherence and integration are weak. The result, the authors postulate, is the emergence of segmented industrial relations in Central and Eastern Europe. Four distinct segments (The State Budget Segment, the Newly Privatised Production Segment derived from the previously owned State production sector, the *ab initio* indigenous Private Sector that has developed since the transition and the multinational sector) are unearthed and the authors provide a nuanced account of the distinct industrial relations dynamic that characterises each of the segments.

Chapter 5 focuses on industrial relations in the Middle East. Here again fairly self-evident hard choices had to be made by the authors about what could and should usefully be covered in order to inform the international reader. Using an analytical framework known as the 'Open and Dynamic Model of Industrial Relations', Amnon Caspi and Ruth Kastiel focus on exploring industrial relations in Jordon, Turkey, Saudi Arabia, Syria and Egypt; the choice of countries being occasioned by, among other things, the availability of data. In advance of a country-by-country summative account of industrial relations, the authors outline the elements of the analytical framework employed in the chapter, including the components of the internal and external environments and the outputs of the industrial relations system, suggesting that, in particular, the analysis points to how the government's involvement in the labour market influences the parties to the industrial relations process and their capacity to achieve their goals in the employment relationship.

In Chapter 6, we turn to industrial relations in Australia and New Zealand. Here, Raymond Harbridge, Benjamin Fraser and Pat Walsh provide an account of historical developments, along with more contemporaneous shifts, most notably the move away from the system of compulsory state arbitration, which have dramatically altered the nature of industrial relations in both countries. They explore the key elements that have allowed significant political and economic realities in the 1980s and 1990s to dramatically alter the nature of the industrial relations in both countries. The historical foundations of the industrial relations regimes in both countries are set down and the differing constitutional and legislative provisions pertaining are discussed. In particular the specifics of constitutional provision for enshrining conciliation and arbitration provisions in the case of Australia are explored. Key institutions and key actors along with their respective roles and interactions are considered. The authors point to the recent significant drop in trade union membership in Australia, accounting for it in the context of a contraction of conventionally highly unionised sectors of the economy and an expansion in 'new' sectors with low membership rates. The Workplace Relations Act 1996 and its radical impact on bargaining across the States are discussed. The abolition of the historically established arbitration system in New Zealand is traced to a number of key recent developments including a loss of employer faith in the system as it failed to deliver industrial stability along with a general rise in individualism. The Employment Contracts Act 1991 abolished exclusive bargaining rights of registered unions and strengthened the hand of employers. Union density, membership and collective bargaining coverage fell significantly during the 1990s. The election of a Labour Government in 1999 saw the introduction of the Employment Relations Act 2000 which some viewed as an attempt to restore union legitimacy as public partners. Overall, the chapter charts key trends and developments in Australia and New Zealand in the context of each country's distinctive path from conciliation and arbitration.

Chapter 7 by Dong-One Kim focuses on industrial relations in Asia and contemporary developments that have occurred in the region as a consequence of macro-economic developments, political democratisation, changes in workforce composition and the Asian financial crisis of the late 1990s. In particular it is argued that two key drivers of industrial relations change are evident in the region, namely regime alignment between industrial relations and the new economic order and a congruence with broader political transformations. Kim selects eleven countries for the analysis presented in this chapter, partly for the pragmatic reason that data were available, but also and perhaps more importantly, because they contrast significantly in terms of levels of development. Against this backdrop, Kim develops a six-fold taxonomy. Thus, Japan is advanced as a co-operative model. Korea and Taiwan are offered as examples of economies on a transition toward pluralism. State exclusionary labour policies and union marginalisation characterise the emerging tiger economies of Malaysia, Indonesia and Thailand. Conversely, State voluntarism is seen to be evident in the Philippines and Hong Kong. Singapore, in Kim's analysis, is offered as an example of Asian corporatism, while China and Vietnam provide examples of regimes operating under Stalinist labour policies. Finally, in pointing to the divergence which characterises industrial relations in these countries, Kim also offers some commonalities which form the basis for some discussion in the chapter.

In Chapter 8, Frank Horwitz advances a comparative analysis of the historical roots of and contemporary developments in industrial relations in Africa. Again, the author made hard choices in terms of country selection for the analysis, with some countries getting rather greater depth of coverage and others being offered as examples of where particular developments have occurred. At the outset, Horwitz draws attention to the contextual uniqueness of Africa, and in particular, the ethno-cultural diversity and the substantially different development trajectories evident in different countries. On the whole, industrial relations regimes are characterised as 'new' and 'evolving'. He notes that while industrial relations in Africa are typically rooted in colonial, or in the case of South Africa, apartheid regimes, political independence has occasioned an expansion in sectors heretofore underdeveloped and resulted in an expanding legislative framework. In many countries developments must be seen against the backdrop of low levels of economic development, low productivity, stagflation and massive external debts. Horwitz notes that the role of government in African industrial relations varies from state control in formally socialist countries such as Ethiopia and Mozambique to state direction in Zambia, to more voluntaristic approaches in countries such as South Africa and Namibia. While there has been a growth in employer associations, the growth in stronger independent labour movements has been diminutive with the consequence that there is a significant need for 'institution building' across Africa to strengthen and buttress industrial relations. Comparing and contrasting developments in selected countries, Horwitz provides an abridged narrative of both the fortunes of the trade union movement and collective bargaining arrangements in operation. In the penultimate section he also offers an account of public sector industrial relations. In concluding, he identifies several diverse developments which have impacted the nature and development of industrial relations in Africa and points to the potential value of joint collaboration in the workplace as a means of generating competitiveness.

The final chapter in Part I examines industrial relations in India, against the backdrop of a dynamic economic policy focused on liberalisation, privatisation and globalisation and an evolving labour market with growing evidence of some casualisation. Vidu Badigannavar sets out the key developments leading to the liberalisation process in India and then treats the Indian institutional framework as the operational platform for industrial relations matters. He describes the dichotomy between the organised and unorganised sectors of the economy with trade unions largely being confined to the organised sector. Union density in this organised sector stands at about 18 per cent. In discussing the workings of collective bargaining in India, Badigannavar draws attention to core legislative provisions that have significantly shaped the industrial relations landscape. He also explores the patterns of industrial relations conflict in India and, in light of the trends, is somewhat less than sanguine about the likelihood of genuine partnership. Finally, he discusses the recent debate concerned with industrial relations reform in India, as a result of the deliberations of the Government appointed National Labour Commission. Here he draws attention to the central plank of the Commission's recommendations, namely the need for the development of a labour–management partnership as the preferred approach to industrial relations reform and change in India.

Part II: Contemporary Debates in International Industrial Relations

Turning from the regional comparisons presented in the first part of this volume, the second part focuses on five key contemporary themes prominent in the international and comparative industrial relations literature.

Chapter 10, by Carola Frege, focuses on International Trends in Unionisation. Without doubt the fortunes of the trade union movement internationally remain somewhat uncertain. Trade unions are declining in membership and power throughout the developed world and as Hyman (1994) notes the weakening of trade unions presents one of the central challenges for explanation in industrial relations. In an earlier contribution Frege and Kelly (2003) have argued that differences in the institutional context of industrial relations, as well as state policies and employer strategies explain some of the major differences in how national unions are responding to the socio-economic challenges facing them. In her chapter in this volume, Frege draws upon the convergence/divergence debate to explore the extent to which union decline is a universal phenomenon. She commences by outlining the difficulties inherent in measuring union density across countries. Then, drawing upon data by Visser, Frege calculates densities for 1985 and 1997. It is estimated that the current total number of union members in the world stands at about 320 million people, or a global union density figure of about 23 per cent. Frege then moves on to explore union membership and density levels in advanced industrial economies and in the transitional economies. The essence of the data leads to two core observations, namely that there is an almost universal trend of union membership decline since the 1980s and that there is no convergence of membership levels across countries. Several observations on the likely reason for these two key trends are made.

Chapter 11 focuses on international labour standards. Thompson (2003), presenting a special issue on industrial relations and global labour standards, based on five selected papers from a session on Industrial Relations and Global Labour Standards held at the 13th World Congress of the International Industrial Relations Association in Berlin, notes that when the 'idea of labour standards is examined, most people in industrial relations think of legal instruments such as those first introduced by the International Labour Organisation in the 1920s. These standards were adopted by a consensus of members of the ILO, which includes private parties, employer and labour organisations'. Broadly this system remains and Thompson argues that it has received greater attention since the transformation of economic and political systems in Europe and Africa, and the expansion of global economic activity. In this chapter, Keith Ewing commences by outlining the core functions underpinning such standards. He then examines how such standards are established and monitored by the International Labour Organisation, drawing attention to the perennial problem that while such standards are addressed mainly to governments, the real custodians of power in a globalised world are major transnational companies.

International Collective Bargaining is the subject of Chapter 12 authored by Jacques Rojot. Following an introduction centred on presenting a usable definition of collective bargaining, he notes that international collective bargaining never really took off, something which he suggests is hardly surprising given international variations in institutional provision, union participation and solidarity, cultural and linguistic barriers. Rojot moves to explore the potential parties to the international collective bargaining process discussing employer associations, multinational firms, and international labour organsiations as key nodes in the international collective bargaining network. He then moves to provide a more detailed treatise on international collective bargaining within the European Union. The past ten years are seen to be characterised by some progress in the direction of a European Social Dialogue, but developments on the European Works Council front are assessed as being relatively weak. Given the underlying looseness in the definition settled on, Rojot suggests that international collective bargaining at an EU level could be conceived of in several different ways including EU-wide global agreements between the social partners, sectoral agreements covering only one industry Europe-wide, or company level agreements for multinationals operating within Europe – each of which he explores in turn.

Accepting that international comparisons of industrial conflict are often very difficult because of different ways of collecting national data, Stokke and Thornqvist (2001) note that one of the main findings from earlier comparative studies of industrial conflict is that strike patterns are closely associated with the structure of collective bargaining and the more decentralised the bargaining system in operation, the higher the risk of strikes, both official and unofficial. Joseph Wallace and Michelle O'Sullivan in Chapter 13 tackle international contemporary strike trends. In their contribution, the authors seek to answer three key questions as follows: To what extent have strikes increased or decreased globally since 1980? Has there been a so-called 'bottoming out' effect between 1991 and 2002? And, to what extent is there evidence of a displacement of strikes to the developing world? The authors commence by juxtaposing the waxing interest in new management strategies and the waning interest in strikes as a social phenomenon. Where a literature on strikes and conflict is identified, the authors identify two common emphases: first, an analysis of the extent of the decline in strike activity; and, second, the overall suitability of strike statistics for getting a handle on levels of industrial conflict. Several methodological shortcomings with the use of comparative strike statistics are presented including missing data, variations in what is included in the count and significant differences in how the data are gathered and reported. On the matter of the first question that Wallace and O'Sullivan sought to answer, the evidence gathered points to a global decline in strikes since 1980. The authors provide an account for both developing and developed economies in this regard. With respect to the bottoming out issue, they move to explore data specifically relating to the period 1991-95 and 1990-2000. Here the data point to a rise in strike activity. In their discussion, the authors present a number of potentially important explanatory factors including the process of trade liberalisation evident since the 1970s and the decline in Keynesian demand management policies.

Chapter 14, by Roger Blanpain, turns to the issue of juridification and the role of labour law in a globalised economy. Gladstone (1997) notes that while the concept of juridification is often not universally understood, despite this there appears to be a reasonably common understanding that it refers to 'the extent to which, in the labour field, matters of interaction in the employment relationship are subjected to regulation through juridical means'. This regulation may be on both substantive and procedural matters and might include legislation, administrative regulation and court decisions. The overarching concern in this regard is the 'legal regulation of employment labour relations' (1997: 2). In this chapter, Blanpain sets the scene by exploring how the global market economy impacts the way in which labour markets function. Several key impacts, along with several prominent examples, are highlighted. He then turns to the role of international, regional and national labour law. The International Labour Organisation, the Council of Europe, the European Union, the Organisation for Economic Co-operation and Development, along with provisions in national labour law and the extent to which they point to convergence or divergence are all explored.

The final chapter by William Cooke focuses on multinational corporations (MNCs) and industrial relations. The rapid growth of internationalisation and global competition have increased the number and significance of MNCs in recent years. Thus, for example, the UNCTAD (2002: 14) estimates that there are some 65,000 transnational firms, with some 850,000 foreign affiliates, engaged in international production. Consequently, MNCs may be viewed as key drivers in the increased internationalisation of business. Indeed, Ferner and Hyman (1998: xiii) have labelled MNCs '… the dominant actors in the internationalization process'. There is long-standing evidence that foreign firms behave differently from their domestic counterparts and that foreign ownership may provide a platform for the diffusion of dominant practices. Indeed, the role of the MNC as a vehicle by which such dominant HR policies and practices may be transported across national boundaries and institutionalised within local contexts is presently one of the most significant lines of enquiry in comparative research. The issue of how MNCs manage industrial relations across borders, the influences of national business systems on this process and the implications for host country industrial relations systems have proven a fruitful line of enquiry (see, for example, Ferner and Quintanilla 2002). In his contribution to this volume Cooke commences by setting out an analytical framework which guides the subsequent analysis. He then explores the business logic underpinning foreign direct investment (FDI) by multinational enterprises and advances several key observations on patterns of FDI by regions. Following this he turns to the nub of his chapter, namely the role of industrial relations considerations when multinationals are making FDI decisions. Here he suggests that choices made will be influenced by both industrial relations ownership advantages that the firm enjoys (which it would legitimately seek to diffuse abroad depending on the cost-benefit calculation of this effort), along with industrial relations system location advantages/disadvantages associated with the host country location. Cooke provides a detailed account of the likely decision-making effort in this regard, citing several examples from the broader literature. On the matter of industrial relations system location advantages, Cooke points to the evidence which shows that the greater the union penetration in a country, the lower the FDI, noting that it is common practice for MNCs to pursue union avoidance strategies and to seek to avoid collective bargaining across subsidiaries, except where the costs of avoidance are perceived as too high. He then seeks to address the response of unions internationally to the growing power of MNCs and outlines the conditions that unions across borders would have to satisfy in order to establish and nurture sustainable partnerships, partnerships which in the current global industrial relations landscape remain relatively uncommon.

References

Ackers, P. and Wilkinson, A. (eds) (2003) *Understanding Work and Employment: Industrial Relations in Transition*. Oxford: Oxford University Press.

Bean, R. and Holden, L. (1992) 'Cross national differences in trade union membership in OECD countries', *Industrial Relations Journal*. 23(1): 52–9.

Baglioni, G. (1990) 'Industrial relations in Europe in the 1980s', in Baglioni, G. and Crouch, C. (eds) *European Industrial Relations: The Challenge of Flexibility*. London: Sage Publications.

Belanger, J., Edwards, P. and Haiven, L. (eds) (1994) *Workplace Industrial Relations and the Global Challenge*. Ithaca, NY: ILR Press.

Berger, P. and Luckmann, T. (1967) *The Social Construction of Reality*. New York: Doubleday.

Beukema, L. and Carrillo, J. (2004) 'Handling global developments, shaping local practices: the interference of the global and the local in work structuring', *Research in the Sociology of Work*. 13(1): 3–20.

Blanchflower, D. and Freeman, R. (1992) 'Unionism in the United States and other advanced OECD countries', *Industrial Relations*. 31(1).

Blyton, P. and Turnbull, P. (1993) *Dynamics of Employee Relations*. London: Macmillan.

Boxall, P. and Purcell, J. (2003) *Strategy and Human Resource Management*. Basingstoke: Palgrave Macmillan.

Brewster, C. (1994) 'HRM: The European dimension' in Storey, J. (ed.) *Human Resource Management: A Critical Text*. London: Routledge.

Brewster, C., Mayrhofer, W. and Morley, M. (2004) *Human Resource Management in Europe: Evidence of Convergence?* Oxford: Butterworth-Heinemann.

Briges, W. and Villemez (1994) *The Employment Relationship: Causes and Consequences of Modern Personnel Administration*. New York: Plenum Publishing Corporation.

Budhwar, P. and Sparrow, P. (2002) 'An integrative framework for understanding cross-national human resource management practices', *Human Resource Management Review*. 12: 377–403.

Cooke, W. (2003) 'Global human resource strategies: a framework and overview' in Cooke, W. N. (ed.) *Multinational Companies and Global Human Resource Strategies*. Wesport, Quorum Books.

D'Art, D. and Turner, T. (eds) (2002) *Irish Employment Relations in the New Economy*, Dublin: Blackhall Publishing.

Due, J., Madsen, J. and Jensen, C. (1991) 'The social dimension: convergence or diversification of industrial relations in the single European market?' *Industrial Relations Journal*. 22(2).

Dunlop, J. (1958) *Industrial Relations Systems*. New York: Holt.

Evans, P., Pucik, V. and Barsoux, J. L. (2002) *The Global Challenge: Frameworks for International Human Resource Management*. New York: McGraw Hill-Irwin.

Fastenau, M. and Pullin, L. (1996) 'Introduction: employment relations: a framework for regional research' in Pullin, L., Fastenau, M. and Mortimer, D. (eds) *Regional Employment Relations: Contemporary Research*. Sydney: University of Western Sydney.

Ferner, A. and Hyman, R. (eds) (1998) *Changing Industrial Relations in Europe, second edition*. Oxford, Blackwell.

Ferner, A. and Quintanilla, J. (2002) 'Between globalisation and capitalist variety: multinationals and the international diffusion of employment relations', *European Journal of Industrial Relations*. 8(3): 243–50.

Fiorito, J., Lowman, C. and Nelson, F. (1987) 'The impact of human resource policies on union organising', *Industrial Relations*. 26.

Flanders, A. (1965) *Industrial Relations: What's Wrong with the System?* London: Faber.

Frege, C. and Kelly, J. (2003) 'Union revitalisation strategies in comparative perspective', *European Journal of Industrial Relations*. 9(1): 7–24.

Frege, C. (2005) 'Varieties of industrial relations research: take-over, convergence or divergence?' *British Journal of Industrial Relations*. 43(2): 179–207.

Galbraith, J. (1967) *The New Industrial State*. London: Hamish Hamilton.

Geppert, M., Matten, D. And Williams, K. (2003) 'Change management in MNCs: how global convergence intertwines with national diversity', *Human Relations*. 56(7): 807–38.

Gladstone, A. (1997) 'Legal perspectives: the juridification of the employment relationship' in Meehan, F. (ed.) *Legal Perspectives: The Juridification of the Employment Relationship*. Dublin: Oak Tree Press.

Gooderham, P., Morley, M., Brewster, C. and Mayrhofer, W. (2004) 'Human resource management: a universal concept?' in Brewster, C., Mayrhofer, W. and Morley, M. (eds) *Human Resource Management in Europe: Evidence of Convergence?* Oxford: Butterworth-Heinemann.

Gooderham, P., Nordhaug, O. and Ringdal, K. (1998) 'When in Rome, do they do as the Romans?' HRM practices of US subsidiaries in Europe', *Management International Review*. 38(2): 47–64.

Guest, D. E. and Hoque, K. (1996) 'National ownership and HR practices in UK Greenfield Sites', *Human Resource Management Journal*. 6(4): 50–74.

Gunnigle, P., Murphy, K. M., Cleveland, J., Heraty, N. and Morley, M. (2002) 'Localisation in human resource management: comparing American and European multinational corporations', *Advances in International Management*. 14: 259–84.

Hall, P. A. and Soskice, D. (eds) (2001) *Varieties of Capitalism: The Institutional Foundations of Comparative Advantage*. Oxford: Oxford University Press.

Hanami, T. (ed.) (2002) Global integration and challenges for industrial relations and human resource management in the twenty-first century: selected papers from the Twelfth IIRRA World Congress', Tokyo: Japanese Institute of Labour.

Harzing, A. W. and Sorge, A. (2003) 'The relative impact of country of origin and universal contingencies on internationalization strategies and corporate control in multinational enterprises: worldwide and European perspectives', *Organizational Studies.* 24(2): 187–214.

Hegewisch, A., Tregaskis, O. and Morley, M. (1997) 'The management of labour in Europe: is human resource management challenging industrial relations? *Journal of Irish Business and Administrative Research.* 18(1): 1–16.

Hoftstede, G. (2001) *Culture's Consequences: Comparing Values, Behaviours, Institutions and Organizations Across Nations.* Thousand Oaks, CA: Sage.

Hyman, R. (1994) 'Theory and Industrial Relations', *British Journal of Industrial Relations.* 32(2): 165–80.

Jackson, S. and Schuler, R. (1995) 'Understanding human resource management in the context of organisations and their environments' in Rosenweig, M. and Porter, L. (eds) *Annual Review of Psychology.* 237–64, Palo Alto, CA: Annual Reviews.

Jacoby, S. (ed.) (1995) *Not the Workers of Nations: Industrial Relations in the Global Economy.* New York: Oxford University Press.

Kaufman, B. (2001) 'What can HR learn from IR?' *Human Resource Management Review.* 11(4) 337–9.

Kerr, C., Dunlop, J. T., Harbison, F. and Myers, G. A. (1960) *Industrialism and Industrial Man.* Cambridge, Mass: Harvard University Press.

Kochan, T., Katz, H. and McKersie, R. (1986) *The Transformation of American Industrial Relations.* New York: Basic Books.

Lane, C. (2000) 'Globalization and the German model of capitalism – erosion or survival', *British Journal of Sociology.* 51(2): 207–34.

Lazonick, W. and O'Sullivan, M. (2000) 'Maximising shareholder value: a new ideology for corporate governance', *Economy and Society.* 29(1): 13–35.

Locke, R., Kochan, T. and Piore, M. (1995) 'Reconceptualizing comparative industrial relations: lessons from international research', *International Labour Review.* 134(2): 139–161.

McGaughey, S. L. and DeCieri, H. D. (1999) 'Reassessment of convergence and divergence dynamics: implications for international HRM', *International Journal of Human Resource Management.* 10(2): 235–50.

Margerison, C. (1969) 'What do we mean by industrial relations? A behavioural science approach', *British Journal of Industrial Relations.* 8(2): 273–86.

Marsh, A. (1969) 'Reviews: industrial relations', *Journal of Management Studies.* 6(2): 261–3.

Marshall, R. (1992) 'Work organisation, unions and economic performance' in Mishel, L. and Voos, P. (eds) *Unions and Economic Competitiveness.* New York: ME Sharpe Inc.

Mitchell, J. and Saidi, M. (1991) 'International pressures on industrial relations: macroeconomics and social concentration' in Treu, T. (ed.) *Participation in Public Policy Making: The Role of Trade Unions and Employer Associations.* Berlin: De Gruyter.

Monks, J. (1994) 'The trade union response to HRM: fraud or opportunity?' *Personnel Management.* September, pp. 42–7.

Morley, M. and Collings, D. (eds) (2004) 'Contemporary debates and new directions in HRM in MNCs', *International Journal of Manpower.* 25(6): 487–591.

O'Sullivan, M. (2003) 'The political economy of comparative corporate governance', *Review of International Political Economy,* 10(1): 23–72.

Piore, M. and Sabel, C. (1984) *The Second Industrial Divide: Prospects for Prosperity.* New York: Basic Books.

Poole, M. (1986) *Industrial Relations: Origins and Patterns of National Diversity.* London: Routledge & Kegan Paul.

Poole, M. (1993) 'Industrial relations: theorising for a global perspective', in Adams, R. and Meltz, N. (eds) *Industrial Relations Theory: Its Nature, Scope and Pedagogy,* Metuchen, NJ: The Scarecrow Press.

Przeworski, A. and Spague, J. (1986) *Paper Stones: A History of Editorial Socialism*, Chicago: University of Chicago Press.

Roche, W. (1986) Systems analysis and industrial relations: double paradox in the development of American and British industrial relations theory', *Economic and Industrial Democracy*. 7(3): 3–28.

Shalev, M. (1980) 'Industrial relations theory and the comparative study of industrial relations and industrial conflict', *British Journal of Industrial Relations*. 18(1): 26–43.

Sorge, A. (2004) 'Cross national differences in human resources and organisations' in Harzing, A. W. and van Ruysseveldt, J. (eds) *International Human Resource Management: second edition*. London: Sage.

Stephans, J. (1990) 'Explaining cross-national differences in union strength in bargaining and welfare', paper read to the XII World Congress of Sociology, Madrid, July 9–13.

Stokke, T. and Thornqvist, C. (2001) 'Strikes and collective bargaining in the Nordic countries', *European Journal of Industrial Relations*. 7(3): 245–67.

Storey, J. (1992) *Developments in the Management of Human Resources*. Oxford: Blackwell.

Storey, J. and Sisson, K. (1993) *Managing Human Resources and Industrial Relations*. Buckingham: Open University Press.

Strauss, G. (1998) Regional studies of comparative international industrial relations: symposium introduction, *Industrial Relations*. 37(3): 273–81.

Streeck, W. (1988) 'Change in industrial relations: strategy and structure', Proceedings of an International Symposium of New Systems in Industrial Relations, Tokyo, Japan Institute of Labour.

Tailby, S. and Whitson, C. (1989) 'Industrial relations and restructuring' in Tailby, S. and Whitson, C. (eds) *Manufacturing Change: Industrial Relations and Restructuring*. Oxford: Blackwell.

Thompson, M. (2003) 'Special issue on global labour standards', *International Journal of Comparative Labour Law and Industrial Relations*. 19(4): 419–20.

Turner. T. and Morley, M. (1995) *Industrial Relations and the New Order*. Dublin: Oak Tree Press.

UNCTAD (2001/2002/2003) *Would Investment Report*. Switzerland: United Nations.

UNCTAD (2004) 'Prospects for FDI flows, transnational corporation strategies and promotion policies: 2004–2007: GIPA Research note 1', Geneva: UNCTAD.

Visser, J. (1992) 'Union organisation: why countries differ', paper read to the IX World Congress of the IIRA, Sydney.

Webb, B. and Webb, S. (1897) *Industrial Democracy*. London: Longman.

Whitfield, K., Delbridge, R. and Brown, W. (1999) 'Comparative research in industrial relations: helping the survey cross frontiers', *International Journal of Human Resource Management*. 10(6): 971–80.

Whitley, R. (1999) *Divergent Capitalisms: The Social Structuring and Change of Business Systems*. Oxford: Oxford University Press.

Part I

Regional variations in global industrial relations

1 Industrial relations in the United States and Canada

RICHARD N. BLOCK

Introduction

The industrial relations systems in the United States and Canada are like siblings; they have similar origins and reflect similar values. The industrial relations system in the United States developed from the economic difficulties of the great depression in the 1930s. Among the premises underlying the founding of the industrial relations system in the United States was that strikes over recognition were disrupting the US economy and the low wages were causing 'underconsumption' and aggravating the economic stagnation. When the modern Canadian industrial relations system was established after the Second World War, it adopted many of the attributes of the industrial relations system of its more populous neighbor to the south.

Yet, like siblings, there are differences as well. This chapter will discuss the commonalities and differences between the two systems, examining:

- the main actors – the state, unions, and employers;
- the nature of collective bargaining in the two countries;
- industrial conflict, and
- conclusions on the state of industrial relations in the two countries as well as future prospects.

The actors in the industrial relations system: the state, union, and employers

The major determinant of the shape and contours of industrial relations in the United States and Canada is the state through its establishment of the legal environment for industrial relations. In both countries, the legal environment provides the basis for determining to which employers and employees the law applies, when an employment relationship is collectivized and bargaining is required, the matters about which the parties must bargain, what constitutes 'bargaining,' what happens when the parties are unable to reach an agreement, and the meaning of an agreement, assuming one is reached. In the United States and Canada, while the state has little direct involvement in determining the terms and conditions of employment established by collective bargaining, by establishing 'the rules of the game' via the legal environment, it can put one party in an advantageous position *vis-à-vis* the other, thereby indirectly affecting terms and conditions of employment.

This chapter will first explore the how the state, via the legal system regulating industrial relations, affects the parties. It will then examine how unions and employers have developed in response to the legal system.

The state

As noted, with their common origins, the United States and Canada share many industrial relations attributes. Despite these similarities, however, there are important distinctions between the United States and Canada. This section will first explore those attributes of the legal system that the countries have in common. It will then examine legal differences between the two countries.[1]

Common legal attributes

The National Labor Relations Act (NLRA), the basic labor legislation covering most private sector employees in the United States, was enacted in 1935, with substantial amendments in 1947 (Hardin and Higgins 2001–2004). The passage of the NLRA in the United States encouraged union pressure for similar legislation in Canada. With the end of World War II and wartime industrial relations regulation, starting in 1948, the federal government in Canada used the NLRA as the model for labor legislation covering employees in interprovincial industries (such as airlines, railroads, and telecommunications). Unlike in the United States, where labor legislation is national, each of the provinces in Canada adopts labor legislation covering the industries in the province that are not interprovincial. All of the provinces except Quebec and Prince Edward Island used the NLRA model for legislation covering employees who worked in industries within the province (Adams 1996–2004: 1–9 to 1–16).

The basic model in the United States and Canada consists of six attributes: employee choice; majoritarianism; decentralization; exclusive representation; bargaining power; written, legally enforceable collective bargaining agreements; and administration by a specialized agency. Each of these attributes will be examined.

Employee choice

The essence of the industrial relations systems in both countries is employee choice. Employees in a 'bargaining unit' determine whether they wish a union to represent them for collective bargaining purposes. There is no presumption in either country that employees wish to be represented by a union or that the terms and conditions of employment in a workplace will be affected or influenced by collective bargaining through extension; indeed, the 'default' in both countries is no union representation. On the other hand, once employees choose representation, the representation stays with the bargaining unit even if the employees change until and unless the current employees indicate a desire no longer to be represented for collective bargaining purposes.

Majoritarianism

Typically, the choice of union or no union is based on a majority of the employees in the designated bargaining unit. In the United States and Canada, sectoral bargaining and corporatist structures by which union-negotiated terms and conditions of employment are extended to all employees in the sector or industry do not exist.

Decentralization

Employees exercise their choice within a designated 'appropriate bargaining unit.' The unit can be a firm, a facility or facilities within a firm, or a craft or occupation within a facility. A unit is considered appropriate if employees in that unit share common employment interests, generally called a 'community of interest.' Employees are considered to have a community of interest if they have similar wage rates, similar duties, similar supervision, and work at the same location – among other matters. Bargaining occurs on a unit-wide basis. This unit-based bargaining results in a decentralized system for both countries, with bargaining agreements covering a single employer or a sub-unit of an employer. Terms and conditions of employment are established at the level of the bargaining unit with little or no government involvement in determining bargaining outcomes. Unless bargaining units agree to be bound in a multi-unit contract, there are no terms and conditions of employment that cover more than one unit. (*Evening News Association* 1965; Block 2003).

Exclusive representation

If a union is chosen by a majority of employees, it represents all employees in the unit, whether they voted for the union or not. The employer must negotiate with that union. Equally important, no other union may represent those employees. Thus, while it is possible for an employer to be required to deal with multiple unions if it deals with multiple bargaining units, for any single bargaining unit, only one union can be the representative at any one time.

The role of bargaining power and industrial conflict

In both countries in the private sector, bargaining power and industrial conflict is an integral component of the bargaining process. Through the system of decentralized, unit-by-unit bargaining, terms and conditions of employment are set at the unit level. Bargaining power, as manifested in either industrial conflict or the potential for industrial conflict, is designed to encourage the parties to come to a settlement (*NLRB* v. *Insurance Agents* 1960). Although in Canada, the state may be required to mediate a dispute if one party requests such mediation, the state rarely has the option of forcing an agreement on private sector parties. As a general rule, outcomes are determined by the bargaining power of the parties, with power exercised by using the protected weapons, i.e. strikes and lockouts. The state has very little influence in directly determining the terms and conditions of employment for employees.

Written, legally enforceable agreements

In both countries, when the parties choose to reduce their agreements to writing, they are legally enforceable for the duration of the agreement and cannot be changed unless both parties agree to a change. While, in theory, collective bargaining agreements could be enforced in court, they are generally enforced through private final and binding arbitration, with only a narrow scope of court review of the decision of the arbitrator (Ruben 2003).

Administration by a specialized agency

In both countries, the law is administered by a specialized agency empowered to interpret the law and to decide matters of representation. This is based on the notion that industrial relations is a specialized area of the law that requires expertise. The relevant administrative agencies in the United States for the private sector are the National Labor Relations Board (NLRB) for all non-agricultural industries except railroads and airlines, and the National Mediation Board (NMB) for railroads and airlines (Block *et al.* 1996; Adams 1996–2005: 2–1 to 2–106, 4–2). In Canada, the laws are administered by various provincial labour relations boards, such as the Ontario Labour Relations Board and the British Columbia Labour Relations Board (Ontario Labour Relations Board undated; British Columbia Labour Relations Board undated). The Canada Industrial Relations

Board administers the national law in Canada for employees in industries involved in interprovincial commerce (Canada Industrial Relations Board undated).

Differing legal characteristics

Whom does the law cover?

A basic question in law in North America is the coverage of the law. The United States makes a distinction between the private sector and the public sector. In Canada, the major distinction is not industrial sectors, but rather the nature of the industry.

Industrial relations in the private sector in the United States are regulated by two laws – the National Labor Relations Act (NLRA) and the Railway Labor Act (RLA). Industrial relations in the public sector are regulated by various state laws.

The NLRA is the basic law in the United States. Initially passed in 1935, and amended in 1947, 1958, and 1974, the NLRA regulates industrial relations in all private sector firms that affect interstate commerce except firms in railroads, airlines, and agriculture, which are not regulated nationally. The RLA covers industrial relations only in the railroad and airline industries.

This bifurcated industrial relations regulatory system for the private sector in the United States is the result of historical factors influenced by court interpretations of the United States constitution. The United States constitution permits the national government to regulate only on matters that affect 'interstate commerce,' leaving the regulation of, presumably, 'intrastate commerce' to each state. Through the mid-1930s, the prevailing judicial view in the United States was that the only industries that the national government could regulate were industries that directly moved goods and persons between states, for example, railroads and airlines. In 1925, the United States decided to regulate industrial relations in the railroads at the national level through the RLA because labor disputes on the railroads were disrupting interstate commerce. Airlines, which also affected interstate commerce, were added to the RLA in 1934. In 1937, however, the US Supreme Court provided an expansive definition of interstate commerce that covered employment, and the NLRA was declared constitutional (Lieberman 1960). Unlike collective bargaining in private employment, collective bargaining in public employment in the United States is not regulated by national law. Individual states regulate collective bargaining for their public employees, including employees of state government, and local government. Twenty-six states have legislation that covers all public employees in the state, twelve states cover some classifications of employees, and twelve states do not provide any collective bargaining rights to employees. Legislation and executive orders regulate collective bargaining for employees of the national government (Wasserman 2006).

As a general rule, public employees in the United States are not permitted to strike. Twenty-six states have legislation that permits at least some public employees to submit unresolved disputes to final and binding arbitration. Public safety employees (police and firefighters) are most often covered by these statutes (Wasserman 2006).

In Canada, the regulation of industrial relations is primarily a provincial matter; employment within a province is not regulated by the federal government in Canada. Thus, each province has its own labor law, although there are basic similarities among them. On the other hand, the federal government does regulate labor relations in industries where the employment is interprovincial in nature, such as airlines and telecommunications (Adams 1996–2005, 2–1 to 2–105). Most provinces have chosen to cover private sector and public sector employees under separate statutes (Adams 1996–2005, 5–39 to 5–40). Canada has generally not mandated compulsory arbitration in the public sector, preferring to deal with disputes that may affect essential services through ad hoc legislation or through labor board action (Adams 1996–2005, 11–57 to 11–61).

Determination of a majority

In the United States, the typical method of determining representation is via a state-supervised 'representation' election in which the employees in a state-determined bargaining unit vote for or against union representation. In the United States, it also possible to establish representation through acquisition of the signatures on authorization cards of a majority of the employees in the bargaining unit. Elections, however, are the preferred method, and, generally, an employer may insist on a representation election as the method of determining whether the employees in the bargaining unit desire union representation (Block *et al.* 1994).

In Canada, there is a greater willingness than in the United States to accept non-election evidence of a majority for union representation. The membership evidence may take the form of signed cards designating the union as a representative, a signed membership application, or payment of dues to the union, taking into account the union's eligibility requirements. Only four provinces, Alberta, British Columbia, Nova Scotia, and Ontario require a vote (Adams 1985 plus supplements).

Judicial review

In the United States, although there is an administrative agency, the NLRB, that hears cases and makes decisions under the National Labor Relations Act, courts have taken an active role in reviewing NLRB decisions. Thus, the agency that is expert in the law must often defer to court decisions. In Canada, on the other hand, courts have but a minimal role to play in reviewing agency decisions. Thus, in Canada, the agencies, who generally have a strong commitment to the collective bargaining system, have the greatest say in the development of law (Block 1994; 1997).

The actors

As noted, the legal environment for industrial relations in Canada is generally based on the legal environment in the United States. Because the legal environment creates decentralized bargaining in both countries, both countries have developed decentralized bargaining for unions and management.

Unions

The general organizational structure of the United States and Canadian labor movements is depicted in Figure 1.1. The two main organizational units that are involved with worker representation are the national/international union and local union. These types of entities are found in all labor organizations that represent employees in the private sector and are colored gray. The central labor body is at the top. Other union structures which exist in some unions, but not others, are designated in white.

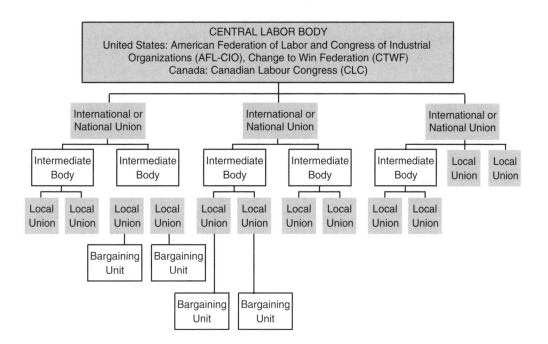

Figure 1.1 Basic structure of United States and Canadian trade union movements

At the top of the chart is the central labor body, the American Federation of Labor and Congress of Industrial Organizations (AFL-CIO) and the Change to Win Federation (CTWF) in the United States and the Canadian Labour Congress (CLC) in Canada. The AFL-CIO was established in 1955 through a merger of two competing central labor bodies, the AFL and the CIO. The CTWF was established in 2005 when seven unions left the AFL-CIO in a dispute over organizing workers (Greenhouse 2005; Burger 2005; Sweeney 2005). Although, early in their history, the AFL, CIO, and the CLC actually established unions by chartering them; over the last fifty years their function has evolved into political action and bringing order to the labor movement, creating rules for relations among member unions.

The basic organizational component in both countries is the national or international union. When examining the structure of the US and Canadian labor movements across unions, organizationally, national and international unions are similar. International unions have members and represent workers in both the United States and Canada, while national unions have members and represent workers in only one of the two countries. International/national unions charter local unions and, through their constitutions, establish the officers of the national/international union, the governing structure of the national/international union, and the level of autonomy of the various parts of the union.

The local union is the entity in the labor movement that is generally responsible for day-to-day workplace representation of union members and workers represented by unions. Local unions are organizational units chartered (established) by national unions for the purpose of direct representation of workers/members *vis-à-vis* employers. Each 'local' generally has a 'jurisdiction,' defined as the scope of workers for whom it may bargain and whom it may represent, assuming it is able to obtain representation rights. In general, national/international unions establish jurisdictions of local unions that are plant/facility-wide, firm-wide, or geographic. Jurisdictions are generally of one type among all locals of the international union. If a local union has been granted a charter with a plant/facility-wide jurisdiction, it may represent only workers at that plant/facility, but may not represent workers at any other plant/facility. Generally, other locals have jurisdiction over other plants and facilities of the same employer. A national/international union may also grant a local a charter covering a single employer. This is generally the case when the union represents workers only at that employer and the employer has either one facility or facilities that are in close geographic proximity. In these cases, the local union is generally synonymous with the bargaining unit; they are generally single-unit locals.

If a national/international union grants a local union a charter with a geographic jurisdiction, the local will be able to represent workers within the designated geographic area, such as a state, province, city, or other delineated region. Such locals normally represent employees working for multiple employers and, in turn, have multiple bargaining units. Organizationally, these multi-unit locals have governing sub-structures for each of the bargaining units. These sub-structures are represented by the boxes at the lowest level of the organizational chart.

At the level between the local union and the international union can be found intermediate bodies. These are entities within the union, generally established by the national/international union, that serve to aggregate the common interests of multiple local unions within the international unions. Sometimes they are industry-based, addressing the common problems of all local unions in the same industry. They may be firm-based, aggregating the interests of all locals that negotiate with a single firm with many facilities, such as General Motors. Some are geographic based, aggregating the regional interests of locals in a geographic area. These latter bodies are generally part of the internal governing structure of the national/international union. Some local unions may not be associated with an intermediate body.

Employer organizations

Decentralized bargaining structures in the United States and Canada mean that there are no broad-based employer organizations that represent the interests of management *vis-à-vis* unions in collective bargaining. The general absence of multi-employer bargaining means that employers generally do not require such structures. There are industries where voluntary multi-employer bargaining does exist, however, and in these specific industries, firms have developed collective structures on the employer side. For example, in the longshore (waterfront) industry on the west coast docks of the United States, the International Longshoremen's and Warehousemen's Union (ILWU) negotiates a common contract for all dockworkers in the ports in the states of California, Oregon, and Washington. Because multiple firms operate in these ports, the firms have established the Pacific Maritime Association to represent 'American flag operators, foreign flag operators, and stevedore and terminal companies that operate in California, Oregon, and Washington ports' (Pacific Maritime Association undated). A similar employer structure, the United States Maritime Association, negotiates for employers operating in the ports on the Atlantic and Gulf (of Mexico) coasts in the United States (International Longshoremen's Association undated; United States Maritime Alliance undated). In addition, construction industry employers in a metropolitan area will generally negotiate as a group with the unions representing the building trades.

The broad-based management structures that do exist generally perform political and/or educational roles for management. For example, the HR (Human Resources) Policy Association (HRPA) in the United States educates its members and the public on the employer perspective of various public policy matters affecting industrial relations (HR Policy Association undated). The HRPA, however, does not bargain for employers.

Summary and conclusions

In the United States and Canada, the state, or more precisely, the state-established industrial relations legal system, creates the framework in which union representation is established and in which collective bargaining occurs. In both countries, the state has established a system characterized by employee choice for union representation, majoritarianism, decentralization of bargaining units, exclusive representation, bargaining power as the main criterion for establishing terms and conditions of employment under collective bargaining, written, legally enforceable agreements, and administration by agency expert in industrial relations.

This decentralized system has created similarly decentralized union and employer organizations. The peak union organizations, the AFL-CIO and CTWF in the United States and the CLC in Canada, are actually federations of unions. Individual unions bargain, with authority divided between the national and local union levels of the union. With the exception of a few industries where the parties choose to engage in multi-employer bargaining, such bargaining rarely occurs. Therefore, there is a minimal incidence of multi-employer bargaining structures.

Collective bargaining in the United States and Canada

Extent of collective bargaining in the United States and Canada

How prevalent is collective bargaining in the United States and Canada? Insight into this question can be obtained by examining data on union density, defined here as the percentage of the labor force in each country covered by unions. These data are presented in Table 1.1.

As can be seen, the percentage of workers represented by unions (union density) in Canada is roughly twice that of the United States. Yet, there are similarities. In both countries, the overall union density rate is roughly one-and-a-half times the private sector rate, resulting from relatively high unionization rates in the public sector. The private sector rate is declining in both countries.

How do these percentages compare with other Western countries? Although unionization rates across different countries are difficult to compare because of differences in definitions of union membership and industrial relations structure, the European Foundation for Employment and Living Conditions attempted to group European countries by categories of unionization levels. Table 1.2 presents 2003 union membership estimates for the United States, Canada, Norway, and fourteen of the fifteen countries that were EU members in 2003.

Table 1.1 Percentage of workers represented by unions, United States and Canada, 1997–2003

| Year | United States | | Canada | |
	Private sector	All workers	Private sector	All workers
1997	10.6	15.6	21.5	33.7
1998	10.3	15.4	21.1	32.8
1999	10.2	15.3	20.0	32.2
2000	9.8	14.9	20.2	32.2
2001	9.7	14.8	20.0	32.2
2002	9.3	14.5	19.6	32.2
2003	9.0	14.3	19.9	32.4

Sources: Statistics Canada
United States Bureau of Labor Statistics
European Foundation for Employment and Living Conditions.

As can be seen in Table 1.2, Austria, with a union membership rate of 40–49 percent, is in the middle of the distribution of these fifteen countries. The unionization rates in Canada would place it just below Austria but still in roughly the middle of the distribution of European countries. The United States, however,

Table 1.2 Estimated union density, fourteen European Union countries, Norway, Canada, United States, 2003

Country	Estimated percentage range
Belgium	80–89
Denmark	80–89
Finland	80–89
Sweden	80–89
Italy	70–79
Norway	70–79
Luxembourg	50–59
Austria	40–49
Canada	30–39
Ireland	30–39
Portugal	30–39
Germany	20–29
Greece	20–29
Netherlands	20–29
United Kingdom	20–29
Spain	10–19
United States	10–19

Sources: Statistics Canada,
United States Bureau of Labor Statistics;
European Foundation for Employment and Living Conditions.

would be at the bottom of the distribution. This suggests that the United States and Canadian industrial relations systems are not as conducive to union membership as many of the European systems, and that the United States variant is even less conducive to union membership than the Canadian systems.

Why might this be the case? First, in both countries, the absence of industry – or sectoral-wide bargaining in the United States means that each plant or facility is generally a separate unit. As new firms are started, or as older firms establish new facilities, the employees in this new firms or establishments will not generally be unionized initially. If these firms or establishments are to be unionized, they must go through the unit-by-unit majoritarian processes discussed above. This is an extremely time-consuming process. Moreover, in the United States, where the representation election is the standard procedure for determining majority status, the unionization process is more difficult than in Canada, where there are often non-election methods for determining majority status. In the United States, the time period prior to the election, usually a period of one to two months, is often characterized by an intense employer campaign against unionization, as the election rules permit the employer to presents its point of view at the workplace, while at the same time barring the union from the workplace (Roomkin and Block 1981; Block, Beck and Kruger 1996; Bronfrenbrenner 1997).

Finally, at least for the United States over the last fifty years, the law of organizing has evolved in a way that has increased the tools available to employers to resist union organization. Thus, if an established facility could avoid unionization until 1956, the employer had an increased capability of resisting unionization. In addition, these same tools were available to new establishments (Block and Wolkinson 1986).

In both the United States and Canada, a bargaining obligation exists only when a union has been certified in accordance with the majoritarian processes discussed above or when a union has been voluntarily recognized by the employer as the representative of its employees. Once a bargaining obligation is created, the decentralized industrial relations system and the principle of minimal government involvement in the bargaining process and the outcomes of bargaining leave the parties generally free to create collective bargaining agreements that reflect their interests and their relative bargaining power. Good faith negotiations and industrial conflict coexist in North American industrial relations. In the United States employers may replace strikers and use the new workforce composition to express a 'good faith' doubt about the union's continuing majority status. Thus, in the United States, there is a set of tools available to the employer that would permit the employer with the inclination and legal resources to eliminate the collective bargaining relationship.

This is less likely to occur in Canada, as the right to replace strikers is more restricted than in the United States (Singh, Zinni and Jain 2005). In addition either side can generally invoke government involvement in the collective bargaining process, through mediation or facilitation. Such involvement generally fosters an industrial relations system that makes it more difficult than otherwise to take extreme positions in bargaining.

That such government involvement in the bargaining process protects the institution of collective bargaining is indicated by the relatively high rate of unionization in the public sectors of both countries. As discussed, in order to avoid strikes, public sector bargaining legislation generally includes mandated impasse procedures pursuant to which the state becomes involved if the parties are unable to agree.

It should also be noted that a fundamental component of industrial relations in the United States and Canada is the written, fixed-term collective bargaining agreement. Generally, negotiations occur in association with the end of the term of the collective agreement. Although the parties may negotiate mid-term adjustments in their agreement if they believe it is in their interest to do so, any obligation to bargain mid-term is generally determined by the collective agreement that has been negotiated.

The definition of 'bargain'

Both the United States and Canada obligate the parties to bargain in 'good faith' and make 'reasonable efforts' toward resolving their differences. For private sector parties, the content of this principle is similar in both countries, in that in neither the United States nor the Canadian jurisdictions does the government have the power to determine what provisions are actually incorporated into the collective bargaining agreement. There is tension between these two principles.

In general, parties have an obligation to meet at reasonable times, to listen to the positions of the other side, and to disclose relevant information to support their respective positions. While there is generally no obligation to agree to a proposal of the other side, or to make a concession, neither can the employer or the union engage in a 'take-it-or-leave-it' approach to bargaining that refuses to recognize the institutional legitimacy of the other party. Ultimately, however, because the parties can use economic weapons and engage in industrial conflict, the bargain on which the parties agree is often heavily influenced either by a strike or lockout, or more frequently, the expected results of a strike or lockout that never occurs.

In the public sector in the United States and Canada, the impasse procedures many states have established as strike 'substitutes' result in far more government involvement in the process and outcomes of bargaining than occurs in the private sector. Indeed, in states in which state-mandated compulsory arbitration is incorporated into the impasse procedure, the arbitrator, who can be considered an arm of the state, has the authority to impose terms and conditions on public sector parties when they are unable to agree.

The subject matter of bargaining: about what must the parties negotiate?

While the United States and the Canadian jurisdictions have adopted basically similar approaches on the definition of bargaining, the countries have diverged on the subjects about which the parties are obligated to bargain.

The United States

The law in the United States generally requires the parties to negotiate only over 'terms and conditions' of employment, or 'mandatory' subjects of bargaining. An employer that must negotiate with a union may not act unilaterally with respect to any mandatory subject of bargaining unless that subject has been a topic of negotiations between the employer and the union. Negotiations over any other legal subject are 'nonmandatory' or 'permissive', and may be discussed only if both parties agree to discuss them. On these nonmandatory issues, the employer may act unilaterally without negotiating with a union.

The result of establishing a set of issues about which the employer must negotiate with a union, and a set of issues on which the employer may act unilaterally, has generated a great deal of litigation before the NLRB on which issues are mandatory and which are permissive. The more issues that the NLRB and courts determine are permissive, the wider the range of employer unilateral action and the less influence unions may have. The most difficult issues under the mandatory-permissive distinction arose when employers found a need to close facilities or effect changes in their capital structure that would result in a reduction of employment. The fundamental question was whether the existence of employment was a 'term or condition of employment'. Over a period of almost thirty years, from the mid-1960s to the early 1990s, the law in the United States evolved to give employers the right to make changes in the capital structures of their business without being required to negotiate those changes with the union, unless the change resulted solely in production relocation. This evolution of the law gave employers wide latitude to restructure their businesses with little union involvement. (cf. *Dubuque Packing Co.*, 303 NLRB 386 (1991).) Employers, however, must negotiate with the union over the effects of such a decision.

Canada

Unlike the United States, the Canadian jurisdictions have never adopted the mandatory–permissive distinction. Although unions and employers may not discuss issues that implicate illegal subjects of bargaining, or that address the internal decision-making processes of the other party, unions and employers in Canada are generally free to negotiate about whatever they wish to negotiate and to use the economic weapons to obtain concessions on these matters (Adams 1996–2004, 10–96 to 10–98). This difference gives Canadian unions a much broader reach in the bargaining process than their United States counterparts.

Bargaining outcomes

In the private sector in both the United States and in the Canadian jurisdictions, the outcomes of bargaining, the content of the collective agreement, is left to the parties to determine. The basic principle is that government should not determine or influence the outcomes of bargaining. In the United States, however, because bargaining is limited to terms and conditions of employment, collective agreements address matters related to terms and conditions of employment. Although Canadian legislation does not limit bargaining to terms and conditions of employment, Canadian agreements look much like their US counterparts (Peirce 2003), suggesting that it is terms and conditions of employment that the parties to collective bargaining are most interested in addressing during the bargaining process.

Because bargaining in the public sector in the US and Canada is basically patterned on the private sector model in both countries, public sector agreements generally address only terms and conditions of employment. Some states may limit the scope of negotiations of the public sector parties.

Collective agreements in both countries are always in writing. They are generally of a fixed duration. For many years, the typical duration was three years, although lately there has been some movement toward four- and five-year agreements in order to reduce the costs associated with bargaining and incorporate increased certainty into the system. In both countries, collective agreements are also enforceable by law; thus they cannot be altered during the term of the agreement unless both parties consent. This principle may be modified in the public sector in some states, depending on state law.

Although the decentralized bargaining structures in the United States and Canada result in differences in the details of collective bargaining agreements among collective bargaining relationships, provisions in collective agreements fall into a few defined categories. Each of these will be briefly examined.

Institutional security

Provisions dealing with institutional security establish the parameters of the bargaining unit and the institutionalization of the union. Thus, a typical agreement will include a 'recognition' provision stating the job classifications or occupations that are covered by the bargain. For example, the 2000 collective bargaining agreement between the UAW and Visteon, the firm that was created when Ford divested its parts facilities, states that the agreement covers 'the hourly rated production, and maintenance employees' at specific facilities listed in the agreement. The contract specifically excludes certain classifications, such as 'office, clerical, nurses' (Agreements 2000).

A component of institutional security is union security, which defines the financial relationship between the employees and the union representing them. In general, the Canadian jurisdictions permit more rigid forms of union security than are permitted in the United States. In the United States, in the twenty-eight states where it is legal, the typical union security provisions negotiated by the parties is the union shop, requiring an employee hired by the employer to join the union or pay the union the equivalent of dues and fees within a specified date of hire, usually from thirty to ninety days. In the twenty-two states in which union shop clauses are illegal, the parties may not negotiate union shop provisions in their collective agreements (National Right to Work Foundation undated).

All Canadian jurisdictions permit parties to negotiate a 'closed shop,' under which a person must be a member of the union prior to being hired (Adams 1996–2004, 14–11). In addition, the parties in Canada may negotiate lesser forms of union security, such as the union shop. In both countries, parties may negotiate a dues checkoff provision, under which the employer deducts union dues from the employee's paycheck and remits the dues to the union.

Rights of the parties

Almost all collective agreements in both countries contain a management rights clause. Such provisions explicitly give the employer the right to make specified decisions, such as what to produce, the means and methods of producing it, production schedules, engineering and design, the number of employees used to produce it, to discipline and discharge employees for just cause, and to adopt reasonable work rules, although work rules are occasionally made part of the collective bargaining agreement. Such rights are typically limited by other provisions of the collective bargaining agreement.

Some agreements provide unions with rights. Typical rights include the right to designate union representatives, the right of those representatives to take work time to deal with issues related to the contract, and the right to attend union conventions without penalty. The rationale for these provisions is that the union must have the right to administer the collective agreement and educate its representatives to perform that duty.

Wage rates and other compensation: fringe benefits

Almost all agreements contain provisions for wage levels of covered employees, generally specifying wage differentials by occupation. The agreements also contain increases for all years of the agreement, which may be in dollar terms or percentages. Some agreements include incentive systems, paying employees based on production. There are also agreements with profit sharing plans.

Typical fringe benefits in the United States include pensions, health insurance, education assistance, and severance pay. Most agreements have provisions for paid time off. This includes vacations, public holidays, and sick leave. (Labour standards in the United States do not provide employees with paid time off by law.) Most collective agreements provide for vacations of greater length depending on seniority, or length of service. Fringe benefits in Canada do not generally include health insurance because health care in Canada is provided by the government.

Job allocation

Although most collective bargaining agreements in the United States and Canada provide management with the right to determine how many jobs shall be performed and the classifications of those jobs, the allocation of those jobs is generally determined by the collective agreement. Put differently, although management generally determines the jobs that will be performed, the collective agreement governs who will receive those jobs.

Most agreements give management the right to determine the shifts that will be worked, but give employees the right to bid periodically on shifts. Generally, shift preference is determined by seniority, or length of service.

Most collective agreements are designed to protect incumbents by creating an internal labor market. New employees are generally assigned entry-level jobs. When promotional opportunities arise, they are usually allocated to incumbents based on a combination of seniority and qualifications. The relative weight given to seniority and qualifications is based on the bargain struck by the parties. Some agreements provide for seniority as a major factor, while other agreements provide that qualifications are the major factor. Unions generally prefer that seniority be used as the determining factor because it is objective and eliminates perceived employer favoritism. Employers prefer qualifications.

Layoffs or job reductions are also generally governed by seniority. Most agreements give employers the right to determine the positions that will be eliminated, either permanently or temporarily. Once a position is eliminated, most agreements provide that a senior employee whose position is eliminated may displace, or bump, a less senior employee whose job has not been eliminated. The extent to which qualifications play a role in who may be bumped is determined by the collective agreement.

Dispute resolution under the collective agreement

A key feature of the collective bargaining systems in both the public and private sectors in the United States and Canada is the use of grievance procedures ending in final and binding arbitration to settle disputes that arise during the collective bargaining agreement. These are considered alternatives to the strike or lockout. In the United States, the use of grievance and arbitration procedures is voluntary, although almost every collective bargaining agreement has one. Once incorporated into a collective bargaining agreement, however, the results of the procedure are enforceable in court. In Canada, the provincial laws require a method for resolving disputes during the term of an agreement without a strike, and, in most cases, the grievance and arbitration procedure serves that purpose (Adams 1996–2004, 12–9).

The typical grievance procedure is common to collective bargaining agreements in both countries. It is a multi-step procedure that is designed to involve representatives of each side who are further removed from the parties involved in the dispute. If the parties are unable to resolve the dispute at the lower levels, the dispute is referred to an arbitrator, although British Columbia, Manitoba, and Ontario provide for the appointment of a grievance mediator as a pre-arbitral step.

The arbitrator normally convenes a quasi-judicial hearing, at which each side presents documentary evidence and witnesses to support its case. The arbitrator is considered to be part of the agreement, and generally the arbitrator is prohibited from modifying the agreement in any way. The arbitrator is also obligated to make a decision based on the record and evidence presented in the arbitration hearing and on the language of the (written) collective bargaining agreement. In both the United States and Canada, there is minimal review of arbitrator's award. This is because the arbitrator is not interpreting the law, but the parties' contract, and the parties agreed that the arbitrator would, if asked, interpret that contract (Peirce 2003).

The Federal Mediation and Conciliation Service, one of the agencies in the United States that provides a list of arbitrators, maintains data on issues in arbitration cases. For the period October 1, 2002–September 30, 2003, 2,717 grievance arbitration awards were issued by arbitrators appointed by FMCS. Of these cases, 1,091 or 40 percent involved discipline or discharge. Other frequent issues involved work assignment (ninety-nine cases), health and welfare plans (sixty-one cases), and pay rates (sixty cases) (United States Federal Mediation and Conciliation Service 2004).

Dispute resolution procedures: resolution before industrial conflict

The United States and Canada have taken opposite approaches to third party dispute resolution in the private sector. In the United States, it is generally voluntary; in Canada, it is generally mandatory.

United States

For most of the private sector in the United States, which is covered by the National Labor Relations Act, there is no requirement that the parties undertake dispute resolution procedures. This is a reflection of the general view in the United States that the collective bargaining process should be free of government involvement. While the United States Government has established the Federal Mediation and Conciliation Service (FMCS) to help resolve disputes, there is no requirement that the parties use its services. The parties are required, however, to notify the FMCS of the expiration of a collective bargaining agreement so that the agency may offer its mediation services to the parties.

There are two exceptions to the general rule. First, firms in the railroad and airline industries are covered under the Railway Labor Act (RLA), which has established mandatory dispute resolution based on the view that strikes on the rails and airlines are especially disruptive to commerce. Thus, the parties in railroads and airlines are required to submit an unresolved contract dispute to mediation by the National Mediation Board (NMB), the agency charged with administering the RLA. Only when the NMB releases the parties from mediation, and after a thirty-day cooling off period, may a strike or lockout occur. In addition, the NMB may recommend to the President of the United States that a special board, an 'Emergency Board' be appointed to make recommendation on resolving the dispute (National Mediation Board undated).

Second, under the National Labor Relations Act, if the president believes a strike or lockout constitutes a national emergency, he/she may appoint a Board of Inquiry which delays the strike or lockout. The Board has sixty days to issue its report on the position of the employer, and the law provides another twenty days for dissemination of the results and voting of the affected employees on the employer's offer.

Canada

Unlike the United States, dispute resolution by the government is an integral part of the Canadian industrial relations systems. The federal jurisdiction, New Brunswick, Newfoundland/Labrador, Nova Scotia, Prince Edward Island, and Ontario require third party involvement as a precondition to a legal strike or lockout. In addition, a mandatory third party process may be initiated by one of the two parties in Manitoba and Ontario. In the federal jurisdiction, Alberta, British Columbia, New Brunswick, Newfoundland, Nova Scotia, and Prince Edward Island, the government has discretion to appoint a conciliator upon application by one of the parties. Quebec and Saskatchewan may appoint a conciliation board on their own authority (Adams 1996–2004, 11–50 to 11–51). While there are differences among the Canadian provinces in the procedures that are used to trigger third party intervention, it is expected that parties in Canada will use third parties in an attempt to resolve their disputes.

Industrial conflict: strikes and lockouts

As noted, bargaining and industrial conflict exist side-by-side in the United States and Canada. The two major forms of industrial conflict are strikes and lockouts.

United States

Economic strikes and lockouts in an attempt to obtain a more favorable agreement from the other party than the agreement would offer in the absence of a strike or lockout are considered 'protected economic weapons' in the United States. During the negotiation of a collective agreement, they may be used only at legal impasse, which is defined as irreconcilable differences after good faith negotiations. The theoretical purpose of a strike or lockout, in an industrial relations sense, is to encourage one or both parties to make concessions so that an agreement can be reached. No strike vote is required, as the United States law would see such a strike vote as an intrusion on the rights of an organization, the union, to establish its own procedures for internal decision-making.

In the United States, just as the strike is considered a protected economic weapon for unions to protect their interests, the employer may, if it wishes, hire replacement workers for economic strikers, with no obligation to terminate the replacements at the end of the strike or if the strikers choose to return to work. While there are certain conditions the employer must meet in order to hire these permanent replacements, the option of hiring replacements does provide the employer with an important tool to offset the union's strike weapon.

In order for the employer to be permitted to hire permanent replacements, the strike must be an economic strike, over differences in proposals for terms and conditions of employment. The employer is not permitted to hire replacements if the purpose of the strike is to protest of, in response to, or is lengthened by an employer's unfair labor practice. In the United States, there is often litigation over whether a strike is an unfair labor practice strike or an economic strike. (See, for example, *Detroit Typographical Union* v. *NLRB* 2001).

Lockouts are somewhat infrequent in the United States, but do occur. In 2002, a recent well-publicized lockout involved the Pacific Maritime Association, the organization representing dock firms on the west coast of the United States, locking out the employees represented by the International Longshoremen's and Warehousemen's Union (Machalaba and Kim, 2002). The 2004–05 National (Ice) Hockey League season was canceled when the league locked out players represented by the National Hockey League Player's Association (Westhead,

2005). The question of whether employers may temporarily replace locked out workers is unresolved.

Canada

Once the parties are unable to agree on a collective agreement, after all attempts at mediation and conciliation are exhausted, the union may strike, and the employer may lockout its employees. Unlike in the United States however, all of the provinces, but not the federal jurisdiction, require a strike vote by the employees involved (Adams 11–47). This is another example of the dichotomy between the United States and Canada. In order to encourage labor peace, the Canadian jurisdictions are more willing to impose governmental requirements on union internal decisionmaking than is the United States.

A second major difference between the United States and Canada is the general availability of first agreement arbitration in the federal jurisdiction: British Columbia, Manitoba, Newfoundland and Labrador, Ontario, Quebec, Prince Edward Island, and Saskatchewan (Adams 1996–2005, 10–137 to 10–142). First agreement arbitration is based on the principle that the inability to agree on first contact is often due to the parties' inexperience and unfamiliarity with collective bargaining; imposing a first agreement with basic terms and conditions of employment will provide the parties with the support they need.

Unlike the United States, the Canadian jurisdictions are divided on an employer hiring permanent replacements during a strike. British Columbia and Quebec, two of the three largest provinces, currently prohibit the employer from using replacement workers during a strike, with replacements defined as new workers and workers transferred from other establishments operated by the employer (Adams 1996–2005, 10–34.1). Ontario and Manitoba permit the hiring of temporary replacements to permit the employer to maintain operations during the strike, but strikers must be reemployed at the end of the strike (Adams 10–41).

Extent of industrial conflict in the United States and Canada

Figures 1.2–1.4 display data on work stoppages in the United States and Canada since 1969. Figure 1.2 presents data on the United States from 1969 to 1981, based on work stoppages involving six or more workers – the vast majority of work stoppages. Figure 1.3 presents data from 1974 to 2003, based on work stoppages in the United States among bargaining units with at least 1,000 workers. Figure 1.4 presents data for work stoppages in Canada for any stoppage that lasted at least ten days.

These figures demonstrate that the trend in both countries is one of declining industrial conflict, at least if industrial conflict is measured by work stoppages. In

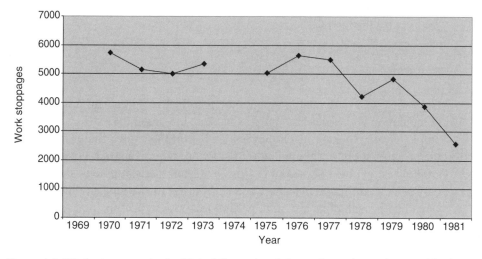

Figure 1.2 Work stoppages in the United States involving at least six workers and lasting
at least one day, 1969–1981
Source: International Labour Organization
Note: No data available for 1974

both United States series, work stoppages started to decline in 1980. Since 1990,
there have been less than fifty strikes per year in units of 1,000 or more workers.
In 2003, there were only fourteen work stoppages affecting 1,000 or more workers.

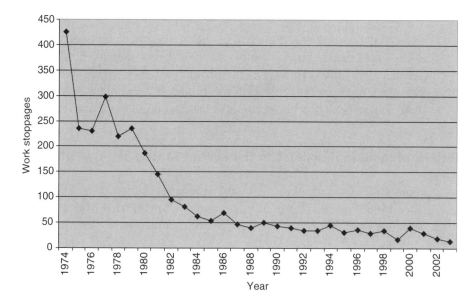

Figure 1.3 Work stoppages in the United States involving at least 1,000 workers and
lasting at least one day, 1974–2003
Source: International Labour Organization

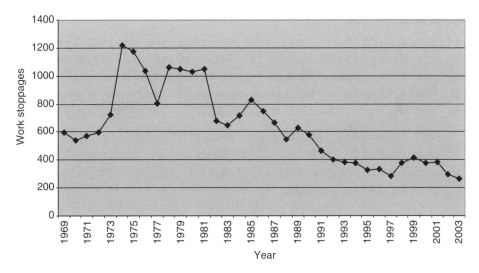

Figure 1.4 Work stoppages in Canada lasting ten or more days, 1969–2003
Source: International Labour Organization

Canadian work stoppages show a generally similar pattern. Following some volatility in the 1970s and early 1980s, work stoppages in Canada have fallen. Despite a slight increase in 1989 and in the late 1990s, currently the level of work stoppages in Canada is well below the level of the 1970s.

Observations

Both the United States and Canada permit private sector parties to engage in industrial conflict, strikes and lockouts, as an element of negotiation of collective bargaining agreements. State-level legislation in the United States generally prohibits public employees from striking, with some states opting for compulsory arbitration as a strike substitute for specific categories of public employees.

Strikes have declined in both countries since 1980. While some commentators attribute the decline in strikes in the US to the well-publicized 1981 decision of then-President Ronald Reagan to replace striking air traffic controllers, the data demonstrate that the declining trend in work stoppages in the United States actually began in 1980, and has generally paralleled the trend in Canada. It is most likely that the decline in work stoppages has been due to the effects of globalization – increasing global competition makes a strike a much less effective weapon than otherwise, as lost market share is less likely to be replaced.

Conclusion

Looking at both the United States and Canada, it is clear that the unionized sector is declining in both countries. The absence of extension and the general principle that employees are not represented by a union unless the unit in which they are employed chooses to be represented is not a hospitable environment for union growth.

In 2004, in the United States, approximately 9 percent of private sector workers were represented by unions (United States Bureau of Labor Stastics 2005). This is roughly the same percentage of workers that were unionized in the 1920s, before passage of labor legislation providing workers with the legally protected right to organize and bargain collectively (Block and Premack 1985).

The situation is more gloomy in the short run for collective bargaining in the United States than for collective bargaining in Canada. The courts in the United States are generally far more supportive of employer property rights than of union rights (Brudney 1996). Moreover, the high value placed on individual rights in the United States tends to favor employer interests (Block *et al.* 2003). Employers in the United States are seen as exercising individual rights, and union engagement in collective action generally involves some compromise of individual rights. In the United States, there is no reason to believe that the downward trend in unionization will change. The conditions that caused this trend still exist, and there is no reason to believe that they will not continue to exist for the foreseeable future.

In Canada, on the other hand, the industrial relations legal system is more supportive of collective bargaining than in the United States. Canadian jurisdictions are far more receptive than the United States to non-election membership evidence, have more latitude to become involved in the bargaining process in order to prevent employers from using the process to eliminate collective bargaining, and have limited court review of labor board decisions, thus protecting the collective bargaining system.

On the other hand, because the structure of collective bargaining is based on the bargaining unit rather than the individual employee, and because bargaining units, once unionized, tend to remain unionized, most of the decline of the union density has occurred in the never-unionized sector rather than in the unionized sector. Put differently, there is no substantial formerly-unionized sector in the United States and Canada. Thus the decline in union density in the United States and Canada has not been associated with a proportional decline in union membership. This is depicted in Table 1.3. Between 1997 and 2003, the percentage of covered employees in the United States declined by 8.3 percent, while absolute union coverage declined by only 2.7 percent. In Canada, while the percentage of covered employees decreased by 3.8 percent, the number of employees covered by collective bargaining increased by 12.4 percent.

Table 1.3 Percentage of workers represented by unions and number of employees covered by union

| | Representation, United States and Canada, 1997–2003 | | | | | | | |
	1997	1998	1999	2000	2001	2002	2003	% Change, 1997–2003
United States								
% union coverage	15.6	15.4	15.3	14.9	14.8	14.6	14.3	–8.3
Employees covered	1,7923.0	17,918.0	18,182.0	17,944.0	18,114.0	17,771.0	17,448.0	–2.7
Canada								
% union coverage	33.7	32.8	32.2	32.2	32.2	32.2	32.4	–3.8
Employees covered	3,843.8	3,847.7	3,882.3	4,024.7	4,109.1	4,200.9	4,318.6	12.4

Sources: United States Bureau of Labor Statistics; Statistics Canada

On the other hand, the never-unionized sector is growing in both countries, representing a challenge for unions and collective bargaining in general. While Canada continues to have a moderate-sized union density rate, that is not the case for the United States. This raises an important question: can one of the great democracies of the world remain truly democratic when almost all of its workers do not enjoy democracy in their workplace?

Note

1 This section will focus on system-wide attributes and the law related to union representation. There is also detailed legal doctrine related to the process of collective bargaining. Because this legal doctrine is so intimately related to the collective bargaining process, it will be discussed in the section of the paper that addresses the bargaining process in the United States and Canada.

References

Adams, George, 1996–2005, *Canadian Labour Law*, Aurora, Ontario: Canada Law Book (with supplements).

Agreements Between UAW and Visteon Corporation, 2000, Vol. 1, June 29.

Block, Richard N., 1994, 'Reforming US Labor Law and Collective Bargaining: Some Proposals Based on the Canadian System,' in *Restoring the Promise of American Labor Law*, Ithaca, NY: ILR Press, pp. 250–59.

Block, Richard N., 1997, 'Rethinking the National Labor Relations Act and Zero-Sum Labor Law: An Industrial Relations View,' *Berkeley Journal of Employment and Labor Law*, Vol. 18, No. 1, pp. 30–55.

Block, Richard N., ed., 2003, *Bargaining for Competitiveness: Law, Research, and Case Studies*, Kalamazoo, Michigan: W.E. Upjohn Institute for Employment Research.

Block, Richard N., Peter Berg, and Dale Belman, 2005, 'The Economic Dimension of the Employment Relationship,' in *The Employment Relationship: Examining Psychological and Contextual Perspectives*, Jackie Coyle-Shapiro, Lynn Shore, Susan Taylor, Lois Tetrick (eds.) Oxford, UK: Oxford University Press, pp. 94–118.

Block, Richard N., John Beck, Daniel H. Kruger, 1996, *Labor Law, Industrial Relations, and Employee Choice*, Kalamazoo, Michigan: W.E. Upjohn Institute for Employment Research.

Block, Richard N. and Benjamin W. Wolkinson, 1986, 'Delay and the UnionElection Campaign Revisited: A Theoretical and Empirical Analysis,' in *Advances in Industrial and Labor Relations, Vol. III*, David Lewin and David B. Lipsky (eds.) Greenwich, CT: JAI Press, pp. 43–82.

British Columbia Labor Relations Board, undated, 'Welcome to the Labour Relations Board', British Columbia Web Site, at http://www.lrb.bc.ca/

Brudney, James, 1996, 'A Famous Victory: Collective Bargaining Protections and the Statutory Aging Process,' *North Carolina Law Review*, Vol. 74, No. 2, pp. 939–1036.

Burger, Anna, 2005, 'Change to Win Founding Convention', statement by Anna Burger, Chair of Change to Win, September 27, at http://www.changetowin.org/index.asp?Type=B_BASIC& SEC={AE1952C4-7F85-48F4-889D-AAEC79FFED34}, accessed January 16, 2006.

Canada Industrial Relations Board, undated, 'About CIRB' at http://www.cirb-ccri.gc.ca/about/index_e.asp

Dana Corporation, 2004, 341 NLRB No. 150 at http://www.nlrb.gov/nlrb/shared_files/decisions/341/341–150.pdf

Detroit Typographical Union v. *NLRB*, 2000, 216 F.3rd 109, CA DC, at http://caselaw.lp.findlaw.com/scripts/getcase.pl?court=dc&navby=case&no=981599A accessed March 28, 2005.

Dubuque Packing Co., 303 NLRB 386 (1991)

Evening News Association, 154 NLRB 1494, 1965.

European Foundation for Employment and Living Conditions, undated, 'Trade Union Membership, 1993–2003,' European Industrial Relations Observatory, http://www.eiro.eurofound.eu.int/2004/03/update/tn0403105u.html

Greenhouse, Steven, 2005, 'Labor Debates the Future of a Fractured Movement,' *New York Times*, July 27.

Hardin, Patrick and John E. Higgins, Jr., Eds.-in-Chief, 2001–04, *The Developing Labour Law*, 4th Ed., Washington, D.C.: Bureau of National Affairs.

HR Policy Association, undated, 'Position Statements,' at http://www.hrpolicy.org/issues/position_statement.asp?IssueID=12

International Longshoremen's Association, undated, 'Proposed Master Contract, May 4, 2004,' at http://www.ilaunion.org/Contracts/USMX_ILA%20%20Masr%20Contract%2004.pdf, accessed March 1, 2005.

Lieberman, Elias, 1960, *Unions Before the Bar: Historic Trials in the Evolution of Labor Rights in the United States*, New York: Oxford Book Co.

Machalaba, Daniel and Queena Kook Kim, 2002, 'West Coast Ports, Dockworkers Set Tentative Deal on Key Issue,' *Wall Street Journal*, November 4.

National Mediation Board, undated, 'NMB Responsibilities and Activities' at http://www.nmb.gov/mediation/mrna.html

National Right to Work Foundation, undated, 'Right To Work States,' at http://www.nrtw.org/rtws.htm

NLRB v. *Insurance Agents International Union*, 1960, United States Supreme Court, 361 US 477, at http://caselaw.lp.findlaw.com/scripts/getcase.pl?court=us&vol=361&invol=477

Ontario Labour Relations Board, undated, 'About Us,' at http://www.olrb.gov.on.ca/english/aboutus.htm

Pacific Maritime Association, undated, 'About PMA,' at http://www.pmanet.org/docs/index.
    cfm/id_subcat/87

Peirce, Jon, 2003, *Canadian Industrial Relations*, 2nd Ed., Toronto: Prentice-Hall.

Roomkin, Myron and Richard N. Block, 1981 'Case Processing Time and the Outcome of
    Representation Elections: An Empirical Analysis,' *University of Illinois Law Review*, Vol.
    1981, No. 1, pp. 75–97.

Ruben, Alan Miles, Ed.-in-Chief, 2003, *Elkouri and Elkouri: How Arbitration Works*, 2003, 6th
    Ed., Washington, D.C: BNA Books.

Singh, P., Zinni, D., & Jain, H., 2005, 'The Effects of the Use of Striker Replacement
    Legislation in Canada: An Analysis of Four Cases', *Labor Studies Journal*, 30:2
    (Summer), pp. 41–86.

Sweeney, John, 2005, "Statement by AFL-CIO President John Sweeney On SEIU, UNITE/
    HERE, IBT and UFCW's Decision to Not Attend AFL-CIO Convention," July 24, at
    http://www.aflcio.org/mediacenter/prsptm/pr07242005.cfm, accessed January 16, 2006.

Statistics Canada, 2003, *Labor Force Historical Review*, 2003.

United States Bureau of Labor Statistics, 1997–2003, 'Union Members in 1997 … 2003,'
    Annual News Release, at http://www.bls.gov/schedule/archives/all_nr.htm

United States Bureau of Labor Statistics, 2005, 'Union Members in 2004,' Annual News
    Release, atftp://ftp.bls.gov/pub/news.release/History/union2.01272005.news.

United States Federal Mediation and Conciliation Service, undated, 'FY 2003 Arbitration
    Statistics' at http://www.fmcs.gov/internet/itemDetail.asp?categoryID=196&itemID=16987

United States Maritime Alliance, Ltd., undated, Website, at http://www.nmsa.us/usmx.htm

Wasserman, Donald S, 2006, 'Collective Bargaining Rights in the Public Sector: Promises and
    Reality,' in *Justice on the Job: Perspectives on the Erosion of Collective Bargaining in the
    United States*, Kalamazoo, MI: W.E. Upjohn Institute for Employment Research,
    forthcoming.

Westhead, Rick, 2005, 'Hockey: NHL Players Overwhelmingly Approve Deal,' *New York
    Times*, July 22.

Suggested key readings

Adams, George, 1996–2004, *Canadian Labour Law*, Aurora, Ontario: Canada Law Book.

Block, Richard N, John Beck, Daniel H. Kruger, 1996, *Labor Law, Industrial Relations, and
    Employee Choice*, Kalamazoo, Michigan: W.E. Upjohn Institute for Employment
    Research.

Bronfrenbrenner, Kate, 1997, 'The Role of Union Strategies in NLRB Certification Elections,'
    Industrial and Labor Relations Review, Vol. 50, No. 2, pp. 195–212.

Clark, Paul F., John T. Delaney, and Ann C. Frost, eds., 2002, Collective Bargaining in the
    Private Sector, Champaign, Illinois: Industrial Relations Research Association.

Dunlop, John T., 1958, *Industrial Relations Systems*, Carbondale, Illinois, Southern Illinois
    University Press.

Freeman, Richard B. and James. L. Medoff, 1984, *What Do Unions Do?*, New York: Basic
    Books.

Godard, John, 2000, *Industrial Relations, The Economy, and Society*, 2nd Ed., North York,
    Ontario: Captus Press, Inc.

Gunderson, Morley and Allen Ponak, eds., 1995, *Union Management Relations in Canada*, 3rd
    Ed., Don Mills, Ontario, Addison-Wesley.

Hardin, Patrick and John E. Higgins, Jr., Eds.-in-Chief, 2001–04, *The Developing Labour Law*,
    4th Ed., Washington, D.C.: Bureau of National Affairs.

Juravich, Tom and Kate Bronfrenbrenner, 1999, *Ravenswood: The Steelworkers Victory and the
    Revival of American Labor*, Ithaca, New York and London: Cornell Press/ILR Press.

Katz, Harry C., 1985, *Shifting Gears: Changing Labor Relations in the US Automobile Industry*, Cambridge, Massachusetts and London, England: MIT Press.

Katz, Harry C. and Thomas A. Kochan, 2004, *An Introduction to Industrial Relations*, 3rd Ed., New York: McGraw-Hill/Irwin.

Kochan, Thomas A., Harry C. Katz, and Robert McKersie, 1994, *The Transformation of American Industrial Relations*, Ithaca, New York: ILR Press.

Lipset, Seymour Martin, *Continental Divide: The Values and Institutions of the United States and Canada*, Toronto and Washington, D.C.: C.D. Howe Institute and National Planning Association, 1989.

Peirce, Jon, 2003, *Canadian Industrial Relations*, 2nd Ed., Toronto: Prentice-Hall.

Thompson, Mark, Joseph B. Rose and Anthony Smith, 2003, *Industrial Divide: Regional Dimensions of Industrial Relations*, Montreal, Quebec and Kingston, Ontario: McGill-Queens University Press.

White, Bob, 1987, *Hard Bargains: My Life on the Line*, Toronto: McClelland and Stewart.

2 Industrial relations in Latin America

HÉCTOR LUCENA AND ALEX COVARRUBIAS

Introduction

Without doubt the countries of Latin America are varied and diverse. This chapter will deal primarily with the most developed countries of the region. As industrial relations are focused on the interactions of labor, political and economic actors, we will outline the historical evolution of the region and the different countries to contextualize later debates on industrial relations (IR) in current times. A significant theme in this regard is that, in the last quarter of the twentieth century, the countries of the region abandoned the economic model based on import substitution, which had traditionally characterized the region, and adopted more open and neo-liberal economic policies. This has had a significant impact on the IR landscape. Indeed, industrial relations have experienced very signifiant evolution since this change in economic policy. Although within Latin America there is a great diversity of economic and political development as well as variety in its socio-cultural traditions, there are recognizable common elements due to their common colonial history.

First, the region is charcterized by high levels of politization or state involvement in IR. This phenomenon derives from the significant role played by the state in the setting and sponsorship of IR actors and institutions. Furthermore, the adoption of the import substitution model was primarily driven by the state elites (Bergquist 1986; Payne 1965; Zapata 1990). In the last twenty-five years, in recognition of the limits of the traditional economic model, the state elites again allowed the international pressures of the international capital and local allies to act to create a more open framework for business. By the beginning of the new century, however, we witnessed the collapse of the open economies of several countries in the region. Furthermore, new forces emerged acting outside of the traditional IR actors, resulting in pressures coming from the informal and other non-formalized urban industrial workers, key actors in the previous stages.

Role of main actors

The state

As was noted above, the state has historically been and remains a key actor in the industrial relations framework of various countries within Latin America. Key in this regard was the state's role in driving high levels of institutionalization in IR. The state was from an early stage heavily involved in the setting of the rules related to IR, with the result that there are permanent close relations between the labor force and the state. The one exception is Uruguay which has enjoyed a more voluntary IR system, based on the autonomy of the labor force and lower levels of institutional constraint on the operation of labor relations.

In outlining the state's relationship with other key IR actors it is important to note that historical differences between countries in the region result in different interactions between state and IR actors in different nations. The significance of the nature of the state's involvement in IR should not be underestimated as it is likely to impact on all other elements of the employment relationship within a country.

During the first decades of the twentieth century, the relationship between the state and the labor force changed dramatically. Previously state repression was a state's main response to the attempts of labor to organize and protest. More recently state and political leaders have legalized labor organizations as a means of institutionalizing industrial disputes. A new pattern of state-labor relations emerged. This 'incorporation' laid the foundations of Latin American corporatism. The political modernization adopted was through the movement known in the literature as 'populism'. Two authors define it as 'A collectivist political phenomenon which is characterized by: an urban environment; a social base integrated by different social classes; an eclectic and ambiguous ideology with a tint of nationalism; and a charismatic leader' (Collier 1979). Another author (Di Tella 1969) sees populism as a political movement that depends on urban workers, but not emanating from any organizational power on their behalf. This author recognizes 'the anti-status quo ideology' characteristic of populism and sees it as having the potential for bringing about significant social change, but does not see the popular masses as exercising an active leadership.

The period of incorporation of the labor movement coincided with the decline of old oligarchies and the rise to power of new elites drawn from the urban commercial and manufacturing sectors. The new elites initiated the reforms and revolutions that gave rise to the 'social constitutions' that later would back the interventionist state. In fact these social constitutions provided the broad framework from which labor law and industrial relations systems regulations would emerge. These laws and regulations shaped a dense web of rules sanctioning work and labor conditions, minimum wages and social security.

Simultaneously, the state was elevated to the category of supreme mediator and arbiter of labor and management disputes and class conflict.

State involvement is primarily evident in the enactment of the first labor legislation, which was intended to facilitate conditions for industrialization, and particularly to regulate and control collective labor relations (Lucena 1989). Although there is evidence of the protection of the workers (individual rights), the state also sought to control social conflict. These two tendencies deepened with time: there was ample protection for the individual worker, with concessions to material benefits, and control of groups or collective actions. This allowed the state ample discretion in the legalization of the unions, the admission of workers' demands and strike regulation (Lucena 1998; Bronstein 1995).

At this time Latin American corporatism developed three distinctive characteristics: (1) a system to control and integrate the labor movement within a non-competitive, compulsory and sanctioned system of interest groups; (2) dependence of these groups on state subsidies; and (3) a system of inducements and constraints to manipulate demands, leaderships and internal governance of labor unions.

For syndicalism the process described in the previous paragraph meant action centered on putting pressure on the state, 'without having responsibility in the production process or in the design of economic policies'. The union battles were in response to redistributional politics based on political negotiation with the state, in either a conciliatory or radical way. Later, when it was necessary to open up the economy, the limitations inherent in this orientation made it incapable of dealing with the crises in the productive systems (Sulmont, D. 1995: 279).

From a political perspective, although the process was common to many of the countries, they achieved it in different ways. Two types of 'incorporation' were apparent: state- and party-led incorporation. In the state-led labor incorporation the primary goal was controlling and depoliticizing the labor movement. In the second type, the party or movement, which later became a party, mobilized labor to generate political support for the urban elites leading modernization. These forms of incorporation provided 'historical legacies' with specific consequences for each nation (Coronil 2002).

Collier and Collier (1991) summarize the key similarities and differences for the eight most important countries of the region. Brazil and Chile are examples of state incorporation with a government basically aiming to control the labor movement. The rest of the countries fall into the category of party incorporation: labor-populism in Argentina and Peru; radical populism in Venezuela and Mexico; and electoral mobilization by traditional parties in Uruguay and Colombia. The cases of Brazil, Mexico, Venezuela and Argentina are discussed in more detail later in this chapter.

Table 2.1 The 'first incorporation' (Collier and Collier 1991). Similarities and differences between pairs of countries

| | *Political similarities during the period of incorporation* | | | |
| | | *Incorporation of party* | | |
Differences, social and economic	*Incorporation of state*	*Mobilization electoral/ traditional party*	*Labor Populism*	*Radical Populism*
Socially more homogenous countries, with greater indicators of modernization per capita	Chile	Uruguay	Argentina	Venezuela[a]
Socially more heterogenous countries, with indicating minors of modernization per capita	Brazil	Colombia	Peru	Mexico[a]

a This ordering of Venezuela and Mexico mainly talks about the period of the 1950s and 1970s. At the end of the nineteenth century and the start of the twentieth century, both countries showed opposed tendencies, but in the 1970s and 1980s the countries tended to converge.
Source: Collier and Collier (1991: 17)

The Trade Unions

The labor movement in the region has been exposed to very restrictive structures and institutions as a result of corporatist traditions. Labor laws put several limits on the rights of workers to organize, go on strike and negotiate collective agreements. According to law, unions were to 'assist' workers with social services and act outside the factory gates, thus limiting their role in engaging with management on issues related to the workplace. The state also reserved powers to control unions at any time and dismiss union leaders at will. As a result, labor was relegated to a position of permanent opposition that would lead to its radicalization. The politicization of the labor movement and its increasing shift to the political left were in many ways a direct result of an industrial relations system that aimed to marginalize unions and place them at a disadvantage at the level of the work place.

Such a system of control and subordination of labor was eventually challenged by a growing insurgency within the labor movement. It came from the most advanced industrial regions and the most skilled workers within those regions. The *coups d'etat* and military rule during the 1960s and 1970s were largely in response to labor unrest. The Brazilian military rule, along with the Chilean, was the largest dictatorship of the whole region. But despite military rule, in the long run, labor protest and unrest did not recede. The major organizations, the United Workers Confederation (CUT) and the General Workers Confederation (CGT), continued to grow, particularly the former. CUT, led by metal and motorcar workers, would go on to create the Party of Workers (PT) as its political arm (French 1992). And together they were instrumental in achieving an end to the military era and the return to democracy. From the rank and file of these movements emerged Luis Ignacio Lula da Silva. When Lula and the PT won the presidential election in 2002, it represented the culmination of labor's three-decade-long struggle for industrial and political democracy.

Collier and Collier (1991) define the party-led incorporation of Venezuela and Mexico as radical populism. This label refers to the electoral mobilization and organization of popular sectors which involved not only the working class but also the peasantry. It produced a political heritage of an 'integrating' party system. In Mexico the party that led the process of incorporation via the mobilization of workers and peasants was the Institutional Revolutionary Party (PRI). Through it, dominant elites set up a one-party dominant system based on a hegemonic, non-competitive industrial and political process. The state and PRI created a complex pattern of negotiation of interests based on the conciliation and accommodation of groups, leaderships and, in the last instance, repression. The control of labor through corporative structures like the Mexican Workers Confederation (CTM) in the first instance, and other workers' organizations, primarily rural sectors through the National Peasants Confederations (CNC) and even other urban popular sectors, gave the Mexican state a great deal of legitimacy.

In Venezuela a somewhat similar picture emerged. But there were some differences. First, the party that initially largely controlled the labor movement, the Democratic Action (AD), later co-operated and shared power with another party, the Social Christian Party (COPEI). From this evolved a political system that had two dominant parties and Venezuelan industrial relations were described as representing a 'limited pluralism'. The Venezuela Workers Confederation (CTV), shaped by militants of both parties, ruled the labor movement. Unionism in practice would become a process of conciliation (Salamanca 1998; Lucena 1998) between management and labor, under the control of the state and the intermediation of the parties. The basics of labor relations were negotiated at state level, between parties and government representatives, giving rise to a system of 'programmed negotiation' (Lucena 2003).

From there, the systems of industrial relations of both countries shared many common features. Labor laws gave powers of intervention to state agencies to approve unions and strikes, as well as to arbitrate in labor/management disputes. Furthermore, the Mexican labor legislation introduced an extensive range of rules to protect labor, along with a set of restrictive conditions on the use of the workforce (De la Garza and Bouzas 1999). These rules remain unchanged and in operation to the current day. In contrast, Venezuelan labor legislation was modified in 1991 and 1997. New labor rules granted greater protection to labor. The same happened with social protection for retired workers. At the same time however, new restrictions on the right to strike were sanctioned (Lucena 2003).

The Venezuelan and Mexican labor laws provide a good example of a well-protected Latin American labor force. In fact, in this respect, it has been argued that Latin American labor laws are unparalleled in many developed countries (Heckman and Pagés 2000; Covarrubias 2000).

Backed by these integrative systems, the political and industrial regimes of Mexico and Venezuela survived and extended their rule until the 1990s. But dramatic changes began to unfold. The persistent work of the political and labor oppositions in both countries, along with mounting social contradictions and unrest related to liberal economic policies and political participation, set the stage for political implosion. Mexico, for the first time, after more than a half-century of single-party domination, had free elections. Perhaps unsurprisingly the PRI lost office. In 2000 the conservative National Action Party (PAN), won the first free election, bringing to a halt the integrative system. Hence, in Venezuela, a new political group stepped forward and swept away the old political domination of AD and COPEI. This group was headed by military leaders that in 1992 were at the forefront of an uprising against the state. They built a broad coalition with several left-wing groups and later on, under Hugo Chavez, they were to take power.

The cost of breaking down the long rule of the integrative system in both countries was high for the traditional rulers. New social forces are coming to the power and divergence is mounting. However, whereas in Venezuela divergence aggravates division, violence and social clash, in Mexico it is taking the form of a toll that a new democratic system must pay. That is, there are now a number of parties contesting for power and government is divided.

Labor-populism in Argentina and Peru paralyzed political and industrial regimes, or created a 'political stalemate' in Collier and Collier's words. In Argentina, Peron and Peronism are to the fore in this regard. Due to populist policies that Peronism followed during the incorporation process, and due mainly to the increasingly authoritarian traits it adopted, Peron was forced from power and exiled. The populist party and Peronist labor movement were banned, leaving labor to follow either an opposition path or to join coalitions in a subordinate role.

Ideologically, financially and structurally speaking, the main organizational base of Peronism was the labor movement. The General Workers Confederation (CGT) was the labor confederation deployed by Peron's Government, which created an industrial relations system with some checks on the power of the workers. Although it even reinforced the right to collective bargaining, it also imposed state intervention on union formation and union agenda and restricted the right to strike. At the same time, a complex system of patronage was put in place, through which union leaders bought and sold favors and protection. The industrial relations system was corrupted. In addition, laws were either selectively or rarely enforced as all were first subjected to Peron's will.

The conflict between Peronists and anti-Peronists would spread from the political arena to the labor relations arena, and to the social sphere, to become the centre of Argentine cultural life. The conflict escalated into a bitter confrontation. The exit of Peron in the midst of violent and bloody confrontations in 1955; his exile for almost eighteen years; the prolongation of confrontations and violence during the following three decades; the prohibition and restrictions on political parties; and the *coups d'etat* of 1962, 1966 and 1976; all demonstrate the extreme antagonism that fractured Argentinian society.

The paralysis of the political and industrial arenas seemed to be at an end when the military left power and the transition to democracy began. For a time the country appeared finally to have reached stability when the radicals of Raúl Alfonsin took the presidency in 1983 and then when the Peronists' Menem won office in 1989, after competing in a free and appeasing electoral contest. Even so, at the end of the 1990s, the nation experienced its greatest paralysis of modern history.

In recent years the trade union movement in Latin America has experienced difficulties similar to those of their counterparts in other regions of the world. This was primarily evidenced in falling union density levels (Rodriguez 1999). Union density rates in the region range from a high affiliation, as in the case of Argentina with 25 per cent, to very low rates in Colombia and the countries of Central America, with rates between 5 and 8 per cent. Similarly, employers' organizations have also endured challenging times. The opening up of the economies has affected productive sectors in different ways. Those that have put into practice effective modernization strategies have adapted better to the

Table 2.2 Union affiliation in selected Latin American countries

Country	Union affiliation	
	1990–1995	*1995–2000*
Argentina	24.4	25.4
Bolivia	30.9	16.4
Brazil	24.9	23.6
Chile	20.8	13.1
Colombia	7.4	6.9
Mexico	22.3	–
Peru	7.5	7.8
Venezuela	25.9	14.9
Latin America average sample	16.8	13.1

Source: OIT, Panorama laboral 2002, Nuevos indicadores para el Indice de desarrollo del Trabajo Decente. Lima

exigencies of internationalization; however, sectors still exist where enterprise companies and unions have not become sufficiently modernized and therefore are also in crisis.

Unionization, democratization and social pressures

We begin by identifying the transitions in the region towards democratization and the impact on the operation of local industrial relations systems. At the beginning of the twenty-first century only two governments in the region, Cuba and Haiti, were not elected through free elections. Today, democracy is widely diffused throughout the entire region.

Nevertheless, signs of turbulence and instability in many countries remain apparent. After being part of 'the third wave of democratization', a number of democratically elected governments have failed to complete their periods in office as public unrest has resulted in ultimately successful demands for their resignation. This picture is familiar to a number of countries within the region: A. Bucaran in Ecuador; Collor de Melo in Brazil; Carlos A. Perez in Venezuela; A. Fujimori in Peru; Fernando De la Rua in Argentina; and lastly, in 2003, G. Sanchez de Lozada and in 2005 Carlos Meza in Bolivia, are all examples.

In the most recent, highly publicized cases – Argentina in 2001 and Bolivia in 2003 and 2005 – democratically elected presidents were dismissed following public riots involving thousands of citizens. Labor unions, in concert with other social sectors, played an active role in the organization of these protests. This indicates that in spite of the problems affecting unions, they remain an important social actor in public life in the region. In both of these countries, the labor movement has played a pivotal role in a complex spectrum of social forces that allied to overthrow their respective governments. What it is important to note is that, as these episodes showed, the labor movement in Latin American currently operates in the midst of a new political and social context. This context comprises a complex mix of new and old social actors. For instance, at the peak of recent social unrest and demonstrations in South America, riots were headed by peasants and farmers in Brazil – 'Movement of People Without Land'; indigenous movements and organizations in Bolivia, among others, the so-called 'Cocaleros'; unemployed, employees of the informal economy and marginalized people in Venezuela among others, the so-called 'bolivarianos' circles; and unemployed and employees of the informal sector in Argentina – the so-called 'piqueteros'.

Although democracy is a key desire and right for any society, 'love with hunger does not last' as the popular saying goes. In the context of high levels of poverty and economic hardship which have characterized the region, transition to democracy in most Latin American countries has been difficult. A number of factors, the most significant of which being external debt, have put an additional pressure on the public budget, taking scarce resources away from promoting development.[1] Simultaneously, governments have been forced by international financial institutions, such as IMF and the World Bank, to apply 'neo-liberal' policies, cutting back social budgets, increasing prices of public tariffs, streamlining government offices, privatizing public enterprises and keeping down wages to stabilize and adjust the economy (Sotelo 2004). This has resulted in a number of critics commenting that 'the treatment has been worse than the disease' (Stiglitz 2002).

It could be argued that presidents have diminished ability to govern, faced with the delicate balancing act of meeting the requirements of international financial creditors and institutions and delivering on election promises to the electorate. De la Rua's presidency in Argentina provides a good example. He was overthrown in December 2001 when the nation defaulted on its international payments and public unrest resulted in damage to and looting of banks and stores. A transitional government led by E. Duhalde and the presently elected government of A. Kirchner have had to set up a meticulous and delicate process of negotiations with financial institutions, making it clear that the government has to attend to social needs and promote development in order to retain governance.

Employers, enterprises and productive systems

Just like their union counterparts it is natural for managers to wish to organize collectively. Similarly, the primary objective of these managerial organizations is to achieve greater bargaining power in their relations with government and more generally with the public bodies with whom they interact. Further objectives include the development of trade, and mutual support and solidarity among their members. One of the most important roles in interactions with state authorities is to act as a pressure group, particularly in the promotion of a pro-business environment and the development of appropriate economic and social policy decisions, of which IR issues often represent an important element.

It is important to consider that in the Latin American region foreign-owned investments have been very important in economic modernization. These investors were characterized by their self-sufficiency in that they did not rely on the state to any great extent in their operation in the country. Thus they often had a relatively powerful bargaining position with government bodies in the host country.

By the end of the 1980s Latin American entrepreneurs viewed the development of market freedom as a victory. These celebrations were, however, tempered somewhat by an emerging fear that by opening their borders to foreign trade, indigenous firms within the region would be faced by a world where the market and new capital – ghastly and autonomous – are the masters and thus their continued operation and profitability would be under threat from foreign competitors. This led to the emergence of a great variety of forms of company and it was no longer possible to speak of a company as a fixed concept. Besides the large companies there are medium and small ones with different objectives and strategies (Raso 2005; Villamil 2001).

In the new Latin American business context old and new managerial models coexist. On the one hand the black economy continues to flourish with archaic production techniques and, indeed, the proportion of illegal work has expanded to previously unknown levels, particularly in 'maquilas', foreign trade zones and other production areas where labor protection does not exist. On the other hand, development and technology are embraced and the industrial landscape has changed significantly. A dual system of production exists in Latin America with a second industrial revolution apparent in certain parts of the economy, co-existing with production models from the first industrial revolution in other parts.

The fragmentation of industrial enterprise has caused the expansion of many small companies. These differ from their larger, longer-established counterparts in having fewer workers with family or personal bonds (same neighborhood, common social origin, etc.), relationships of solidarity depending on non-traditional hierarchies, limited capital requiring the substitution of advanced technologies or specially skilled workers to add value and a tendency to depend on a limited number of buyers purchasing significant percentages of the production output. The small company is not eliminated from the system. On the contrary it has found new work opportunities, either supplying major companies, or finding niche markets. Such companies are important employment generators, although often jobs are precarious and not covered by labor law. These have given rise to new workers' associations dedicated to promoting different kinds of co-operatives in Colombia, Peru, Uruguay and Venezuela. (In the last two-and-a-half years more than sixty thousand new co-operatives have been registered in Venezuela.) In general, co-operatives have lower overhead costs that favor their extension in the labor market (Lucena 2005; Raso 2005).

Latin America, USA and the Free Trade Agreement

During the Clinton era, as neo-liberal policies established themselves in country after country, a plan was formulated to create a large free trade zone throughout the entire American continent, from Alaska to Patagonia – the Free Trade Agreement of the Americas (FTAA). The idea of FTAA gained momentum with the USA, Canada and Mexico signing the 1994 North American Free Trade Agreement (NAFTA). But creating the FTAA has proven to be a more difficult task than creating bilateral or sub-regional agreements. Thus, despite the fact that during the last round of talks a statement was made to the effect that negotiations were to be concluded in January 2005 and membership come into force no later than December 2005, real progress has yet to be achieved.

Historical inequalities for the countries of the region in trade with the USA have not been satisfactorily resolved for Latin American. Given this, and in view of the greater obstacles to advancing the FTAA proposals, the USA has decided to promote bilateral agreements, and indeed it already has made agreements with certain countries in the region (for example Chile and Costa Rica). In addition to the FTAA negotiations, previous experience of constructing a regional block has been gained with the Mercade Común del Sur (Southern Common Market – MERCOSUR), and it has played an important role in promoting political partnerships. MERCOSUR originally consisted of Brazil, Argentina, Uruguay and Paraguay – but more recently Chile and Bolivia have also been included, and Venezuela and Mexico are in the process of joining.

The development of economic relations with the USA is a fundamental priority for the region, as it needs US investments as well as the US market for its products. However, this must be in the context of fairness and political recognition. Recently these concerns are being more often voiced by the regional governments, as political democratization proceeds and public executives are held accountable for economic success or failure. There are movements in some countries in the region supporting the idea of referendums to decide whether they should join the FTAA or not.

Collective labor relations: Conflicts and collective bargaining

The end of the cold war and the fall of commumism had serious implications for the trade union movement in the region. In general, unity between the various stakeholders was needed for the region to adjust to this change. This also raises the question of whether the union movement was prepared to operate in the new political environment. The perception predominates that the union movement also requires reconstruction (Portella and Wachendorfer 1995).

While globalization has resulted in increased mobility of capital, technologies, companies and products, labor remains a somewhat less mobile commodity. Globalization also presents challenges for the labor movement. In neo-liberal societies companies have the freedom to produce where the wages are lowest and sell where the wages are high.

The union movement's response to neo-liberalism was different to its operation within the previous model of accumulation, which gave rise to a predominantly corporative syndicalism in most Latin American countries, and to majority classist unionism in a few. In most Latin american neo-liberal societies the union movement has not enjoyed sufficient influence to be able to bring about classist syndicalism as it had operating within the previous economic model.

Figure 2.1 illustrates strike trends in the region over the last twenty-three years. It is important to note, however, that there is a clear tendency to understate strike levels in the region. This is valid even in the case of Brazil, a country whose propensity to strike is the greatest on the continent. In Mexico, where the information is more complete, the trend towards fewer strikes in the two decades is more than clear; it is irrefutable.

The dynamic technological development associated with globalization has impacted upon the productive systems of the region, and given rise to new productive profiles. The relationship between the productive system and the markets has also changed, as of course has the relationship with the state. The unions adapted to these changes. Nevertheless, over the years union power has diminished in South America for the same reasons it has in many parts of the world.

Under the previous economic model public sector companies and administrative service organizations enjoyed high levels of union membership. Many of these have since been privatized and others have adopted private employment policies, limiting the union's traditional role. The most visible transformation derived from privatization is seen in the area of industrial relations and specially in the issues included in the collective agreements; additionally, management behaves in a more professional manner in the area of human resources (Walter 1998; Walter and Senen 1998; Iranzo and Ritcher 1999).

The transformation of IR in these privatized institutions can also be seen as an advance given the generalized malfunctioning of the services and activities undertaken by state companies. Interested parties have taken advantage of the situation to fortify the private sector, placing responsibility for economic

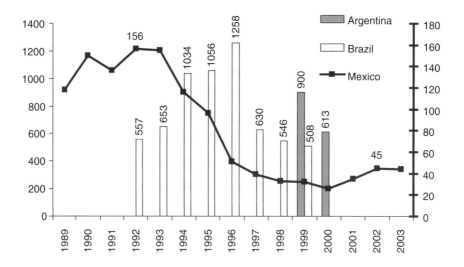

Figure 2.1 Strikes (Brazil, Mexico and Argentina)
Source: Figures given by the Secretaría del Trabajo y Previsión Social, Mexico.

problems on poor industrial relations practices. The result has been to strengthen individual bargaining power at the expense of collective interests. Industrial relations are thus conducted at company level or at establishment level. Only Brazil and Argentina have managed to develop advanced industrial relations practices at sectoral or industrial levels, while in other countries response to the transformation has seen sectoral and national level agreements diminishing.

The region has historically assigned special importance to the construction of an official framework. In Latin America, the tradition has seen the ratification of a high number of the International Labour Office (ILO) approved treaties. This stands in contrast to the more developed countries of North America where the USA and Canada have only ratified twelve and twenty-nine ILO agreements respectively. But at the same time, the high number of ratified agreements has meant a high number of breach and violation complaints. The Committee of Union Freedom of the ILO (Rodríguez 2001) provides the following data for the ten-year period 1990–2001:

- 52 per cent of complaints come from Latin America (1,022)
- 31.88 per cent of Latin American complaints come from Andean countries (338)
- As much in Latin America as in the Andean countries, most of the complaints arise from anti-union discrimination: 32 per cent in both cases.
- Of the six greatest violators of union freedom five are Latin American countries representing 42 per cent of the total. The complaint figures are: Argentina, 40; Peru, 38; Colombia, 28; Venezuela, 26; and Guatemala, 23.
- Of the 320 thoroughly analyzed cases, 64 per cent involved Latin America governments. The second greatest violators were private companies and the third public companies.

Treaties in the region are often modified. These changes alter both collective agreements and conditions of work in general. This has happened historically in the small companies, but now occurs in great transnational companies, even with the knowledge of the relevant departments of public authorities. The phenomenon of modification to working condition agreements – 'labor flexibility' – derives from the need for significant segments of the working population to secure some income to solve their subsistence problems. If the normative or regulatory schemes are too protective of workers' rights, the labor market will erode the good intentions behind the regulations. This leads to extreme casualization: large factories either hire workers with limited labor rights, part-time workers, for instance, or outsource work to third parties that hire labor under even more precarious employment conditions. The point is that in a context of weak labor markets with high unemployment rates, workers have no choice – they have to accept these informal job opportunities.

Collective bargaining takes many forms. In some large nations, like Brazil, Argentina, Mexico and Uruguay, negotiations are centralized. With the exception of Uruguay, all of them are permeated by state intervention. In other countries, like Chile, Peru, Venezuela and Colombia, negotiations are decentralized and at company level (O'Connell 1999).

The region has witnessed a high degree of deterioration of its labor markets. This works against the development of collective bargaining (BID 2004; Cepal 2004). In the 1970s, Latin America could have provided a showcase for unusual working arrangements, the most prevalent being informality (Candia 2003; Mesa-Lago 2000). Today Latin America remains a region that offers the most diverse forms of work, that is to say forms of survival. Some are obliged to accept informality as the norm even though they once worked as formal employees; others do not know what protected employment is, and few experience more enlightened practices.

As a whole, informality accounts for over 50 per cent of the economically active population. Of course, statistical averages include societies where the figure exceeds 60 per cent. Scholars working from different perspectives established a variation from 35 to 60 per cent in the non-formal sector of the economy (OIT 1999; Portes and Hoffman 2003).

What implications have these phenomena for IR? First that the number of employees enjoying the benefits of enlightened IR concepts and traditional forms of welfare have diminished. It is not only the diminution of unionization and collective bargaining that is worrying – that is a global trend – but still more disquieting is the diminution in the creation of jobs. This alert has been raised by U. Beck (2000), who believes that reasons for the job losses experienced by the developed capitalist world are already implanted in the Latin American region.

Conclusion

The end of the twentieth century and the beginning of the twenty-first found the industrial relations of the region in the process of fundamental reform and many of these changes have been alluded to in this present chapter. In drawing together this contribution, it is worth focusing the attention of the reader on a number of key issues.

Conventionally, industrial relations were seen as important to support the development of the region, and in some respects they became a platform for development. Although development was accompanied by conflict and social unrest with labor acting against the forces of capital, there is no doubt that some workers and some employers would have preferred to operate without rules, outside of the established institutions and without democratically elected leaders or spokesmen. Many employers, however, quickly saw the necessity of the recognition of a leader who could be seen to be a consistent representative of the workers. Part of the backdrop, therefore, to the development of industrial relations was the overcoming of resistance. The industrial relations that developed are indicative of a common denominator on the continent in terms of rules, institutions and mechanisms. However, it is necessary to note that industrial relations and its instruments and systems did not extend to all the productive areas. They have materialized in the modernized segments of the manufacturing and services economy, including certainly the most important producers and contributors in terms of GNP makeup. Many of the benefits of regulations and institutions involved in industrial relations have also extended to other sectors. This occurred through general legislation of social and labor subjects, as well as through labor and social public policies that adopted best practices from those sectors which had establised processes of negotiations or institutions that were seen to be mutually beneficial.

By the end of 1970s it was apparent that the import substitution model era had fallen apart. Growth had slowed throughout the region and investment was shrinking as external debt, unemployment, poverty and inflation rates skyrocketed. Countries then turned to the export-oriented industrialization model promoted by the IMF, the World Bank and the Washington Consensus, focused on outward orientation policies and creating unregulated-free markets and labor relations. After more than two decades of economic, political, and labor transformations in Latin America industrial relations have changed. The state-directed system of labor relations has receded. Labor markets and labor unions are in crisis. The former is affected by a non-formal economy that is growing in the context of privatization and deregulated state and labor relations. The latter is being challenged by neo-liberal policies and flexible production systems that demand more from workers. Yet unions have lost momentum. A new free industrial relations system and a new labor unionism have yet to be constructed in the region.

Note

1 The external debt made the following progression: In the 1970s, US$ 200 billion; in the 1980s, 400 billion; in the 1990s, 800 billion. The external debt reached 43 per cent of GNP in 2002 and 180.5 per cent of export of goods and services (CEPAL – Economic Commission for Latin America; 2004: 38–39).

References

Banco Interamericano de Desarrollo BID (2004) *Informe de progreso económico y social. Se buscan buenos empleos. Los mercados laborales en América Latina*. Washington.

Beck, Ulrich (2000) *Un nuevo mundo feliz. La precariedad del trabajo en la era de la globalización*. Edit. Paidos, Barcelona.

Bergquist, Charles (1986) *Labor in Latin America: Comparative Essays on Chile, Argentina, Venezuela and Colombia*. Stanford, California: Stanford University Press.

Bronstein, Arturo (1995) 'Cambio social y relaciones de trabajo en América Latina: balance y perspectivas' en *Revista Internacional del Trabajo*. OIT, Ginebra, 114(2): 184–209.

Candia, Jose Miguel (2003) 'Sector Informal ¿treinta años de un debate bizantino? *Nueva Sociedad*. Nº 186 Julio, Agosto. Venezuela, pp. 36–45.

CEPAL (2004) *Estudio económico 2002–2003. AL y el Caribe. Situación y perspectivas*. Santiago.

Collier, Ruth and David Collier (1991) *Shaping the Political Arena. Critical Junctures, the Labor Movement, and Regimen Dynamics in Latin America*. USA: Princeton University Press.

Collier, David (ed.) (1979) *The New Authoritarism in Latin America*. USA: Princeton University Press.

Coronil, Fernando (2002) *El Estado mágico. Naturaleza, dinero y modernidad en Venezuela*. 1era edic. en castellano, edit. Original en Inglés 1997; Edit. Nueva Sociedad-UCV, Caracas.

Covarrubias, V. Alex (2000) *Mercados de trabajo y subsistemas de empleo en México y Brasil: Un modelo analítico y dos estudios de caso en la Industria Automotriz*. El Colegio de Sonora. Hermosillo, Sonora.

Di Tella, Torcuato (1969) 'Populism and reform in Latin America' in Claudio Veliz (ed.) *Obstacles to Change in Latin America*. Oxford University Press: Oxford.

French, John D. (1992) *The Brazilian Workers' ABC. Class Conflict and Alliances in Modern Sao Paulo*, The University of North Caroline Press.

Garza, E. de la and Bouzas, A. (eds) (1999) 'Cambios en las relaciones laborales. Enfoque sectorial y regional', Vol. I, Edit. UAM, UNAM, FAT, AFL-CIO.

Heckman, James J. and Carmen Pagés (2000) 'The cost of job security regulation: evidence from Latin American labor markets', *National Bureau of Economic Research*, Working Paper, Washington.

Iranzo, Consuelo and Ritcher, Jacqueline (1999) *La privatización ¿ruptura en las Relaciones Laborales?* Edit CENDES-UCV: Caracas.

Lucena, Héctor (1989) 'The paper of the State in the industrial relationships in Latin America' in *Relations Industrielles*, 44(1) Edit. Quebec, Canada: Université Laval.

Lucena, Héctor (1998) (first edition 1992) *Las Relaciones Laborales en Venezuela*. Caracas: Edit. Centauro.

Lucena, Héctor (2003) *Las Relaciones de Trabajo en el nuevo siglo*. Edit. Tropykos, Caracas.

Lucena, Héctor (2005) 'Propuestas alternativas en las relaciones de trabjao Venezolanas: la cogestion y el cooperativismo', en *Libro Memoria del I Congreso Latinoamericano sobre Gerencia, Ley y Jurisprudencia Laborales*, Caracas, Edit. Iltras y Unimet, pp. 133–158.

Mesa-Lago, Carmelo (2002) *Buscando un modelo económico en América Latina. ¿Mercado, socialista o mixto? Chile, Cuba y Costa Rica*, Editado por Nueva Sociedad y Florida Internacional University, Caracas.

O'Connell, Lesley D. (1999) 'Collective Bargaining Systems in 6 Latin American Countries: Degrees of Autonomy and Decentralization. Argentina, Brazil, Chile, Mexico, Peru, and Uruguay', Working paper No. 399, May, Inter-American Development Bank, Washington, D.C.

Organización Internacional del Trabajo (OIT) (2002) *Panorama laboral 2002, Nuevos indicadores para el Indice de desarrollo del Trabajo Decente*, Lima: OIT.

Organización Internacional del Trabajo (OIT) Tokman, V y Martinez D (1999) *Flexibilización en el margen: la reforma del contrato de trabajo*. Lima: OIT.

Payne, James L. (1965) *Labor and Politics in Peru*. New Haven: Yale University Press.

Portella, M.S. and Wachendorfer A (ed.) (1995) *Sindicalismo Latinoamericano. Entre la renovación y la resignación*. Edit. Ildis-Fes y Nueva Sociedad, Caracas.

Raso D, Juan (2005) *Una mirada global al mundo del trabajo*. Universidad Nacional del Uruguay.

http://www.rau.edu.uy/universidad/inst_derecho_del_trabajo/raso.pdf , accessed March 22, 2005.

Rodríguez C, Eduardo (2001) *Perfil del comité de libertad sindical. 50 años como garante internacional*. Edit. Lima: OIT.

Rodríguez, Leoncio Martins (1999) *Destino do Sindicalismo: crisis o declinio?* Edit. USP, Sao Paulo.

Salamanca, Luis (1998) *Obreros, movimiento social y democracia en Venezuela*. Edit. Universidad Central de Venezuela, Facultad de Ciencias Jurídicas y Políticas; Caracas, p. 420.

Sotelo Valencia, Adrián (2004) 'Crisis de la deuda externa y reestructuración del mundo del trabajo' En *Revista Trabajadores*, No. 41, Año 8, Marzo-Abril. Editada por Universidad Obrera de México, México, pp. 37–41.

Stiglitz, Joseph (2002) *El malestar en la globalización*. Edit. Buenos Aires: Taurus.

Sulmont, Denis (1995) 'Transformación productiva y opciones para el trabajo' en *Revista del Centro de Investigación y Acción Social*, Año XLIV, No. 444, Julio; Buenos Aires; pp. 277–92.

Villamil, Robert (2001) *El papel de los gremios empresariales en los albores del siglo XXI*. Cartagena de Indias, Colombia, http://www.iberpymeonline.org/documentos/sep2001_uruguaytexto.pdf, review the March 22, 2005.

Walter, J and Senen, C (ed.) (1998) *Privatizaciones y relaciones laborales en la telefonía latinoamericana*. Edit. Eudeba, Buenos Aires.

Walter, Jorge (1998) 'Privatizaciones y relaciones laborales en la telefonía latinoamericana' in *Revista Latinoamericana de Estudios del Trabajo*, Año 4, No. 8, Sao Paulo, pp. 89–107.

Zapata, Francisco (1990). *Ideología y Política en América Latina*. El Colegio de México.

Suggested key readings

Bergquist, Charles (1986) *Labor in Latin America: comparative essays on Chile, Argentina, Venezuela and Colombia*. Stanford University.

Collier, Ruth and David Collier (1991) *Shaping the Political Arena. Critical Junctures, the Labor Movement, and Regimen Dynamics in Latin America*. Princeton University Press. USA.

De La Garza Toledo (ed.) (2000) *Tratado latinoamericano de sociología del trabajo*. Primera Edición. México.

Dombois, Rainer and Pries, Ludger (2000) *Relaciones laborales entre mercado y Estado. Sendas de transformación en América Latina*. Edit. Nueva Sociedad.

French, John D. (1992), *The Brazilian Workers' ABC. Class Conflict and Alliances in Modern Sao Paulo*. The University of North Caroline Press.

Labarca, Guillermo (ed.) (1999) *Formación y Empresa. El entrenamiento y la capacitación en el proceso de reestructuración productiva*. Edit. OIT, CINTERFOR Y CEPAL, Montevideo.

Lucena, Héctor (2003) *Las Relaciones de Trabajo en el nuevo siglo*. Edit. Tropykos, Caracas.

Mesa-Lago, Carmelo (2002) *Buscando un modelo económico en América Latina. ¿Mercado, socialista o mixto? Chile, Cuba y Costa Rica.* Editado por Nueva Sociedad y Florida Internacional University, Caracas

Portella, M.S. and Wachendorfer A (1995), *Sindicalismo Latinoamericano. Entre la renovación y la resignación.* Edit. Ildis-Fes y Nueva Sociedad, Caracas.

3 Industrial relations in Western Europe

COLIN GILL

Introduction

From the 1970s onwards all Western European economies have faced a number of common developments which have fundamentally shaped the evolution of industrial relations. Western European economies have been undergoing a structural transformation in the transition from manufacturing to services. As services have expanded there has been a significant shift from manual to white-collar employment. At the same time, developments in international trade have meant that European economies have become increasingly integrated into a global economy dominated by large multinational companies. The emergence of the single market in the European Union (EU) can be seen as an element in these developments, as European businesses seek to enhance their competitiveness in world markets. As new technological innovations based on microelectronics and telecommunications have developed, European firms have sought to compete by moving away from mass standardized production to customized, quality 'high-tech' products which are aimed at niche markets.

Superimposed on these developments has been the inexorable rise in unemployment which has abated only slightly throughout the European Union (EU) in recent years. By March 2004 (Eurostat 2004), unemployment in the EU had gradually started to fall. In the fifteen member states of the EU as a whole, before enlargement, it stood at 8.0 per cent, with levels of 9.3 per cent in Germany, 9.4 per cent in France and 11.1 per cent in Spain, while in Sweden, which had historically prided itself on its low unemployment levels, it had gradually fallen to 6.4 per cent. This has been one of the main factors responsible for a shift in the balance of power against labour over the past decade or so, both at the political level and within labour markets, although the effects of this shift have been uneven across different European countries. One consequence of this is that there has been a marked refocusing of European social policy away from seeking to extend workers' rights to concentrating on employment creation and 'employability'.

Major political changes have also affected Western European countries. The post-war consensus between management and labour has continued to erode and there have been ongoing reductions in government expenditure on social welfare. European countries have had to face growing budget constraints, and an endemic fiscal crisis of the welfare state has severely limited their ability to offer concessions to trade unions in exchange for restraint in wage claims. Many governments in EU member states have been forced to adapt to a tighter international monetary regime, particularly those in the Euro-zone.

Trade unions in Europe have had to adapt to a much more diverse constituency of groups and interests as a result of these economic and political changes. Apart from the shift of employment to the services sector and the increasing importance of 'knowledge' or white-collar workers, they have had to accommodate themselves to: increasing rates of female participation within the workforce; transformations of the traditional family structure; the growing individualization of lifestyles; and the expansion of 'atypical' work, e.g. part-time, temporary, agency and seasonal work. This means that European trade unions have to appeal to an ever more heterogeneous population across a range of diverse interests.

Associated with the introduction of new technology has been the trend towards 'flexibility': flexibility in hours, flexibility in pay, flexibility in tasks and a move towards company-specific rather than industry-specific training. The recession in Europe in the early 1990s encouraged management to embark on a process of 'downsizing' in order to contain labour costs, and a new wave of rationalization and downsizing started to appear following the financial crisis in Asia in 1998.

Linked with moves towards greater flexibility has been a trend towards a devolution of industrial relations issues to lower levels, often as a result of management using their enhanced bargaining power and exercising their prerogative to shift bargaining from a national or industry-wide level down to the level of the enterprise. While managements have frequently taken the initiative towards decentralization, major political and economic forces have also been at work, such as the growth of international competition coupled with the growing volatility of international markets.

The tendency towards decentralization of industrial relations has been accompanied by organizational changes in companies such as the growth of 'business units' with their own profit centres and autonomy in conducting the management of employee relations. All this means that European unions find it difficult to bring their own organizational strength to bear.

It would be a mistake, however, to assume that the nature and extent of decentralization has been uniform across Europe. While it has been most pronounced in the UK, and generally less so in countries like France, Italy,

Portugal and Spain, there have been few signs of change in collective bargaining structures or the introduction of 'human resource management' initiatives in certain others like Austria. Similarly, although there is some evidence that there has been increased devolution of industrial relations issues to workplace level in countries such as Germany and Denmark (both of which are renowned for their relatively high degree of centralization of collective bargaining and extensive regulation of their labour markets), such changes have generally been accommodated within existing procedures.

The European Social Model

The European Social Model really developed after the end of the Second World War. A political consensus was observed right across Europe from those forces that had opposed Fascism. The most important of these political groups was the Christian Democrats. It was accepted at the most fundamental level that Europe had to avoid the social conflicts of the inter-war period. The new Europe could not be allowed to become either a completely authoritarian dictatorship or go to the other extreme of uncontrolled capitalism.

All this led to the development of the European welfare states, a defining feature of Western Europe. The Anglo-Saxon model in the UK differs from that of its Continental neighbours in that its welfare state is based on selected provisions. Moreover, its version of 'shareholder' capitalism contrasts with 'stakeholder' capitalism on the Continent.

There are also different versions of the Social Model in Continental Europe itself. The social democratic Scandinavian model is based on the provision of universal rights which cannot be taken away. The most common model, the Continental model, is a mixture of state corporatism and family tradition. It places great importance on financial labour contributions both from the state and from employers. The newer Mediterranean model is similar to the Continental model but places much more emphasis on the role of pensions and the function of the family as a safety net. However, all versions of the European Social Model are based on common principles and values such as social justice and social citizenship. Citizens have a right to education, health care, social security etc. The use of the word 'rights' is important here. Rights cannot be taken away and are enforceable. There is an acceptance of a public sphere. This is that area of society that belongs to all citizens. In this sphere things are not done for profit but for the general good.

In Continental Europe social policy is also recognized as a productive factor. Social partners (trade unions and employers) are accepted as principal actors in social development. Companies are seen as social entities. Both political and religious arguments give firms a social obligation to the community. The idea of economic citizenship is also developed. European employees also have greater rights of participation in the enterprise in which they work. These can start from the basic (and not necessarily just European) rights of representation within the workplace, the right to health and safety etc. Employees also have the greater right to be informed about decisions both at a workplace and company level. They have a right to influence decisions that affect them and a high level of job security. Central to this philosophy is the theme of partnership that is meant to encourage employee commitment. This is epitomized in the German tradition of *Mitbestimmung* (co-determination). In this scheme workers are given wide levels of representation but their representatives must also consider the enterprise's interests. Trade unions also have an important role in the European Social Model. Although there has been a decline in trade union membership in recent years (see following section), trade unions still have an important representative and legitimate function in European enterprises with much co-operation with management.

Trade unions

Trade unions across Europe have not been immune from the general turbulence and restructuring that has been affecting industry and services. The long-term changes in the sectoral distribution of the labour force are continuing to undermine some of the key strongholds of traditional trade unionism and trade union organization. They have responded to these challenges by being at the forefront of change and have had to confront fundamental issues in the process.

Trade union membership

The long-term trend established since the mid-1980s towards a decline in trade union membership appears to be continuing but there are wide variations across Western Europe. It is necessary to state at the outset that reliable and accurate comparative figures on union membership are hard to find. The table below has been compiled from trade union density percentages given in a European Industrial Relations Observatory survey in July 2002 (tn0207104f).

Table 3.1 Three clusters of union density (percentages) in 2002.

High	%	Medium	%	Low	%
Denmark	88	Ireland	45	Portugal	29
Sweden	79	Austria	40	UK	29
Finland	79	Italy	36	Netherlands	27
Belgium	69	Greece	33	Spain	15
Luxembourg	50	Germany	30	France	9

Source: European Industrial Relations Observatory, July 2002.

Table 3.1 above does not indicate the substantial fall in trade union membership across Western Europe from 1993–2003. Across the EU, recent evidence points to distinct problems in different countries. In Portugal there has been a drop of 40 per cent over the past decade and in France membership has hit an all-time low. Germany experienced a hemorrhage of membership: between 1993 and 2003 it lost 24 per cent of its members. Austria also experienced a significant membership decline of 13 per cent. One relevant question is whether such changes are pushing more national situations closer to the low cluster and away from the high and medium ones.

The high-water mark for union density in Germany was reached after reunification and a significant decline has been felt in the East. However, closer analysis shows that this is a partial picture, and recent losses and union reorganization plans, locate the problems across the whole of the German economy and not simply in one geographical part. The heaviest fall in membership has been in the leather industry followed by textiles, wood and plastics and mining and energy. The recession and job losses in Eastern Germany account for some of this but much of it is attributed to increased competition and the employers' restructuring of the 'value chain' with the consequent use of outsourcing strategies. It appears that all the membership boost resulting from reunification has melted away. In the UK, the 2003 Labour Force Survey showed a similar picture with a 20 per cent drop in membership in the 1990s (to 7.2 million). There has been a slight increase since 2001, but density is still only 27 per cent.

The Nordic countries stand out as the exceptions to these trends. In Norway, union density rose by 13 per cent from 1993–2003. Swedish trade union density was largely static at just below 90 per cent and Denmark reported a density increase of 2 per cent for the same period.

Union responses

Union responses have tended to fall into three categories – mergers, new recruitment strategies and 'Europeanization'. The first option is clearest in Austria and Germany where already large industrial unions are amalgamating still further. The Austrian union confederation (ÖGB) plans a reduction to only three unions representing manufacturing, services and the public sector. A newly merged union in Germany was formed from five unions in the postal, media, commerce and banking, white-collar professionals, transport and public services to create the Unified Service Sector Union (*Vereinigte Dienstleistungsgewerkschaft, ver.di*) with around 2.8 million members.

The end result is a very slimmed-down DGB (German Trades Union Confederation) with eight unions in membership in 2003 with a total membership of 7.7 million. There is also much restructuring taking place among unions affiliated to the British Trades Union Congress (TUC), particularly in the finance and white-collar sectors. In the Netherlands, a Dutch 'super union' was formed representing 500,000 members from the industrial, services, transport, agricultural and foodstuffs sectors.

Finally, some unions have considered organizing at the European level and breaking with nationally dominant systems of representation. A first step in this direction has been taken by the British GMB union and the German IG Chemie-Papier-Keramik which have signed a reciprocal membership agreement.

Collective bargaining

Collective bargaining has long been the dominant way of determining pay and working conditions in Europe. From the end of the Second World War up to the end of the 1970s, elements of the employment relationship which had traditionally been regarded as the prerogative of management were gradually drawn into the bargaining process. Such collective bargaining, generally over pay, took place at the national or sectoral level and was seen as providing a stable framework for the institutionalized management of conflict in European developed industrial societies, although there were wide variations in practice.

Both employers and trade unions supported centralized forms of collective bargaining for a number of reasons. The unions saw it as a means of controlling and sometimes reducing wage differentials – between firms, sectors and regions as well as between occupational and skill groups; this enabled them to cater to the great diversity of their membership. Since centralized bargaining favoured large over small firms, it also had the support of the large corporations because they realized that it was less prone than workplace bargaining to interfere with managerial prerogative at the point of production.

Governments too, supported the centralization of both collective bargaining and union organization. As far as they were concerned, it enabled them to monitor wage agreements so that settlements were 'reasonable', were not excessively inflationary and could be reconciled with democratic capitalism's core commitment to maintain full employment.

However, from the 1980s onwards there were growing pressures from employers and some governments to decentralize elements of the bargaining process in order to promote more flexibility. The initiative for such change came largely from employers and increased in intensity throughout the 1990s. This trend, however, has not been uniform across Western European countries. For example, the level of bargaining in Austria and Finland is still relatively centralized. Although collective bargaining in Germany remains at industry-wide level and at regional levels, there is evidence that the rise of company bargaining, 'site pacts' and flexibility agreements driven by specific sectoral and company demands for cost-cutting and adaptability are severely testing the limits of such standardized pay and conditions.

The coverage of collective bargaining in Western Europe is much wider than is the case in Japan and the United States. For example, the number of workers, unionized or not, which have their pay and employment conditions determined by a collective agreement, as a percentage of all workers is above 90 per cent in Austria, Belgium, France and Sweden. In Germany, Denmark, Spain and Norway it is above 80 per cent.

Overall, while there has been a general trend towards a greater emphasis on enterprise-level industrial relations, decentralization has taken a different form in each country. The general trend towards decentralization has also involved critical decisions on how work is to be organized and labour to be deployed on a more flexible basis, as well as how management is to be devolved within the enterprise.

The emergence of human resource management

Some commentators have argued that collective bargaining itself is threatened not only by the decline of trade unions and trends towards decentralization but also by the rise of human resource management (HRM) in a European context. HRM emphasizes individualism rather than collectivism by seeking to foster the commitment of individual employees to the aims of the business in which they work. Opinion is sharply divided on the implications of HRM for the future of collective bargaining. Legge (1991) has argued that the emergence of HRM is a reflection of the rise of the 'new Right': 'our new enterprise culture [in Britain] demands a different language, one that asserts management's right to manipulate, and ability to generate and develop resources'. The proponents of HRM present it as being concerned with 'a coherent positive and optimistic philosophy about management ... built around the possibility of achieving personal growth in an integrated, human organization' (Guest 2001).

HRM has taken a different form in Western Europe from that in the USA, where it has been more closely associated with either anti-union activities or alternatives to collective bargaining. In Europe, unions and collective bargaining are retained partly as a result of the legal framework, partly due to higher levels of unionization, and partly as a feature of the 'social democratic' version of HRM at the macro-level, as represented by the approach taken in the European Union's Employment Chapter of the EU Treaty.

Human Resource Management (HRM) is about making people committed to a company by satisfying their needs and giving them a means to express themselves in the enterprise. This idea of satisfaction and the right of expression is not too different to some of the ideas of the European Social Model as described earlier.

Concepts such as keeping employees informed, providing effective communications channels to management are some of the most important concepts in Human Resource Management. Proponents of HRM would say that these benefits would encourage employees to have a sense of responsibility towards the organization they work in, just the kind of responsibility expected from them by the European Social Model. In this sense therefore, HRM and the European Social Model appear to have much in common.

However, the main problem is that, unlike in the European Social Model, the facilities provided to employees by HRM in itself are not *rights*. Employees are treated as a resource, especially by those employers who adopt the 'hard' model of HRM, which is common in the UK (Cully *et al.* 1999). HRM represents a move towards individualism, which is in stark contrast with one of the key elements of the European Social Model – *partnership*. HRM is associated with the deregulation of labour markets and consequently increases the power of employers: hence the contrast between the two philosophies of employment protection on the one hand, and imposed flexibility on the other.

Unlike in the US, European HRM also takes into account things like culture, the role of the state, and legislation. A good example of this kind of blending together of the two models can be seen in the field of participation. HRM favours a more direct participation approach, whereas the European Social Model would seek to maintain some form of indirect participation, through legal means if necessary. However there is no reason why both direct and indirect participation cannot co-exist. Indeed, the 1998 Workplace Employee Relations Survey (WERS98) (Cully *et al.* 1999) clearly shows that 'softer' forms of HRM are most successful when combined with some kind of collective bargaining. Many commentators would argue that successful European companies adopt a socially responsible HRM based on high commitment management practices with elements of collective bargaining and social partnership.

In sum, HRM as practised in Europe is very different from the American model; the Europeans tend, in their HRM systems, to take account of more factors than the Americans – cultural factors, the role of the state, difference in company shareholding, and extensive employment protection legislation.

The changing nature of participation

There has been considerable debate throughout Europe for a considerable time about the most appropriate forms of employee participation in decision-making within the enterprise. Until the 1980s, the main emphasis was on *indirect* forms of participation through works councils, co-determination and collective bargaining. In this context, trade unions were generally the main channel of representation for employees. During the 1980s there was a switch in focus to *direct* forms of participation, which have been defined by Geary and Sisson (1994:2) as:

> opportunities which management provide, or initiatives to which they lend their support, at workplace level for consultation with and/or delegation of responsibilities and authority for decision-making to their subordinates either as individuals or as groups of employees relating to their immediate work task, work organization and/or working conditions.

Indirect participation

Indirect forms of participation have a long history in many European countries. In Germany, the Co-determination Act (1951) and Works Constitution Act (1952) extended a range of rights to employees to participate in decision-making. These were considerably extended and consolidated during the 1970s. The main instrument for this is the works council, elected by all employees in a firm regardless of their union affiliation, and operating on a defined legal status. Works councils of various kinds now play an important role in many European countries; eleven of the fifteen member states of the European Union had some form of works council in 2003. At European level, European Works Councils have been set up affecting all companies in the EU and the European Economic Area (EEA) which employ over 1,000 workers in the host country and at least 150 workers in two or more other countries.

During the 1970s and early 1980s a number of countries adopted legislation on employee participation, although few were as extensive as the German model. In Sweden, which traditionally favoured national collective agreements, new rules for indirect participation were established in the 1976 Co-determination Act including employee directors on company boards. Legislation was enacted in the Netherlands, France and Belgium that provided for some form of indirect participation. In Denmark, the role of co-operation committees was strengthened in 1982, but through collective agreements rather than through legislation.

The introduction of new technology into enterprises is central to the concerns of employees. Research on the diffusion of participation in new technology in the then twelve member states of the European Union in 1990 (Gill and Krieger 1992) reported a wide diversity of levels of participation throughout the EU. The authors of this study, under the auspices of the European Foundation for the Improvement of Living and Working Conditions, concluded that five variables play a crucial role in shaping the opportunities for participation in new technology. These include: management's reliance on the workforce to achieve its objectives for introducing new technology; management style and culture; the bargaining power of organized labour; regulatory provisions including legislation providing for participation; and the degree of centralization of the industrial relations system in the particular country. Although the authors warn that these variables are no more than generalizations, their study provides an important reminder of the complex array of factors that influence the types and levels of participation found in Europe.

European legislation, based on the EU Directive (2002/14/EC) establishing a general framework for informing and consulting employees in the European Community now applies at Member State level. All undertakings with at least fifty employees (or establishments with at least twenty employees) must inform and consult employee representatives about business developments, employment trends and changes in work organization.

Direct participation

Until the early 1990s, compared to indirect participation, little was known about the extent and significance of *direct participation* in Europe. In 1993 the European Foundation for the Improvement of Living and Working Conditions launched a major investigation into its extent and nature focusing on all the twelve member states of the European Union as well as the three countries that subsequently joined the Union in 1995 – Austria, Finland and Sweden. The results indicated that direct participation is particularly likely to be found in organizations that compete in international markets and are in close competition with Japanese firms. More advanced forms of direct participation are also more likely in firms that produce high value-added, high quality, customized goods rather than in establishments concerned with high volume, low value-added, labour-intensive products. However, while a subsequent large survey of enterprises found that there has been an increase in the incidence of direct participation in Europe, only a small number (around 2 per cent) of organizations in the ten EU member countries covered by the survey were pursuing high-intensity group work with a qualified workforce and with a high training intensity (European Foundation for the Improvement of Living and Working Conditions 1997).

Recent direct participation initiatives tend to be far more coherent and strategic in nature than older experiments. They concentrate on enhancing competitiveness and tend to go hand-in-hand with a set of HRM techniques. It seems that many organizations in Europe adapt particular strands of HRM techniques to suit their own circumstances.

Some of the examples of direct participation identified by the European Foundation highlight the fact that direct and indirect forms of participation may be complementary. Indeed, it appears that a strong institutional basis for indirect participation stimulates the emergence of direct forms. The lesson that might be drawn from this is that, on their own, the individualistic approach of direct participation and the collectivist approach inherent in indirect participation are unlikely to succeed. There is a need for a mixture of both; examples from the European Foundation suggest that successful organizations tend to have integrated *both* forms of participation in their employment policies.

The European Union: the social dimension

No discussion of industrial relations in Western Europe would be complete without considering the growing influence of the European Union on industrial relations.

The European Union has been going through a period of consolidation recently, attempting to implement existing commitments such as the 1995–97 Social Action Programme and other outstanding pieces of legislation. The substantive area is now dominated by the concern over employment and employability first systematically articulated at the Essen Summit in 1994, which culminated in the provisions of the Treaty of Amsterdam. Procedurally the main development has come in the development of a 'negotiation track' within the social dialogue process.[1]

Social dialogue

In 1996 and 1997 the social dialogue began to bear fruit following the very first framework agreements between the social partners on parental rights and part-time work. This 'negotiation track' offers a real chance for European collective agreements to become a key mechanism for European social reform.

Attempts to give closer involvement to the social partners – now joined by the public sector representatives (CEEP) – became more pressing following the social policy agreement and social protocol of the 1991 Maastricht Treaty, especially on issues likely to be sensitive. The Commission is required to consult on 'the possible direction of Community action' and later, if it considers such action advisable, on 'the content of the envisaged proposal'. These changes have helped to unblock a host of measures previously vetoed and led directly to the development of mechanisms to translate the Social Charter into concrete reality. The 'negotiation track' allows the social partners to negotiate a European-level framework agreement that is then enforced through a directive. If negotiations fail, the 'consultation track' allows the views of the social partners to be taken into account by the Commission which then draws up its own directive.

Since then several initiatives have either been fed into this process or have emanated from the European Commission. Some have already become law and others are in the process of being adopted:

- Health and Safety Framework Directive
- Parental leave
- Part-time work – legal right to equal treatment with full-time workers
- European Works Councils
- Working Time – extension to cover transport workers and junior doctors
- Temporary Agency Workers – equal treatment with permanent workers
- 'Works Councils' at national level – information and consultation
- Fixed Term Contracts – equal treatment of fixed-term employees
- Posted workers – provisions for employees working in another EU state
- Equal Treatment for gender, disability, age, gender, ethnicity, sexual orientation, religion etc.

The most important innovation of the Treaty of Amsterdam in 1997 was the insertion of a new Chapter on Employment and explicit references to the EU's role in promoting the 'co-ordination between employment policies of the member states with a view to enhancing their effectiveness by developing a co-ordinated strategy for employment' in order to promote job creation. While each member state retains its autonomy in formulating and implementing its own labour market policy, member states are now required to submit an annual report to the Commission and Council on the steps they have taken to meet the guidelines to be adopted every year by the Council on employment policy.

The guidelines adopted by the Council fall under four main headings. These have now been described as the four 'pillars' of EU employment policy. These are:

- improving employability
- developing entrepreneurship
- encouraging adaptability
- promoting equal opportunities.

These are seen as essential to combat unemployment and to promote job creation.

There has now been a clear shift in the EU away from legislation and regulation on industrial relations towards *employability*, *adaptability* and *flexibility* in labour markets. Globalization in general, technological change and the Single European Market in particular have created pressures requiring a rethinking at all levels – intersectoral, sectoral and company. These pressures have themselves built up in the context of major long-term trends affecting European labour markets, including the growth of the services sector, increasing female participation rates and increasing forms of so-called 'atypical' work.

There is now a gradual but nevertheless distinct emergence of an EU model of industrial relations based on agreement at intersectoral, sectoral and company levels and reinforced, at the intersectoral level, by legislation in the form of directives whether or not agreement can be reached. Europe has therefore not turned its back on regulation in favour of laissez faire flexibility. It is true that there was a period of uncertainty – especially from 1991–97 between Maastricht and the defeat of the Conservative Government in the UK – but now Europe is beginning to rethink regulation. It is embracing new patterns of work, but acknowledging that flexibility must not lead to a free-for-all. On the contrary, workers must be protected from the excesses of adaptability and efficiency (for which many read 'exploitation') through the regulation of working time, parental leave and European works councils, among other areas. This is often linked to a greater awareness of the need to integrate working and family life.

To this extent EU social policy has been refocused: from the rights of workers it now embraces the interests of non-workers – the unemployed whose numbers stood at just under 9 per cent of the EU labour force by Autumn 2004.

This rethinking at EU level to a large extent reflects similar developments within member states. Action is now being taken in most countries to rectify perceived rigidities in labour markets, but in many cases they involved consultations between the social partners and a measure of negotiated re-regulation, all of which are attempts within their respective national frameworks to bring a degree of security back into labour markets that, subject to pressure and turbulence, looked increasingly insecure.

Finally, what is the legal position in relation to employment rights legislation now that the new Employment Chapter is in operation? The situation is that qualified majority voting (QMV) in the EU Council is required in

- working conditions
- information and consultation of workers
- equal pay.

Unanimity is still required on:

- social security
- protection for unfair dismissal
- protection for non-EU workers
- financial schemes for job creation.

The following matters are *excluded* from the Employment Chapter:

- pay
- the right of association
- the right to strike or to impose a lock out.

Conclusions

Despite the initiatives that have emanated from the European Union to facilitate the integration of social and economic policies among member countries, many of the influences on industrial relations within Europe are coming from *outside* Europe. As was outlined earlier, markets have become globalized and segmented, so that production and the provision of services are now often organized on an international, if not global, level. The global trend towards more customized products and services has accentuated the search for improved labour and capital flexibility.

Linked with this trend are perhaps the two key issues facing Europe into the twenty-first century – the problems of rising unemployment and European competitiveness in world markets. The European employers (UNICE) argue that the relatively high labour standards in Europe, compared for example with the USA, are a contributory factor to the problems facing European companies when competing in world markets and have led to a rise in unemployment. The European trade unions (ETUC) maintain that European companies can best compete in the newly emerging high-technology markets with a highly skilled, well-paid and highly trained labour force. They also claim that the problem of unemployment cannot be solved by lowering labour standards.

Note

1 The Social Dialogue was originally initiated in 1985 when Jacques Delors was President of the European Commission. It was introduced partly as a means of circumventing the lack of progress on European social and employment legislation during the 1980s. It consists of a dialogue between the ETUC and the European Employers' Confederation (UNICE) and the European Public Sector Employers (CEEP) whereby EU employment proposals are considered by the parties with a view to arriving at an agreement between themselves before the European Commission acts.

References

Cully, M., Woodland, S., O'Reilly, A., Dix, G. (1999) 'Britain at Work: as depicted by the 1998 Workplace Employment Relations Survey'. London: Routledge.

European Foundation for the Improvement of Living and Working Conditions (1997) *New Forms of Work Organization: Can Europe Realise its Potential?: Results of Survey of Direct Participation in Europe.* Dublin.

Gill, C. and Krieger, H. (1992) 'The diffusion of participation in new information technology in Europe: survey results', *Economic and Industrial Democracy* 13(3).

Guest, D. (2001) 'Industrial Relations and Human Resource Management', in Storey, J. (ed.) *Human Resource Management: A Critical Text.* Thomson Learning: London.

Legge, K. (1991) 'Human resource management: a critical analysis', in Storey, J. (ed.), *New Perspectives on Human Resource Management.* Routledge: London.

Statistical Office of the European Communities (2004) Luxembourg.

Suggested key readings

Atkinson, J. and Meager, N. (1986) *Changing Patterns of Work*. London: NEDO.

Brewster, C. (1992) *The European Human Resource Management Guide*. London: Academic Press.

Carley, M. (1998) 'Board-level employee representation in Europe', *Transfer, European Review of Labour and Research* 4(2) (Summer): 281–96.

Cressey, P., Gill, C. and Gold, M. (1998) 'Industrial relations and social Europe: a review', *Industrial Relations Journal: European Annual Review 1997*, September.

Cully, M. *et al.* (1999*)*, 'Britain at Work: as depicted in the 1998 Workplace Employment Relations Survey'. London: Routledge.

European Foundation for the Improvement of Living and Working Conditions (1997) *New Forms of Work Organization: Can Europe Realise its Potential? Results of Survey of Direct Participation in Europe*. Dublin.

Ferner, A. and Hyman, R. (1992) *Industrial Relations in the New Europe*. Oxford: Blackwell.

Ferner, A. and Hyman, R. (1994) *New Frontiers in European Industrial Relations*. Oxford: Blackwell.

Geary, J. and K. Sisson (1994): *Conceptualising Direct Participation in Organisational Change – The EPOC Project,* Luxembourg: Office for Official Publications of the European Community.

Gill, C. and Krieger, H. (1992) 'The diffusion of participation in new information technology in Europe: survey results', *Economic and Industrial Democracy* 13(3).

Gill, C., Krieger, H. and Fröhlich, D. (1993) *Roads to Participation in the European Community: increasing prospects of employee representative involvement in technological change*, Vol 1, Second Report on the attitudinal survey on technological change, European Foundation for the Improvement of Living and Working Conditions, Office for Official Publications of the European Communities, Luxembourg.

Gill, C.G. and Krieger, H. (1999) 'Direct and representative participation in Europe: recent survey evidence', *International Journal of Human Resource Management* 10(4) (August): 572–91.

Goetschy, J. and Pochet, P. (1997) 'The Treaty of Amsterdam: a new approach to employment and social affairs?', *Transfer* 3(3): 607–20.

Gold, M., Cressey, P. and Gill, C.G. (2000) 'Employment, employment, employment: is Europe working?', *Industrial Relations Journal (European Annual Review 2000)* September.

Hall, M., Carley, M., Gold, M., Marginson, P. and Sisson, K. (1995) *European Works Councils: Planning for the Directive*, Industrial Relations Research Unit, University of Warwick and Industrial Relations Services, London.

Storey, J. (1991) *New Perspectives on Human Resource Management*. London: Routledge.

Tüselmann, H. and Heise, H. (2000) 'The German model of industrial relations at the crossroads: past, present and future', *Industrial Relations Journal* 31(3) (September): 162–77.

Websites

http://www.eiro.eurofound.ie/ – the website of the European Industrial Relations Observatory in Dublin which contains a wealth of material on Britain and other European Union countries. There are extensive links to other useful industrial relations websites in Europe.

http://europa.eu.int/comm/eurostat/ – (Eurostat) the latest and the most complete statistical information on the EU and the Euro-zone.

4 Industrial relations in Central and Eastern Europe

RODERICK MARTIN AND ANAMARIA M. CRISTESCU-MARTIN

Introduction

This chapter examines recent trends in industrial relations in Central and Eastern Europe (CEE). The focus is on developments since 1989, when the fall of Socialism in the region led to a series of revolutions in politics, economics, and society. The analysis relates to developments in seven countries: Bulgaria, the Czech Republic, Hungary, Poland, Romania, Slovakia, and Slovenia. In the Socialist period, from the end of the Second World War to 1989, the institutional arrangements in the seven countries were broadly similar, with the state, on behalf of the Communist Party and in the name of the proletariat, largely determining the pattern of industrial relations. Trade unions were 'transmission belts' to assist in the implementation of state policies (Pravda and Ruble 1986). Since 1989 the institutional uniformity has disappeared, with different countries following different paths, in industrial relations institutions as in other spheres. The divergences have become so great in the case of the former Yugoslavia and the former Soviet Union that they fall outside any common analysis. The disintegration of Yugoslavia has resulted in the destruction of the former system of industrial democracy, and the creation of different systems in the successor states. In Russia a catastrophic decline in living standards, rising unemployment, and a large disparity between the relative prosperity of small groups in major metropolitan areas, employees in the oil and gas sector, and the rest, sidelined industrial relations institutions (Standing 1996; Clarke 1999).

The fall of Socialism in 1989 led to a series of revolutions in politics, economics, and society in CEE. In politics, the dominant role of Communist parties was destroyed, and multi-party, parliamentary democracies were established. Elections became free, and governments frequently lost power. The economies of the region were transformed. International trade was reoriented from the former Soviet bloc to global (primarily West European) markets. State-owned enterprises were privatised, and planned inter-firm relations gave way to market exchange. Society also changed. The values of solidarity and economic equality, which – if often ignored, in practice – had been the formal values of Socialism, gave way to greater individualism and emphasis on incentives and individual success.

Industrial relations were also revolutionised. This chapter reviews the emerging industrial relations systems against a background of EU accession, incorporation into global production systems, continuing economic growth, and gradual – if, at times, artificial – improvement in real incomes.

This chapter is divided into the following sections.

Following this Introduction, the second section, 'Sources of industrial relations system integration', identifies the mechanisms – institutions and shared values – that have the potential to generate cohesive, integrated industrial relations systems at national level; the theme is the continuing fragility of such mechanisms.

The third section, 'Segmentation', examines the process of segmentation, even fragmentation, that has led to the development of four distinct systems of industrial relations, only imperfectly linked to one another due to overstretched, quasi-corporatist structures and trade unions. Industrial relations in the region are characterised by subordination to distinct pressures and incentives rather than to an effective, comprehensive, higher authority, and, consequently, by distinct actor priorities. The four industrial relations systems are the state sector, the privatised or about to be privatised state sector, the private sector, and the multinational corporations (MNCs).

Finally, the Conclusion, the last section, discusses possible future trends in industrial relations in the region, as well as their likely future impact on industrial relations in Western Europe.

EU accession considerations

Eight CEE countries, the Czech Republic, Estonia, Hungary, Latvia, Lithuania, Slovakia, Slovenia, and Poland, joined the EU on 1 May 2004. Two others, Bulgaria and Romania, hope to follow suit in 2007.

In the build-up towards EU membership, many changes affecting industrial relations in CEE have already been implemented. Although the principle of subsidiarity (that EU decisions 'should be taken as closely as possible to the citizens of the Union') means that many industrial relations issues will remain a matter of national rather than EU legislation, EU accession will, in practice, further impact upon industrial relations in the region. At national level, EU accession stimulates and accelerates CEE integration into the global economy. Guarantees of institutional rectitude remain major facilitators for investment in South-Eastern Europe (Raiffeisen Zentralbank Group 2003), and achieving the *acquis communautaire* has acted as a quality check for potential foreign investors. EU accession confirms basic institutions as meeting the Copenhagen criteria, including democracy and 'a functioning market economy' and, hence, as not posing a high political risk. At enterprise level, EU accession involves overarching industrial relations legislation, in CEE as well as elsewhere in Europe. As new members of a, until very recently, very exclusive club, the new accession countries are likely to show – and experience – stronger commitment to 'the rules of the game' than well-established club members.

Thus, aspects of industrial relations policy such as the strengthening of multi-level tripartite institutions, consolidation of employee representation rights, and greater attention to the enforcement of anti-discrimination legislation are likely to change. Other aspects of industrial relations policy such as international labour mobility and migration are difficult to foresee. And other aspects of industrial relations policy such as processes of wage determination are unlikely to change.

Economic considerations

After a catastrophic decline in the early 1990s, the economies of the region revived and, by 2000, the GDP of the seven countries exceeded the level of 1989. Growth rates in 2004 were substantially higher than in Western Europe. Real incomes rose in the early twenty-first century, and productivity increased. However, unemployment remained high, especially in Poland, the region's largest economy, where it reached 19.4 per cent by 2003; Hungary, with 5.8 per cent unemployed in 2003, performed best (United Nations Economic Commission for Europe 2003: 22–3). Several countries, including Hungary and Poland, allowed imports and public sector deficits to rise, in order to finance increases in real incomes, especially for public sector workers.

Sources of industrial relations system integration

The industrial relations system is often conceived as an integrated whole, as a set of institutions and practices that regulate relations among employers, employees, and the state, within given economic, technological, and cultural environments (Dunlop 1958: 7). The industrial relations system may itself be more or less integrated, and the industrial relations system may be more or less integrated into its environments. The argument of this chapter is that the level of integration both within the industrial relations system and between the industrial relations system and its environments is low. In CEE the overarching national institutions and ideology that provide integration are at best fragile and often absent. This section discusses four sources of integration: the state itself, tripartite social partnership structures, national level industrial relations institutions, and shared core values.

The state

The legitimacy of the role of the post-Socialist state in industrial relations was questionable. On the one hand, to varying, but everywhere extensive, degrees throughout CEE, including in Hungary, the region's most effectively pluralist state, the state was involved in labour code maintenance and detailed regulation of employment issues, including detailed regulation of collective bargaining at enterprise level. The state was also involved in negotiating EU accession agreements and in taking multi-level industrial relations initiatives. Moreover, to ensure the achievement of EU standards in areas such as health and safety and discrimination, as well as to foster effective social partner representation, the European Commission sought to strengthen the state's administrative apparatus in industrial relations.

On the other hand, depoliticising economic life, including limiting the role of the state, was the overall objective of the post-Socialist transition.

Employers, as well as trade unions – albeit less frequently – questioned the state's involvement in the detailed operation of the industrial relations system. Multinational employers in particular, most significantly in Poland, saw left-leaning governments as too responsive to union opinion. Trade unions, as in Hungary under Prime Minister Orban, often saw governments as favouring neo-liberal policies at the expense of the social wage.

Tripartite social partnership structures

The contribution of tripartism (joint institutions comprising representatives of employers' organisations, trade unions, and the state) to developing integrated industrial relations systems in CEE was equally questionable.

By some accounts, tripartism was an emergent form of neo-corporatism, with separate interests co-ordinated into a unified political agenda through a process of political exchange (Iankova 2002). More fully, traditional neo-corporatism involved developing centralised organisations for interest representation, with representational monopolies and privileged access to government, and social partnership between business and labour (Lehmbruch 1984). Sympathising with and refining this analysis, Iankova (2002: 11) highlights three elements distinguishing CEE tripartism from West European forms: political negotiations rather than negotiations on purely economic and social issues, involvement of a broader range of civic groups than the restricted representation of business, labour, and state (co-opting of interest group leaders involved in neo-corporatist institutions weakened internal representational linkages), and multi-level bargaining structures.

By some other, more sceptical, accounts, tripartism was merely 'a political shell for a neo-liberal economic strategy,' involving no significant concessions to union representatives (Thirkell *et al.* 1998: 166). Similarly, the Hungarian political scientist Lajos Héthy (1994: 94) saw tripartism as window dressing only, a relic of the unitarist assumptions of the Socialist period, of some short-term political value, but of no long-term economic importance: 'Old political forces trying to secure their survival and new ones looking for a foothold, often tend to look upon tripartism as an interim solution providing room for short-lived and narrow political compromises and for a mutual reinforcement of legitimacy, representativeness and public support ... Tripartism appears to be based on pragmatism on the part of the social partners and its existence has very little, if any[thing] to do with the essential political and economic philosophies of the new regimes in the region.'

Tripartism nomenclature differed among countries, but 'reconciliation' was a common theme, initially, and implied more than just the right of consultation, but less than the right of veto (Ladó 1996: 163). By the late 1990s, however, this easily evolved into EU-characteristic, social partnership, language. The tripartite organisational sophistication and the significance of the issues discussed varied throughout the decade too, and differed between countries.

The Hungarian National Council for the Reconciliation of Interests, established in 1988 and relaunched in 1990 as the Interest Reconciliation Council, was the earliest tripartite institution. Similarly, Councils of Economic and Social Agreement were established in the Czech Republic and Slovakia in 1991; the Bulgarian National Council for Co-ordination of Interests was founded in 1990 and then placed onto a more substantial legal basis with the new 1993 Labour Code; and the Polish National Negotiating Commission was launched in 1993. In Romania, tripartism was less strongly developed, but joint government and union discussions were held from 1990 onwards.

The tripartite institutions discussed three types of issues. The first was specific industrial relations issues, especially wages, governments stressing wage restraint and trade unions expressing concern over the national minimum wage level and, especially in the early 1990s, cost of living adjustments. The second was broader public policies, especially social welfare issues. The third was nationally significant industrial disputes.

National level tripartite institutions were complemented by sectoral and enterprise level arrangements. The EU saw integration among the three levels as necessary for effective implementation of agreements on social welfare issues. But Ghellab and Vaughan-Whitehead (2003: 1) observed that '[t]he small number of collective agreements, the lack of communication between social partners at this level, and the failure so far to develop the requisite legal and institutional framework are clear signs of the lack of dialogue at the sectoral level'. Although usually reluctant to draw attention to shortcomings in its own schemas, the EU recognised the weaknesses of sectoral level social dialogue in CEE and the consequent lack of articulation between national and enterprise level developments.

The level and form of sectoral integration differed between countries, with, for example, greater formal institutionalisation in Bulgaria than in Poland. Reflecting economic and political differences as well as the level of local initiative, there were also differences among sectors within individual countries (Iankova 2002: 19).

It was impossible to reconcile conflicting political and economic objectives, that is, the governments' objectives for institutional transformation, control of public sector expenditure, and wage restraint with the unions' objectives for employment security and defence of living standards. Thus, the impact of tripartite structures on economic performance in CEE – their independent 'added value' – was negligible.

Even so, tripartite institutions provided mechanisms for increasing institutional integration, enhancing regime legitimacy, and reducing industrial conflicts, at least in the short run. Commenting on the 'historic role' of Hungarian national tripartism, Ladó (2003: 258) concluded that it had 'contributed to peaceful transition in at least three different ways: (1) smoothed economic and social change; (2) facilitated the development of the social partners and their learning process; and (3) helped the government to withdraw gradually from the economy'.

Thus, tripartism achieved the short-term objective of providing institutions for reconciling interests, reducing the threat of social conflict, and increasing the legitimacy of the new post-Socialist regimes, but this success was transient.

Four conditions needed to be met, for tripartism to be effective in the long-term (adapted from Héthy 1996: 150). The first condition was for strong government, with firm electoral support and sufficient economic headroom to buy the support of business and labour. The second condition was for strong and united partners, able to ensure that agreements were supported by their members and could be made to 'stick.' The third condition was for complementarity – not necessarily identity – among the parties' political and economic objectives. The fourth condition was for appropriate institutional and legal frameworks to enable effective negotiations among the parties. Such requirements were rarely met in CEE. If they had been met, tripartism might not have been necessary. Most importantly, tripartite institutions remained subject to political pressures, their success heavily dependent upon the attitudes, inconstant, even erratic, adopted by political leadership groups. Martin and Cristescu-Martin (1999: 392–4) discuss tripartism in CEE in further depth.

Industrial relations institutions

In CEE, strong, nationally coherent industrial relations institutions, with secure and disciplined membership, were notably lacking.

Trade unions were the most effectively organised, with membership levels remaining above West-European levels and ranging, in the larger EU accession states, from 41 per cent in Slovenia, 40 per cent in Slovakia, 30 per cent in the Czech Republic, and 20 per cent in Hungary, to 15 per cent in Poland (Ladó 2002: Table 4.1). Nevertheless, union movements were highly fragmented, especially between post-Communist successor unions and anti-Communist unions: in Hungary, there were nine union federations, for example.

Also, throughout the period, there were high levels of membership dissatisfaction with their unions (Martin et al. 1998).

The degree of fragmentation among employers was even greater than among trade unions. Employers' organisations emerged rapidly, after 1989, partly due to government stimulus, with a view to populating emergent tripartite institutions, and partly due to the development of more independent firms. But the variety of forms of ownership (state, corporatised, privatised, municipal, co-operative, as well as private and mixed) contributed to fragmented, and competitive, systems of employers' representation, throughout the period. Not including the state itself, the Hungarian Interest Representation Council included nine employers' associations, for example, and the Czech Council of Economic and Social Agreement comprised seven.

Core values

In the absence of firmly grounded institutions, shared values – a commitment to democracy – could have been related to the industrial relations system, or to the political system as a whole, and could have provided an alternative basis for system cohesion. However, the widespread relevant values provided little support for an effective industrial relations system.

Scepticism about the very usefulness of organisational participation was one such widespread value. Based on surveys and 'experiential' research, Howard (2003: 10) concluded that '(1) most post-communist citizens still strongly mistrust and avoid organizations ... ; (2) many of the private and informal networks that developed under communism . . . still persist ... and they serve as a disincentive for many people to join formal organizations; and (3) many post-communist citizens are extremely dissatisfied with the new political and economic system ... and this disappointment has caused them to withdraw even further from public activities.' Rose et al. (1998: 155) reached similar conclusions: 'scepticism dominates popular evaluations of post-Communist institutions ... In post-Communist societies people are not only anti-government but also "anti-social".' Scepticism about trade unions (9 per cent trust) and political parties (5 per cent trust) was particularly widespread, the church and the army enjoying the lowest levels of scepticism (30 per cent trust) (ibid.). Most CEE citizens were committed to democracy, but only on the surface: 'the median groups are ambivalent; either they compliantly favour both old and new regimes or are sceptical about both. Together, sceptics and compliant make up 44 per cent of NDB [New Democracies Barometer] respondents; this constitutes a large and potentially shifting middle ground' (Rose *et al.* 1998: 202). Even where trade union membership remained high, scepticism about formal organisations led to low levels of organisational participation.

Not entirely surprisingly, voting levels in the European elections in spring 2004 were low – scepticism and distrust of organisations reflected high levels of privatisation and there was a focus on family and informal network, social atomism and low levels of trust (Roney 2000).

Commitment to 'the market' was another, widely shared, value. The early 1990s saw discussion of the 'social market,' but the 'social' epithet was dropped by the mid-1990s, and private property relations, competition, and broad acceptance of managerial authority, especially foreign, became market principles. The interpretation of 'market' was often neo-liberal ('Americanised'), involving, as in Poland, low levels of regulation (Meardi 2001: 6). CEE echoed only relatively weakly the Russian questioning of managerial authority, although corruption and mafia links were seen as especially widespread in South Eastern Europe. Trade unions like the Polish Solidarity proselytised for the market (Ost 2001: 83–4) – employment security was clearly subordinate to market values.

Thus, commitment to 'market principles' undermined, rather than supported, an integrated national industrial relations system, members often viewing their unions as part of the enterprise organisation, rather than an independent means of representing their interests effectively.

With low levels of trust in organisations, particularly in industrial relations organisations, shared values were unlikely to contribute to integrated national industrial relations systems.

The forces leading to cohesion in industrial relations systems in CEE remained fragile. Neither the state nor tripartite institutions nor shared values provided the basis for integration. While the national trade union movements provided the major unifying influences, such movements were themselves threatened both from outside, by employer hostility and neo-liberal governments, and from inside, by division, decline in union membership, and high levels of dissatisfaction with union performance.

Inevitably, such weak pressures for coherence and integration resulted in the development of segmented industrial relations systems. As the next section shows, there were four major segments, each characterised by its own particular requirements and matching participant priorities and pressures.

Segmentation

The concept of a segmented industrial relations system emerged from research into Scandinavian industrial relations (Esping-Andersen 1992). Parts of the industrial relations systems in Sweden and Finland were integrated into the international global economy, with wages and employment conditions linked to the international business strategies of major international firms. International business competition obliged firms to develop high performance/high value-added approaches to labour utilisation. These pressures, however, did not apply in the public service sector, and the long-standing Swedish system of centralised bargaining, bureaucratised structures, and high social wages could be maintained, at least in the short run. Spill-over between the two systems was limited. Parallel differentiations between the private and public sectors are found in other systems, including the US.

In extent as well as degree, CEE segmentation is greater than Scandinavian, and requires a more finessed approach. Four segments exist in CEE. The first is the state budget sector, comprising central and local government administrations, education, health services, police, and armed services. The second comprises the privatised, or about to be privatised, state production sector, involving the major extractive and manufacturing industrial sectors, including coal mining, iron and steel, transport (encompassing, in some countries, railways), engineering, and telecommunications. The third contains the emergent private sector, involving mainly small- and medium-sized firms operating in services, including marketing, retail distribution, tourism and hospitality, and much of financial services, together with small-scale manufacturing. The fourth includes the multinational corporate sector, involving multi-national manufacturing and retail firms, integrated into international production and supply chain systems. The motor industry, including motor industry component suppliers, is a particularly important constituent within this segment. The four segments are substantially self-contained, and operate according to different dynamics.

The state budget segment

With relatively high salaries, relaxed work regimes, access to state facilities, and job security subject to political loyalty, employees in this segment had been privileged in the Socialist period. The *nomenklatura* system operated at the higher and more politically sensitive levels, appointments being made by the Communist Party. Pay determination was centralised and related to job classifications and credentials. Trade union membership was universal.

The implosion of the Communist Party and collapse of the Socialist regime led to crisis in this segment. Senior officials were dismissed, demoted, or sidelined, as being associated with the Communist Party. The system of centralised pay determination survived, but its ability to provide for employees was destroyed by rapid inflation and crises in public sector finances. Trade union membership continued at relatively high levels, but with much lower levels of unity than under Socialism; 'reformist' unions were especially strong among professional state employees in health and education. State budgetary crises led to wages falling seriously behind, with inflation and, in some cases, inability to pay wages at all.

The result was a continuing crisis in the state budget segment, with the quality of performance deteriorating sharply from the already low levels of public services provided in the late Socialist period. Exit was the major response to the collapse. Where it was possible to get employment in the private sector or vanish from the labour market, state officials resigned. In capital cities, young officials with good connections and good command of foreign languages, especially English, left for well-paid posts in finance. Frequent, usually short-term demonstration, strikes occurred among health workers, education workers in Hungary, Poland, Slovenia, and Romania, and even among judicial officials in Romania. Governments sought to control state deficits by enforcing wage restrictions on public sector workers, at the cost of increased labour turnover, ever lower morale, increased corruption and payment for 'services rendered,' encouragement to multiple job holding, and industrial action. In the longer-term, governments sought to reduce – or, at least, redistribute – costs by decentralisation and divestment; policies encouraged as 'rolling back the state' by international agencies (Allison 1998).

Industrial relations in the state budget segment have thus been in continuing crisis since 1989. The crisis involved a sharp decline in the living standards of state budget employees, high levels of discontent, and sporadic industrial action. Centralised wage determination continued, but employees' reliance upon users' payments for services rendered and multiple job holding eroded its significance. In the absence of effective voice, exit was the solution, with high levels of voluntary resignations, with a resulting decline in service quality. Despite the size of the segment, state budget employees did not mobilise the political influence that their position might have been expected to warrant.

The privatised segment

The privatised, or about to be privatised, state production segment comprised the major extractive and manufacturing industrial sectors, involving coal mining, iron and steel, transport (encompassing, in some countries, railways), engineering, and telecommunications.Under Socialism, this segment provided the working class elite. Post-Socialist experience has varied.

Industrial relations were determined by the bargaining power of the groups involved, in turn determined by product markets, labour markets, and political leverage. To facilitate response to changing market requirements, and in line with transition policies, bargaining moved from national to sectoral and enterprise levels. Hence, unions in industries with expanding product markets were able to maintain employment levels and earnings, while unions in industries with contracting product markets saw sharp employment contraction. Even Bulgaria, which faced a major currency crisis in 1997, experienced a sharp contrast between telecommunications, where employment stabilised and relative earnings increased, and electronics, where employment and earnings collapsed with the loss of Council for Mutual Economic Assistance (CMEA) markets (Iankova 2002: 124). Overall, the privatisation of manufacturing resulted in an employment decline.

Nevertheless, the development of sectoral and enterprise level bargaining did not always result in responsiveness to product market trends. Unions successfully used political pressure and industrial action to protect employment levels, even in sectors with declining demand, such as coal mining and iron and steel (Martin and Cristescu-Martin 2000: 353–8). Polish and Romanian coal miners were more successful than their West European counterparts in maintaining levels of employment and relative earnings, despite successive reorganisation and restructuring financed by World Bank loans designed to reduce the size of the industry. For example, in 2001, the Romanian miners secured highly favourable voluntary redundancy terms; subsequently, when the jobs they had anticipated securing failed to materialise, these were successfully renegotiated. Polish miners were similarly successful in extracting a high restructuring compensation. In 2003, the number of employees in mining and quarrying was only slightly lower than in 2000: 253,000 compared with 292,000 in Poland and 141,000 compared with 163,000 in Romania (National Institute of Statistics 2003: Table 4.1). (Attempts to protect employment levels on the railways were less successful.) Earnings also remained relatively high. In January 2004, Romanian workers in mining and quarrying earned £182.06 gross equivalent per month, while in manufacturing £103.61 (Table 4.1).

Industrial relations have thus been turbulent in the privatised segment. Bargaining decentralisation to sectoral and enterprise levels increased flexibility and facilitated rationalisation and restructuring. With strong external financial support, some restructuring was achieved, but progress was slow. Restructuring was accompanied by major industrial conflicts in both Poland and Romania, especially amongst coal miners – the shock troops of Socialism, to misquote British trade union leader Arthur Scargill.

The private segment

The emergent private segment involves mainly small- and medium-sized firms operating in services, including marketing, retail distribution, tourism and hospitality, and much of financial services, together with small-scale manufacturing.

Table 4.1 Average Romanian earnings distribution (January 2004)*

	Gross (ROL**)	Percentage of average (rounded)	Net (ROL)	Percentage of average (rounded)
Overall	8,006,308	100.00	5,771,049	100.00
Agriculture	5,188,347	64.80	3,982,426	69.00
Industry	7,034,696	87.90	5,253,220	91.00
Mining and quarrying	11,103,876	138.70	8,020,204	139.00
Manufacturing	6,319,216	78.90	4,772,436	82.70
Tobacco	16,694,567	208.50	10,733,039	186.00
Textiles	5,073,231	63.40	3,941,294	68.30
Chemicals	9,520,912	118.90	6,860,666	118.90
Road transport equipment manufacturing	7,839,871	97.90	5,914,075	102.50
Construction	5,834,673	72.90	4,408,191	76.40
Hotels and restaurants	4,736,681	59.20	3,627,036	62.90
Post and telecommunications	16,794,948	209.80	10,711,072	185.60
Financial intermediation	21,317,029	266.30	13,373,993	231.70
General government	15,234,052	190.28	10,142,675	175.80
Education***	11,140,324	139.10	7,673,215	132.00
Health and social assistance	7,302,283	91.20	5,342,510	92.60

* Based on National Institute of Statistics (2004b).
** ROL = lei (Romanian currency); £1 = ROL60,990 on 16.01.2004.
*** Major pay award made in December 2003.

With new, private firms providing the major source of employment growth, this segment is increasingly important: small- and medium-sized enterprises contributed 69 per cent to employment according to a 2001 Hungarian survey (Martin and Cristescu-Martin 2002: 527). Employment in real estate, renting, and business activities, for example, continued to expand in all CEE countries: between 2000 and 2003, it increased from 89,000 to 113,000 in Bulgaria; from 266,000 to 284,000 in the Czech Republic, from 205,000 to 265,000 in Hungary; from 531,000 to 686,000 in Poland, from 132,000 to 151,000 in Romania, from 47,000 to 52,000 in Slovenia, and from 91,000 to 108,000 in Slovakia (National Institute of Statistics 2003: Table 4.1). Tourism, especially rural tourism, where the small private firm plays a major role, is seen as a sector where CEE countries may have a long-term competitive edge.

In this segment, collective organisation is limited amongst both employers and employees. Where it does exist, employers' collective organisation is oriented towards trading issues, commercial organisation, and marketing. Industrial relationships are informal, based on personal networks. Work organisation is similarly informal.

The level of earnings, in this segment, is highly variable. A minority of firms in financial services, trade, and property development are making substantial profits, with high earnings for some employees, primarily in capital cities. In Romania, for example, average earnings in the finance sector were more than double the national average (266: 100), significantly higher than the next highest sector, posts and telecommunications (209: 100). In some firms, there is a high level of exploitation, including 'self-exploitation,' single-person firms working long hours for erratic rewards. At £77.66 gross equivalent per month (59 per cent of average gross earnings in Romania in January 2004), earnings in hotels and restaurants were especially low.

The multi-national corporate segment

CEE became incorporated into global capitalism in the 1990s, but the terms of that incorporation remain contentious. It has been argued that the region is acquiring a 'maquiladora' status, analogous to the North Mexican regions bordering the US: a provider of cheap labour for low value added manufacturing and service industries in Western Europe. Much of the German clothing industry production was transferred to the Czech Republic and Poland, for example, through both outward processing arrangements and direct investment (United Nations Economic Commission for Europe 1995: 117).

Through privatisation acquisitions, joint ventures, and greenfield investments, German companies were the most active in the region, although there were also major investments by US, French, and, to a lesser extent, British and Japanese companies. In the car industry, for example, CEE became a major centre for the manufacture of cars designed for entry level customers, a strategy initiated as early as 1990 by Volkswagen (VW) with its investment in the Czech motor manufacturer Škoda. Hungary was initially the major destination for foreign direct investment (FDI), and remained the largest recipient of FDI in per capita terms throughout the transition, but Poland, the largest economy in the region, has now received the largest cumulative level of investment.

In CEE, multi-national corporations sought to follow their international human resource policies and practices, with reductions in employment levels, rationalisation of work organisation, and increased flexibility, both internally and externally. The extent of employment reduction varied, and, although there is no comprehensive data, case study research (Makó *et al.* 1998; Estrin *et al.* 2000) illustrates the large scale and processes involved. Foreign acquisition resulted in job losses even in telecommunications: in 2002, 8,500 jobs were lost when the Greek OTE (as the Hellenic Telecommunications Organization is known on the New York Stock Exchange [NYSE]) acquired the Romanian Romtelecom. Newly introduced industrial relations practices included increased flexibility, new payment systems, and time limited in place of indefinite employment contracts – a 'Trojan horse' for the introduction of similar measures in Western Europe argued Meardi (2002), although the evidence is still slight.

Collective organisation in multi-national corporations was low. Multi-nationals did not favour collective organisation: the formal policies adopted towards trade unions reflected the original national characteristics of the multi-national, with US firms ideologically opposed to union membership and European firms committed to partnership philosophies. The earnings of multi-national employees were, indeed, at least on a par with those in nationally owned firms, but multi-national employers sought higher levels of work effort, and greater commitment, and CEE employees were left in an exposed position. Thus CEE trade unions looked to EU accession as a means of strengthening their bargaining power: at national level, through social partnership arrangements, at sectoral level, through sectoral level social dialogue, and at enterprise level, through the development of European Works' Councils (Meardi 2003). The EU fostered closer links between CEE unions and West European unions as a way of increasing the strength and sophistication of CEE unions.

Industrial conflict differed from segment to segment, and we argue here (4.3.2) that, for political, institutional, and economic reasons, collective conflict is likely to be higher in the second segment. This is confirmed by Romanian evidence. In 2001, 271,291 employees participated in industrial disputes. Of these, 58.66 per cent were in the energy sector (electricity, thermal energy, gas, and water) and 23.00 per cent in manufacturing. Within manufacturing, there was little conflict in textiles, clothing, footwear and furniture – sectors mainly in private ownership. In 1999, there was a much higher level of industrial conflict: 1,029,500 employees were involved. Of these 22.81 per cent were in mining and quarrying, 31.52 per cent in manufacturing, and 10.68 per cent in energy (National Institute of Statistics 2004a: Table 3.2.4). Despite acute financial pressures in the state budget segment, the overall level of conflict was low, except for education. The level of conflict remained low in agriculture, too, despite poverty. Unfortunately, there are major difficulties in using international comparative data, with major differences among countries in definitions, methods of data collection, and reliability. After collating data on strikes in Hungary, Poland, Slovakia, and Slovenia, the European Industrial Relations Observatory (2003: 8) concluded that 'the data … do not seem to be reliable enough to compare the countries involved'. The four segments operate according to different dynamics, themselves responding to different political and economic pressures.

In the state budget segment, the dynamics are governed by state budgetary policy, itself heavily influenced by international agencies, especially when countries face major economic crises. Hence, the dynamics are governed by political, including international relations, and macroeconomic considerations. CEE governments are thus constrained by international pressures and public sector budgetary limitations. State budget segment industrial relations are characterised by continuing crisis.

In the privatised segment, the dynamics are both economic and political, with the major operating forces – product market demand levels especially – being economic. At global level, this is reflected in the contrast between sectors with expanding product markets, such as telecommunications, and sectors with declining product markets, such as electrical engineering. However, there remains a significant political influence, with key groups of workers able to exert political as well as economic pressures. Groups such as coal miners, in Poland and Romania, and transport workers, in Hungary and Slovakia, successfully defended their positions, at least in the short term.

The dynamics of the third, private segment are economic, responding primarily to changes in national product markets, and to the demand and supply of labour. The level of collective organisation is low and labour force flexibility is high. The high level of demand for financial services and low level of supply of qualified labour resulted in high earnings in some private services, while labour surplus allowed earnings to fall in other sectors, such as retail distribution.

Finally, industrial relations in the multinational corporate segment responded to the strategies of MNCs, themselves subject to changes in international product markets, and in the relative costs of labour internationally.

Conclusion

This chapter sought to provide an overview of industrial relations in CEE, after a decade and a half of post-Socialist development. The chapter examined the forces contributing to cohesion and those leading to segmentation in CEE industrial relations systems. The guiding hypothesis was that the emerging systems of post-Socialist industrial relations are highly segmented, and that the process of segmentation is being consolidated.

The major potential sources of cohesion are the state itself, the tripartite institutions sponsored by governments and the EU, and the representative institutions for employers and, especially, employees. Trade unions were the most influential supporters of national industrial relations systems. However, overall, the institutions supporting integration are fragile. Even trade unions are weak, for both internal and external reasons. In practice, unable to cover the full range of segments, CEE unions were most heavily involved in the second, privatised segment, where they proved effective in mobilising both economic and political powers, in limited circumstances. However, their successes are likely to be short-lived, since they were primarily defensive in character, concerned with minimising the impact of restructuring upon employees.

The reasons behind the particular form of segmented industrial relations systems emerging in CEE after 1989 lie partly in the international situation and partly in specific features of the CEE context.

At the time of the collapse of Socialism, the post-WWII 'consensus' had already disintegrated. Neo-liberalism had become the dominant ethos, even if the Washington consensus was less than complete. In the Anglo Saxon economies, collective bargaining systems had eroded, while there was diminishing confidence in the Rhenish model, involving macroeconomic consensus building and social partnership. Post-Socialist governments were anxious to follow in 'Western' footsteps, while being presented with alternative Western models, pushed by different international agencies and governments. Of these, the International Monetary Fund and the World Bank were the most powerful and persuasive. The conflicting tendencies in post-Socialist industrial relations thus reflected the international situation.

Internal developments strengthened the tendency towards segmentation. Communist party dissolution removed the major form of institutional integration in CEE. Inevitably, the process of de-legitimising Socialism involved in regime change also de-legitimised the state itself. Post-Socialist states' capacity to construct effective institutions was thus small. Popular scepticism and distrust of governments, political parties, and trade unions reflected this ineffectiveness. In the early 1990s, the post-Socialist governments' objective was to create internationally acceptable 'market' economies, while avoiding major social conflicts. The creation of long-term social arrangements for reconciling conflicting interests was subordinate to that objective.

Thus, the initiative for the creation of industrial relations institutions lay with employers and trade unions. However, employers had little interest in creating nationally integrated industrial relations systems, since flexibility suited them better: decentralised, fragmented systems favour the powerful, on the principle of divide and rule. Moreover, there were profound differences among employers, in the different industrial relations segments. Trade unions would have benefited from nationally integrated industrial relations institutions, unity providing strength. However, the political and economic circumstances of post-Socialism created wide differences between the interests of different groups, exacerbated by ideological conflicts between 'successor' and 'reformist' union movements and institutional rivalries. International, regional, and national influences thus combined to consolidate segmentation – a fuller statement of the argument is made in Martin and Cristescu-Martin (2004).

What of the future? The effects of EU accession on the future pattern of CEE industrial relations are not yet evident. CEE states will retain features distinctive from Western Europe – the heritage of forty years of Communist government will not disappear quickly, especially its cultural values (Howard 2003). National differences will continue to be linked to both country histories during the Socialist period and the political and economic developments of the 1990s.

The boundaries between politics and economics will remain indistinct and permeable. Employers' organisations will remain fragile, operating within, rather than between or over, the four segments of the industrial relations system. Trade unions will continue to operate primarily in the first and second segments, with centripetal modes of operation and limited membership involvement at enterprise and establishment levels. The earnings levels in CEE will be likely to remain far below West European levels.

However, in industrial relations, there are already some signs of convergence between CEE and Western Europe – in practices, if not in outcomes. The first three segments do experience common problems, but the primary shared experience is in the fourth segment.

Multi-nationals follow internationally co-ordinated production systems, using CEE primarily as a base for serving local markets (especially in Poland, with its large domestic market) and/or West European markets (as in Hungary and the Czech Republic, with small domestic markets). Western acquisition of CEE enterprises through privatisation purchases resulted both in the transfer of production from Western Europe to CEE and in the consolidation of production in Western Europe. This Western consolidation is especially likely in sectors with high levels of capital investment in advanced technology and low proportion of labour costs in overall production costs. Thus, CEE started to experience consequences (otherwise long since experienced in Western Europe) of international product market changes. In Hungary, exports by foreign-owned multi-nationals (for example in office equipment) deteriorated in 2003, with local job losses. At the same time, VW bosses accused Czech workers of seeking wage increases likely to bring Czech labour costs close to German labour costs and thus endangering jobs in the Czech Republic as a whole. For sectors where labour costs represent a high proportion of total costs, there are already signs of the drift of jobs further eastwards, with, for example, Hungarian firms developing production facilities in Romania. In the fourth industrial relations segment, as CEE labour costs rise to approach West European levels and the full range of EU policies impacts on the cost structure of CEE firms, there are clearly problems for firms and employees alike.

This process of 'Europeanisation' of industrial relations in CEE may have an impact on Western Europe (Biagi *et al.* 2002). Enlargement could increase the scope for 'coercive comparisons' across Europe, leading to a European-wide deterioration in labour standards. The fear of EU enlargement undermining the European social partnership model is especially strong in Germany, where FDI was interpreted as a means of 'blackmailing' German workers into accepting greater flexibility (Lane 2001: 195). VW Group's investment in its new Audi plant in Györ, Hungary, was seen as an experiment in new production methods, explicitly intended for re-export back to Germany. However, such trends are neither unique nor inevitable. Existing processes of international competition already show the transferability of production methods among firms, as in the widespread use of lean production systems that followed the 'Toyotaism' successes, in the 1980s. Moreover, the oncosts (pensions and benefits costs) of employing Hungarian workers are already substantial, making lower labour costs only short-term advantage. Furthermore, workers in CEE are as aware as their Western European colleagues that a 'race to the bottom' would not be in their own interests.

EU enlargement does not represent a unique Trojan Horse for new employment practices in Western Europe – just the current stage of development reached in the internationalisation of industrial relations. The accession of the eight post-Socialist states into the EU marks an important stage in CEE integration into the international economy. The price of that integration is not yet clear.

References

Allison, Christine H. (1998) 'Discussion,' in László Halpern and Charles Wyplosz (eds) *Hungary: Towards a Market Economy*. Cambridge: Cambridge University Press.

Biagi, Marco, Michele Tiraboschi and Olga Rymkevitch (2002). *The 'Europeanisation' of Industrial Relations: Evaluating the Quality of European Industrial Relations in a Global Context – A Literature Review*. Dublin: European Foundation for the Improvement of Living and Working Conditions.

Clarke, Simon (1999) *New Forms of Employment and Household Survival Strategies in Russia*. Coventry: Centre for Comparative Labour Studies, University of Warwick.

Dunlop, John T. (1958) *Industrial Relations Systems*. New York: Holt, Rheinhart and Winston.

Esping-Andersen, Gosta (1992) 'The Emerging Realignment between Labour Movements and Welfare States,' in Marino Regini (ed.) *The Future of Labour Movements*. London: Sage.

Estrin, Saul, Xavier Richet and Josef C. Brada (2000) *Foreign Direct Investment in Central Eastern Europe: Case Studies of Firms in Transition*. Armonk, NY: M. E. Sharp.

European Industrial Relations Observatory (EIRO) (2003) 'Labour Dispute Settlement in Four Central and Eastern European Countries.' EIRO On-Line. http://www/eiro.eurofound.ie/2003/01/study/tn0301101s.html. Accessed 19.02.2004.

Ghellab, Yousef and Daniel Vaughan-Whitehead (eds) (2003) *Sectoral Social Dialogue in Future EU Member States: The Weakest Link*. Geneva: International Labour Office.

Héthy, Lajos (1994) 'Tripartism – Its Chances and Limits in Central and Eastern Europe,' in Timo Kauppinen and Virpi Köykkä (eds) *Transformation of the Industrial Relations in Central and Eastern Europe*. Helsinki: International Industrial Relations Association (IIRA) Fourth Regional Congress.

Héthy, Lajos (1996) 'Negotiated Social Peace – An Attempt to Reach a Social and Economic Agreement in Hungary,' in Attila Ágh and Gabriella Ilonski (eds) *Parliaments and Organised Interests: The Second Steps*. Budapest: Hungarian Centre for Democracy Studies.

Howard, Marc Morjé (2003) *The Weakness of Civil Society in Post Communist Europe*. Cambridge: Cambridge University Press.

Iankova, Elena A. (2002) *Eastern European Capitalism in the Making*. Cambridge: Cambridge University Press.

Ladó, Mária (1996) 'Continuity and Changes in Tripartism in Hungary,' in Attila Ágh and Gabriella Ilonski (eds) *Parliaments and Organised Interests: The Second Steps*. Budapest: Hungarian Centre for Democracy Studies.

Ladó, Mária (2002) 'Industrial Relations in the Candidate Countries.' http://www.Eurofound.IE/2002/07/FeatureTN0297102F.html. Accessed 19.02.2004.

Ladó, Mária (2003). 'Hungary: Why Develop Sectoral Social Dialogue?' in Yousef Ghellab and Daniel Vaughan-Whitehead (eds) *Sectoral Social Dialogue in Future EU Member States: The Weakest Link*. Geneva: International Labour Office.

Lane, Christel (2001) 'Understanding the Globalization Strategies of German and British Multinational Companies,' in Marc Maurice and Arndt Sorge (eds) *Embedding Organizations*. Amsterdam: John Benjamins.

Lehmbruch, Gerhard (1984) 'Concertation and the Structure of Corporate Networks', in John H. Goldthorpe (ed.) *Order and Conflict in Contemporary Capitalism*. Oxford: Oxford University Press.

Makó, Csaba, Peter Novoszáth and Àgnes Verèb (1998) 'Changing Patterns of Employment and Employee Attitudes at the Firm Level: The Hungarian Case', in Roderick Martin, Akihiro Ishikawa, Csaba Makó and Francesco Consoli (eds) *Workers, Firms and Unions: Industrial Relations in Transition*. Frankfurt am Main: Peter Lang.

Martin, Roderick and Anamaria M. Cristescu-Martin (1999) 'Industrial Relations in Transformation: Central and Eastern Europe in 1998,' *IRJ* (*Industrial Relations Journal*) 30 (4): 387–404.

Martin, Roderick and Anamaria M. Cristescu-Martin (2000) 'Industrial Relations in Central and Eastern Europe in 1999: Patterns of Protest,' *IRJ* (*Industrial Relations Journal*) 31 (4): 346–62.

Martin, Roderick and Anamaria M. Cristescu-Martin (2002) 'Employment Relations in Central and Eastern Europe in 2001: An Emerging Capitalist Periphery', *IRJ* (*Industrial Relations Journal*) 33 (5): 523–35.

Martin, Roderick and Anamaria M. Cristescu-Martin (2004) 'Consolidating Segmentation: Post-Socialist Employment Relations in Central and Eastern Europe.' *IRJ* (*Industrial Relations Journal*) 35 (6): 629–46.

Martin, Roderick, Akihiro Ishikawa, Csaba Makó and Francesco Consoli (eds) (1998) *Workers, Firms and Unions: Industrial Relations in Transition*. Frankfurt am Main: Peter Lang.

Meardi, Guglielmo (2001) 'What Does 'Normal' Industrial Relations Mean? Models and Mirages in Central Eastern Europe.' Conference paper. Helsinki: Fifth European Sociological Association Conference.

Meardi, Guglielmo (2002) 'The Trojan Horse for the Americanization of Europe? Polish Industrial Relations Toward the EU', *European Journal of Industrial Relations* 8 (1): 77–99.

Meardi, Guglielmo (2003) 'Foreign Direct Investment in Central Eastern Europe and Industrial Relations: Lessons from the European Works' Councils in Poland'. Conference paper. Berlin: IIRA (International Industrial Relations Association Thirteenth World Congress.

National Institute of Statistics (NIS, Romania) (2003) 'CANSTAT Statistical Bulletin No. 3/2003.' http://www.insse.ro/canstat_q3/canstat.htm. Accessed 19.02.2004.

National Institute of Statistics (NIS, Romania) (2004a) 'Romanian Statistical Yearbook 2002: Time Series 1990–2001.' http://www.insse.ro/download/anuar_2002/aseng2002.htm. Accessed 25.06.2004.

National Institute of Statistics (NIS, Romania) (2004b) 'Earnings by CANE Divisions, Press Release No. 13.' http://www.insse.ro/com_casti/a04/cs01e04.pdf. Accessed 19.02.2004.

Ost, David (2001) 'The Weakness of Symbolic Strength: Labor and Union Identity in Poland 1989–2000,' in Stephen Crowley and David Ost (eds) *Workers after Workers' States: Labor and Politics in Postcommunist Eastern Europe*. Lanham: Rowman and Littlefield.

Pravda, Alex and Blair A. Ruble (eds) (1986) *Trade Unions in Communist States*. Boston: Allen and Unwin.

Raiffeisen Zentralbank Group (RZB) (2003) *South East Europe in the Spotlight*. Vienna: Raiffeisen Zentralbank Group (RZB).

Roney, Jennifer Lynn (2000) *Webs of Resistance in a Newly Privatized Polish Firm: Workers React to Organizational Transformation*. New York: Garland Publishing.

Rose, Richard, William Mishler and Christian Haerpfer (1998) *Democracy and Its Alternatives: Understanding Post Communist Societies*. Cambridge: Polity Press.

Standing, Guy (1996) *Russian Unemployment and Enterprise Restructuring: Reviving Dead Souls*. Basingstoke: Macmillan.

Thirkell, John, Krastyu Petkov and Sarah Vickerstaff (1998) *The Transformation of Labour Relations: Restructuring and Privatization in Eastern Europe and Russia*. Oxford: Oxford University Press.

United Nations Economic Commission for Europe (UNECE) (1995) 'Outward Processing Trade between the European Union and the Associated Countries of Eastern Europe: The Case of Textiles and Clothing'. *Economic Bulletin for Europe* 47: Ch. 5. Geneva: UNO (The United Nations Organization).

United Nations Economic Commission for Europe (UNECE) (2003) *Economic Survey of Europe* No. 2. Geneva: UNO (The United Nations Organization).

Suggested key readings

EUROPA (The European Union On-Line) http://europa.eu.int. Various documents (for comprehensive information on EU accession).

European Industrial Relations Observatory (EIRO) http://www.eiro.eurofound.ie. Various documents (for up-to-date news items on industrial relations in CEE).

Iankova, Elena A. (2002) *Eastern European Capitalism in the Making*. Cambridge: Cambridge University Press.

IRJ (*Industrial Relations Journal*) Various years (for comprehensive annual reviews of industrial relations in CEE).

Martin, Roderick (1999) *Transforming Management in Central and Eastern Europe*. Oxford: Oxford University Press.

Martin, Roderick and Anamaria M. Cristescu-Martin (2004) 'Consolidating Segmentation: Post-Socialist Employment Relations in Central and Eastern Europe.' *IRJ* (*Industrial Relations Journal*) 35 (6): 629–46.

Meardi, Guglielmo (2002) 'The Trojan Horse for the Americanization of Europe? Polish Industrial Relations toward the EU'. *European Journal of Industrial Relations* 8 (1): 77–99.

5 Industrial relations in the Middle East

AMNON CASPI AND RUTH KASTIEL

Introduction

This chapter attempts to describe industrial relations in Middle Eastern countries, the conditions in which the players in these relations operate, and their ability to achieve their goals. The focus is on a selected number of countries, namely Jordan, Turkey, Saudi Arabia, Syria and Egypt (these countries being chosen according to the availability of data). The discussion on each country is based on the Open and Dynamic Model of industrial relations developed while designing an academic course on Industrial Relations for the Open University of Israel.

The nature of a nation's industrial relations system is related to several socio-cultural and institutional contextual factors including the overall degree of democracy which characterizes the state. One important characteristic of democracy is civil society. The essential characteristics of civil society are its structures of voluntary association, networks of public communication and norms of community co-operation. A strong and autonomous civil society is a necessary and central condition for democracy. In terms of the functions of civil society, many organizations in the Middle East have been among the most effective means of challenging government authority and responding to citizens' needs and concerns (Fuller 1991). But Arab-Islamic culture has its own distinctive features with regard to state/society and public relationships (Ayubi 1996), an important aspect of which refers to the ongoing exploration of, and debate on, the principles of democracy and the process of democratization.

Liberal and democratic societies can be grouped with reference to two main categories of actors: individuals and classes. While individualism has different meanings in different situations, one view is that it establishes the rights and the dignity of individuals who enter into social relationships of their own free will.

This type of relationship also governs the individual's connection with the state through mechanisms such as elections and representation. Classes are social groups that join together individuals who occupy similar positions with regard to the means of production and the relations of production in society. Through their collective action they are presumed to influence strategic decision-making in society. Ayubi (1996) argues that in a number of Middle Eastern states the individual is partly a member of his primary group and partly a member of an emerging class structure. In such a situation, the state cannot derive or deduce anything from the contractual relationship that binds the individual to the government in a liberal and democratic society.

According to Bellace (1994), 'the question no longer is whether the state acts on behalf of the ruling class, which owns the means of production. Rather, the state acts to restrain the inherent power of employers, so that workers have a reasonable opportunity to participate in decisions that affect them'. We argue that this may be the case in many situations, but one must also take account of the dominant philosophy and ideology of the governing party and its approach to the employment relationship. The approach of this stakeholder will likely be important in determining the extent to which the power of the different parties to the employment process is restrained and curbed or buttressed and supported.

Analytical framework

The 'Open and Dynamic Model of Industrial Relations' (which was developed while designing an academic course on 'Industrial Relations' for the Open University of Israel by Amnon Caspi) presented here reflects an open and dynamic system in which interrelationships depend on time and change with time (see Figure 5.1). In contrast, the static closed system is by definition cut off from its surroundings and does not interrelate with the external environment. The open system continuously interrelates with its surroundings, affects them and, most important, is influenced by elements of the external environment. Within the open system, there is a process of change that radiates to the surroundings and affects the other linked systems. The output of these systems and sub-systems, in turn, influences the open system.

Further to what prior research has suggested (e.g. Shirom, 1994), this Open and Dynamic Model of Industrial Relations advocates taking into consideration not only adjacent systems – political, legal, economic, etc. – but also distant variables and systems such as the level of technology, quality of life, standard of living, etc. Similarly, processes of globalization bring into question the value of democracy defined in terms of the nation state.

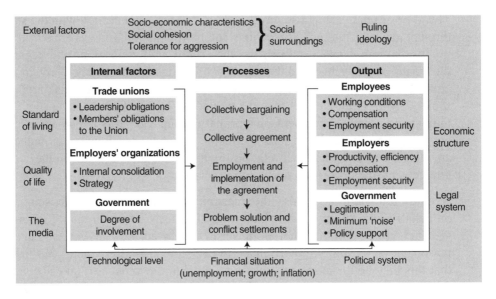

Figure 5.1 Open and dynamic model of industrial relations

Even in consolidated democracies, increasing regional and global connectedness of states and markets means that national governments no longer enjoy exclusive political and economic sovereignty in their own territory, and that their decisions and policies may affect the decision-making capacity of other states beyond their borders. Moreover, democratic procedures on the national level have become less significant in a context where transnational economic and political power grow ever stronger, free from democratic accountability.

The open and dynamic model presents the main components of the complex Industrial Relations system. It includes the components of the internal environment – employers, employees' representatives and the government, the interrelationships among them (the change process), the players' goals (the output), and the external factors that influence them all. These external factors are not only dynamic but also mutually influential. The dominant ruling ideology influences the political system which together designs the legal system, the economic structure, the level of technology, the social structure etc. All these nourish one another and play a role in the economy of the state: inflation, growth, unemployment and recession are not independent elements but the result of all the factors mentioned above.

Since the surrounding components are not static, the relative weight of each component changes, as does its influence on the other components. If we add the strong effect of globalization and other international factors mainly in the economic field, we perceive a chaotic, rapidly changing environment.

As can be seen from the model, the collective bargaining, the collective agreements, the implementation of the collective agreements and the settling of conflicts are influenced not only by components of the external surroundings, but by internal factors as well. The ideology of each player influences the topics that are negotiated as well as the tactics and actions taken to achieve their goals (industrial actions, strikes, etc.).

The output of the industrial relations system reflects the extent to which the players in the system achieve their goals in the employment relationship. The emphasis is naturally on the extent, because the external and internal components enable 'Zero Game' results. In other words, they enable results in which only one player achieves his goals and the other gains nothing. The nature of the output derives from the players' goals: the workers strive for better wages and employment security; the employers seek increased productivity, flexibility and efficiency. The government's goals are, of course, minimal 'noise' in the labour market and legitimation of its economic labour market policy.

This analysis of industrial relations in Middle Eastern countries drawing upon an exploration of key relationships postulated in our open and dynamic model will show how the links between the government's involvement in the labour market influence the players and their capability to achieve their goals in the employment relationship.

Industrial relations in Jordan

During the 1980s, Jordan experienced a regression in economic growth and a reduction in the bargaining power of labour. This was due to growing unemployment and the competition of foreign workers who accepted jobs for lower wages and fewer benefits. As a result, the trade union movement faced challenges – including the restriction of the migration of foreign workers to Jordan and the preservation of wage levels. Following a policy aimed at neutralizing the political influence of opposition forces within the Labour movement, the authorities disregarded violations of democratic union practices. This led to the emergence of union elements that profited from dominating the leadership of the trade unions and of the General Federation; it also prevented the emergence of young union leaders. The workers lost confidence in the prospect of enhancing their living conditions and distanced themselves from the unions. In the 1990s the fall of the USSR and its satellites in Eastern Europe, representing the end of the Cold War, left a strong imprint on the structure of the Jordanian Labour Movement. This impact was greatest on the unity and cohesion of the left wing of the Labour Movement and its ideology. Many leftist parties active in the Trade Unions split off, causing a decline of their influence in several trade unions, which they had dominated for years (al-Hourani 2002).

Internal factors

Structure of the Jordanian trade movement

In terms of its organizational structure, on the national level the Jordanian Labour Movement consists of a united framework, the General Federation of Trade Unions in Jordan, which currently includes all seventeen labour trade unions. In 2001 the General Federation had about 230,000 members (see Table 5.1).

The current legal basis for the Federation rests on the New Labor Law of 1996, according to which the Ministry of Labor is the government agency entrusted with dealing with the General Federation and all trade unions, with monitoring elections, registering member unions, and mediating in disputes between employers and unions. The unions accepted the new Labor Law with reservations, and the leaders of the General Federation submitted objections to about twenty of its one hundred and forty-two articles. Their objections and requests for modification related to points such as the right to 'terminate work contracts after an unlimited period, either fully or partially, or to suspend them …'. Some feared that the article could lead to arbitrary dismissal of workers, without compelling or technical justification. Subsequent clauses regulated and moderated its implementation by requiring the

Table 5.1 Membership of trade unions 2001

Union	*Number of members*
General Trade Union of Construction Workers	2,500
General Trade Union of Petroleum and Chemicals Employees	3,647
General Trade Union of Municipality Employees	1,500
General Trade Union of Private Education Employees	1,850
General Trade Union of Public Services and Free Professions	1,156
General Trade Union of Health Service Employees	4,600
General Trade Union of Railway Employees	1,505
General Trade Union of Food Industries Employees	7,000
General Trade Union of Printing, Photography and Paper Employees	2,100
General Trade Union of Textile Industry	987
General Trade Union of Electricity Employees	3,742
General Trade Union of the Employees of Banks, Insurance and Auditing	4,715
General Trade Union of Mines and Mining Employees	6,500
General Trade Union of Commercial Stores Employees	2,812
General Trade Union of Ports and Clearance Employees	6,500
General Trade Union of Air transport and Tourism Employees	3,700
General Trade Union of Land Transport Employees and Mechanics	175,000
Total	229,814

Source: Survey conducted by Al Urdun Al Jadid Research Center, Spring

formation of a tripartite committee to oversee the propriety of the procedures underpinning any termination action.

The law also did not clearly stipulate equal wages for men and women, despite Jordan's ratification of a number of international treaties and the International Declaration of Human Rights, which stress equal wages for men and women.

The general goals of the Federation are to:

- Contribute to converting society from a society of consumption to a productive society, and to invest in national wealth and resources by participating in political and economic decision-making;
- Strive to guarantee the right to fair pay and stable work, to provide equal employment opportunities and to exert efforts to counteract and put an end to the problem of unemployment;
- Raise the efficiency of workers, improve the means of production, and develop methods of vocational training;
- Enlighten workers and develop union awareness, project the role of workers as serving the public interest, to stress the importance of achieving social justice in building national unity, and to strive to develop social laws and legislation on a continuous basis;
- Work to attain solidarity among the various trade unions, between trade unions and their branches, and between trade unions and workers, and to promote a co-operative spirit and amicable conflict resolution;
- Strengthen national unity by combating any manifestation of division based on ethnicity, sex, color or religion;
- Maintain the unity of the Jordanian Labour Movement, while respecting freedom of opinion, ideology and expression, by instituting democratic methodology and practices;
- Develop and maintain union liberties and rights, supporting these through all legitimate means, and to protect public freedoms and human rights;
- Strengthen the ties of brotherhood, co-operation and unity among the workers of the Arab world, to co-ordinate and mobilize their nationalist and political efforts to serve nationalist causes within the framework of the International Confederation of Arab Labour Trade Unions.

The Central Council of the Federation plays only a limited role in supporting the member trade unions of the General Federation in labour disputes. Usually, this support is restricted to listening to the trade union representatives' reports during their meetings, while leaving each trade union to manage the negotiation processes that concern it.

Degree of government involvement

In the early 1970s, the General Intelligence Service created a special department for labour trade unions. Since then, the government-union relationship has had a flagrant security role making it difficult to achieve these goals. Despite the change in the political climate in the country, the government still retains the same approach in its management of trade unions and has been seen by some as seeking to remove all radical and politically 'mistrusted' elements from trade unions. Generally, the authorities supported the employers in resisting the establishment of unions, and even utilized the army and security forces to disperse strikes and to destroy attempts to achieve union organization (al-Hourani 2002). Presently within Jordan, the General Federation is considered by professional associations, public federations and opposition parties as something of a conservative force with somewhat diminished influence and power. Although the Federation enjoys representation in many national bodies such as the Social Security, Employment, Training and Economic Consultative committees, its influence on the policies of these institutions and committees remains limited and more circumsribed than was the case previously, leading in some quarters to a questioning of its independence and its capacity to realise its objectives for its affiliated unions and for broader Jordanian society.

Processes

Labour disputes do occur, typically in the following circumstances:

- When the assets of companies are impounded or restricted due to losses, the rights of employees and workers are affected, for example, by delaying payment of due wages;
- In cases of dismissal of employees or the threat to dismiss a certain number of workers from companies and factories subject to privatization;
- When failing companies claim that the existence of economic or technical circumstances compelled them to terminate work contracts and dismiss large numbers of employees;
- In cases of mismanagement of employee savings, with losses incurred by the institutions that manage funds for their workers;
- When worker demands for increase of wages and promotions are rejected.

During the last decade of the twentieth century, the number of labour disputes increased because the influx of migrant workers continued to threaten the job opportunities and wage levels of Jordanian workers. The majority of the migrant labour force is of a low educational and professional level, suited to manual labour and attracting relatively low wages. In parallel, the Jordanian government intensified privatization in the public sector, resulting in the sale of some public institutions to the private sector, or introducing strategic partners who began to play a primary role in formulating the policies of privatized companies. This resulted in the dismissal of workers, curbing their privileges, or the threat of the discharge of scores of employees, either immediately or in the future. Nevertheless, the number of cases that were settled by collective agreements was limited, and included only a very small percentage of the workforce.

Output

The structure of the labour movement has not advanced in correspondence with the developments that are the result of the rise of new industries. The inflexible structure has not undergone any change since 1976 (al-Hourani 2002).

This structure is the outcome of policies that aim to control the trade unions and to regulate the workers in practising their right to organize and unionize. The intervention of government authorities, by introducing a classification of crafts, professions and industries related to each trade union, in practice revokes the workers' freedom to establish new union organizations. For example, the Ministry of Labour rejected an application submitted by the Jordan Telecom company to establish a company trade union and justified this rejection by claiming that workers could join the Public Services trade union. Likewise, employees in government institutions, agricultural workers, those working for day wages outside regulated institutions, and foreign workers are deprived of the right to organize.

The organizational structure of the trade unions does not allow member workers to practise membership rights and perform duties in an active and continuous manner. The constitutions of the trade unions restrict the right of candidacy for election to leadership bodies, and allow the union members to vote only once every four years, which means that their only mission is to grant authorization to the Executive Committee to represent them. This is not accompanied by any other rights or responsibilities for members.

Currently, the General Federation of Trade Unions does not represent the unity of the Labour movement. Instead, it prevents pluralism and limits the independence and freedom of the member trade unions. A significant number of the existing trade unions appear to be fictitious and seem to have no legal legitimacy because of the lack of periodic elections and the fact that their leaders resort to illegal methods to maintain their positions. These leadership groups fail their members by not opening the door to candidates on administrative committees, or run fictitious elections in the presence of a minority of General Assembly members, or declare the victory of a list of names in uncontested elections, claiming that no other candidates were nominated. In this, the leadership benefits from the Ministry of Labour turning a blind eye and providing security for them.

Apparently, this led to the existence of fictitious inflated membership rolls in many trade unions which are completely isolated from the sectors they represent. This explains the absence of active participation of the union base in elections, as well as the absence of an actual role for the trade union in defending its members' interests.

Industrial relations in Turkey

Turkish industrial relations were affected by important historical developments. They also reflect the present structure of institutions and influence the attitude of social partners, trade unions, employers and government. The roles of industrial relations actors in Turkey and industrial relations practices such as collective bargaining, industrial conflict, etc., have historically grown in tandem with an interventionist tradition of industrial relations through state intervention and extensive legislative regulation. The establishment of the industrial relations system in general was regarded by the government not as an instrument of collective representation for employees and employers, but rather as an essential part of the apparatus of the government's industrialization and of the economic development of the country (Buyukuslu, 1998–1999).

The legalization of unions under the Trade Union Law of 1947 paved the way for the slow but steady growth of a labour movement that evolved in parallel with multi-party politics. The principal goal of unions as defined in the law, was to seek the betterment of members' social and economic status. Unions were denied the right to strike or to engage in political activity, either on their own or as political parties. In spite of these limitations, trade unions gradually acquired political influence. The Confederation of Turkish trade unions (*Turk-Is*) was founded in 1952. Under the tutelage of *Turk-Is*, labour evolved into a well-organized interest group; the organization also functioned as an agency through which the government could restrain workers' wage demands. The labour movement expanded in the liberalized political climate of the 1960s, especially after a union law enacted in 1963 legalized strikes, lockouts, and collective bargaining.

However, workers' dissatisfaction with *Turk-Is* as the representative of their interests led to the founding of the Confederation of Revolutionary Workers' trade unions of Turkey (*DISK*). *DISK* leaders were militants who had been expelled from *Turk-Is* after supporting a glass factory strike opposed by the *Turk-Is* bureaucracy. Both *Turk-Is* and the government tried to suppress *DISK*, whose independence was perceived as a threat. However, a spontaneous, two day pro-*DISK* demonstration by thousands of workers in Istanbul (the first mass political action by Turkish workers), forced the government in June 1970 to back away from a bill to abolish *DISK*. For the next ten years, *DISK* remained an independent organization promoting the rights of workers and supporting their job actions, including one major general strike in 1977 that led to the temporary abolition of the military-run State Courts. By 1980 about 500,000 workers belonged to unions affiliated with *DISK* (Library of Congress 1995).

On September 12, 1980, the army took over the country and abolished the 1961 constitution, and closed down three union confederations: *DISK*, *HAK-IS* and *MISK*. *Turk-Is* was not shut down but was not allowed to engage in trade union activity. Wages were also immediately frozen. Until new trade union legislation was passed, collective bargaining activities were undertaken by the Supreme Arbitration Council established by the National Security Council (governed by the army). The Arbitration Council deliberately kept nominal wage increases below the annual inflation rates for about four years (Buyukuslu 1998–1999).

Following the 1980 coup, the military arrested hundreds of *DISK* activists, including all of its top officials. In a series of trials that lasted until December 1986, the secretary general of *DISK* and more than 250 other defendants received jail sentences of up to ten years. Meanwhile, the more compliant *Turk-Is* worked with the military government and its successors to depoliticize workers. The 1982 constitution permits unions but prohibits them from engaging in political activity, thus denying them the right to petition political representatives. As the government-approved labour union confederation, *Turk-Is* benefited from new laws pertaining to unions. A law issued in May 1983 restricted the establishment of new trade unions, placed constraints on the right to strike by banning politically motivated strikes, general strikes, solidarity strikes and any strike considered a threat to society or to national well-being. University students and faculty members could not be members of political parties or become involved in political activities. Youth branches of political parties were forbidden. Political activity by trade unions was banned, but they were allowed to make known their opposition to or support of political parties and government policies. Collective bargaining and strikes were regulated, so unions needed government permission to hold meetings and rallies (Library of Congress 1995).

However, in 1986 the unions experienced a resurgence. In February several thousand workers, angered by pension cutbacks, held a rally – labour's first such demonstration since the 1980 coup – to protest against high living costs, low wages, high unemployment, restrictions on union organizing and collective bargaining. Since 1986 workers have conducted numerous rallies, small strikes, work slowdowns, and other manifestations of dissatisfaction. By the early 1990s, an average of 120,000 workers per year were involved in strike activity (Library of Congress 1995).

Trade union membership dropped sharply during the 1980s and 1990s, falling from 24 per cent to 15 per cent by unofficial estimates. It seems that Turkish trade unions have been mainly influenced by anti-union policy measures of employers such as the growing number of sub-contracted workers hired, extensive lay-offs, increasing numbers of skilled workers, supervisors, and professionals not covered by collective bargaining, and the extensive use of seasonal and temporary workers (Ozkaplan 2000).

Employers

The Turkish Trade Association (*Turkiye Odalar Birligi – TOB*) has represented the interests of merchants, industrialists, and commodity brokers since 1952. In the 1960s and 1970s, new associations representing the interests of private industry challenged the *TOB*'s position as the authoritative representative of business in Turkey. The Union of Chambers of Industry was founded in 1967 as a coalition within *TOB* by industrialists seeking to reorganize the confederation. The Union of Chambers of Industry was unable to acquire independent status but did achieve improved co-ordination of industrialists' demands. By setting up study groups, the union was able to pool research on development projects. In addition, the union organized regional Chambers of Industry within the *TOB*.

Business interests also were served by employers' associations that dealt primarily with labour-management relations and were united under the aegis of the Turkish Confederation of Employers' Union (*Turkiye Isveren Sendikalari Konfederasyonu – TISK*). This confederation was established in 1961, largely in response to the development of trade unions, and was considered the most militant of the employers' associations. By the end of 1980, *TISK* claimed 106 affiliated groups with a total membership of 9,183 employers. Although membership of *TISK* was open to employers in both the private and the public sectors, it was primarily an organization of private sector employers. When the military regime took power in 1980, trade union activities were suspended, but *TISK* was allowed to continue to function. Employers supported the subsequent restrictive labour legislation which appeared to be in accordance with *TISK* proposals.

Another representative of business interests, the Turkish Industrialists' and Businessmen's Association (*Turk Sanayicileri ve Is A damlari Dernegi – TUSIAD*), was founded by the leaders of some of Turkey's largest business and industrial enterprises soon after the military coup. Its aim was to improve the image of business and to stress its concern with social issues. At the same time, *TUSIAD* favored granting greater control of investment capital to the large industrialists at the expense of the smaller merchant and banking interests that were usually supported by *TOB*. *TUSIAD*'s leaders were also concerned about widening economic inequality between regions and social classes and opposed *TISK*'s extreme anti-labour policies, which they perceived as jeopardizing Turkey's chances of entering the European Union.

Privatization

The privatization of public enterprises became a key strategy in the government's market-oriented approach. Basically, the privatization programs were designed to reduce the size and scope of the public sector and to strengthen market forces in the economy. The sell-off philosophy has been a central pillar of Turkish government economic policy since 1984, though the results so far have sometimes been less than convincing and, more important, have had a negative impact on trade unions.

The government took two major, seemingly crucial steps in the privatization process. First, key state companies, including a tourism chain, Turkish National Airlines, and an airline catering company were identified for privatization. But since these companies were very profitable and productive, it was somewhat unlikely that through privatization they would become more productive, which was the government's expectation. Second, the government identified major foreign investors, rather than domestic ones, as candidates for company acquisitions. In addition, in its relations with privatized industry, the government's approach was to reshape the industrial relations system (Buyukuslu 1995).

In the Turkish public sector, a system of 'tripartite political exchange' between the public sector, the unions and the government had developed but was diminishing due to the abolition of the 'workers' participation scheme' in the State Economic Enterprises (SEEs) in 1983. The SEEs encompass around 750,000 employees. There is no doubt that the privatization program affected *Turk-Is*, as it was largely organized in the public sector. A review of the various publications of the unions shows that, in general, they all considered the privatization effort a move aimed at undermining the trade union movement. The unions also criticized the policy on the grounds that the government sold the most profitable companies to private capital, particularly to foreign companies. Most unions claimed that there were significant changes in the status of the unions and in collective bargaining arrangements, increases in unfair dismissals, and that unionized workers were the first to be dismissed after the privatization of most companies (Buyukuslu 1995).

Processes

The late 1980s bought an increase in strikes and the beginning of a period of intense conflict with the government. For the first time, workers of different affiliations, religious and ethnic roots and geographical regions, established a legal and independent mass movement in order to pursue the broad economic and political interests of the working class. This mass movement forced the trade unions towards a new position in relation to the government and employers. In 1989, 600,000 public sector workers carried out widespread action known as the 'Spring Mobilization', including street demonstrations with the objective of tipping the scales in their favor in collective bargaining. In response to the ban on strikes, the trade unions in the public sector adopted a series of new tactics for collective action that fell within the law, such as slow-downs, lunch boycotts, false requests for medical examinations, not working overtime, etc.

This development resulted in a set of collective bargaining agreements which enabled workers to make up for the post-1980 losses. In 1990 the real wages of unionized workers increased above the pre-1980 level, despite opposition by employers and the government. As a result of successful collective bargaining in 1990 and 1991, wages increased by 81.7 per cent (taking the 1983 index as the base for real wages). In this period, multi-plant bargaining with single enterprise agreements was widespread and collective bargaining tended to be more centralized, particularly in the public sector. One of the important reasons for the successful conclusion of the 1989–1992 collective agreements was collective action by trade unions affiliated with the *Turk-Is* confederation which responded with a disciplined display of unity under a *Turk-Is* directive. All public sector unions agreed to enter into negotiations as one unit, agreeing that no union would sign an individual agreement (Buyukuslu 1998–1990).

Thirteen years later, in March 2004, the Turkish government is still using the decree to ban strikes:

> The national tyre workers union, Lastik-IS, was due to hold a nationwide strike earlier in the week to protest against a slide in pay and conditions at world famous tire manufacturers including Pirelli. However, on 21 March 2004, the Turkish authorities enacted a government decree signed by Prime Minister Recep Erdogan which effectively bans the planned protest … This reflects the Turkish authorities' consistent approach; relying on anti union tactics rather than respecting the core labor rights enshrined in the UN's International Labor Organization Conventions 87, 98 and 158, all of which the Republic of Turkey has ratified.
>
> (International Confederation of Free Trade Unions 2004)

Industrial relations in Saudi Arabia

Before the discovery of oil in the Kingdom of Saudi Arabia, the pattern of employment shows that in the main areas of economic activity such as pasturage, agriculture and commerce, the employed manpower was unspecialized. However, after the discovery of oil, the development of the petrochemical industry led the way to industrialization and economic expansion. This resulted in a shortfall in a wide variety of labour skills, which led to substantially higher wage rates than those in many other countries. The higher wages attracted high-quality foreign workers. Consequently, the labour market gained one of its features – a large influx of expatriate workers. A report by the Manpower Council (established in 1980, headed by HRH Prince Naif Bin Abdul Asziz, the Interior Minister, to be responsible for manpower planning in the Kingdom), indicates that the total civil manpower in Saudi Arabia reached 7.2 million by the end of 1997 – 4.7 million foreign workers, and 2.5 million Saudi workers (Alzalabani 2004).

As the pace of industrialization increased, relations between employers and employees became more important because of the unique features of industrial relations in Saudi Arabia. The government controls all aspects of industrial relations in the country: there are no trade unions; collective bargaining is prohibited; employers set wages, which vary according to the labour market and worker's nationality; and strikes are forbidden. It is illegal to provoke a strike for any reason. Indeed, these features are shared by most of the Gulf States. Officials say that trade unions are unsuited to their traditional form of society (ibid.).

In 2001, the government approved the establishment of an employees' committee in any company with more than one hundred Saudi employees. The purpose of the committee, which can be considered a foundation of collective bargaining, is to provide the company management with its recommendations with regard to the work conditions, products and any work-related issues which may help to improve production and the work environment. This committee should have between three and nine members, usually selected from among the workers. Its aim is to create a channel of communication between management and employees and help employees to raise complaints and exercise their rights (*Al-Eqtisadiah* 2001).

Industrial relations in Egypt

In 1993, a new labour law was approved that included new guidelines for hiring and firing, the right to strike, and collective bargaining. However, the law was not expected to allow workers to establish independent trade unions and, according to the US Department of Labor, the government-run trade union federation will probably remain the sole representative of Egyptian workers (1993).

There is only one legally recognized labour federation, the Egyptian Trade Union Federation (ETUF), to which all unions must belong (Pugh 1993). The current labour law allows the government to render illegal any trade union by revoking, or declining to register its charter (US Department of State 1994). Under the law, unions in the public sector may negotiate work contracts only if the public sector enterprises agree to negotiate. Otherwise unions lack bargaining power in the state sector. As a matter of fact, collective bargaining does not exist in any meaningful sense because the government sets wages, benefits and job classifications (ibid.).

According to the US Department of State (1992: 1,385), the government considers strikes a form of public disorder, not a contractual dispute. Hence, they are *de facto* illegal. Nevertheless, strikes do occur. The trade union leadership keeps its distance from workers who organize job actions because the law empowers the government to remove from office any union executive board member who provokes a strike. Strikers may be sentenced to up to two years in jail, and those who incite others to strike may receive additional penalties.

Privatization

Under pressure from the World Bank and the International Monetary Fund, the government took its first half-hearted steps in 1990 to begin the sale of its publicly owned enterprises, which the banks believed were a major cause of Egypt's economic woes. Among Egypt's problems were an excessive demand for subsidized goods, serious inflation, balance of payments deficits, growing international indebtedness and foreign exchange shortages. Selling companies was only a part of the problem. Privatization requires a flexible banking system, an active stock exchange and a supportive legal environment for success. Although the government began to improve all these areas of the market system, no one was ready to handle a rush of new private, or newly privatized, companies. Workers in state-owned industries feared losing their jobs if their companies were sold into private hands. In addition, according to Napoli (1995), one factor that everyone quietly acknowledged but few publicly discussed, was the rampant corruption that was prevalent in Egyptian society.

It seems that the situation of the workers has not changed much since 1995. In 2004, the owner of an asbestos company, many of whose workers had contracted cancer, stopped paying workers' salaries in response to the government demand that it implement safety measures regarding asbestos exposure (Kazan-Allen 2004). With no income, the injured workers looked to the Government for assistance. However, the Health Insurance Institution refused to recognize their illnesses as occupational diseases; thus preventing the workers from receiving compensation and medical treatment.

Industrial relations in Syria

Since the revolution in 1963, Syria has been governed by the Baath Party and the Assad family. The actual executive core of the Baath Party was the twenty one-member Regional Command, also headed by Assad, which directed Baath activities in Syria. Through its People's Organizations Bureau, the Baath Party administered a number of organizations, including the Revolutionary Youth Organization, Union of Students, the Women's Organization, the Peasants' Federation and the General Federation of Trade Unions. Each organization was supervised by a member of the Regional Command. These organizations inculcated Baath values in their members, provided new recruits, and extended services to various social groups. The party has been working for years to increase the number of peasants and workers in its ranks and claimed that union membership was growing by 30,000 a year (Library of Congress 1987).

Since 1963, the Syrian middle class has remained remarkably stable, both as a percentage of the workforce and in terms of the standard of living and social mobility of its members. Because Syria has not yet developed a large industrial sector, it lacks a true proletariat of wage-earning factory workers. The number of persons employed by private and public sector industry in 1980 was 207,000 or 12 per cent of the working population (according to statistics compiled by the Syrian General Federation of Trade Unions – ibid.). As of 1983 about 15 percent of non-labour was unionized (222,203 members in 179 unions). Union membership was largest among government, construction, textile and land transportation workers. The government encouraged and supported labour organizations but closely supervised their activities, restricted their political influence and economic power, and minimized labour disputes. Labour achieved a voice in management of public enterprises through the participation of workers' representatives in committees at each plant, but the managers headed the committees. In an effort to increase production and productivity, production councils were established, consisting of the business manager and representatives of the Baath Party, the union, and the plant workers (Library of Congress 1987).

Conclusion

At the beginning of this chapter we argued that the degree of democracy in the country influences the industrial relations systems. The main characteristic of all the countries discussed above is a low degree of democracy reflected in the fact that the two main categories of actors in a democracy, individuals and class, are for the most part unable to influence strategic decision-making in society. This is even more the case in the field of industrial relations. The Middle Eastern governments described intervene in the industrial relations systems in each country, not as one of the actors but as the sovereign. As can be seen above, by involving the armed or the security services, government intervention can be quite direct. Furthermore, there are laws that enable very close supervision of the actors – workers and unions – and do not allow employees or employers freedom to achieve their goals. The employees' representatives sometimes have an unpalatable and difficult choice: to represent the employees faithfully and thereby endanger themselves, sometimes risking arrest or even potential loss of life; or to become incorporated, submissively accepting the dictates of the government but thereby undermining its power to act independently. Nevertheless, labour disputes and strikes occur, and in most cases are ended through the use of emergency decrees or aggressive involvement of the security services sent in by the government.

In the context of the current discussions on Turkey's potential membership of the European Union an important question that presents itself is whether the EU will accept the current regulatory environment in Turkey and the restrictions on trade union activity. In the other Middle Eastern countries, the position of the trade unions remains uncertain. The International Confederation of Free Trade Unions (ICFTU), which seeks to promote freedom of association throughout the world argues that truly independent trade unions remain rare in the Middle East with union activity throughout the region remaining controlled by the State or ruling party. It is noted that of the IFCTU's more than 230 international afffiliates, only some 19 are in the Middle East.

Unfortunately, very little published data on industrial relations in Middle Eastern countries is available. Consequently, it is very important to perform further research in this area, both in order to understand the situation that currently reigns in these countries, and also, hopefully, to highlight the existing problems and thereby promote change.

References

Al-Eqtisadiah (2001). 'Development of labor committee in organizations recruiting Saudis'. *Al-Eqtisadiah* 3732 (3 April).

al-Hourani, Hani (2002). *The Jordanian labor movement: History, structure and challenges.* Bonn: Friedrich-Ebert-Stiftung.

Alzalabani, Abdulmonem H. (2004). 'Industrial relations and the labor market in Saudi Arabia'. Paper presented at the conference of the International Industrial Relations Association (IIRA), Seoul, Korea, June 23–26.

Ayubi, Nazih N. (1996). *Over-stating the Arab state: Politics and society in the Middle East.* New York, NY: I.B. Tauris.

Bellace, Janice R. (1994). 'The role of the state in industrial relations'. In J. R. Niland, C. Verevis and R. D. Lansbury (Eds.), *The future of industrial relations: global change and challenges.* London – Newbury Park: Sage.

Buyukuslu, Ali Riza (1995). 'The evolution of privatization in Turkey and its impact on Turkish trade unions'. *IBAR – Irish Business and Administrative Research* 16.

Buyukuslu, Ali Riza (1998–1999). 'The changing nature of Turkish trade unions since 1980'. *IBAR – Irish Business and Administrative Research* 19–20 (1).

Esposito, John L., and James P. Piscatori (1991). 'Democratization and Islam'. *Middle East Journal* 45 (3): 427–440.

Fuller, Graham (1991). 'Respecting regional realities'. *Foreign Policy* 83: 39–46.

International Confederation of Free Trade Unions (ICFTU) (2004). *ICFTU Online* 29.3.2004. Retrieved from: http://www.icftu.org/displaydocument.asp?Index=991219133 &Language=EN

Kazan-Allen, Laurie (2004). Victimization of Egyptian asbestos workers. *International Ban Asbestos Secretariat (IBAS)* June. Retrieved from http://www.btinternet.com/~ibas/ Frames/f_lka_vict_egypt_asb_wrks.htm

Library of Congress (1987). *Country Studies – Syria*, Section 123 of 5000 (April).

Library of Congress (1995). *Country Studies – Turkey*, Section 35 of 5000 (January).

Napoli, James J. (1995). Cairo communiqué: 'Mubarak slows Egypt's privatization drive'. *The Washington Report on Middle East Affairs* 13 (5): 50, 111.

Ozkaplan, Nurcan (2000). 'Trade unions' responses to globalization: A case study of the Turkish labor market'. *Management Research News*, 23 (2–4).

Pugh, Deborah (1993). 'Professionals denounce bill to curb Egyptian trade unions'. *The Guardian*. London, 17 February.

Shirom, Arie (1994). The system perspective in labor relations: Toward a new model. In D. Lewin, D. Sockell and D. B. Lipsky (Eds.), *Advances in Industrial and Labour Relations*. Greenwich, CT: JAI Press, pp. 37–62.

US Department of Labour (1993). *Foreign labour trends, Egypt*. Washington, DC: Bureau of International Labour Affairs.

US Department of State (1992). *Country reports – Egypt*. Washington, DC.

US Department of State (1994). *Country reports – Egypt*. Washington, DC.

Industrial relations in Australia and New Zealand: the path from conciliation and arbitration

RAYMOND HARBRIDGE, BENJAMIN FRASER AND PAT WALSH

Introduction

The paths away from conciliation and arbitration of industrial relations matters in Australia and New Zealand are now well established. Yet the paths adopted are quite different. In this chapter we explore how these two countries moved away from common systems. For most of the twentieth century Australia and New Zealand were internationally known for their unique national industrial relations system of compulsory state arbitration (Bray and Walsh 1998). The myriad of changes that occurred in both the political and economic arenas in the late 1980s and early 1990s had a profound impact upon the nature of conciliation and arbitration in both countries. This chapter will explore the key elements that have allowed these changes to alter dramatically the nature of industrial relations in both countries. First, the historical foundations of industrial relations in both Australia and New Zealand will be examined. Second, the key legislation that underpins the nature of each system will be analysed, with an emphasis upon the role of the constitution as a method of enshrining the principles of conciliation and arbitration. Third, the key institutions that govern industrial relations in Australia and New Zealand will be considered in the light of their ability to influence the interpretation and direction of conciliation and arbitration. Fourth, the role of the key actors in the process will be analysed, including the important role that the states in Australia have played in defining the path of collective bargaining. Finally, trends and developments in Australia and New Zealand will be considered in light of the similarities and differences between each country's distinctive path from conciliation and arbitration, and their implications for the future.

Australia: The foundations

In 2001, the Commonwealth of Australia celebrated a centenary of Federation. Australia is still a comparatively new country, but its short history reflects many innovative attempts to balance what has traditionally been viewed as a tenuous model of co-operative federalism. The States and Territories that agonised over the 'how' of Federation decided naturally, to have a constitution embedded in law, the *Commonwealth of Australia Constitution Act 1901*. As is true throughout the world, constitutions are remarkably robust, embodying principles of how the country will be managed, and extraordinary means are required for them to be altered. They are legislated within an economic and social framework that has radically altered, yet our forefathers (and in rare cases, foremothers) were able to use a one-off opportunity to pre-determine how employment in our society would be managed, virtually forever. The management of industrial relations in Australia fell within that gambit of opportunity, and saw the development of a constitution for the Commonwealth that would come to govern industrial power for the next hundred years.

Australia: The legislation

The decade before Federation saw unprecedented levels of industrial disputes and unrest (Hawke and Wooden 1997). Accordingly, industrial dispute resolution was placed firmly on the constitutional agenda, and the Commonwealth was given an industrial power defined by parliament within the *Commonwealth of Australia Constitution Act 1901*. The Commonwealth Parliament's industrial power contained in Section 51 (xxxv) of the Constitution was the result of a compromise during the Federation debates, which limited parliament to make laws 'with respect to conciliation and arbitration for the prevention and settlement of industrial disputes extending beyond the limits of any one State'. The framers of the constitution did not have any clear idea of how industrial power was to be exercised by the Commonwealth, although there was wide consensus that it would involve the resolution of disputes that were national in concern by an independent tribunal. Three states (Victoria in 1896, Western Australia in 1900, and New South Wales in 1901) had passed legislation to establish industrial tribunals before the Commonwealth (December 1904). It was anticipated that the Commonwealth's power would apply to only a handful of industries (such as shearing and maritime) where inter-state disputes had spread beyond state borders (Ford 1997). A clear vision was only reached during the passage of the *Conciliation and Arbitration Act 1904*, where the judicial model was firmly adopted (Frazer 2002). Since the system was primarily concerned with dispute resolution (rather than a legislative function of industrial regulation), an approach based on adjudicative arbitration was thought to be a natural one. As it was envisaged that the Act would apply to national disputes within national industries, the States developed their own industrial relations systems to deal with state level disputes.

Australia: The institutions

Over the next century, the approach and functions of the arbitration system were modified in response to the changes in the industrial relations environment. Attempts to engineer fundamental change to the system have, however, been of limited success because of the constitutional and political constraints of Australia's complex federal system. The federal approach to industrial conciliation and arbitration had developed some important characteristics. During the period 1918–1990, the federal and state tribunals regulated employment for over 80 per cent of the workforce. While the exact proportions have changed over time and by region, in general terms the ratio of 50:50 between federal and state has been largely maintained. The precise nature of the relationship between federal and state tribunals and awards has been largely governed by High Court decisions regarding the interpretation of Section 51 (xxxv) of the Constitution (Ford 1997). Questions such as, 'what is conciliation and arbitration?' (it is not collective bargaining); 'what is an industrial dispute?' (and therefore what is an industry and an industrial matter, etc.) have been before the courts. The federal constitution provides that federal laws (including awards created by conciliation and arbitration) override state laws to the extent of any inconsistency. This does not, however, empower the federal jurisdiction to legislate to compel unions and employers to use the federal arbitration system because of the inherent limitations of Section 51 (xxxv). Clearly, many employers and unions have chosen not to bring their disputes into the federal system. Attempts to abolish arbitration either federally or at a state level appear pointless. Repeal of either system simply creates a vacuum, which would be filled by the other system procedure, as happened in the state of Victoria when it abolished its system at state level in 1992.

Australia: The actors

With Federation in 1901, the concept of conciliation and arbitration was written into the Constitution and subsequently embodied in federal legislation in 1904. This legislation encouraged the organisation of representative bodies of employers and employees. This official recognition of trade unions strengthened the position they had developed in Australia during the latter half of the nineteenth century. In 1907, the High Court of Australia established the guidelines for a 'fair and reasonable' minimum weekly wage. This gave unions the impetus to lobby the federal government for national wage rises and improvements to working conditions through the industrial tribunal framework. With the creation of the Australian Council of Trade Unions (ACTU) in 1927,

Australian unions had one centralised body which could be used to represent employee interests before the Federal Industrial Commission (later the Australian Industrial Relations Commission) and other federal and state tribunals. The relationship between the ACTU and government reached its peak in the 1980s, with the adoption of the Prices and Incomes Accord (the Accord) by the Labour government. The basic premise behind the Accord process was that in return for union co-operation in setting national wages policy, the government would develop social and economic policies encouraging full employment and a rise in living standards. With the shift towards restructuring and enterprise bargaining in the early 1990s, unions turned their attention to enterprise-level industrial relations. While the unions supported the devolution of the industrial relations process, there remained an ongoing commitment to a safety net for those workers unable to receive wage increases through direct negotiations. With the election of the Coalition government in 1996 and the introduction of the *Workplace Relations Act 1996*, the ability of the ACTU to influence government policy was effectively curtailed and its influential position as the unions' supreme body was diminished by the significant decrease in union membership encountered during this time (Cooper 2004).

The most significant drop in trade union membership in Australia occurred between 1992 and 2002. By August 2002, there were 1,833,700 employees who were members of a trade union, which represents 23.1 per cent of the workforce (ABS 2002). Table 6.1 illustrates the decline in union membership between 1992 and 2002. This trend appears to be continuing. By August 2004 there were 1,842,100 employees who were members of a trade union, a 1 per cent decrease since August 2003 (Cooper 2004).

The decline in trade union membership in Australia is in part due to changes in the composition of the labour market, with job growth tending to occur in

Table 6.1 Trade union membership to 30 August 2002

Year	Trade union members (thousands)	Proportion of total employment (%)
1990	2,659.6	40.5
1992	2,508.8	39.6
1994	2,283.4	35.0
1996	2,194.3	31.1
1997	2,110.3	30.3
1998	2,037.5	28.1
1999	1,878.2	25.7
2000	1,901.8	24.7
2002	1,833.7	23.1

Source: Trade Union Members, Australia (ABS Cat. No. 6325.0); Employee Earnings, Benefits and Trade Union Membership, August 2003 (ABS Cat. No. 6310.0)

industries (particularly in the services sector) where the trade union membership rate has always been relatively low. Conversely, there has been a decline in jobs in industries that were traditionally highly unionised, such as mining and manufacturing. In 2003, the unionisation rate was highest in electricity, gas and water supply, at 54 per cent, and the lowest unionisation rate was in agriculture, forestry and fishing, at 5 per cent (Cooper 2004). The largest decrease in the trade union membership rate was in the communication services industry, from 74 per cent in 1993 to 31 per cent in 2003 (Cooper 2004).

The Australian industrial relations system has fostered similar collective representation for employers as it has for employees. The system of conflict resolution and the administration of awards and agreements have been historically based on the assumption that a large numbers of manufacturers are members of employer associations. Employers have constructed a complex web of national and state industry-level associations which are linked through a pattern of cross-affiliations. A major activity of these associations has been to service member organisations when they appear before industrial tribunals. Along with this activity, most employer associations are engaged in the provision of a range of

Table 6.2 Trade union membership by industry to 30 August 2003

ANZSIC by employee	Employees (%)	Unionisation rate (%)
Agriculture, forestry and fishing	2.2	5.2
Mining	0.9	29.1
Manufacturing	12.5	25.7
Electricity, gas and water supply	1.0	53.7
Construction	6.0	26.5
Wholesale trade	4.9	8.5
Retail trade	15.5	17.3
Accommodation, cafes and restaurants	5.2	8.7
Transport and storage	4.5	38.2
Communication services	1.9	31.2
Finance and insurance	4.0	18.7
Property and business services	11.6	7.0
Government administration and defence	5.0	38.4
Education	8.3	41.8
Health and community services	10.6	29.8
Cultural and recreational services	2.3	13.3
Personal and other services	3.6	28.7
Total	100.0	23.0

Source: Employee Earnings, Benefits and Trade Union Membership, August 2003 (ABS Cat. No. 6310.0)

additional, specialist services to keep members abreast of any relevant government policy or legislative proposals, as well as offering advice on a range of workplace related issues. Australia now has three major national employer bodies, with the formation of the Australian Industry Group (AIG) in 1998. Together with the Australian Chamber of Commerce and Industry (ACCI) and the Business Council of Australia (BCA) the three represent employer interests at the national level. The BCA comprises around eighty chief executives of Australia's largest firms, and was instrumental in the push for enterprise-based industrial relations in the 1980s. The aim of the BCA was to foster an industrial relations climate at the enterprise level which is based upon direct employer–employee communication. Not surprisingly, many see this as a disguised attempt to marginalise, if not eliminate, trade unions from the process. The ACCI was instrumental in putting together the Coalition's industrial relations agenda prior to the 1996 election (and has also played a large part in subsequent elections) and has been vigorous in lobbying for further legislative amendments and the creation of a unified industrial relations system. The AIG has not been as militant as the other two national bodies in pushing for increased change – rather it has focused upon providing professional support services to assist its 10,000 member organisations.

Australia: Trends in industrial relations post-Workplace Relations Act 1996

The current Federal Coalition Government has been committed to the continued reform of industrial relations arrangements and processes after the introduction of the *Workplace Relations Act 1996* (MacDermott 1997). This commitment to change has sought to enhance the emphasis on enterprises, workplaces and individuals in the bargaining process, with a consequential reduced role for the Australian Industrial Relations Commission (AIRC) (Callus and Lansbury 2002). Changes to the regulatory framework have resulted in the system of rule-making changing from one which relied exclusively upon union representation in bargaining, to one that provides a range of possibilities – union, non-union collective or individual employee–employer bargaining (ACCIRT 1999). The distribution of employee coverage by type of industrial instrument is presented in Table 6.3. The data show the falling importance of multi-employer awards (whether federal or state), the growth of enterprise-level bargaining, the failure of registered individual agreements to penetrate the system, and the dominance of unregistered individual agreements.

The *Workplace Relations Act 1996* restricted the AIRC's role in determining wages and conditions, and union negotiated awards were stripped back to permit only twenty allowable matters to be heard before the Commission (Rimmer 1997). These changes have coincided with the rise of somewhat sophisticated

Table 6.3 Distribution of employee coverage by industrial instrument, Australia, May 2000 and 2002

Type of instrument	% employee coverage 2000	% employee coverage 2002
Awards (state and federal)	23.2	20.5
Federal registered collective agreements	21.7	24.2
State registered collective agreements	13.5	13.9
Registered individual (federal)	1.0	1.0
Registered individual (state)	0.8	0.8
Unregistered collective	1.5	2.2
Unregistered individual	38.2	39.3

Source: Employee Earnings and Hours, Australia, May 2000, 2002 (ABS Cat. No. 6305.0)

human resource management practices that have been underpinned by a view of the Australian workplace from a unitaristic standpoint. This is in stark contrast to the traditional view of the Australian workplace, which had embraced many elements of collectivism, elements which had in turn influenced the systems, structures and institutions that governed Australian industrial relations (Costa 1997). There are still remnants of this traditional approach to employment relations at both the state and federal levels, although the changes at the federal level have been far more significant (Nolan 1998).

While the pace and shape of institutional reform is dependent on the political process, the ability of governments to resist change is argued to be weak (Rimmer 1997). In particular, a return to a highly centralised system for the determination of wages and employment conditions appears to be neither a realistic nor sustainable option given the significant changes that have occurred, starting with the introduction of the *Workplace Relations Act 1996*. The *Workplace Relations Act 1996* has established two principal employment bargaining pathways – Certified Agreements (CAs) and Australian Workplace Agreements (AWAs). Figure 6.1 outlines the three bargaining and agreement processes operating in the federal system. AWAs are probably the most significant fact of the Act, and because of their emphasis on individual employee bargaining, they represent a radical change from past processes. An AWA is an individual contract between employer and employee – unions can be used in a much reduced role as 'bargaining agents', and then only with the direct approval of the employee(s) concerned. Before they are approved, AWAs are not, in most circumstances, scrutinised by the AIRC but by the newest player in the industrial relations process, the Office of the Employment Advocate (OEA). Once approved by the OEA, an AWA replaces all other awards or agreements for the employee(s) covered by the AWA. The international evidence suggesting both a gradual gravitation downward in the level of workplace bargaining and a decline in trade union density provides support for the argument that a reversal in the reform process is unlikely (Creighton 1997). The Australian evidence is still open to interpretation, as the adoption of AWAs has not met initial expectations of broad take-up by employers and employees (McCallum 1997). There has, however, been a significant rise in the use of standard form, common law contracts (Wailes and Lansbury 1999). AWAs apply to less than two per cent of employees whereas non-union certified agreements currently apply to around eight per cent. Individual contracts are not vetted by the Office of the Employment Advocate and are not subject to union scrutiny. Data obtained from government sources show that as at June 2004, 1,305,500 employees were covered by union certified agreements, 166,100 by non-union certified agreements and 273,400 by AWAs. AWAs are most prevalent in the retail trade, property and business services, and manufacturing. At September 2004, over one-third of all AWAs occurred in Western Australia, with 20 per cent in New South Wales and 14 per cent in Victoria.

The reforms that have been introduced over the last decade, beginning with the enactment of the *Workplace Relations Act 1996*, raise a number of questions regarding the effect that such reforms have had upon job security, increasing working hours and rising wage inequality. The link between decentralisation of wage bargaining and rising earnings inequality is quite strong, and has significant implications for government (Wooden 2000). Again, the question as to the role and function of the AIRC needs to be considered, as the gap between high and low wage earners continues to increase.

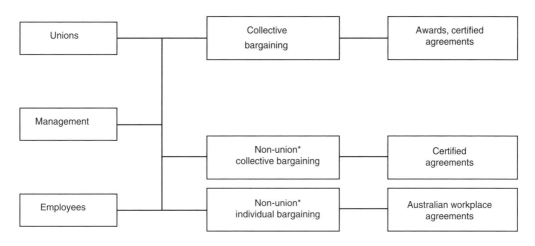

*Unions can only act as 'bargaining agents'

Figure 6.1 Summary of federal bargaining processes

Australia: The states

Around 25 per cent of Australian full-time employees are covered by awards, enterprise agreements and dispute settlement processes of the tribunals and commissions established at the state level (ABS 2002). The states are not bound by the constitutional restrictions that have influenced the development of the conciliation and arbitration power at the federal level. With the introduction of the *Workplace Relations Act 1996*, the Federal Coalition government attempted to extend the alignment of the federal and state systems through the use of complementary legislation to ensure that the full impact of the changes took place (Callus 1997). The response of the various state governments at the time was patchy to say the least, even though conservative governments were in power in all Australian states except New South Wales (Kollmogen 1997). Only the state of Queensland passed the requisite legislation in 1996, which was subsequently amended. As a result, five distinct state systems remain an integral part of Australian industrial relations. The two most populous states are New South Wales (33 per cent of the working population) and Victoria (25 per cent), followed by Queensland (19 per cent) and Western Australia (10 per cent). Of all the states, Victoria has undergone the most significant industrial relations changes. In March 1993, Victoria took the first step towards the decentralisation and individualisation of workplace relations, reflecting the prevailing ideological moves towards the individualisation of the workplace and the sidelining of unions from the negotiation process. With the introduction of the *Employee Relations Act 1993*, Victoria became the first state to abolish the conciliation and arbitration process (Forsyth 1995). The aim of legislation in Victoria was to minimise regulation of the employment relationship and to support individual employment agreements as the preferred means of determining workers' terms and conditions. An award could only be made if the employer and employees agreed that the employment relationship would continue under an award, yet employer associations were resistant to continuation of the award system (Forsyth 1995). This approach caused a great number of employees in Victoria to attempt to avoid these changes by escaping from the Victoria state system through federal award coverage.

A further development occurred in Victoria with the passage of the *Commonwealth Powers (Industrial Relations) Act 1996* (Vic), which had the effect of referring the vast majority of the Victoria Parliament's powers with respect to industrial relations matters, to the Commonwealth. The terms of Section 51 (xxxvii) of the Constitution empower the Federal Parliament to make laws with respect to 'matters referred to the Parliament of the Commonwealth by the Parliament or Parliaments of any State or States, but so that the law shall extend only to States by whose Parliament the matter is referred'. Relying on these powers, the Federal Parliament enacted Part XV of the *Workplace Relations Act 1996*, dealing with matters referred by Victoria. By the terms of these various enactments, the industrial relations system of Victoria was abolished, with the Victoria government handing the conduct of industrial relations in that state to the Federal Parliament. This change was historic indeed.

Federal award coverage has always been wider in Victoria than in states like Queensland and New South Wales which operate industrial tribunal mechanisms similar to those under federal law. For example, in May 1990 almost 40 per cent of Victoria employees had their wage rates and terms and conditions of employment regulated by federal awards. State awards also covered approximately 40 per cent of the Victoria workforce, with the remaining 20 per cent of employees being award free. At that point in time, by way of contrast, only 26.5 per cent of New South Wales employees and 23.2 per cent of Queensland employees were governed by federal awards. This high level of federal regulation in Victoria was largely due to two factors. Victoria has always been the heartland of the manufacturing industry in Australia, and large-scale manufacturing easily lent itself to federal coverage through the creation of interstate industrial disputes. As a result, a significant sector in Victoria, manufacturing, has been regulated under federal awards. In addition, the focus of the Victoria wages board mechanism was on the minimum wages and the terms and conditions of employees of small employers, and of those engaged in small-scale industry. Its awards were almost always applied as a common rule right across an industry. As a consequence, employees and employers in larger enterprises who preferred more enterprise-specific arrangements gravitated towards the federal system. With the abolition of state awards in early 1993, Victoria trade unions took action to move the industries over which they had coverage from Victoria to federal regulation. This movement of significant numbers of employees, in particular nurses, teachers and other public sector areas, substantially increased federal award penetration in Victoria. So great was the shift that by July 2000 it appeared that approximately 67 per cent of Victorian employees had their minimum terms and conditions of employment governed by federal awards, compared with 37.9 per cent in 1990.

The practical effect of Part XV of the Federal *Workplace Relations Act* is essentially to create an intrastate industrial relations system within the AIRC jurisdiction. The changes brought about by Victoria ceding its powers in relation to industrial relations matters fall into two broad areas. The first area relates to the exercise of the AIRC's functions and powers in the absence of an interstate industrial dispute, concerning matters in Victoria. Federal agreements, such as certified agreements and AWAs, may also be entered into by Victoria employers and employees under these provisions. Protection from unfair dismissal contained within the *Workplace Relations Act* is also extended to Victoria employees. The second area relates to minimum conditions of employment. Previously, under the former Victoria *Employee Relations Act 1993*, certain minimum conditions of employment were prescribed. Section 500 of the *Workplace Relations Act* now provides for these minimum conditions of employment. Additionally, the function of establishing minimum wages has also been transferred to the AIRC. As a reform measure, the Victoria Parliament passed the *Federal Awards (Uniform System) Act* in 2003. This Act enabled the Commonwealth, and in certain circumstance, the Victoria Civil and Administrative Tribunal to make common rule awards for 130,000 award-free workplaces in Victoria. The changes brought about by these developments in Victoria are unique in the Australian context. The extent to which other states may consider a similar course in the future remains to be seen.

Australia and New Zealand: The process of change

The current international trend towards labour market deregulation and the resultant impact upon the employment relationship has been used as an attempt to circumvent Section 51 (xxxv) of the Constitution (Hancock 1999). This is one aspect of Australian industrial relations which is in marked contrast to the New Zealand experience. In the 1890s, New Zealand had considered, but rejected, joining the Commonwealth of Australia. Nonetheless, similar forces were at work and, a decade earlier than Australia, New Zealand had adopted the *Industrial Conciliation and Arbitration Act 1894* as its method of managing industrial relations. New Zealand, however, had no constitution in which to embed the principles of conciliation and arbitration. So when the forces of labour market deregulation gathered momentum nearly a decade later, a unicameral parliament, with remarkably few checks and balances, was easily able to abolish the applicable legislation and deregulate through the *Employment Contracts Act 1991* (Harbridge and Walsh 2000). No such easy option has been available in Australia. Nonetheless, Australian legislators have attempted to modify and overcome the inherent limitations of Section 51 (xxxv). Referendums have been tried and failed (most notably in 1929 where the referendum to repeal the *Commonwealth Act* not only failed but the Government also lost the election). If a Federal Government wanted to deregulate industrial relations by providing for non-union agreements free from tribunal surveillance, then it had a problem. One problem was solved when the *Workplace Relations Act 1996* made provision for Australian Workplace Agreements (AWAs) and non-union collective agreements (Birmingham 1997). The power to achieve this legislation was through the constitutional authority of the *corporations power* (Section 51 (xx)). Surveillance was placed largely in the hands of the Office of the Employment Advocate (OEA) and unions could effectively be shut out of the process (van Barnevald and Waring 2002).

Various responses have attempted to overcome the perceived constitutional limitations, align federal and state jurisdictions and extend the adjudicative model of arbitration to include a wider regulatory function. Each response failed after facing strong opposition from state-based political forces from a variety of quarters. Likewise, many plans to convince the states to transfer their powers over employment matters have proved fruitless (apart from the recent example of Victoria in 1996). Alignment was successful in the area of joint appointments of presidents and members of state and federal tribunals, and the widespread acceptance by the states of federally determined wage principles adopted under the Indexation and Accord policies of the 1980s and 1990s. This is best seen as friendly co-operation rather than any dismantling of the system.

It has been argued that the result has been the use of more direct forms of legislative regulation using the external affairs and corporations powers in recent years (Wailes and Lansbury 1997). The use of such powers indicates a decline in government confidence in the value of the arbitration tribunal's autonomy and expertise. The trend of federal legislation in industrial relations shows an increasing tendency of governments to influence arbitral decision-making through procedural checks and by requiring the consideration of public policy issues such as the state of the economy. The consideration of these external pressures has allowed successive governments to mask their true intentions in relation to the industrial relations framework.

New Zealand: The arbitration regime

The regulatory system that governed industrial relations in New Zealand for almost a century was the national arbitration system established by the *Industrial Conciliation and Arbitration Act 1894*. The logic of the arbitration system was an exchange of concessions to trade unions and constraints upon them. This tied into the key objectives of the system – to redress inequality and to stabilise industrial relations (Harbridge and Walsh 2000). The system constrained the capacity of unions to engage in industrial action at the same time as it reduced their desire to do so by setting limits to the exploitation of workers by employers. The Act regulated employer and employee representation and the negotiation of employment conditions. It established a system of union registration and gave a registered union the exclusive right to bargain on behalf of workers in the occupations or industries that came within its coverage rules. The Act also required the formation of unions of employers to bargain with their worker counterparts, and where employers were reluctant to participate in this process, the state appointed representatives to take on this role. From 1936, union membership was compulsory, either directly through legislation or through negotiations, for any worker covered by an award (Harbridge and Walsh 2000). Registered unions secured exclusive rights to represent workers covered by their membership rule. They also gained exclusive access to compulsory bargaining forums, called conciliation councils, chaired by a state conciliator. An unsettled dispute was referred from the conciliation council to the Court of Arbitration that issued binding awards. Through this process, the state effectively guaranteed that union members would receive at least minimally acceptable conditions of employment (Holt 1986). The third major concession to unions was a guarantee by the state that an award would apply to all employers of workers covered by the award. This constituted one of the arbitration system's great attractions for unions since it meant they did not have to negotiate separately with each employer. In addition, the state not only required the universal application of an award, it also accepted responsibility for its enforcement.

New Zealand: The actors

The representation and negotiation systems established by the arbitration system constituted substantial concessions for unions. But they came at a high price. Compulsory membership and compulsory arbitration robbed many unions of their organisational vitality by eliminating the recruitment and negotiating challenges faced by union movements elsewhere (Harbridge and Honeybone 1996). Other aspects of the system reinforced their relative lack of vitality. The system of union registration set strict limits on a union's occupational and geographical jurisdiction and on the fees they could charge. This ensured that the New Zealand union movement was made up of literally hundreds of small weak unions. The arbitration system paid little attention to procedures to resolve employment disputes until the latter part of the twentieth century (Harbridge and Walsh 2000). From 1905, all strikes and lock-outs were illegal in the arbitration system and successive governments took the view that disputes procedures were therefore unnecessary. Instead the focus was on punitive measures to punish unions for unlawful industrial activity. By the 1970s, however, the level of industrial disputes had grown to an alarming degree. As a result, statutory procedures were established to resolve employment disputes, including personal grievance procedures to resolve disputes arising out of dismissals that were the cause of a high proportion of strikes. The inclusion of these procedures in awards and collective agreements was made mandatory (Holt 1986).

In the second half of the twentieth century, support for the arbitration system declined for a number of reasons. Of crucial importance was the loss of employers' faith in the system and their growing willingness and capacity to challenge its legitimacy (Harbridge and Honeybone 1996). Employers had been its reluctant supporters. They did not relish the protections enjoyed by unions but accepted them so long as the system delivered industrial stability and moderate wage increases. By the 1970s and 1980s, it delivered neither of these. Those unions whose size and membership solidarity would have allowed them to succeed without the protections of the arbitration system capitalised on the long period of post-war prosperity and labour scarcity to negotiate directly with employers and bypass the Court of Arbitration. The result was a steep rise in industrial conflict, high levels of wage inflation and industrial disorder on a remarkable scale.

Two other significant developments signalled the death-knell of the system. A radical programme of economic deregulation initiated by the Labour government of 1984–90 generated even more pressure for the abolition of the arbitration system. It was argued that the continued determination of wages on an occupational basis without regard for the economic circumstances facing particular industries and firms was untenable in a deregulated economy (Nolan and Walsh 1994). Alongside economic deregulation, the rise of individualism and associated values challenged the continued existence of the collectivist principles underpinning the arbitration system. The Labour government made a number of changes to the system in an effort to ensure its long-term survival. These included the abolition of compulsory arbitration but in most other respects retained the system's key features. The election of the conservative National government in 1990 heralded a shift to a radically different regulatory regime.

New Zealand: The contracting regime, 1991–2000

Rarely has one labour market regulatory regime been replaced by another so fundamentally at odds with its predecessor. In 1991, the National government enacted the *Employment Contracts Act*. The Act and associated legislation and the case law which supported them formed a regulatory regime based on the philosophy that the labour market involves freely contracting individuals of equivalent market power and that the potential for exploitation is relatively low (Dannin 1997).

The new regime denied legitimacy to unions and, far from facilitating collective organisation and practice, the new regime placed significant obstacles in their path (Hince and Vranken 1991). The consequence was greatly heightened employer resistance to all aspects of union activity. The Act made no mention of unions although it did refer to 'employee organisations'. The premise of the Act was that the activities of trade unions had no greater public policy significance than those of the local golf club. The Act abolished exclusive bargaining rights for registered unions and made the negotiation of any form of compulsory membership unlawful. Employers were given the right to veto union access to a workplace for the purpose of recruiting members, although unions did have rights of access to discuss negotiations with members for whom the union had established authority to recruit. No statutory procedures governed the negotiation of either individual or collective contracts of employment. The blanket coverage provision, by which awards were extended to all employers within its coverage, was abolished, requiring unions to negotiate separately with individual employers. The Act gave employers the capacity to veto any attempt to negotiate multi-employer contracts by outlawing strikes to support multi-employer bargaining.

These legislative provisions posed significant difficulties for unions seeking to pursue collective negotiations on behalf of their members. These difficulties were compounded by the development of case law under the Act which allowed employers to pursue aggressive de-unionisation strategies. Unions lacked effective counters to these strategies and their successful implementation and the judicial support they received discouraged workers from contemplating a collective response. For example, case law sanctioned the presentation of draft contracts to employees with, on occasions, financial incentives to sign, and, often related to this, a 'take or leave it' negotiating stance; a refusal to negotiate or even to meet, and 'captive audience' speeches by employers to workers. Above all, the Act imposed a higher standard for the courts to set aside employment contracts than for any other commercial contract. The normal contractual test of 'unfair' or 'unconscionable' contractual behaviour was replaced by the requirement that the contract must have been procured by 'harsh and oppressive behaviour'. The combined effect of legislative and judicial sanctioning of these approaches made for a bleak industrial landscape for unions and imposed severe impediments to effective collective organisation.

The consequences for unions were profound. With the shift from multi-employer to enterprise bargaining, unions struggled to negotiate many times more separate contracts on behalf of fewer members and with fewer resources. In many cases employers emboldened by the new legislative regime and by the development of supporting case law sought harsh changes to employment conditions. Union membership fell hugely and precipitately during the 1990s. Union density fell from 52 per cent of wage and salary earners in 1991 to 21 per cent in 1999 (May *et al.* 2003). Collective bargaining fell at a similar rate. Collective bargaining coverage fell from 50 per cent of the labour force to 25 per cent during the decade. Multi-employer bargaining which had dominated bargaining under the arbitration system fell to 15 per cent of total collective bargaining coverage (Walsh and Harbridge 2001). The consequences for workers of a gravely weakened union movement were equally profound. Unions were unable to resist employer determination to downgrade employment conditions. Radical changes were made to a wide range of employment conditions, particularly in the areas of working time and premium pay for overtime, weekend and evening work (Walsh and Harbridge 2001).

The employment contracts regime made radical changes to the resolution of employment disputes. Under the arbitration system, disputes and personal grievance procedures had been available only to union members employed under an award or collective agreement negotiated by the union. This could not be the criterion governing access to these procedures under the *Employment Contracts Act* since the Act made no reference to the existence of unions. Since the Act applied to the negotiation of all employment contracts, whether of the chief executive or the tea person, it required that all employment contracts, including individual contracts, must contain effective procedures to settle personal grievances and disputes, culminating if necessary in arbitration by one of two specialist institutions, the Employment Tribunal or the Employment Court. Thus, for the first time, all employees in New Zealand had access to compulsory state arbitration to resolve any dispute that arose in connection with their employment relationship. By any standard, this was a remarkable extension of the role of the state in industrial relations.

New Zealand: The employment relationship

The Labour Government, elected in 1999, was determined to restore some balance to the industrial relations system. In pursuit of these objectives, it enacted the *Employment Relations Act* in 2000 (Rasmussen 2004). The most important changes made by the this Act concern representation and negotiation. It retains the voluntary membership provisions of the *Employment Contracts Act*. Labour judged that the decade of voluntary membership had established public opinion irrevocably in opposition to compulsion. However, it does restore a system of union registration and confers upon registered unions the exclusive right to negotiate collective agreements. Those agreements cover union members only. The employer's veto right over union access to the workplace is eliminated. However, the blanket coverage bargaining provisions of the traditional award system are not restored and there is no return to compulsory arbitration nor any compulsion to settle a collective agreement. The obstacles to multi-employer bargaining in the *Employment Contracts Act* are removed.

A key to the new regime is that unions are seen as legitimate, significant and positive institutions that can contribute to the achievement of important public policy objectives. However, the Act does not restore anything resembling the full range of protections that unions enjoyed under the arbitration regime. Instead, the Act aims to give New Zealand's unions the opportunity to repair some of the damage done to their movement during the last decade. The evidence to date suggests that unions have had only limited success in achieving this objective (Harbridge *et al.* 2002). Union membership has risen slightly from 302,000 to 330,000 but as a proportion of wage and salary earners, the increase is only from 21 to 22 per cent. Collective bargaining coverage has actually decreased, falling from 399,000 to 332,000 (Thickett *et al.* 2003). What accounts for the lack of change? First, with regard to union membership, some of the explanation lies in the continuing legacy of the employment contracts decade. The huge loss of membership has driven the resources of many unions down to a level where maintaining current levels of activity exhausts all available resources. Second, a decade has passed in which a generation of new workers entering the labour force simply did not consider joining the union, while a generation of new firms has been established without a union presence. Third, more sophisticated human resource management has softened the edges of management practice and for many workers has weakened their sense of needing union protection. With regard to collective bargaining coverage, one consequence of the *Employment Relations Act* has been to reduce free riding. Free riding occurs when workers legitimately enjoy the benefits of an agreement negotiated collectively by a union of which they are not a member – a free ride. The *Employment Contracts Act* tolerated and even encouraged free riding in two ways. It permitted non-union collective bargaining that by 2000 had grown to cover 14 per cent of those covered by a collective contract. Second, it allowed non-union members to be covered by a union-negotiated collective contract. The result was that by 2000, 27 per cent of those covered by a collective contract were not union members. The *Employment Relations Act* prohibits this by assigning the exclusive right to negotiate collective agreements to registered unions and by limiting coverage to union members only. The intent behind this was to encourage non-members to join unions. It is evident that this has not been successful.

Australia and New Zealand: The path from concilation and arbitration

Over a hundred years ago, Australia and New Zealand adopted a unique approach to the resolution of industrial disputes – conciliation and arbitration. During the past two decades, both countries have sought a path away from that approach. The fundamental issue in any employment relations regime is the degree to which it legitimises unions and facilitates collective organisation. The more it does this, the less the capacity of employers to resist union activity. In New Zealand, the arbitration and contracting regimes adopted radically different systems of representation and negotiation. As a result, the arbitration regime legitimised unions and greatly facilitated their operation; the contracting regime did the reverse. In Australia, the two levels of the industrial relations system permitted the development of a strong union movement at both state and federal level and gave arbitration as an institution a large measure of legitimacy as well as popular support. New Zealand had no particular difficulty legislatively abandoning conciliation and arbitration: the *Employment Contracts Act* achieved that in 1991. Australia, on the other hand, has had insurmountable difficulty achieving the same result due to conciliation and arbitration being embedded in the Constitution. Regardless, both countries reached a broadly similar position by 2003 as to levels of trade union density, and thus penetration and effectiveness. In Australia, the trade union membership rate has also declined over the last fifteen years, from 42 per cent in 1988 to 23 per cent in 2003. In New Zealand, union membership has dropped from slightly over 50 per cent in the late 1980s to 22 per cent in 2003. In part, the decline in trade union membership in both countries is due to changes in the composition of the labour market, with job growth tending to occur in industries (particularly in the services sector) where the trade union membership rate has always been relatively low. Conversely, there has been a decline in jobs in industries that were traditionally highly unionised, such as mining and manufacturing. Coinciding with these changes has been an increase in casual and part-time employment, both of which have tended to have lower unionisation rates. These factors, when combined with the substantial changes to the industrial relations environment over the past decade have had a significant impact upon unions. The emphasis on decentralised bargaining and the opening up of both collective and individual bargaining to workers not represented by unions have reduced the role of unions in the wage negotiation process. In Australia, other changes, such as the restriction of federal awards to certain allowable matters, and the exclusion of union preference clauses from awards, have led to a shift in employee attitudes towards trade unions and their role in the workplace.

New Zealand's employment relationship regime, established in 2000, does not go as far in either direction as its predecessors. It offers unions a degree of legitimacy and support for collectivism which was lacking under the employment contracting regime. However, it has not yet achieved the same degree of change that the other two regimes did in their early years. Under both arbitration and contracts, the industrial relations landscape was recast in a very short period of time. Under the employment relationship regime, change has been much less dramatic in its first few years. This suggests that patterns of behaviour in industrial relations become heavily embedded and resistant to change. Regardless of the degree of opposition to a regime when it is introduced, the regime's impact on resources and, as a result, the strategic options open to the parties, mean that the parties adjust to a new regime and map their structures and modes of operation onto it even while some continue to express their opposition to it. The introduction of a new regime does not change behaviour unless it also reallocates resources and thereby changes power relations to a degree that opens up new strategic options. In this lies the explanation for the limited change wrought under the employment relationship regime. By steering a middle ground between the arbitration and employment contracting regimes, the new regime does not affect the shift in resource allocation and power relations that is needed to make possible radically different strategic options for the parties.

Conclusion

For much of Australia and New Zealand's history, the responsibility for balancing the interests of employers and employees has fallen on the shoulders of the government. The industrial unrest before Federation led to the incorporation of industrial powers in the Constitution and the ensuing establishment of Australia's conciliation and arbitration system. New Zealand, however, had no constitution in which to embed the principles of conciliation and arbitration, which has resulted in a markedly different path for industrial relations legislation. State and federal governments in Australia, acting on behalf of 'public interest' have played a major part in shaping the framework for industrial relations through legislation. From 1904–1988, the Australian industrial relations framework changed little, but over the past two decades successive federal governments have introduced major industrial relations legislative changes. In addition, all Australian states have undergone industrial relations legislative reforms, with Victoria being the most notable example. The industrial relations landscape in New Zealand, under both the arbitration and contracting regimes, was recast in the same short period of time. The judicial system in Australia, particularly the High Court, has had significant impact through its interpretation of the legal framework which governs the industrial relations system and the manner in which the framework operates. Similarly, the courts in New Zealand have always had a profound impact on the operation of the system. The continued existence of a specialist Employment Court, supported by institutions with mediation and arbitral authority, means that the system's outcomes are significantly shaped by judicial opinion and decision.

An ongoing issue in Australian industrial relations has been the next step in the path from conciliation and arbitration – whether the state systems of industrial relations can be unified nationally. It has been argued that the current arrangements are complex and produce inconsistent outcomes. Many are persuaded by this argument, although consensus over the best approach to a national system remains difficult to achieve. The referral of Victoria's industrial relations powers to the Commonwealth was intended to represent the first step towards a unitary industrial relations system in Australia. There were high hopes that the other states would follow suit, eventually creating a unitary, national system but to date, no other state has done so. It remains to be seen how far reaching the implications of Victoria's march towards a unitary industrial relations system will be. Will the other states follow Victoria's lead? A review of recent history would indicate that this is highly unlikely. However, this needs to be tempered with the recognition that the current Federal government enjoys a majority in the House of Representatives, and in July 2005 will extend this majority to include the Senate. Sweeping industrial relations changes have been mooted. The only certainty is further change. In New Zealand, the industrial relations policy debate has muted in recent years. Although the opposition National party contests aspects of the Coalition government's most recent legislative amendments, the fundamentals of the *Employment Relations Act* are largely accepted, albeit grudgingly on the part of the National party, and further radical legislative change appears unlikely in the medium-term future.

References

ABS (2002) *Employee Earnings and Hours, Australia*, May 2002, ABS Cat. No. 6305.0, Canberra: Australian Bureau of Statistics.

ACCIRT (1999) *Australia at Work*. Sydney: Prentice Hall.

Birmingham, A. (1997) 'A Guide to the Workplace Relations Act 1996', *Australian Bulletin of Labour*, 23 (1): 33–47.

Bray, M. and Walsh, P. (1998) 'Different paths to neo-liberalism? Comparing Australia and New Zealand', *Industrial Relations*, 37 (3): 358–387.

Callus, R. (1997) 'Enterprise bargaining and the transformation of Australian industrial relations', *Asia Pacific Journal of Human Resources*, 35 (2): 16–25.

Callus, R. and Lansbury, R. (2002) *Working Futures: The Changing Nature of Work and Employment Relations in Australia*. Leichhardt: Federation Press.

Cooper, R. (2004) 'Trade unionism in 2003', *Journal of Industrial Relations*, 46 (2): 213–225.

Costa, M. (1997) 'Union Strategy Post–Workplace Relations Act', *Australian Bulletin of Labour*, 23 (1): 48–58.

Creighton, B. (1997) 'The Workplace Relations Act in international perspective', *Australian Journal of Labour Law*, 10 (1): 31–49.

Dannin, E. (1997) *Working Free: The Origins and Impact of New Zealand's Employment Contracts Act*. Auckland: Auckland University Press.

Ford, W. (1997) 'Reconstructing Australian labour law: a constitutional perspective', *Australian Journal of Labour Law*, 10 (1): 1–30.

Forsyth, A. (1995) 'Employee Relations Amendment Act (Vic)', *Australian Journal of Labour Law*, 8 (2), 154–166.

Frazer, A. (2002) *The Federal Conciliation and Arbitration Power: From Cradle to the Grave?*, Australian Parliamentary Library Research Paper No. 15 2001–02.

Hancock, K. (1999) 'Labour Market Deregulation in Australia'. In Richardson, S. (ed.) *Reshaping the Labour Market*. Melbourne: Cambridge University Press.

Harbridge, R. and Honeybone, A. (1996) 'External legitimacy of unions: trends in New Zealand', *Journal of Labor Research*, 27 (3): 425–444.

Harbridge, R. and Walsh, P. (2000) 'The evolution of collective enterprise bargaining in New Zealand', *Labour & Industry*, 11 (1): 1–22.

Harbridge, R., Walsh, P. and Wilkinson, D. (2002) 'Re-regulation and union decline in New Zealand: likely effects'. *New Zealand Journal of Industrial Relations*, 27 (1): 65–77.

Hawke, A. and Wooden, M. (1997) *The Changing Face of Australian Industrial Relations*. Adelaide: National Institute of Labour Studies.

Hince, K. and Vranken, M. (1991) 'A controversial reform of New Zealand labour law: The Employment Contracts Act 1991', *International Labour Review*, 130, (4): 475–493.

Holt, J. (1986) *Compulsory Arbitration in New Zealand: The First Forty Years*. Auckland: Auckland University Press.

Kollmorgen, S. (1997) 'Towards a unitary system of industrial relations? Commonwealth Powers Industrial Relations Act 1996 (Vic)', *Australian Journal of Labour Law*, 10 (1): 158–169.

MacDermott, T. (1997) 'Industrial legislation in 1996: The reform agenda', *Journal of Industrial Relations*, 39 (1): 52–76.

McCallum, R. (1997) 'Australian workplace agreements: an analysis', *Australian Journal of Labour Law*, 10 (1): 50–61.

May, R., Walsh, P., Harbridge, R. and Thickett, G. (2003) 'Unions and union membership in New Zealand': Annual Review for 2001, *New Zealand Journal of Industrial Relations*, 28 (3): 314–325.

Nolan, D. (ed.) (1998) *Australasian Labour Law Reforms: Australia and New Zealand at the End of the Twentieth Century*. Leichhardt: Federation Press.

Nolan, M., and Walsh, P. (1994) 'Labour's leg-iron? Assessing trade unions and arbitration in New Zealand'. In P. Walsh (ed.), *Trade Unions, Work and Society: The Centenary of the Arbitration System*, Palmerston North: The Dunmore Press.

Rasmussen, E. (ed.) (2004) *Employment Relationships: New Zealand's Employment Relations Act*. Auckland: Auckland University Press.

Rimmer, M. (1997) 'The Workplace Relations Act 1996: an historical perspective', *Australian Journal of Labour Law*, 10 (1): 69–81.

Thickett, G., Harbridge, R., Walsh, P. and Kiely P. (2003) *Employment Agreements: Bargaining Trends and Employment Law Update 2002/2003*. Wellington: Industrial Relations Centre, Victoria University of Wellington.

Wailes, N. and Lansbury, R. (1997) 'Flexibility vs collective bargaining: Patterns of Australian industrial relations reforms during the 1980s and 1990s', ACCIRT Working Paper No. 49, Sydney: ACCIRT.

Wailes, N. and Lansbury, R. (1999) *Flexibility vs Collective Bargaining: Patterns of Australian Industrial Relations Reforms during the 1980s and 1990s*. Sydney: ACCIRT.

Walsh, P. and Harbridge, R. (2001) 'Re-regulation of bargaining in New Zealand: The Employment Relations Act 2000', *Australian Bulletin of Labour*, 27(1): 43–60.

Wooden, M. (2000) *The Transformation of Australian Industrial Relations*. Leichhardt: Federation Press.

Useful websites

Federal Australia
www.dewr.gov.au
www.workplace.gov.au
www.airc.gov.au
www.oea.gov.au
www.worldlii.org/catalog/1.html

New Zealand
www.dol.govt.nz
www.worldlii.org/catalog/2050.html

Victoria
www.irv.vic.gov.au

New South Wales
www.industrialrelations.nsw.gov.au

Queensland
www.dir.qld.gov.au

South Australia
www.eric.sa.gov.au

Tasmania
www.justice.tas.gov.au/tic/index.htm

Western Australia
www.wairc.wa.gov.au

Suggested key readings

Bray, M. and Walsh, P. (1998) 'Different Paths to Neo-Liberalism? Comparing Australia and New Zealand', *Industrial Relations*, 37 (3): 358–387.

Callus, R. and Lansbury, R. (2002) *Working Futures: The Changing Nature of Work and Employment Relations in Australia*. Leichhardt: Federation Press.

Deery, S. and Mitchell, R. (1999) *Employment Relations: Individualisation and Union Exclusion - An International Study*. Leichhardt: Federation Press.

Hawke, A. and Wooden, M. (1997) *The Changing Face of Australian Industrial Relations*. Adelaide: National Institute of Labour Studies.

New Zealand Journal of Industrial Relations, 28 (2), June 2003. Symposium on Collective bargaining under the Employment Relations Act.

Nolan, D. (ed.) (1998) *Australasian Labour Law Reforms: Australia and New Zealand at the End of the Twentieth Century*. Leichhardt: Federation Press.

Rasmussen, E. (ed.) (2004) *Employment Relationships: New Zealand's Employment Relations Act*. Auckland: Auckland University Press.

Rimmer, M. (1997) 'The Workplace Relations Act 1996: An Historical Perspective', *Australian Journal of Labour Law*, 10 (1): 69–81.

van Barnevald, K. and Waring, P. (2002) 'AWAs: A Review of the Literature and Debates', *Australian Bulletin of Labour*, 28 (2): 104–119.

Wooden, M. (2000) *Union Wage Effects in the Presence of Enterprise Bargaining*. Melbourne Institute Working Paper No. 7.

7 Industrial relations in Asia: old regimes and new orders

DONG-ONE KIM[1]

Introduction

The purpose of this chapter is to document the current status of industrial relations (IR) in Asian countries, examine the magnitude and direction of changes in IR, and provide some analysis of prospects for the future. IR in Asia are changing for various reasons, such as the new global economic order, political democratization, changes in the composition of industry and the labour force, and the 1997–98 Asian financial crisis and the resultant economic and financial restructuring.

Since the mid-1990s, two major forces appear to have driven changes in IR in Asian nations both of which continue unabated. The first of these is the drive to resolve the inconsistencies increasingly apparent between the existing IR systems in these countries and the new economic order. This new order is characterized by heightened international competition, changes in industry and labour force composition, the recent financial crisis, the pursuit of labour flexibility, and efforts to restructure economic systems including financial institutions.

The second of these forces is the changing relationships between IR actors. The conflicts of interest among IR actors in this region have been intensified mainly because of the advent of political democratization in several countries and the transition from planned economies to market economies (Kim and Kim 2003). Consequently, a gradual or abrupt transformation of IR systems can be expected because of the mismatch between political and industrial structures and IR systems.

Over-reliance by many experts on official statistics has created an impression that the Asian labour movement has been weak and its influence is declining. However, a careful analysis of newly emerging labour movements in several Asian countries such as South Korea (Korea, hereafter), Taiwan, Indonesia,

Thailand, Malaysia, China, and Vietnam, leads to the conclusion that the Asian labour movement is neither universally weak nor universally declining. Whereas it may be true that IR in Asia has been underdeveloped and under-institutionalized until now, Asia is very likely to have a dynamic labour movement over the next few decades.

This discussion of IR in Asia covers eleven countries which are selected because data on them are readily available. However, these eleven cover much of the Asian landmass from East Asia to South Asia – and show the region's diversity, both in economic development and in types of economies. This diversity ranges from Japan, one of the most affluent capitalist economies, to Indonesia, an underdeveloped but developing country, and, again, from capitalist Japan to ex-Communist countries such as China and Vietnam which are in transition to market-governed economies.

Table 7.1 shows the extreme variation in population – from 1,288 million in China to 4.3 million in Singapore – and the disparity in per capita GDP, which ranges from US$33,819 in Japan to only US$417 in Vietnam.

Table 7.1 Economic and social indicators

Country	Population (in thousands, 2003)[a]	Per capita GDP ($US, 2003)[b]	Industry structure, % of GDP (2001 or 2002)[c]			Literacy rate (%, 2001)[d]
			Agriculture	Industry	Services	
China	1,288,400	1,100	14.5	51.7	33.7	85.8
Hong Kong	6,816	22,618	0.1	13.4	86.5	93.5
Indonesia	214,471	944	17.5	44.5	38.1	87.3
Japan	127,210	33,819	2.0[f]	36.0[f]	62.0[f]	99.0
Korea	47,912	11,059	4.0	40.9	55.1	97.9
Malaysia	24,774	4,227	9.1	48.3	46.4	87.9
Philippines	81,503	1,005	14.7	32.5	52.8	95.1
Singapore	4,250	21,195	0.1	33.6	66.6	92.5
Taiwan	22,520[e]	12,588[e]	1.9	31.0	67.1	92.5[e]
Thailand	62,014	2,273	9	42.5	48.5	95.7
Vietnam	81,314	471	23.0	38.5	38.5	92.7

Source
a The World Bank. 2004. *World Development Indicators Database*, September. *http://www.worldbank.org/data/databytopic/POP.pdf*. Accessed 5 Nov., 2004.
b The United Nations. 2004. *Social Indicators. http://unstats.un.org/unsd/demographic/products/socind/inc-eco.htm* Accessed 6 Nov., 2004.
c The Asian Development Bank. 2003. *Key Indicators 2003*. *http://www.adb.org/Documents/Books/Key_Indicators/2003/default.asp* Accessed 6 Nov., 2004.
d The United Nations. 2003. *Human Development Report 2003*. New York: Oxford University Press.
e The Directore General of Budget, Accounting and Statistics. 2003. *Statistical Yearbook of the Republic of China 2003*.
f The World Bank. 2001. *World Development Indicators 2001*. Washington, D.C.: The World Bank. (The 1999 Statistics were reported.)

The present chapter is composed of several sections. The first classifies the eleven countries under discussion into six typologies based upon their industrialization strategy and the characteristics of their IR actors (i.e. state, labour, and employers). The succeeding sections consist of an analysis and synthesis of the variety of developments that exist within Asian labour relations; this analysis and synthesis, in turn, become the basis for a presentation of several common trends in Asian IR.

Six typologies of Asian IR

The eleven countries included in the present study show wide variations in terms of the economic characteristics and industrialization strategy and in the nature of the three industrial relations actors: state, labour, and employers. The eleven countries were classified into the six sub-groups: (1) Japan; (2) Korea and Taiwan; (3) Malaysia, Indonesia, and Thailand; (4) the Philippines and Hong Kong; (5) Singapore; (6) China and Vietnam.

IR based upon informal agreement: Japan

Although most industrialized countries suffer from the post-industrialization syndrome characterized by de-industrialization and the decline of manufacturing, Japan borders on being an exception. This is because the Japanese economy's manufacturing sector retains its world-class competitiveness in such industries as automobiles and electronics.

One peculiar characteristic of Japanese labour relations is the underlying consonance between the state, employee groups and the labour centre, which makes Japanese labour relations unusually co-operative and free of overt and extreme labour–management conflicts. The state plays the role of neutral referee in labour relations.

Recently, the three pillars of the Japanese system – long-term employment, seniority-based pay, and enterprise unions – have been noticeably weakened. Although the three pillars benefited only regular male employees in large firms (irregular employees such as part-time workers, seasonal workers and immigrant workers were excluded); they represented the norm in Japanese labour relations. Some scholars interpret the recent large-scale layoffs, the adoption of performance pay, and the continuing decline of enterprise unionism as marking the end of Japanese-style labour relations (Whittaker 1998). Indeed, union membership and density have declined steadily since 1970. The main causes of this weakening may be the shift of employment from the industrial sector to the service sector and decreasing union loyalty from workers. Most unions conduct pay negotiations during Shunto in April and May of each year, but the relative importance of these negotiations in national wage bargaining has declined. Furthermore, the number of labour disputes has been falling, which implies that the significance of unionism in Japan is becoming weaker and weaker.

In contrast to scholars who see Japanese-style labour relations disintegrating, another group thinks that the essence of the system is still intact (Berggren and Nomura 1997; Kuwahara 1998). These authors regard the typical Japanese firm as a quasi employee-managed firm or corporate community. That is, most directors of these firms are ex-employees, some of whom were leaders of enterprise unions when they were rank and file employees. It is assumed that Japanese-style employee-managed firms seek to maximize the dividend or net income per worker, while typical capitalist firms seek to maximize total profit. In addition, an employee-managed firm implies a type of participatory management in which member–workers hold ultimate decision-making rights. This interpretation explains why Japanese employers are extremely reluctant to fire permanent employees. Its perspective of the corporate community as the essence of the Japanese system and the three pillars as merely surface phenomenon also supports a conclusion that the Japanese system has not been transformed.

As for the labour movement, the new Rengo[2] was established in 1989 and has pursued co-operative labour–management relations. The Rengo attempted to unify the industrial federations of enterprise unionism to respond effectively to industrial- and national-level employment issues. However, the Rengo has been unsuccessful in coping with either industrial-level restructuring drives or declines in unionism.

Uneven transition toward pluralism: Korea and Taiwan

IR in Korea and Taiwan share many similarities, but also differ significantly. Industrial development in Korea, which has relied on large corporations in the heavy engineering and chemical industries and has concentrated them in certain geographical regions, has been conducive to the formation of a strong working class. This is because larger firms help to shield workers from direct employer surveillance and facilitate close co-operation among the workers, and geographical concentration allows better cross-union collaboration. In contrast, small- and medium-sized companies typically based upon family ties have mainly been in the forefront of economic development in Taiwan. Until very recently, the boundaries between workers and small employers have remained vague. Moreover, many workers in Taiwan have regarded their jobs as an apprenticeship for their own entrepreneurial undertakings, and as a result many workers never developed a strong identity with the working class. Consequently, workers in Taiwan were poorly organized before the democratic transition in the late 1980s, whereas workers in Korea were able to organize autonomous unions as early as 1970 (Chu 1998).

Currently, Korea and Taiwan are in transition to high value-added industrial societies as they move from labour-intensive industries to capital- and technology-intensive enterprises and from manufacturing-based to service-based economies. As this transition occurs, labour-intensive employers in both countries have relocated their operations to China and to South East Asian countries such as Thailand, Malaysia, Indonesia, and the Philippines, to escape increased labour costs.

Both countries have moved out of their long periods of state corporatism and now experiment with a new industrial order that can incorporate state, labour and employers under one overarching ideology. In Korea and Taiwan, the labour movement enjoys greater freedom after a long period of suppression. Both countries seem to be moving slowly toward pluralistic systems under newly elected democratic regimes. However, the transition from authoritarian political systems to more democratic ones has been uneven and has been accompanied by intensified labour–state conflict that has increased the number of labour disputes.

Korea

Economic growth in Korea was led by large indigenous private organizations that were closely guided by the state and were recipients of its support in various forms. The Korean economy has been heavily dependent upon *chaebols*,[3] such as Samsung, Hyundai, LG, and SK. Employment practices in Korea can be characterized by principles of seniority-based wages and long-term employment. Since the mid-1990s, however, these principles have frequently been violated. This was particularly true during the 1997–98 financial crisis, which made employers eager to adopt an alternative employment principle based upon labour flexibility.

During the rapid economic growth of the 1960s and 1970s, the government suppressed the independent labour movement. Although labour gained some legal rights in the 1980s, the labour law now in effect still prohibits union activities by public employees and university professors. It also requires compulsory arbitration by the Ministry of Labour of disputes in some private industries.

The freedom of the labour movement in Korea has been closely related to political circumstances at the national level. After 1949, the government recognized the Federation of Korean Trade Unions as the only legal national-level union federation; this organization was generally subordinate to the government. A turning point in the representation of labour came in the late 1980s, ignited by the Democratization Declaration issued in June 1987 by President Noh Tae Woo. This declaration led to the greatest labour turmoil in Korean history. There were 3,749 strikes in 1987, a thirteen-fold increase over the previous year. This unprecedented magnitude of labour strife led to an expansion of the Korean union movement, which was rapidly acquiring members. Union membership increased during 1987–89 from 11.7 to 18.6 per cent of employment. This expansion was followed in the early 1990s by the formation of the Korea Confederation of Trade Unions, a militant and illegal national federation. After the largest general strike in Korean history in early 1997, the trade union law was revised in 1999 to allow the Korea Confederation of Trade Unions to become a legitimate union federation (Kim and Kim 2003).

Although most Korean unions are enterprise unions (accounting for approximately 95 per cent of union members in the mid-1990s), industrial unionism is a notable recent trend. The 1997–98 financial crisis, and the resultant waves of layoffs, led union leaders to take note of the limitations of enterprise unionism. Since then they have increasingly realized that enterprise-based unions cannot effectively respond to industrial- and national-level employment issues, such as industry-level restructuring plans led by the government (Kim and Kim 2003).

The movement toward industrial unionism is a highly significant strategic choice by labour in Korea. Between 1998 and 2000, almost twenty industrial unions were formed. The combined membership of these industrial unions accounted for approximately one-third of the total union membership in Korea in 2005. Industry-level bargaining, however, is conducted only in a limited number of sectors, such as the metal and health industries. This is largely because employers in other sectors refuse such bargaining.

Since the financial crisis, strike activities have increased by all measurements. As shown in Table 7.3, the number of strikes increased from 78 in 1997 to 320 in 2003 and involved more workers and more working days lost. One notable outcome of the financial crisis of November 1997 was the formation of the Tripartite Commission by labour, employers, and the state. Without such a crisis, such a commission would not have been possible because of the traditional animosity between labour and the state. Creation of the Tripartite Commission implied that the Korean government regarded labour at least as a partner for negotiations and compromise. On 9 February 1998, the Tripartite Commission agreed to major agenda items and publicly announced a Social Compact. The key ingredient of the Social Compact was additional legalization of basic labour rights for unions and workers in return for accepting immediate implementation of layoffs of redundant labour forces. This Social Compact was the first agreement ever reached in Korea by labour, management, and the state, in which each party acted autonomously (Kim and Bae 2004).

Taiwan

The main actors in Taiwanese economy have been small- and medium-sized enterprises usually based upon family ties. Most of the country's large corporations, such as petroleum and chemical companies, are typically government-owned. Small corporations, which are in the majority in Taiwan, are usually privately owned. The Chinese Management Association is the most powerful employer organization.

The Kuomintang traditionally maintained an iron-fisted labour policy that can be characterized as state corporatism. Although the state passed the Labour Standards Act in 1984 to specify employment standards for individual workers, some basic union rights were not provided. For example, until martial law was ended in 1987, strikes were illegal, and unions were not permitted to bargain over the introduction of either new technology or new work standards. The end of martial law in July 1987 signalled the beginning of democratization. In 1987, the Council of Labour Affairs was created for the explicit purpose of enforcing the Labour Standards Act.

Before the start of the democratization movement in the mid-1980s, trade unions were merely auxiliary institutions and administrative arms of government. The major union organization, the Chinese Federation of Labour, represented state-controlled or employer-controlled trade unions. However, after the democratization movement in 1987, independent unions were formed, such as the Federation of Independent Unions, the National Federation of Industrial Unions, and the Taiwan Labour Front. These independent unions criticized the Chinese Federation of Labour as too subordinate to the state and employers, and worked on behalf of an autonomous labour movement that would be more independent of the state and employers.

In 2000, the former mayor of Taipei, Shui-Bian Chen, was elected as President, and the Democratic Progressive Party replaced the Kuomintang which had ruled Taiwan for fifty-five years. However, the Trade Union Law still dictates that the state has the right to dissolve unions or change their leadership if they disturb the peace and public order. Strikes are allowed only after mediation and arbitration by local officials, which serve to make most strikes illegal. Moreover, teachers and government employees are forbidden to form unions. Thus, Taiwan retains elements of state corporatism in its labour policy.

After Shui-Bian Chen won the presidency, independent unions were legalized by presidential edict. The rise of a new federation, the Taiwan Confederation of Trade Unions, has divided the labour movement. Forced by the Taiwan Confederation of Trade Unions to compete for workers' loyalty, the mainstream trade unions affiliated with the Chinese Federation of Labour have tended to become more autonomous. As a consequence of democratization, a new attitude by government, and a more aggressive labour movement, unions in Taiwan today enjoy more power, and their influence is widely felt. In this sense, the decline in union membership does not mean a decline in union strength. Union influence has, in fact, been increasing. The growth of democracy has weakened the government's control over unions, allowing them greater autonomy (Lee 2000). As union influence has increased steadily since the late 1980s, so has the number of labour disputes (including strikes, lockouts, and unresolved labour-management conflicts).

Emerging tigers under the state exclusionary labour policy: Malaysia, Indonesia and Thailand

These three countries have in common state exclusionary labour policies bent on union marginalization. The objectives of labour suppression are twofold: (1) to maintain low labour costs in order to attract foreign investment and to guarantee price competitiveness in the international market; and (2), to prevent possible political challenges from organized labour groups.

Malaysia

Malaysia has been one of the fastest growing economies in the world since the 1980s. Twenty years of sustained economic growth based upon relatively cheap and docile labour made Malaysia one of the largest manufacturers of semiconductors and a sizeable producer of electronic products and textiles. The population is composed of Malays (approximately 54 per cent of the population), Chinese (37 per cent), and Indians (16 per cent). The government maintains policies to protect Malays' interests, but industry continues to be dominated by ethnic Chinese.

Given that neighbours like Cambodia, Vietnam, and Laos offer lower-cost alternatives, Malaysia is trying to forge an industrialization strategy based upon highly skilled labour requirements and high value-added products. With its suppressive labour policy still in place, the government has not yet devised human resources and IR policies more consonant with this high value-added economy (Kuruvilla and Arudsothy 1995).

Indeed, IR in Malaysia has been severely repressed. The government excludes trade unions from decision-making at the national level, and they exert very little influence in the workplace. Although unions are legal, Malaysian unions are tightly controlled by the state through the union registration process. To prevent the rise of militant unions, the Registrar of Trade Unions has wide discretion over the process of officially recognizing unions. Top-level labour organizations such as the Malaysian Trade Union Congress are incorporated as societies, not as union federations. Furthermore, in order to keep the labour movement fragmented, the state effectively bans the effort of labour federations to unite into a single federation.

Collective bargaining is also highly restricted. Unions are not allowed to bargain on employee transfers, promotions, job assignments, or layoffs. Collective bargaining actually covers only a small minority of the urban workers. Collective bargaining in export processing zones is circumscribed, and unions in the electronics sector are allowed to operate only on an in-house basis, which is a part of the government's strategy to maintain the competitive advantage of low-cost exports. Strikes are legal only under limited conditions that include mandatory strike ballots and advance notice of intent to strike. Strikes are prohibited once the dispute had been referred to arbitration by the Minister of Labour (Kuruvilla and Arudsothy 1995).

During the financial crisis, the government set up the Tripartite National Advisory Council with the participation of the Malaysian Trade Union Congress to draw up guidelines on how to handle industrial restructuring and the introduction of performance-based pay. Although the results of the Tripartite Accord of 1996 seemed insignificant, it did show the intent of the Malaysian government to handle the employment issue in a tripartite manner (Frenkel and Kuruvilla 2002; Kuruvilla and Erickson 2002). Currently, the Malaysian government plans to create a knowledge-based economy (popularly called 'Vision 2020'). However, the current highly controlled and iron-fisted approach to IR does not seem to match with the K-economy plan (Todd *et al.* 2004), which must utilize employees' discretionary efforts, voluntary commitment, and creativity.

Indonesia

Indonesia is the world's largest Muslim country, and its population ranks fourth in the world. Like other emerging tigers, until the 1997–98 financial crisis, Indonesia had shown significant economic growth in the preceeding decades (see Table 7.2). Its industrialization strategy is based upon inexpensive labour with a strong work ethic and on the export of low-priced products.

The state's repression of the union movement has a long history. The suppressive labour policy began in the latter years of Sukarno's Old Order (1945–66), and continued during the New Order (under Suharto, 1966–1998). During these periods, the state tightly controlled the independent labour movement, especially because of labour's links with the communists. In 1974, the Suharto government devised the Pancasila IR system that emphasized industrial peace and harmony between workers, management and the government. However, the Pancasila IR system did not recognize industrial disputes. After the 1997 financial crisis and the fall of Suharto in May 1998, Indonesians witnessed democratic reforms that loosened the authoritarian reins of government (Suwarno and Elliott 2000).

During the New Order, the Federasi Serikat Pekerja Seluruh Indonesia/Federation of All-Indonesia Workers' Unions (FSPSI) was the government-sponsored labour entity. The government encouraged enterprise-based unions and allowed only a single union in each plant. Despite the monopoly of the state-backed organizing

Table 7.2 Unemployment rate[a] (growth rate of GDP)[b]

	China	Hong Kong	Indonesia	Japan	Korea	Malaysia	Philippines	Singapore	Taiwan[c]	Thailand	Vietnam
1980	4.9 (6.0)	3.8 (10.1)	– (9.9)	2.0 (2.8)	5.2 (-2.1)	– (7.4)	4.8 (5.1)	3.0 (9.7)	1.2 (7.3)	0.8 (4.8)	– (-4.8)
1981	3.8 (5.7)	3.6 (9.2)	– (7.9)	2.2 (2.8)	4.5 (6.5)	– (6.9)	5.4 (3.4)	2.9 (9.6)	1.4 (6.2)	1.3 (5.9)	– (4.0)
1982	3.2 (9.6)	3.6 (2.7)	– (2.2)	2.4 (3.2)	4.4 (7.2)	– (6.0)	5.5 (3.6)	2.6 (6.9)	2.1 (3.6)	2.8 (5.4)	– (8.7)
1983	2.3 (10.9)	4.5 (5.7)	– (8.8)	2.6 (2.3)	4.1 (10.7)	– (6.2)	4.9 (1.9)	3.2 (8.2)	2.7 (8.5)	2.9 (5.6)	– (6.3)
1984	1.9 (15.2)	3.9 (10.0)	– (7.0)	2.7 (3.8)	3.8 (8.2)	5.8 (7.8)	7.0 (-7.3)	2.7 (8.3)	2.5 (10.6)	2.9 (5.8)	– (8.4)
1985	1.8 (12.6)	3.2 (0.4)	– (2.5)	2.6 (4.6)	4.0 (6.5)	6.9 (-1.1)	6.1 (-7.3)	4.1 (-1.6)	2.9 (5.0)	3.7 (4.6)	– (6.2)
1986	2.0 (8.5)	2.8 (10.8)	– (5.9)	2.8 (2.9)	3.8 (11.0)	8.3 (1.1)	6.4 (3.4)	6.5 (2.3)	2.7 (11.6)	3.5 (5.5)	– (2.9)
1987	2.0 (11.2)	1.7 (13.0)	– (4.9)	2.8 (4.4)	3.1 (11.0)	7.3 (5.4)	9.1 (4.3)	4.7 (9.7)	2.0 (12.7)	5.9 (9.5)	– (4.0)
1988	2.0 (10.7)	1.4 (8.0)	– (5.8)	2.5 (6.5)	2.5 (10.5)	7.2 (8.8)	8.3 (6.8)	3.3 (11.6)	1.7 (7.8)	3.1 (13.3)	– (5.2)
1989	2.6 (4.1)	1.1 (2.6)	– (9.1)	2.3 (5.2)	2.6 (6.1)	6.3 (9.2)	8.4 (6.2)	2.2 (9.6)	1.6 (8.2)	1.4 (12.2)	– (4.7)
1990	2.5 (2.7)	1.3 (3.4)	– (9.0)	2.1 (5.2)	2.4 (9.0)	5.1 (9.0)	8.1 (3.0)	1.7 (9.0)	1.7 (5.4)	2.2 (11.1)	– (5.1)
1991	2.3 (10.6)	1.8 (5.1)	– (8.9)	2.1 (3.3)	2.3 (9.2)	– (9.5)	9.0 (-0.6)	1.9 (6.8)	1.5 (7.6)	2.7 (8.6)	– (6.0)
1992	2.3 (14.3)	2.0 (6.3)	– (7.2)	2.2 (1.0)	2.4 (5.4)	3.7 (8.9)	8.6 (0.3)	2.7 (6.7)	1.5 (7.5)	1.4 (8.1)	– (8.6)
1993	2.6 (13.5)	2.0 (6.3)	– (7.3)	2.5 (0.3)	2.8 (5.5)	3.0 (9.9)	8.9 (2.1)	2.7 (12.3)	1.5 (7.0)	1.5 (8.3)	– (8.1)
1994	2.8 (12.8)	1.9 (5.5)	– (7.5)	2.9 (1.0)	2.4 (8.3)	– (9.2)	8.4 (4.4)	2.6 (11.4)	1.6 (7.1)	1.3 (9.0)	– (8.8)
1995	2.9 (10.5)	3.2 (3.9)	– (8.2)	3.2 (1.9)	2.0 (8.9)	3.1 (9.8)	8.4 (4.7)	2.7 (8.0)	1.8 (6.4)	1.1 (9.2)	– (9.5)
1996	3.0 (9.6)	2.8 (4.3)	4.0 (7.8)	3.4 (3.4)	2.0 (6.8)	2.5 (10.0)	7.4 (5.8)	3.0 (8.1)	2.6 (6.1)	1.1 (5.9)	2.7 (9.3)
1997	3.0 (8.8)	2.2 (5.1)	4.7 (4.7)	3.4 (1.8)	2.6 (5.0)	2.5 (7.3)	7.9 (5.2)	2.4 (8.5)	2.7 (6.7)	0.9 (-1.4)	– (8.2)
1998	3.1 (7.8)	4.7 (-5.0)	5.5 (-13.1)	4.1 (-1.1)	6.8 (-6.7)	3.2 (-7.4)	9.6 (-0.6)	3.2 (-0.9)	2.7 (4.6)	3.4 (-10.5)	– (5.8)
1999	3.1 (7.1)	6.2 (3.4)	6.4 (0.8)	4.7 (0.1)	6.3 (10.9)	3.4 (6.1)	9.6 (3.4)	4.6 (6.4)	2.9 (5.4)	3.0 (4.4)	– (4.8)
2000	3.1 (7.9)	4.9 (10.2)	6.1 (4.9)	4.7 (2.8)	4.2 (9.3)	3.0 (8.3)	10.1 (6.0)	4.4 (9.4)	3.0 (5.9)	2.4 (4.6)	– (6.8)
2001	3.6 (7.5)	5.1 (0.5)	8.1 (3.4)	5.0 (0.4)	3.8 (3.1)	3.5 (0.4)	9.8 (3.0)	3.4 (-2.4)	4.6 (-2.2)	2.6 (1.9)	2.8 (6.8)
2002	4.0 (8.0)	7.3 (2.3)	9.1 (3.7)	5.4 (0.1)	3.1 (6.3)	3.5 (4.1)	– (4.4)	5.2 (2.2)	5.2 (3.6)	1.8 (5.4)	– (7.0)
2003	– (9.1)	7.9 (1.5)	– (4.1)	5.3 (2.7)	– (3.1)	3.6 (5.2)	– (4.5)	5.4 (0.5)	5.0 (-)	1.5 (6.7)	2.3 (6.0)

a The International Labour Organization. 2004. LABORSTA Internet. http://laborsta.ilo.org. Accessed 8 Nov., 2004
b The United Nations. 2004. National Accounts Main Aggregates Database. http://unstats.un.org/unsd/snaama/Introduction.asp Accessed 6 Nov. 2004.
c Directorate General of Budget, Accounting and Statistics. 2003. Statistical Yearbook of the Republic of China 2003.

vehicles, independent labour organizations often operated secretly in the 1980s and 1990s in conjunction with labour-based non-governmental organizations (NGOs).

For example, in 1992, an independent union centre, the Serikat Buruh Sejahtera Indonesia/Indonesian Prosperity Trade Union (SBSI) (i.e. a rival to the existing FSPSI) was formed and challenged the government to provide greater opportunities for workers to create an independent labour movement. In 1994, a third union centre, the Pusat Perjuangan Buruh Indonesia/Centre for Indonesian Working Class Struggle (PPBI), was organized to set up links between student and worker groups in Indonesia (Hadiz 2001).

Despite the advent of these independent labour organizations, the labour movement was severely suppressed until the late 1990s. The police, the army, and employers' groups pressured union activists with the threat of dismissal. Under these circumstances, the NGOs urged the government to take into consideration international labour standards as stipulated in the International Labour Organisation (ILO) conventions and recommendations. The persistent and continuing violation of union rights in Indonesia attracted international attention, and these issues were discussed several times in the ILO in the 1990s (Suwarno and Elliott 2000).

After the fall of Suharto in May 1998, the Indonesian Reformation Government (May 1998 to October 1999), led by President Habibe, took a significant step to improve basic labour rights. The government ratified the key ILO conventions on freedom of association and the right to organize. The ratification and subsequent implementation of the ILO conventions resulted in a significant increase in union activity. The independent SBSI was legally accepted as a union in 1998 (Suwarno and Elliott 2000), whereupon the previously state-sponsored FSPSI underwent rapid decline (Hadiz 2001). Since the ratification of the ILO conventions in 1998, workers' organizations have been expanding along with a sudden rise in the number of work stoppages and demonstrations (Soeprobo 2004).

Indeed, the late 1990s saw a resurgence of labour activism in Indonesia, involving an expansion of the labour movement, an increase in strike activities, and the proliferation of semi-formal labour-organizing vehicles (Hadiz 2001). Although the high level of unemployment after the 1997 Asian economic crisis diminished the bargaining power of workers, strike statistics for Indonesia showed a high level of activity in the following years (see Table 7.3).

Indonesia has been one of the few countries to show increasing levels of union density and of strike activities. The sheer size of the country and its population underscore the significance of these developments.

Table 7.3. Frequencies of strikes, lockouts, and labour disputes

	China[a]	Hng Kng[b]	Taiwan[c]	Indone.[b,d]	Japan[b]	Korea[b]	Malaysia[b]	Philip.[b]	Singap.[b]	Thailand[b]
1980	-	37	626	198	1,133	206	38	62	0	18
1981	-	49	891	125	955	186	31	260	0	54
1982	-	34	1,153	224	944	88	28	158	0	22
1983	-	11	921	-	893	98	25	155	0	28
1984	-	11	907	29	596	114	19	282	0	17
1985	-	3	1,443	78	627	265	25	371	0	4
1986	-	9	1,485	73	620	276	23	581	1	9
1987	-	14	1,609	37	474	3,749	13	436	0	10
1988	-	8	1,314	39	498	1,873	9	267	0	7
1989	-	7	1,943	17	362	1,616	17	197	0	11
1990	-	15	1,860	61	284	322	17	183	0	9
1991	-	5	1,810	130	310	234	23	182	0	14
1992	-	11	1,803	251	263	235	17	136	0	33
1993	-	10	1,878	185	252	144	18	122	0	23
1994	1,482	3	2,061	296	230	121	15	93	0	15
1995	2,588	9	2,271	276	209	88	13	94	0	39
1996	3,150	17	2,659	346	193	85	9	89	0	18
1997	4,109	7	2,600	234	178	78	5	93	0	23
1998	6,767	8	4,138	278	145	129	12	92	0	8
1999	9,043	3	5,860	125	154	198	11	58	0	16
2000	8,247	5	8,026	273	118	250	11	60	0	13
2001	9,847	1	10,955	194	90	235	13	43	0	5
2002	11,024	0	12,393	220	74	322	4	36	0	-
2003	-	1	9,869	-	-	320	-	-	0	-

* In the cases of China and Taiwan, the numbers of labour disputes were reported. Labour disputes including strikes, lockouts, and any unresolved disagreements between labour and management. For all other countries, the number of strikes and lockouts were reported.
a The National Bureau of Statistics and Ministry of Labour and Social Security, P. R. C. 2003. *China Labour Statistical Yearbook 2003*. Beijing: China Statistics Press.
b The International Labour Organisation. 2004. *LABORSTA Internet. http://laborsta.ilo.org*. Accessed 8 Nov. 2004.
c Directorate General of Budget, Accounting and Statistics 2003. *Statistical Yearbook of the Republic of China 2003*.
d Soeprobo (2004) for the Indonesian strike data from 1990 to 2002.

Thailand

As one of the emerging tigers, the Thai economy has grown rapidly in recent years, averaging about 10 per cent GDP growth during the 1987–96 period, and then slowing to 4 per cent to 6 per cent after the 1997–98 Asian financial crisis (see Table 7.2). Thailand adopted a strategy of export-oriented industrialization involving light manufacturing such as textiles, clothing, toys, and assembly of electronic products. Employers have adopted cost-reduction measures based upon numerical flexibility and labour suppression, using several methods to achieve these ends. These have included casualization – the replacement of permanent employees with temporary and short-term workers; subcontracting; preventing or weakening unions; dismissal of union organizers; and temporary plant closures followed by selective re-employment of former workers (Deyo 1995).

IR in Thailand suffered a series of repressions related to the military coups until the early 1990s. Thai workers have been engaged in an ongoing battle to gain recognition from the state of the right to organize. Before the 1980s, the Thai government considered labour issues as one aspect of national security. Suppression of labour organizations was justified as a way to maintain political stability (by preventing challenges from left wing groups) and ensure a healthy economy (by keeping labour costs low).

Within this overall atmosphere of repression of organized labour, there has been an ebb and flow in the degree of hostility on the part of the government. For example, after 1976, when the Chatichai government was democratically elected, the government showed greater official acceptance of trade unionism, an attitude that persisted throughout the 1980s (Brown and Frenkel 1993). This changed, however, with the February 1991 military coup, after which all state enterprise unions were banned. The democratically elected Chatichai government was disbanded, the constitution abrogated, and martial law imposed. Despite the repeated military coups that followed, Thailand is a country with an unusually dynamic citizens' movement. Indeed, the citizens' struggle for democracy after the 1991 military coup was followed by the retreat of the military government, and democratic order was restored in May 1992. A new democratic constitution was approved in October 1997 during the 1997–2000 economic crisis, which was linked to the July 1997 collapse of the Thai Baht.

Thai unions are generally enterprise based. They are relatively powerful in the state enterprise sector and weak in the private sector. The comparatively more powerful state-enterprise unions were at the forefront of the general struggles for basic labour rights in the 1980s, assisting private sector unions in campaigns to force employers to abide by the law and protecting workers against unfair labour practices. In some cases, powerful state-enterprise unions have been successful in halting the privatization of state enterprises. Despite some successes, however, the Thai union movement is generally weak and fragmented. Although less than 5 per cent of the work force is organized, this membership is spread among more than 700 unions and five major labour centres (Brown and Frenkel 1993). Only a small minority of employees in the state-enterprise sector are covered by collective bargaining. Reflecting this weakness, the level of officially recorded strike activity, which has never been very high, has declined further since the 1997–98 financial crisis (see Table 7.3).

Fragmented labour movement under voluntaristic labour policy: The Philippines and Hong Kong

In general, heavy state intervention characterizes Asian labour relations. The Philippines and Hong Kong have been exceptions. Both countries have traditionally maintained a voluntaristic labour policy that implied minimal state intervention in labour affairs. Nevertheless, in both countries the labour movement has remained fragmented and in some senses weak. Although Hong Kong became a part of China in 1997, the IR system in Hong Kong did not change significantly when this occurred and has retained the voluntaristic tradition rooted in the British system. Thus, it is fair to classify Hong Kong with the Philippines rather than to group it with either China or Vietnam.

The Philippines

The Philippines has an open market economy with a large urban informal sector. Since the 1970s, the Philippines has pursued an export-oriented industrialization strategy. The main human resource strategy of employers has been to focus on numerical and wage flexibility. The 1997–98 financial crisis gave new impetus to this strategy which has been implemented by such measures as layoffs, labour casualization, subcontracting, and labour-only contracting. In the export processing zones, regional governors have enforced a de facto informal non-union policy as a way to attract foreign investment (Erickson *et al.* 2003). The government tolerates 'no union, no strike' policies and labour-only contracting practices in order to facilitate implementation of the export-oriented industrialization strategy. The state lacks the political will to enforce its laws, particularly when enforcement may mean challenging large economic entities (Skene 2002). Although most Philippine employers are focused on numerical flexibility, a small minority of firms such as US-owned semiconductor factories are clearly moving towards functional flexibility.

The Philippines operates US-model labour relations systems because of the country's history as an American colony. Indeed, the Industrial Peace Act of 1953 resembled the US National Labor Relations Act of 1935, which bequeathed a decentralized collective bargaining system to the Philippines. During the Marcos dictatorship and its use of martial law (from 1972 to 1986), however, labour relations policies were extremely suppressive. After the assassination of Senator Benigno S. Aquino in August 1983 and the 'people power' revolution in February 1986, democratization began. During the subsequent Aquino and Ramos governments, democratization led to the removal of the restrictive labour policies of the Marcos era. However, remnants of the suppressive labour policy of their predecessors remain in labour laws and are exemplified by several restrictions on the ability of unions to strike. Overall, the basic underlying concept of a voluntaristic IR system has remained strong, although it was dormant under the Marcos regime (Kuruvilla and Erickson 2002).

The weakness of the labour movement in the Philippines lies in its increasingly fragmented trade unions. Approximately 145 competing labour federations are affiliated with rival labour centres, including, to name some of the largest, the Trade Union Congress of the Philippines, the Kilusang Mayo Uno, the Federation of Free Workers, and the Lakas Manggagawa Labour Center. Almost all the labour federations are engaged in general unionism, which means organizing across industries. This explains why union-raiding (i.e. 'organizing the already organized') has been popular (Ofreneo 1995).

The economic crisis in the late 1990s, which led to waves of layoffs, labour casualization, subcontracting, and labour-only contracting, has made many unions and workers bitter towards the companies, resulting in a few highly contentious and visible strikes, such as the labour disputes at Philippine Airlines in 1998 over job security. Since the 1997 Asian economic crisis, the most strike-prone industries have been in transportation, utilities, and the hotel industries (Erickson *et al.* 2003). The prominence of these recent disruptions, however, should not obscure the downward trend throughout the 1990s in the number of strikes, statistics that document the weakening of labour activism.

During the 1997–98 financial crisis, the Employers Confederation of the Philippines and the government managed to bring labour into a tripartite forum to discuss ways to adjust to the crisis. The Tripartite Social Accord issued in February 1998 tried to ease restrictions on layoffs as a means of promoting economic restructuring and simultaneously to expand social security to give workers more protection from the effects of layoffs (Erickson *et al.* 2003; Frenkel and Kuruvilla 2002). However, the Accord seemed merely symbolic because the government did not propose any actual policies for its enforcement.

Hong Kong

Hong Kong has been characterized as a highly industrialized society with an underdeveloped system of IR. The economic competitiveness of Hong Kong lies in the service sector, which accounts for 86.5 per cent of GDP. The manufacturing sector continues to rely on relatively unskilled human resources that produce low value-added products.

Although British colonial rule was terminated on 1 July 1997, and Hong Kong was officially returned to China, the voluntaristic tradition (i.e. minimal regulation by the government) derived from the influence of British colonialism continues as a distinct characteristic of IR in Hong Kong (Chiu and Levin 1996). However, a signal of a more active role by the new Chinese-appointed government may have come in the repeal of the trade union laws[4] passed by the outgoing British-appointed government on the eve of the transfer of sovereignty.

IR in Hong Kong is characterized by a limited scope of trade union representation in which no more than 4 per cent of the labour force is covered by collective bargaining, which has led some observers to call it 'the near absence of collective bargaining' (Chiu and Levin 1996). Most Hong Kong unions are small – and labour federations, rather than individual unions, play a key role in labour movement (Snape and Chan 1997).

The labour movement in Hong Kong is fragmented through competition among three labour centres, each of which has a very different ideology. The largest of the three is the pro-China Hong Kong Federation of Trade Unions, which subscribes to the traditional dual role of unions in communist states: a representative function (protecting and advocating employees) and a production function (educating workers and co-ordinating productivity campaigns).

The second largest, the Hong Kong Confederation of Trade Unions, was established in 1990, and has shown radical and adversarial approaches that emphasize union democracy. The Hong Kong Confederation of Trade Unions has generally been apolitical, keeping its distance from both China and Taiwan. The third largest labour federation, the pro-Taiwan, Hong Kong and Kowloon Trade Union Council (TUC) has been passive and has been in a vulnerable position in the years since Hong Kong was officially returned to China in 1997.

Despite this fragmentation of the labour movement, union membership has increased in Hong Kong from 17 per cent in 1988 to 21.5 per cent in 1999 (see Table 7.4).

Although few strikes have occurred since 1997, the increasing union density in Hong Kong is noteworthy because it implies that the Chinese-appointed government tolerates an autonomous labour movement. Whether the voluntaristic tradition of IR in Hong Kong will remain intact will be the biggest question in the years ahead.

A city state under state corporatism: Singapore

Singapore has only 4.3 million people, and 76 per cent of them are Chinese. Singapore has been a centre of multi-national companies in Asia, and its economy depends heavily on foreign investment. Consequently, by creating a

Table 7.4 Union density*

	China[a]	Hng Kng[a]	Japan[a]	Korea[a]	Philip.[a]	Singap.[a]	Taiwan[a]	Thailand[b]
1980	82.1	-	30.8	21.0	27.0	26.8	-	-
1981	83.6	-		20.8	30.2	23.7	-	-
1982	85.4	-	30.5	20.2	30.7	22.2	-	-
1983	87.0	-	29.7	19.4	26.2	20.8	-	-
1984	87.8	-	29.1	18.1	23.8	19.4	-	-
1985	88.4	-	28.9	16.8	24.1	20.6	-	-
1986	89.5	-	28.2	16.8	24.6	20.7	-	-
1987	89.7	-	27.6	18.5	23.2	20.5	-	-
1988	89.6	17.0	26.8	19.5	22.8	19.9	-	-
1989	90.1	17.8	25.9	19.8	29.4	19.5	38.6	3.8
1990	90.8	18.8	25.2	18.4	29.7	15.5	43.3	1.7
1991	91.5	20.0	24.5	17.2	29.7	16.4	48.0	1.9
1992	92.0	21.2	24.4	16.4	29.5	16.8	48.1	2.0
1993	91.6	20.9	24.2	15.6	29.6	17.1	49.5	2.0
1994	90.5	22.2	24.1	14.5	31.0	16.4	48.9	2.3
1995	91.9	21.1	23.8	13.8	30.2	15.7	46.6	2.3
1996	91.3	22.3	23.2	13.3	27.6	17.1	44.6	2.1
1997	90.3	21.9	22.6	12.2	26.8	16.4	42.2	2.0
1998	91.7	21.5	22.4	12.6	27.4	16.9	41.1	-
1999	89.7	21.5	22.2	11.9	-	18.0	40.0	-
2000	90.3	-	21.5	12.0	-	-	38.5	-
2001	-	-	-	12.0	-	-	39.4	-
2002	-	-	-	11.6	-	-		-

* Membership as percentage of total paid employees
Sources
a The International Labour Organization, Bureau of Statistics. 2003. *Statistics of Trade Union Membership.*
  (unpublished). *http://www.ilr.cornell.edu/library/downloads/FAQ/UNIONSTATS2002.pdf* . Accessed 5 Nov. 2004.
b The Japan Institute for Labour Policy and Training. 2003. *Main Labor Economic Indicators*, July
  http://www.jil.go.jp/estatis/eshuyo/200307/eshuyo.pdf. Accessed 5 Nov., 2004.

docile and co-opted labour movement, the state developed IR policies that were highly attractive to foreign investors.

Before 1959, IR in Singapore was plagued with industrial strife because of the political struggle between the communist-controlled unions and the colonial government. The People's Action Party was established in 1959 and initiated tight pre-emptive controls over organized labour through the government-dominated National Trade Union Congress. The current government, which operates under a one-party system, still maintains a state-corporatist IR structure. The state co-opts and includes unions in national policymaking, which compromises the independence of labour. The National Wages Council, a tripartite body, was set up in 1972 to establish general guidelines on wage policy and regulate wage increases. Although IR policies are formally an expression of this tripartite system, the unequal status of labour in this so-called partnership between trade unions, employers, and state makes the legitimacy of this tripartite system doubtful.

In 1979, the government began aggressively pursuing a second phase of industrialization aimed at achieving high value-added production and product technologies (Begin 1995). However, this upgrading of the economy faltered, and in 1985 Singapore experienced a negative GDP growth rate of 1.8 per cent, the first negative rate of growth since national independence. To counter the economic crisis, the government introduced new labour policies. First, the state accelerated the adoption of Japanese-style employee involvement systems, such as work excellence committees, work improvement teams, and quality control circles, all of which had begun to be introduced in the early 1980s. Despite the emphasis placed on experimentation with these models, they yielded mixed results, which seems partly attributable to cultural differences between Singaporeans and Japanese (Wilkinson 1994). A second reaction to the economic crisis was acceleration of the transformation of Singapore's unions. In 1980, the government had begun pressing the traditional general unions (called 'omnibus' in Singapore) and industry unions to become enterprise unions after the Japanese-style co-operative model. By the early 1990s, enterprise unions accounted for forty-five per cent of all unions (Frenkel 1993). Finally, in the mid-1980s, the National Wage Council abandoned its policy of recommending uniform wage increases, a decentralization that has given employers considerably more flexibility in the workplace.

The Labour movement in Singapore is unquestionably subordinate to the government. The upper echelons of the National Trade Union Congress are still dominated by People's Action Party members of Parliament, and the National Trade Union Congress is incapable of acting independently of the government or of challenging the regime's ideological parameters (Barr 2000). Union activities are limited by government regulations, too. The scope of collective bargaining is restricted. Bargaining over transfers, promotions, layoffs, and job assignment is not allowed. Strikes are prohibited in industries such as gas, electricity and water supply, deemed essential to economic development (Leggett 1993).

The Singaporean IR system has a strong paternalistic element. For example, during the 1997–98 financial crisis, layoffs were minimized as a result of a tripartite agreement in which employers received financial incentives if they avoided layoffs (Kuruvilla *et al.* 2002). As Deyo (1989) indicated, whether the degree of corporatist control in Singapore can be maintained depends on how long Singapore can keep up the economic growth required to sustain the materialistic needs of its population.

Stalinist labour policy under increasingly pluralistic economies: China and Vietnam

China and Vietnam have much in common. In each case, they have undergone a transition from a centrally planned economy to an emerging socialist market system by pursuing a so-called 'third way' (socialist market economy) between a command economy and the capitalist alternative. A socialist market economy is characterized by the operation of a market mechanism within the context of economic dominance by public ownership and the political dominance by the Communist Party (Zhu and Fahey 1999). Although society has undergone significant change in both countries, both are also still groping toward a socialist market economy that offers a satisfactory balance between ideology and a market mechanism. In both countries, major tasks of reform have been the rationalization of state-owned enterprises and the introduction and expansion of domestic and foreign private enterprises. Although the pre-reform system has been tentatively dismantled in China and in Vietnam, an IR system consonant with their newly emerging socialist market economies has not yet appeared.

China

Before the start of the transition from a centrally planned economy, the system of three 'old irons' existed: the iron rice bowl (guaranteed life-time employment), the iron chair (selection based on political orientation, absence of punishment for poor business performance), and iron wages (a state-administered, inflexible wage structure and low wage policy) (Ding and Warner 2001). Under this system, most employees were assigned to state-owned enterprises and received state-guaranteed lifetime employment; endemic to the system were such problems as overstaffing, lack of motivation, low morale, absenteeism, inefficient use of labour, reluctance to learn job skills, and high wastage of energy and raw materials.

The programme of post-Mao economic reforms (the open door policy) began in 1978. In the 1980s, a rapid shift began from a policy of import-substitution industrialization to one oriented towards exports. In the 1980s, the reform initiatives were defined as the breaking of the 'three irons' and the establishment of three new systems, including the establishment of a labour contract system, a floating wage system, and a manager engagement system (i.e. decentralizing economic decision-making powers so that managers had increased authority and responsibility). Since 1992, reform of the employment system has accelerated (Zhu and Warner 2000), resulting in the further weakening of guaranteed lifetime employment.

On paper and in terms of legal status, labour is tightly controlled in China, but in recent years cracks have begun to appear in what is designed as a monolithic structure. China is a one-party state and does not allow unions autonomy from the state. The government bans independent unions and any form of labour disputes.

State-controlled unions exist at the enterprise, industry and regional levels. The unified 1994 labour law mandates labour unions in every enterprise, and the Trade Union Law enacted in October 2001 stipulates that all establishments must deal with the All-China Federation of Trade Unions. Although some forms of collective bargaining exist at the enterprise level, no legal right to strike is acknowledged: The right to strike was removed in 1982 from the Chinese Constitution.

The All-China Federation of Trade Unions, which was established by the Communist Party, clings to a traditional Leninist notion of trade unions under party control (Leung 1997). The All-China Federation of Trade Unions plays the role of transmission belt: (1) to transmit the Party's current ideological line and policies to the urban working class and to secure workers' support and compliance, and (2) to protect the interests of workers and staff members. Double posting in which union officials hold simultaneous positions in local Party and government organs is popular. Thus, the All-China Federation of Trade Unions is considered a Stalinist union operating within an increasingly pluralistic market socialism (Leung 1997).

The operational dilemma faced by the All-China Federation of Trade Unions in the midst of China's rapid changes was further sharpened by the recent proliferation of alternative, independent organizations, such as the Workers' Autonomous Federation. Although thousands of leaders and members of the Workers' Autonomous Federation have been fired since 1989, the independent labour movement continued in 1992 in the form of the Free Trade Unions of China. More than 800 unofficial workers' organizations, operating like underground organizations and secret societies, were identified in 1994. These organizations argued that workers were losing out under the reforms that were occurring and identified the All-China Federation of Trade Unions as part of the problem, not the solution (White 1996).

An increasing level of labour disputes has been reported in recent years. Collective disputes (including strikes) have increased almost every year since 1994. The number of labour disputes rose from 1,482 in 1994 to 11,024 in 2002, a more than seven-fold increase in eight years (see Table 7.3). In particular, the escalation of widespread resistance by workers to both management and the government was reported during 2000–2003. Collective strikes, picketing, mass assemblies, parades, demonstrations, sit-down protests, outright challenges to management and local authorities were common (Cheng 2004; Siegel 2004).[5]

The real problem in the Chinese IR system seems to be the absence of a mechanism for representation of the various interests present in the increasingly pluralistic economic system. Despite this pluralism and market orientation, the party-state still rejects any development of pluralistic political and interest representation systems (Leung 1997). For example, the Chinese government did not legalize the growing independent labour organizations that represent the interests and concerns of many workers. The lack of any power balance between the traditionally dominant actor (i.e. the state) and the emerging actors (i.e. labour and employers) in labour relations seems to worsen the current problems. One of the urgent tasks for the Chinese government seems to be to developing a more pluralistic IR system that is a better match with the country's emergent market economy.

Vietnam

After the Vietnam War (1960–1975), Vietnam remained a centrally planned economy until the late 1980s. The movement towards a socialist market economy began during the early stage of the *Doi Moi* reform (1988–1991), and foreign investment has increased exponentially since the introduction of the Foreign Investment Law promulgated in January 1988. The end of the US trade embargo in 1994 accelerated foreign investment. Foreign investment declined temporarily as a result of the Asian financial crisis, but quickly resumed. Before the economic reforms, the reward system had only an indirect relationship to enterprise efficiency and individual labour effort. The state rewarded labour on the basis of seniority and of service to the Party and the war effort. Because it has a shorter history of Communism, state-owned enterprises in Vietnam have played a less significant role than in China in terms of employment and contribution to GDP. Since the *Doi Moi* reforms, the system of lifetime employment has weakened, and the movement of labour to major urban centres has escalated. However, the transition to a contract employment system has been relatively slow. Only new employees are on the contract system (Zhu and Fahey 1999).

The current Labour Code, which came into effect in 1995, provides guidance for workers and employers in establishing harmonious and stable labour relations and mutual co-operation at workplaces. The Labour Code signalled a loosening of the previously tight control exercised by government over wages and working conditions. Individuals are now able to enter private contacts, and wage flexibility is increasing. The operation of the Labour Code, however, is mainly confined to state enterprises, their joint ventures with foreign firms, and to a limited number of private sector firms (employing more than ten persons).

Under the Labour Code, workers for the first time have the right to strike. Vietnam is more progressive than China in this respect. Although the right to strike can be only exercised in limited circumstances (after two weeks' notice and only in non-essential businesses) (Zhu and Fahey 1999), the number of strikes is increasing, particularly within foreign-owned enterprises. Other labour problems and issues are emerging as the long-established Communist system of legal and economic controls is gradually dismantled. There are criticisms that the Labour Code tends to be ignored in workplaces and that there is limited enforcement of the code by the state (Lansbury 2004).

Although the role of unions is still limited and they are not completely independent from the state, the Vietnamese General Confederation of Labour, which traditionally performed only as a transmission belt, is trying to increase the degree of separation between the party and the union movement. Although the Confederation's effort to become more independent and self-reliant seems to be genuine, its level of independence is still questionable (Zhu and Fahey 1999). Like China, Vietnam does not seem to have a complete blueprint for an IR system consonant with an emergent socialist market economy.

Common trends in Asian IR

Although the eleven Asian countries discussed here show extremely diverse patterns of economic and political systems, one can still find some commonalities between them. At the risk of over-simplification, this section identifies some universal trends (with some significant exceptions, of course) that can be identified in Asian countries.

The determining role of state and suppressive labour policies

The state has been the most important factor in determining the nature of IR in Asia, and the state remains the dominant influence on IR in many countries. The state provided the impetus for economic development in most Asian countries because of the lack of accumulated industrial capital for investment in initial industrialization. Consequently, in each country, the state designed IR and economic policies suited to its economic development plan. The desire for political stability and the need for low labour costs encouraged governments to impose stringent constraints on labour (Deyo 2001). As a few authoritarian states such as Korea, Taiwan, Indonesia, the Philippines, and Thailand, move toward democracy, however, a suppressive labour policy can no longer be maintained, and more pluralistic IR systems are expected to emerge. Also, the political changes from planned economies to socialist market systems in China and Vietnam, for example, are expected to have a significant impact on IR in these countries.

In most Asian countries, the rights of individual workers (such as a minimum wage and workplace labour standards) are relatively well-protected by labour laws, although the degree of enforcement varies widely (Kuruvilla and Venkataratnam 1996). However, group-level labour legislation severely limits union activity. Suppressive labour policies remain the norm in most countries except in Japan. In most Asian countries – even those that are economically advanced – the ability of trade unions to organize, engage in genuine collective bargaining and pursue legal industrial action is generally restricted.

The right to organize has been severely limited in several countries. For example, the Korean government still prohibits government employees from organizing and bans the existence of multiple unions within a single firm. In Taiwan, government employees and teachers are not allowed to form unions. In Malaysia, trade union federations are registered as societies, not unions, and union mergers are effectively barred.

Restrictions are also common on the types of issues subject to bargaining. In Korea, Taiwan, Singapore, and Malaysia, collective bargaining is not allowed on such issues as transfers, promotions, work assignments, introduction of new technology, layoffs, and employment restructuring. The governments of Singapore and Malaysia even require collective bargaining agreements to be certified by an industrial court.

The most severe restrictions are on the right to strike. The governments of a few countries attempt to minimize the occurrence of strikes because they are believed to hamper economic development. In Singapore, Vietnam, and Korea, the right to strike is prohibited in essential private enterprises and in public industries such as oil refining, banking, transportation, railroad, and electricity utilities. Third party mediation, conciliation, or arbitration is required before a strike or lockout can begin in Korea, Singapore, Malaysia, Vietnam, and Taiwan. Also, labour laws require a strike vote by secret ballot in Korea, Taiwan, and the Philippines. In China, the word 'strike' does not even appear in any labour laws, and strikes are strictly prohibited.

In recent years, however, the trend of globalization seems to have weakened suppressive labour policies (Kim and Kim 2003). As the world economy is increasingly globalized, the roles of international organizations such as the ILO and the Organisation for Economic Co-operation and Development (OECD) tend to be more important in the enforcement of labour standards. The ILO and the OECD recommend to their member countries internationally accepted labour standards, monitor violations, and publish (sometimes embarrassing) reports to force member countries to improve labour standards. Furthermore, some industrialized countries (i.e. the United States and European Union nations) at the World Trade Organisation (WTO) Conferences make proposals, although unsuccessfully, to impose trade sanctions against countries that violate internationally accepted labour standards (WTO 2001). Indeed, international organizations such as the ILO and the OECD have continually raised the issue of the violation of union rights in Asian countries, and since the late 1990s there has been some progress in improving union rights in Korea (e.g. the legalization of teachers' unions in 1999) (Kim and Kim 2003) and Indonesia (e.g. the ratification of ILO Convention No. 87 in 1998) (Soeprobo 2004).

Because of democratization in several countries, resort to old-style labour subordination to obtain labour's consent in employment matters has not been plausible even in crisis situations. Thus, in Korea, the Philippines and Malaysia, the state initiated tripartite systems to help overcome the 1997–98 financial crisis. However, except in the case of Korea, these state-initiated experiments turned out to have little real impact and failed to produce lasting results.

Enterprise unions, under-institutionalised labour movement, and spontaneous labour disputes

Most countries in Asia – Japan, Korea, Taiwan, Thailand, Malaysia, Indonesia, and Singapore – have enterprise unions. In Japan, where enterprise unionism is well-known, its exact origin has been debated. However, in many Asian countries, enterprise unionism can be considered a consequence of government policy (Frenkel 1993). For example, in Korea, Singapore, Indonesia, and Malaysia, the government intentionally forced the reorganization of labour into enterprise unions in the 1980s to induce Japanese-style labour-management co-operation.

Many observers are of the impression that unions in Asia are weak and declining (Kuruvilla and Venkataratnam, 1996; Kuruvilla *et al.* 2000). However, careful observation of Asian unionism leads to a different conclusion. Among the eight Asian countries for which official statistics are available (see Table 7.4), union density has risen in one of them since the 1980s (China) and two since the 1990s (Hong Kong and Singapore). In two (the Philippines and Taiwan), union density has changed little. Thus, declining union density is obvious only in Japan and Korea, whereas in most other countries it is either increasing or stable.

In several countries such as Korea, Taiwan, Indonesia, China, and Malaysia, traditional, co-opted labour centres are clearly declining or stagnating, but newly emerging independent unions are expanding or gaining popularity. For example, in Korea the traditionally co-opted Federation of Korean Trade Unions has been in decline, but the more independent Korea Confederation of Trade Unions has gained momentum. In Taiwan, the influence of the old-style Chinese Federation of Labour tends to be weakening at the same time as the newly emerging Taiwan Confederation of Trade Unions is strengthening. The Chinese workers' indifference toward the All-China Federation of Trade Unions and the rise of independent unions echoes this situation. Some may think that the divided labour movement in these countries will weaken the influence of labour. I disagree. I believe that the rise and proliferation of new independent unions and the eclipse of old unions subordinate to the government destabilizes the suppressive industrial order fostered by authoritarian regimes and makes way for a democratic labour movement. This has the potential to elicit genuine commitment from workers and attract uncorrupted labour activists (as shown in Korea and Taiwan) and in the long run fosters a healthy labour movement.

Also, more strikes have occurred in several of the Asian countries (see Table 7.3). Among the ten Asian countries for which official strikes statistics are available, four – China, Taiwan, Korea, and Indonesia – have recorded increases. In a fifth, Vietnam, persistent reports reveal that strikes are increasing (although supporting statistics are absent from Table 7.3). In only three countries, Hong Kong, the Philippines, and Japan, the number of strikes decreased. In Singapore, Thailand, and Malaysia the trend is less clear. Thus, in a majority of Asian countries strike activities seem to be increasing (or at least not declining as in their Western counterparts).

One noteworthy observation is that strike activities in Asia seem inversely related to the degree of the suppressive, controlling power of the state over labour. Indeed, many strikes coincide with periods of democratization of authoritarian regimes and with political turbulence and crises. For example, it is well-known that in Korea the peaks of strike activities have coincided with the occurrence of every political crisis in Korean politics from 1910 to 1990 (Kim 1993). In Taiwan, the Philippines, Indonesia, and Thailand, series of strikes have occurred in periods of democratization, and in China and Vietnam waves of strikes accompanied turbulence in the wake of changes from a planned economy to a market economy. In periods of political crises, democratization, and economic change, the state may not completely control the activities of independent labour organizations because of the weakening of its legitimacy. Future studies should investigate this proposition more thoroughly.

A noteworthy feature of these strikes is their under-institutionalized nature. In China, all strikes are illegal, whereas in Korea, Taiwan, Indonesia, Thailand, and Vietnam, a significant number of the strikes were technically illegal and resulted in the arrest and imprisonment of strikers. Also, these strikes are witness to increasing levels of spontaneous worker protests and to the politicization of labour movements. For example, in the Philippines the economic crisis of the 1980s precipitated a rise in militant unionism whose depth and breadth was without parallel in the country's history and culminated in the democratic coup of 1986 (Deyo 2001; Ofreneo 1995). Moreover, in Indonesia and Korea during the financial crisis of the late 1990s co-operation between various popular non-governmental organizations and student activists were new patterns of labour protest.

As observed above, the Asian financial crisis of the late 1990s led to the politicization of the labour movement. The spontaneous protests of one form or another that accompanied this politicization lacked an institutional underpinning to ensure longevity. Whether these spontaneous outbreaks can transform themselves into institutionalized labour movements (as happened in Korea and Taiwan) remains to be seen. Overall, it is fair to say that the Asian labour movement continues to be under-institutionalized (rather than weak), which suggests great potential for future changes.

In Asia, labour organizations have been generally decentralized as indicated by the almost universal existence of enterprise unions. Currently, a trend to centralization is under way in Korea and to a lesser degree in Japan and the Philippines. The centralization trend is most significant in Korea where enterprise unionism and enterprise-level bargaining were traditionally the norm. Since the financial crisis, the shift to industrial unionism and industry-level bargaining has accelerated. Most of these industrial unions were formed by merging individual enterprise unions, and the combined membership of these industrial unions has become approximately 30 per cent of the total union membership in Korea (Kim and Kim 2003). Industry-level bargaining is currently conducted in some industries such as metal, hospital, and banking.

In Japan, the movement towards strengthening peak-level federations through mergers, co-ordination arrangements and union mergers such as Ui Zensen Domei[6] has already begun. Union consolidation and co-ordination occurred in the Philippines where a highly fragmented union structure has been one of labour's hallmarks. These centralization trends in Asia contrast with the decentralization argument by Katz (1993), which was based upon evidence from Western countries.

Limited role of employers and pursuit of flexibility

The role of employers in IR has been relatively limited in Asia, but has become more significant in recent years, especially as employers have pursued flexibility in the face of the trend towards globalization. As globalization proceeds, governments increasingly rely on the interests of employers to keep firms competitive and efficient in an era of unlimited global competition (Frenkel and Peetz 1998). Thus, globalization has led states to adopt labour policies designed to increase flexibility to the benefit of employers.

The polarization of employment policies is evident in some countries. On the one hand, there has been increasing attention to training, skill-building, and performance-based human resource systems (especially for core workers in high value-added sectors). Training and human resource investment, however, have not been accompanied by increased worker participation (as will be discussed later). On the other hand, the size of contingent employment seems to be rising in all Asian countries. In particular, in labour-intensive, export-oriented industrial structures, managers have sought to meet these new competitive pressures through cost-cutting tactics like increased use of temporary and contract labour and greater production outsourcing (Deyo 2001).

Another characteristic of Asian management is limited worker participation. Although joint consultation and quality circles figure in several countries, self-managing teams and strategic participation by unions, both of which provide greater empowerment of labour, are seldom introduced. Also, except in Japan, success stories on joint consultation and quality circles seem rare in Asian countries.

The reasons for limited employee participation may be two-fold. First, in most developing Asian countries, employee input or creativity is not needed under highly structured and low value-added industrial conditions. Second, innovation-based industrialization, which is observed in advanced economies, relies on development of a stream of new products and technologies for changing markets that require employee creativity, knowledge, and commitment to debug the errors in the development processes. By contrast, existing technology-based industrialization, common to most Asian countries, except Japan, depends on local adoption of technologies and products developed elsewhere (Amsden 1989). In this type of imported technology-based industrialization, already debugged production processes and products minimize the need for an extensive involvement of workers in dealing with shop-floor production problems (Deyo 2001), which explains the limited usage of empowered employee participation in Asia.

Conclusion

The 1997–98 financial crisis had a huge economic impact, and the Asian economy is still recovering from the shock as shown by the V-shape on a graph of economic activity over time (see Table 7.2). The eleven-country average GDP growth rate for the 1992–97 period (the six years before the financial crisis) was 6.94 per cent, whereas the eleven-country average GDP growth rate for the 1998–2003 period (the six years after the financial crisis) was 3.32 per cent. Unemployment rates show an opposite trend, illustrated by an inversed V-shaped recovery pattern. The eleven-country average unemployment rate for 1992–97 was 3.09 per cent and 4.73 per cent for 1998–2003. Thus, both GDP growth rate and the unemployment rate show the Asian economy is recovering from the 1997–98 financial crisis, but remains below the level of the pre-crisis period.[7]

The official statistics and anecdotal reports discussed in the previous section show that Asia is one of the few continents where union density and strike activities are not universally decreasing, but are, in fact, actually increasing in several countries. Among the Asian countries where official statistics are reported, declining union density is clearly occurring only in Japan and Korea; in the other countries discussed here, union density is either increasing or stable (see Table 7.4). Furthermore, in several countries such as Korea, Taiwan, Indonesia, China, and Malaysia, traditionally co-opted labour centres seem to be stagnating or losing popularity, while newly emerging independent labour centres have become more active. Also, strike activities keep increasing in several Asian countries (see Table 7.3) such as China, Taiwan, Korea, Indonesia, and Vietnam. Thus, Asian countries have in recent years shown unusually dynamic labour movements and union activities that contrast with patterns of labour activity in Western countries.

In the next section, I will suggest some possible future scenarios for the three actors in Asian IR. Concerning the state, although authoritarian governments exist in some Asian countries, a gradual improvement in labour rights seems inevitable because advances in information technology such as the Internet have resulted in greater exchanges of information about labour conditions across international boundaries. Information about the violation of basic labour rights, such as the exploitation of child labour and harsh working conditions for women and minority workers, can be easily disseminated across national borders and attract international attention. Also, the continuing process of democratization in developing countries and the advent of non-government organizations have led to more active monitoring of morally unacceptable labour practices and an increased risk of consumer boycotts and other means of retaliation (Kim and Kim 2003; Lee 1997). Thus, suppressive labour policies in some countries may not last long, and the changes that follow them may lead to more pluralistic IR systems.

As for employers, if unlimited global competition continues, their role in IR areas may be expanded. The need for greater flexibility inevitably leads employers to modify rigid employment systems in both the union and non-union sectors, which implies that employers can be the initiators of strategic changes in IR. As an economy grows and the economic activities within it become more complicated, it becomes too big and too complex for a government to monitor all of its various industrial sectors. Consequently, to some extent, the role of employers may replace the role of the state as a rule setter for IR.

Finally, the future of Asian unionism is a focus of attention against a background of its decline elsewhere in the world. Both negative and positive forces are shaping its future. According to the negative perspective of the labour's future, structural changes, including employers' drive toward employee head count flexibility, a shift from manufacturing to services, and a universal increase in contingent labour will all have detrimental effects on Asian labour. For example, the furthering of labour flexibility in the Philippines has had negative effects on an already fragmented labour movement. A continuing increase in contingent labour poses a particularly serious problem for enterprise unions in Asia. It is particularly hard for enterprise unions to organize contingent employees because of their short tenure and weak attachment to the enterprise. Furthermore, many enterprise unions do not consider contingent workers as their jurisdiction and do not even attempt to organize them, as witnessed in Japan and Korea. Consequently, in Korea, only 2 per cent of contingent workers are union members.

There are also positive forces influencing future unionism in Asia. First, the universal trend of democratization, which is associated with the expansion of basic labour rights, is very likely to boost unionism. Political democratization tends to promote industrial democracy, and in the long run, the expansion of independent trade unions will continue in Asia. For example, as Taiwan and Korea become democratized, there are strong possibilities that teachers' unions and government employees' unions in Taiwan and government employees' unions in Korea, currently banned, will be soon permitted. As a result, sizeable surges in union density are expected in both countries. The legalization of independent unions in China might surely change the landscape of IR in China, although it is unlikely to happen soon.

Second, international pressures from the ILO and the OECD will strengthen labour rights, which in turn helps trade unions. For example, the ratification in Indonesia of the ILO conventions on freedom of association and protection of the right to organize resulted in a significant increase in union activity. The legalization of teachers' unions in Korea was also heavily influenced by the ILO and the OECD (Kim and Kim 2003).

Finally, job insecurity during and after the financial crisis increased popular support for unions and politicized the labour movement in several Asian countries. As the financial crisis increased job insecurity, workers in Korea and Taiwan have become more committed to their unions (Kim and Kim 2003; Chen *et al.* 2003). A major challenge for labour is to take advantage of this popular support to form solid, enduring formal organizations.

Overall, IR systems in Asia are relatively unstable. That is, in most countries, the IR systems and the political and industrial structures are out of balance. In Japan, the traditional three pillars seem to lag increasingly flexible employment practices; and Taiwan and Korea retain under democratically elected governments such vestiges of authoritarian labour policy as the arrest and imprisonment of labour activists. In Malaysia and Singapore, the pursuit of knowledge-based industry clashes with current authoritarian labour policies. In China and Vietnam, the old Stalinist unions are misfits with their emerging market economies. In sum, none of these countries has built IR systems consonant with their rapidly changing economic and political environments. These facts imply that abrupt changes in Asian IR systems are possible in the future, if enough tensions between these conflicting forces are allowed to build up. Since unstable periods provide more room for strategic choices by IR actors than are possible during stable periods in which institutions are more resistant to changes, Asian countries can be expected to show very dynamic IR over the next decades.

Notes

1 The author thanks Yoon Ho Kim, Sung Hyun Lim, and Chae Ho Lee for their excellent research assistance.
2 Rengo (Japanese Trade Union Confederation, JTUC) is the predominant top-level union federation in Japan. When Rengo was established in 1989 by combining both private and public sector unions, it had seventy-eight industrial federations with nearly 8 million members (Kuwahara 1998).
3 The Korean *chaebol* indicates a conglomerate of many companies clustered around one parent company. The companies usually hold shares in each other and are often run by one family.
4 The trade union laws gave employees the right to individual representation by a union.
5 The precise number of strikes cannot be found in official statistics. The only data reported are the numbers of labour disputes (including bargaining impasses, strikes, and plant lock-outs) without specific identification.
6 In September 2002, Zensen (Japanese Federation of Textile, Garment, Chemical, Mercantile, Food and Allied Industries Workers' Unions), CSG Rengo (Japanese Federation of Chemical, Service and General Trade Unions) and Sen-I Seikatsu Roren (Japan Federation of Textile Clothing Workers' Unions of Japan) were merged into the Ui Zensen Doemi.
7 There are two views on the causes of the crisis (Lee 1998). Some attribute blame to the globalization of international financial markets, whereas others see domestic factors as the primary cause. For the former, the crisis is understood as a consequence of the liberalization of international financial markets. In a globalized market, there are virtually no effective instruments for dealing with a large increase in capital inflows and outflows, which occurred before and

during the crisis. The susceptibility of international financial markets to self-fulfilling panic can be the catalyst for a sudden shift from boom to bust. The latter perspective holds that a defective Asian model of development, which can be characterized by a deviation from the principles of free market economics such as widespread political interference with market processes, moral hazard and corruption, caused the financial crisis. The general conclusion is that the crisis was caused by many factors, including the two cited above and the inter-reaction between them.

References

Amsden, A. (1989) *Asia's New Giant: South Korea and Late Industrialization*. Oxford: Oxford University Press.

Barr, M. D. (2000) 'Trade unions in an elitist society: the Singapore story'. *Australian Journal of Politics and History*, 46(4): 480–496.

Begin, J. P. (1995) 'Singapore's industrial relations system: is it congruent with its second phase of industrialization'. In S. H. Frenkel and J. Harrod (eds), *Industrialization and Labor Relations: Contemporary Research in Seven Countries*: 64–87. Ithaca, NY: ILR Press.

Berggren, C. and Nomura, M. (1997). 'Employment practices: a critical analysis of the 'three pillars''. In C. Berggren and M. Nomura (eds), *The Resilience of Corporate Japan: New Competitive Strategies and Personnel Practices*: 66–94. London: Paul Chapman Educational Publishing.

Brown, A. and Frenkel, S. (1993) 'Union unevenness and insecurity in Thailand'. In S. Frenkel (ed.), *Organized Labor in the Asia-Pacific Region*: 82–106. Ithaca, NY: ILR Press.

Cheng, Y. (2004) 'The development of labour disputes and the regulation of industrial relations in China'. *International Journal of Comparative Labour Law and Industrial Relations*, 20(2): 277–295.

Chen, S.-J., Roger Ko, J.-J., and Lawler, J. (2003) 'Changing patterns of industrial relations in Taiwan'. *Industrial Relations*, 42(3): 315–340.

Chiu, S. and Levin, D. A. (1996) 'Prosperity without industrial democracy? Developments in industrial relations in Hong Kong Since 1968'. *Industrial Relations Journal*, 27(1): 24–37.

Chu, Y.-W. (1998) 'Labor and democratization in South Korea and Taiwan'. *Journal of Contemporary Asia*, 28(2): 185–202.

Deyo, F. C. (1989) *Beneath the Miracle: Labour Subordination in the New Asian Industrialism*. Berkeley: University of California Press.

Deyo, F. C. (1995) 'Human resource strategies and industrial restructuring in Thailand'. In S. H. Frenkel and J. Harrod (eds), *Industrialization and Labor Relations: Contemporary Research in Seven Countries*: 23–36. Ithaca, NY: ILR Press.

Deyo, F. C. (2001) 'The social construction of developmental labour systems: South-East Asian industrial restructuring'. In G. Rodan, K. Hewison, and R. Robison (eds), *The Political Economy of South-East Asia – Conflict, Crises and Change*, 2nd ed.: 259–282. Oxford: Oxford University Press.

Ding, D. Z. and Warner, M. (2001) 'China's labour-management system reforms: breaking the "three old irons" (1978–1999)'. *Asia Pacific Journal of Management*, 18(3): 315–334.

Erickson, C. L., Kuruvilla, S., Ofreneo, R. E. and Ortiz, M. A. (2003) 'From core to periphery? Recent developments in employment relations in the Philippines'. *Industrial Relations*, 42(3): 368–395.

Frenkel, S. (1993) 'Variations in patterns of trade unionism: a synthesis'. In S. Frenkel (ed.), *Organized Labor in the Asia-Pacific Region*: 309–346. Ithaca New York: ILR Press.

Frankel, S. and Kuruvilla, S. (2002) 'Logics of action, globalization, and changing employment relations in China, India, Malaysia, and the Philippines'. *Industrial and Labor Relations Review*, 55(3): 387–412.

Frenkel, S. J. and Peetz, D. (1998) 'Globalization and industrial relations in East Asia: a three-country comparison'. *Industrial Relations*, 37(3): 282–310.

Hadiz, V. R. (2001) 'New organising vehicles in Indonesia'. In J. Hutchison and A. Brown (eds), *Organizing Labour in Globalising Asia*: 108–126. London: Routledge.

The ILO. (2003) *The Yearbook of Labour Statistics*. Geneva, Switzerland: the ILO.

Katz, H. (1993) 'The decentralization of collective bargaining: a literature review and comparative analysis'. *Industrial and Labor Relations Review*, 47(1): 3–22.

Kim, D.-O. (1993) 'Analysis of labour disputes in Korea and Japan: the search for an alternative model'. *European Sociological Review*, 9(2): 139–154.

Kim, D.-O. and Bae, J. (2004) *Employment Relations and HRM in Korea*. London: Ashgate Publishing Co.

Kim, D.-O. and Kim, S. (2003) 'Globalization, financial crisis, and industrial relations: the case of South Korea'. *Industrial Relations*, 42(3): 431–367.

Kuruvilla, S. and Arudsothy, P. (1995) 'Economic development strategy, government labor policy and firm-level industrial relations practices in Malaysia'. In A. Verma, T. A. Kochan, and R. D. Lansbury (eds), *Employment Relations in the Growing Asian Economies*: 158–193. London: Routledge.

Kuruvilla, S., Das, S., Kwon, H., and Kwon, S. (2002) 'Trade union growth and decline in Asia'. *British Journal of Industrial Relations*, 40(3): 431–461.

Kuruvilla, S. and Erickson, C. L. (2002) 'Change and transformation in Asian industrial relations'. *Industrial Relations*, 41(2): 171–227.

Kuruvilla, S. and Venkataratnam, C. S. (1996) 'Economic development and industrial relations: the case of South and Southeast Asia'. *Industrial Relations Journal*, 27(1): 9–23.

Kuwahara, Y. (1998) 'Employment relations in Japan'. In G. J. Bamber and R. D. Lansbury and N. Wailes (eds), *International and Comparative Employment Relations*. London, Thousand Oaks, New Delhi: Sage Publications.

Lansbury, R. D. (2004) 'Rapporteur's report: emerging patterns of employment relations in the Asia-Pacific region'. Paper presented at the IIRA 5th Asian Regional Congress, Seoul.

Lee, E. (1997) 'Globalization and labour standards: a review of issues'. *International Labour Review*, 136(2):173–189.

Lee, E. (1998) *The Asian Financial Crisis: The Challenge for Social Policy*. Geneva: International Labor Organization.

Lee, J. S. (2000) 'Changing approaches to employment relations in Taiwan'. In G. Bamber, F. Park, C. Lee, P. Ross, and K. Broadbent (eds), *Employment Relations in the Asia-Pacific*: 100–116. Sydney: Thomson Learning.

Leggett, C. (1993) 'Singapore'. In S. Deery and R. Mitchell (eds), *Labour Law and Industrial Relations in Asia*: 96–136. Melbourne: Longman Cheshire.

Leung, T. W.-Y. (1997) 'Trade unions and labor relations under market socialism in China'. In G. Schienstock, P. Thompson, and F. Traxler (eds), *Industrial Relations Between Command and Market: A Comparative Analysis of Eastern Europe and China*. New York: Nova Science Publishers, Inc.

Ofreneo, R. E. (1995) 'Philippine industrialization and industrial relations'. In A. Verma and T. A. Kochan and R. D. Lansbury (eds), *Employment Relations in the Growing Asian Economics*: 194–247. London: Routledge.

Siegel, J. S. (2004) 'Labor relations in the emerging chinese economy'. Paper presented at the IIRA 5th Asian Regional Congress, Seoul.

Skene, C. (2002) 'The impact of external constraints on labour rights: the case of the philippines'. *International Journal of Human Resource Management*, 13(3): 484–500.

Snape, E. and Chan, A. W. (1997) 'Whither Hong Kong's unions: autonomous trade unionism or classic dualism?' *British Journal of Industrial Relations*, 35(1): 39–63.

Soeprobo, T. B. (2004) 'Indonesian industrial relations: a continuing learning process'. Paper presented at the IIRA 5th Asian Regional Congress, Seoul.

Suwarno, S. and Elliott, J. (2000) 'Changing approaches to employment relations in Indonesia'. In G. Bamber, F. Park, C. Lee, P. Ross, and K. Broadbent (eds), *Employment Relations in the Asia-Pacific*: 129–141. Sydney: Thomson Learning.

Todd, P., Lansbury, R., and Davis, E. (2004) 'Industrial relations in Malaysia'. Paper presented at the IIRA 5th Asian Regional Congress, Seoul.

Wilkinson, B. (1994) *Labour and Industry in the Asia-Pacific: Lessons from the Newly-Industrialized Countries*. New York: Walter de Gruyter.

White, G. (1996) 'Chinese trade unions in the transition from socialism: towards corporatism or civil society?' *British Journal of Industrial Relations*, 34(3): 433–457.

Whittaker, D. H. (1998) 'Labour unions and industrial relations in Japan: crumbling pillar or forging a 'third way'?' *Industrial Relations Journal*, 29(4): 280–294.

Zhu, Y. and Fahey, S. (1999) 'The impact of economic reform on industrial labour relations in China and Vietnam'. *Post-Communist Economies*, 11(2): 173–192.

Zhu, Y. and Warner, M. (2000) 'Changing approaches to employment relations in the People's Republic of China (PRC)'. In G. Bamber, F. Park, C. Lee, P. Ross, and K. Broadbent (eds), *Employment Relations in the Asia-Pacific*: 117–128. Sydney: Thomson Learning.

The WTO. (2001) *Press Brief: Trade Labour Standards*. *http://www.wto.org/english/thewto_e/minist_e/min96_e/labstand.htm*. Accessed 30 Nov., 2004.

Suggested key readings

Chen, S.-J., Roger Ko, J.-J., and Lawler, J. (2003) 'Changing patterns of industrial relations in Taiwan'. *Industrial Relations*, 42(3): 315–340.

Deyo, F. C. (1989) '*Beneath the Miracle: Labour Subordination in the New Asian Industrialism*'. Berkeley: University of California Press.

Deyo, F. C. (2001) 'The social construction of developmental labour systems: South-East Asian industrial restructuring.' In G. Rodan, K. Hewison, and R. Robison (eds), *The Political Economy of South-East Asia - Conflict, Crises and Change*, 2nd ed.: 259–282. Oxford: Oxford University Press.

Erickson, C. L., Kuruvilla, S., Ofreneo, R. E., and Ortiz, M. A. (2003) 'From core to periphery? recent developments in employment relations in the Philippines.' *Industrial Relations*, 42(3): 368–395.

Frenkel, S. (1993) 'Variations in patterns of trade unionism: a synthesis'. In S. Frenkel (ed.), *Organized Labor in the Asia-Pacific Region*: 309–346. Ithaca, NY: ILR Press.

Kim, D.-O. and Kim, S. (2003) 'Globalization, financial crisis, and industrial relations: the case of South Korea'. *Industrial Relations*, 42(3): 431–367.

Kuruvilla, S. and Erickson, C. L. (2002) 'Change and transformation in Asian industrial relations'. *Industrial Relations*, 41(2): 171–227.

Kuwahara, Y. (1998) 'Employment relations in Japan'. In G. J. Bamber and R. D. Lansbury and N. Wailes (eds), *International and Comparative Employment Relations*. London, Thousand Oaks, New Delhi: Sage Publications.

White, G. (1996) 'Chinese trade unions in the transition from socialism: towards corporatism or civil society?' *British Journal of Industrial Relations*, 34(3): 433–457.

Zhu, Y. and Fahey, S. (1999) 'The impact of economic reform on industrial labour relations in China and Vietnam'. *Post-Communist Economies*, 11(2): 173–192.

8 Industrial relations in Africa

FRANK M. HORWITZ

Introduction

Sandwiched uneasily between the two larger domains of the East and West, the industrial relations (IR) problems and challenges of Africa have not been adequately addressed in the mainstream literature (Kamoche *et al.* 2004). In many cases the state still plays a dominant role in driving industrial and economic development through institutional, state-directed industrial relations systems, investing in state-owned enterprises (SOEs), soliciting foreign aid, and public works programmes seeking to improve employment creation. When most African countries were gaining independence, particularly in the 1960s and 1970s, these measures proved critical as colonial administrations of the time had failed to establish a broad-based and thriving private sector. This chapter provides a comparative analysis of historical roots, contemporary developments and trends in industrial relations, focusing on the main actors in selected countries and includes a section on the public sector. The latter is considered particularly significant given the strong role it has played in industrial relations in Africa. Africa has over fifty nations. It is therefore impossible to include them all. Those included are the subject of varying degrees of analysis; some cited as examples and others treated in more detail. Countries included range from those in sub-Saharan Africa like Botswana, South Africa and Zimbabwe; North Africa, such as Tunisia; East Africa, such as Kenya and Tanzania – as well as West African countries like Nigeria and Ghana. The available literature on IR in Africa tends to focus on certain countries considerably more than others, for example Kenya and South Africa.

Analysts make broad generalisations about industrial relations in Africa ignoring the unique features of each country. The diversity of Africa cuts across many dimensions: ethnically, with some 2000 different ethno-cultural communities; historically, depending on whether their colonial background is British, French or

Portuguese, for example; politically, with dictatorships and democracies; and economically, with several high-income countries amid a poverty-stricken majority. It is erroneous to assume homogeneity within specific countries, too, as many African countries have diverse ethno-cultural communities struggling to establish an identity as a nation-state (Kamoche *et al.* 2004: xvi). In countries like Zambia and Ghana with extensive privatisation of state-owned enterprises (SOEs), the IR landscape has been reshaped in significant and enduring ways. Many Zambian SOEs, for instance, have been bought by South African companies, whose managers apply employment practices based on those of their parent company. The Southern African region (particularly Botswana and South Africa) has emerged as a catchment area for talent from other parts of Africa, in particular East and Central Africa.

There are many challenges facing workers as well as managers in Africa today. Forced to open their markets as part of World Bank and IMF structural adjustment programmes (SAPs), and finding many foreign markets closed to their products, organisations have borne the brunt of globalisation, resulting in plant closures and high unemployment. In the worst cases, countries like the Democratic Republic of Congo and Somalia have been so ravaged by war that they have no real economy, and do not function as modern nation states. However, there are more democratically elected governments in Africa today than fifteen years ago. Matanmi (2000) summarises the major elements of industrial relations in emergent or transitional economies as having elements of colonial impact, nationalism, post-colonial states and crises of development; enduring the impact of structural adjustment programmes, the democratic challenge, and the emergent demands of social partnership (Matanmi 2000: 95–96).

Industrial relations regimes are relatively new and evolving. The International Labour Organisation (ILO), for example, has a number of advisors working with African national governments to establish industrial relations systems, legislative frameworks, collective bargaining and dispute resolution systems based on International Labour Organisation (ILO) conventions. Since its launch in 2000, the ILO Project based in Pretoria has made considerable progress in initiatives to strengthen social dialogue in six SADC countries – South Africa, Namibia, Lesotho, Botswana, Swaziland and Zimbabwe – by seeking to create tripartite forums and designing industrial relations and dispute resolution systems (Anstey 2004: 59). As emergent economies, many African countries show uneven patterns of development and under-development, with low average per capita national income, low living standards and poorly developed social welfare. In IR terms, African countries are not monolithic. The contiguous sub-Saharan African countries differ in levels of infrastructural development or acquisition of expanding wage employment and industrial sectors. Unevenness in this regard widens when comparing regionally faster-growing and more rapidly industrialising South Africa with other African countries like Ethiopia (Matanmi 2000: 96). Industrial relations in Africa are often rooted in colonial or apartheid

(South African) regimes which created wage work in the exploitation of primary natural resources, such as gold, diamonds, and emergent manufacturing sectors such as clothing and textiles, in countries like Kenya and South Africa. Political independence expanded the wage employment sectors (largely public, but also private sectors), creating legislative frameworks legitimising to varying degrees trade union rights.

The role of main actors – government

The role of government in African IR varies from state control in formally socialist states such as Ethiopia and Mozambique, and state direction in countries like Zambia, to a strong legislative framework permitting more voluntary systems such as in South Africa and Namibia. Under colonialism or apartheid, trade union movements could be characterised in part, as social movements often mobilising workers against an existing political regime. South Africa was a good example of this. Leadership development emerged from trade union movements to assume subsequently prominent political and business leadership roles following democratisation. But when government becomes hegemonic, for reasons of ineptitude or malfeasance, labour policies are sometimes inconsistent and unenforced (Fashoyin *et al.* 1994).

In Nigeria, the degree of robustness of labour rights has been a function of the dispositions of successive national governments from colonialism to the present era of protracted military dictatorship. In some African countries public policy on industrial relations has reflected the state's tendency for taking complex industrial and labour relations decisions by fiat (for example, wage determination in the public sector, with often serious inflationary consequences), rather than allowing industrial relations institutions that do exist to operate independently. This has accounted for the poor record of collective bargaining in the public sector, which represents the largest proportion of the wage-earning population, and from which the first three trade unions – of civil servants, railway workers and teachers – emerged during the colonial period. Yet a culture of collective relations has endured in the private sector.

In most cases, newly independent sovereign states though pluralistic lacked a democratic culture and tolerant political leadership to carry along the wider populace. The pursuit of often parochial interests in the face of widespread poverty and scarcity soon fanned the embers of inter-ethnic confrontation. However, there are pressures for significant change through democratisation and good governance. The New Partnership for African Development (NEPAD) is a political initiative taken by African governments to foster democracy, economic development and poverty alleviation on the continent. It has a peer review mechanism to exert pressure on governments whose actions fail to meet its normative requirements. It is a potentially important development in Pan-African democratisation if the collective political will of its members is applied. It is premised on the notion of a self-directed social, economic and political Renaissance for Africa.

The state and structural adjustment programmes

Many emerging economies in Africa were under one or another form of structural adjustment programme (SAP) by the mid-1980s, comprising several policy measures aimed at finding effective solutions to macroeconomic problems. The problems generally include a lack of self-reliant growth and development, low productivity and stagflation, serious imbalance of payments, huge external debts, and government budget deficit. Moreover, the SAPs have often been prescribed by the Bretton Woods institutions (the International Monetary Fund and the World Bank), on whom the crisis-laden economies of these nations are dependent for development credit and finance (Matanmi 2000: 100). The prescriptions usually comprise: devaluation, removal of subsidies on basic commodities, reduction of government expenditure, labour market reforms, reduction of trade protection, and increased incentives for the traditional sector (agriculture and mining). These measures have not so far produced obvious signs of recovery. Matanmi concludes that the effects of SAPs on industrial relations have been unfavourable. These include union membership decline with contracting formal employment, growing informalisation and casualisation, a hardening of employer positions in collective bargaining with increasingly precarious, unprotected and insecure employment models being adopted. Privatisation and deregulation have also been opposed by unions in countries such as South Africa. Fluid, and at times, volatile political economies have militated against trade union growth and stability. There is a vital need for institution building in African countries to strengthen industrial relations systems. This underlines a need to extend the IR agenda to the arguably most important challenges facing Africa, that of human resource development, building managerial capacity, investing in training and development and, sound human resource management practices.

Employers

The emergence of seemingly powerful industrial unions in critical sectors of many of these countries – for example, Ghana, Nigeria and Zimbabwe – has also influenced the proliferation of employers' associations and federations. Many African economies are experiencing a transition from large and often over-staffed public corporations to enterprises that are more publicly accountable and private firms that have to compete globally and be profitable (Jackson 2002: 999). Modern organisations in Africa fall into three categories (Fashoyin 2000). The first is public enterprises, in which the state controls 50 per cent or more of the share capital. Organisations in this category are set up to discharge specific functions and attain objectives which are more readily achievable outside the civil service system. In African economies like Tanzania, Nigeria and Zambia this has been a dominant type of organisation in the modern sector. Extensive privatisation programmes have substantially reduced the role of the state in business enterprises in this category. The second category includes private indigenous enterprises, an area in which African entrepreneurs are dominant. These often occur in the informal sector of most economies, for example the large pavement hawker sector in Nigeria and SMMEs (small, medium and micro-enterprises) in South Africa's townships. Enterprises in this category are comparatively small in size and are prominent in commerce, manufacturing and services. In this same category are a large number of informal micro-enterprises. This informality has been particularly prominent since the introduction of economic reforms and industrial restructuring which have led to substantial contraction of formal enterprises since the 1980s. In this category of African businesses, management principles are marginally or informally practised. The third category includes multi-national companies such as Johnson & Johnson, most oil MNCs, such as Shell and BP, foreign subsidiaries and joint-venture organisations. Organisations in this latter category occur in all sectors, particularly in manufacturing, textiles and automobile assembly. Several African nations subscribe to ILO conventions on freedom of association and the right to collective bargaining. However, implementation is often not strongly supported. Trade unions are sometimes restricted in the scope of their activities due both to the limited spread of wage or paid employment and to unfavourable state policies which impede their ability to use bargaining machinery effectively. In an authoritarian–paternalistic management environment, collective bargaining does not always receive management approval (Fashoyin 2000: 172–173). The Ghana Employers Association (GEA) with some 330 members is a major player in IR. Established in 1959, the GEA represents employers' interests to the government, promotes good relations and better understanding between employers and employees, and assists affiliated employers in negotiations with organised labour. The GEA co-ordinates and represents the views and reactions of its members on industrial relations problems and reactions to proposed legislation. Through the ILO's 'improve your business project', the GEA has helped members to address the business and management problems of small enterprises (Aryee 2004: 130). Down-sizing in the public sector, the traditional bastion of unionism, has led to a decline in unions.

The effects of ethnicity are not well documented regarding its impact on IR in Africa (Nyambegera 2002). Managerial styles, human resource management (HRM) practices and preferences for particular types of conflict resolution, may be mediated by ethnic factors, including the degree of cultural ethnocentrism, and tolerance or intolerance of diversity. Company-level employment practices in some countries like Kenya and South Africa have in some sectors reflected preferences for particular ethnic groups or family members of an ethnic group. Historical–political factors such as apartheid and colonialism have seen post-independence governments promoting policies variously referred to as Africanisation, localisation and employment equity, for which employer compliance is required. In South Africa for example, trade unions have to be consulted by employers on the latter's employment equity plans, under the terms of the Employment Equity Act (1998). Since the 1980s an increasing number of enterprises in Africa have taken a more accommodating stance towards workers' unions. Increasingly, managers are realising both the positive role of the union and also the inevitability of a workers' organisation to provide a workers' voice. Thus, what the future portends for labour relations is how to balance the organisational interests of the workers with the commitment to corporate effectiveness and competitiveness (Fashoyin 2000: 173).

Trade unions

Trade union density decline has occurred in most Western countries (Verma *et al.* 2002). Developing countries have seen similar patterns, this despite the notion that increasing political democratisation would be accompanied by stronger independent labour movements. Other than in South Africa, this has generally not been the case (Table 8.1). In Kenya trade union density dropped by no less than 60 per cent to 17 per cent, while in Mauritius the decline was more moderate with union density in 1997 still at approximately a quarter of the labour force. South Africa is one of the few countries which has contradicted this trend. Union density rose by no less than 40 per cent, between 1950 and 1997 but was still relatively low at 22 per cent in 1997, and subsequently has declined in key sectors such as building, construction, clothing, textiles and mining.

Regarding unions, other forms of employee participation, and state direction of IR, the trade union movement in Zimbabwe, for example, grew to some 1.5 million members under the Labour Relations Act (1985). Minimum wages were legislated and labour representation enhanced labour practices. Recently, the Zimbabwe Congress of Trade Unions has strongly opposed aspects of government policy having an adverse impact on union rights and has been viewed by the state as a social movement increasingly under pressure to conform rather than to oppose state interests (Tamangani and Muranda 2000). In contemporary Zimbabwe the union movement occurs alongside works councils and against a backdrop of decentralisation and local government reforms (Muhandu 2000). Similarly, under former President Dr Kenneth Kaunda, a policy called industrial participatory democracy was established in Zambia aimed at active involvement of workers, though unions are also active. South African labour legislation makes provision for work place forums. But these have been largely ignored or opposed by unions viewing them as potentially co-opting and a threat to traditional shop steward organisation.

Table 8.1 Statistics on trade unions in selected African countries

Country	Pop (000s)	HDI (Human Dev. Index)	Labour force (000s)	TU members (000s)	% of labour force (union density)	% non agric. labour force (union density)	% formal sector wage earners
African states							
Mauritius	1,129	83		478	22.1	25.9	36.6
South Africa	42,393	71	16,635	3,154	18.9	21.8	51.9
Botswana	1,484	67	654	45	6.8	11.5	19.3
Namibia	1,575	64	650	55	8.4	22	
Egypt	63,271	61	23,203	3,313	14.2	29.6	38.8
Swaziland	881	59	315	21	6.6	19.1	
Zimbabwe	11,439	50	5,281	250	4.7	13.9	21.7
Cameroon	13,560	48	5,500	250	4.5	14.7	
Ghana	17,832	47	8,393	700	8.3	25.9	
Kenya	27,799	46	13,953	500	3.5	16.9	33.3
Nigeria	115,020	39	45,565	3,520	7.7	17.2	
Zambia	8,275	37	3,454	273	7.9	12.5	54.5
Cot d'Ivoire	14,015	36	5,526	300	5.4	13	77.9
Tanzania	30,799	35	15,793	470	2.9	17.4	
Senegal	8,532	34	3,815	184	4.8	21.9	54.8
Uganda	20,256	34	10,084	63	0.6	3.9	
Malawi	9,845	33	4,807				
Ethiopia	58,243	25	25,392	152	5	41	22.3
Comparative statistics							
USA	269,444	92.7	136,884	16,360	11.9	12.7	
UK	58,144	91.8	28,967	7,280	25.1	26.2	
Germany	81,922	90.6	40,935	9,300	22.7	29.6	
Sweden	8,819	92.3	4,769	3,180	66.6	77.2	
Argentina	35,219	82.7	13,809	3,200	23.1	25.4	65.6
Brazil	161,087	73.9	73,733	15,205	20.6	32.1	6.6
Chile	14,421	84.4	5,740	684	11.9	15.9	3.3
South Korea	45,314	85.2	22,399	1615		9	

Source: ILO 1997. World Labour Report 1997–8: Industrial relations, democracy and social stability. Geneva: ILO
The ILO Swiss Project in Pretoria (2003) advised that these are its most updated statistics.

Ethiopia, like Zimbabwe, shows how an initially independent union movement can become subsumed under a state-directed system with various governments over time, including military and 'imperialist' regimes requiring union movement to support their particular aims. In 1962, the government in Ethiopia issued a Labour Relations decree, which allowed the establishment of trade unions. In 1963, the first trade union, the Confederation of Ethiopian Labour Unions (CELU), was recognised by authorities. CELU was made up of twenty-two industrial labour groups. The lack of national structure and constituency has limited its effectiveness (Mekonnen and Mamman 2004). The failure to follow government demands led to its abolition. It was replaced with the Ethiopia Trade Union (AETU) in 1977. The intention of the government was made clearer when it declared that the main purpose of AETU was to educate workers about the need to contribute their share to national development by increasing productivity and building socialism.

In Africa, single and multi-union systems occur variously in different countries. As in Mauritius, there are several unions in the Ivory Coast which has a tradition of employer–union adversarialism. Here the major unions are UGTCI (General Union of Workers of Ivory Coast), Centrale Dignité (Dignity Central), SYNARES (a union of university professors), and the SYNESCI (a union of middle school and high school teachers), to name the most popular. Although these unions did not play a key role during the independence struggles, they were instrumental in contributing to multi-party elections and democracy in the early 1990s. Specifically, the SYNARES and the SYNESCI were instrumental in allowing the multi-party elections in 1990 and the liberalisation of political discourse. The labour–management relationship may symbolise a cultural pattern in that it helps us understand how those who have power and control resources view employees in the workplace. In countries where labour–management relations are adversarial, one may expect a 'them versus us' mentality (Beugré 2004).

The multi-unionism of Mauritius, South Africa and Zimbabwe is in contrast with Tunisian unionism which is characterised by a single national organisation (The Tunisian General Employment Union (UGTT)) established in 1946. It represents 30 per cent of the Tunisian workforce; with 60 per cent of members in the public sector. The UGTT is composed of 7,000 unions distributed throughout the country, of which, twenty-three are regional unions, twenty are professional federations, and thirty are national unions, with the rest being local unions. As in Zimbabwe and several other African countries, pre-independence unions had strong features of a social movement collaborating with nationalist political organisation by mobilising workers in a struggle for independence (Yagoubi 2004). After independence, the UGTT became more of an administrative institution than an independent organisation of workers, and its leaders belonged to the government structure occupying functions in national and regional administration. Today, Tunisian unionism is undergoing a transformation. In Mauritius the history of the labour movement dates to the plantation days of tyranny, where repression and even execution were the lot of workers seeking industrial relations rights, especially in the 1970s. The socio-political environment has changed much since, with the flourishing economy and quasi-full employment lasting from the early 1980s. Multi-union membership is widely spread across sectors, industries, and occupations, although generally speaking, union activities are not backed by popular support, and their role as political change agents has not so far carried much weight either. The Industrial Relations Act and the Trade Unions and Labour Relations Act provide mostly for an interventionist approach, regulating the legal environment within which unions operate. However, this legislation itself has been contentious for decades now, with successive governments promising to review it (Ramgutty-Wong 2004).

Unions in Mauritius lack concerted action due to their lack of critical mass – a high proportion of them have fewer than 100 members. As in some other African countries, negotiations for annual salary compensations are conducted under a tripartite system involving the state and employer groups, but the multi-union groups tend not to be equal players. Fragmentation within the union movement makes it difficult to exercise much bargaining power. Thus, the current framework of industrial relations in Mauritius is neither adequately enabling nor particularly repressive (Ramgutty-Wong 2004).

In several African countries, union membership appears to be weakening with some anti-union sectors, individualistic cultural values and a new-found and materialistic orientation (Ramgutty-Wong 2004: 66). Following the overthrow of the socialist government in 1991, trade unions in Ethiopia have become relatively more independent. However, they still remain polarised and ineffective, largely due to internal strife, national economic problems, and the increasingly market-oriented economy. High unemployment and the growing privatisation of state-owned enterprises have also resulted in lower trade union membership (Mekonnen and Mamman 2004: 111).

In South Africa, up until this last five years, manual and semi-skilled workers have represented over 60 per cent of total union membership, but sub-contracted labour, casual and short-term contracts are having an adverse impact and employment is increasingly precarious. Building, construction, clothing and mining industries have been particularly affected, as employers have increasingly used labour-only sub-contractors (firms whose main purpose is to supply labour for particular projects on a temporary or ad hoc basis). In South Africa it is estimated that employment losses in traditionally highly unionised industries have resulted in a drop of union membership by over 20 per cent in the past three years. In the mining industry, coverage by collective agreements has dropped to below 50 per cent from 58 per cent in 1997 (Theron and Godfrey 2000: 116).

As in South Africa, the trade union movement in Tanzania was actively involved in the anti-colonial struggles. However, after independence, relations between the trade union leaders and the government were strained over the future role of the labour movement. Following a military mutiny in 1964 and the alleged involvement of some prominent trade union leaders, the government dissolved and banned the Tanganyika Federation of Labour (TFL). In its place, the government created an economic development oriented/state institution union called the National Union of Tanganyika Employees (NUTA). In 1997, the merger of the political parties on the Tanzania mainland (formerly Tanganyika) and Zanzibar was accompanied by the merger of the trade unions in both places. The new labour movement was subsequently integrated into the new political party. With multi-party politics, the Tanzanian labour movement freed itself from the state apparatus and became autonomous. It evolved into a number of trade unions under one umbrella organization in April 2001, and in1998 gained legal status with the enactment of the Trade Union Act which allowed freedom to form trade unions. By April 2002 seventeen trade unions on the mainland had registered with the registrar of trade unions. In Tanzania, although trade unions are recognised, the complex dispute settlement procedures make it extremely difficult for unions to call strikes in the public sector and many work stoppages are considered illegal by public authorities and tribunals. There are procedures for compulsory arbitration or adjudication when bipartite negotiations between employer and employees fail.

In recent years, trade unions in sub-Saharan Africa, have focused attention on addressing problems arising from enterprise restructuring programmes and privatisation, child labour, and the impact of HIV/AIDS on employment. As in Kenya, Botswana and South Africa, HIV/AIDS is a serious problem. Trade unions are working in conjunction with the government and NGOs to educate workers on prevention measures. Tanzanian trade union leaders have mounted vociferous attacks on the negative impacts of the ongoing privatisation programme. Since the initiation of the privatisation programme in the 1990s, there has been massive retrenchment of workers in the public sector in Tanzania. The privatisation programme has resulted in changes in conditions of service and deterioration and lack of enforcement of minimum employment standards legislation. Market-oriented reforms, as in many other African countries, have weakened the ability of trade unions to contest successfully policies and practices detrimental to workers' interests (Debrah 2004).

Collective bargaining and dispute resolution

Siddique (1989: 85) points out that most developing countries exhibit a dualistic economic structure, where a pre-capitalist economic system mainly dominates the scene, with a small industrial sector and a related numerically small working class. Other features include a segmented labour market, with a sharp dualism both between modern and traditional manufacturing sectors and between large and small firms; the dominance of the state in the industrial sector; weak trade unions and weak collective bargaining. Further, Siddique argues that IR in developing country settings can be explained in two ways: the popular culture-based explanation and the role of the state in these systems. The state's influence is manifest through the dominant role in industrialisation and the labour market, as in Kenya and Zimbabwe.

In Africa, where the state has traditionally been dominant in economic management, triparthite collective bargaining is rare. However, tripartite organisations have increasingly included members of unions, employers' associations and government. A further development has been the deregulation or decentralisation of collective bargaining, mainly as a result of the recession and slow economic development. The original centralised structures of bargaining have been strained and rendered unviable, with the implication that aspects of national labour contracts, even under multi-employer bargaining, are increasingly being subjected to individual employment contracts. Although this is one dimension of a new flexibility in the labour markets, it is an important instrument of the ascendancy of concession bargaining, and the new economy-imposed challenge of employer–employee co-operation, in these countries (Matanmi 2000: 100).

Collective bargaining frameworks vary including public policy level negotiations in tripartite structures in some countries. Kenya for example inherited the British Colonial Office 'voluntary' industrial relations system with decentralised plant level unionism and collective bargaining. Shortly after independence, the government moved towards tripartism by adding a government conciliation service and a labour court to provide binding arbitration. South Africa similarly has a tripartite form of societal corporatism, the National Economic Development and Labour Council (NEDLAC) which is established by statute. It has various chambers including one in which the social partners negotiate proposed labour laws or amendments to them, prior to tabling them in parliament. Employment creation initiatives are important issues addressed at NEDLAC. Major legislative reforms after the demise of apartheid, such as the Labour Relations Act (1995), Employment Equity Act (1998) and Skills Development legislation were first negotiated at NEDLAC between the three social partners, Government and organised labour and business. The Labour Relations Act also requires certain types of industrial action to be 'sanctioned' or otherwise by NEDLAC.

Tripartite co-operation of the labour market partners also occurs in Ghana. The Industrial Relations Act of 1965 consolidated the law relating to trade unions, collective bargaining, settlement of disputes involving certified trade unions, strikes and lockouts, and unfair labour practices. Trade unionism in both the private and public sectors has existed in Ghana since the introduction of wage employment by the colonial government and a labour federation, the Trades Union Congress (TUC), was established in 1945. The labour movement advanced the interests of its membership through legislation in return for embracing the development objectives of the government. The 1965 Act sought to conform to International Labour Organisation (ILO) regulations (Aryee 2004).

The Act provides for the recognition of a central labour movement, the Trades Union Congress (TUC), as a sole representative of the labour movement and the structure and functioning of the labour movement. To address the fragmented state of the labour movement, the 1965 Act structured unions along industrial lines and allowed for the affiliation of seventeen national industrial unions to the TUC. The TUC does not, however, participate in the negotiation of collective bargaining agreements on behalf of its affiliates. It provides advice on issues relating to the employment relationship, co-ordinates the activities of affiliates, and represents the interests of workers through its membership of national bodies. Collective bargaining is at the enterprise level and covers both procedural and substantive issues. The substantive component of the collective bargaining agreement sets conditions and terms of employment. The 1965 Act provides for procedures governing terminations, and dismissals, issues which are also covered in the collective bargaining agreement under discipline. The Act also provides for mechanisms for dispute resolution. Disputes which are not settled even after arbitration may then lead to strikes or lockouts.

The origins of collective bargaining in certain African countries are traceable to colonial times when unions emerged as key players in confronting oppressive colonial policies. Examples include Kenya and Tanzania. After independence in 1963, the Kenyan government found it necessary to choreograph the union movement by arguing that the nascent industrialisation needed to be protected from activism and disruptive activity. Employer organisations like the Kenyan Federation of Employers were drawn into this effort in order to ensure industrial stability. Kamoche *et al.* (2004) argue that the government's policy towards IR was that of exercising restraint in order to ensure the industrial stability that was deemed necessary for economic growth. However, given the deteriorating trust between the government and employees, militancy came to characterise IR. In recent years, this has covered a wide range of industries, for example air traffic controllers and the Kenyan Union of Teachers (KNUT). Factors that have kept the militancy in check include fear of dismissal given high unemployment, frequent retrenchments, business failures, and past government interference in labour disputes 'to rescue the economy'.

Labour market negotiations in many African countries are governed by rules contained in labour codes and in collective agreements. In Tunisia, for example, these are negotiated by tripartite committees every three years with the aim of avoiding industrial conflicts. Collective agreements determine, among other things, the level of wages and their growth over the next three years. While strikes used to be an instrument of the union struggle, unions in Tunisia are also involved in contractual policy, through periodic negotiations with an employers' association. At the enterprise level, despite social and economic changes, the union still occupies a less important place. Conflict resolution occurs primarily at the workplace, not necessarily involving an independent union. Countries like Egypt and Somalia also have labour codes containing various provisions. Ghana, Nigeria, Kenya, Zambia and Mauritius – to mention just a few – have adopted specific industrial relations Acts that also recognise certain labour rights (ILO 1997: 28–29). The scope of both labour policy or legislation and collective relations was rather limited until the 1970s or 1980s, depending on the individual country. For example, in Africa even now, with the exception of Egypt, Ethiopia, Libya, South Africa and Tanzania, existing legislation has yet to include rural (traditional) and informal or casual wage employment regulation (Matanmi 2000).

In Africa, reasons for the restriction of collective relations have included: unequal bargaining power relations, especially in the context of development and largely unfavourable economic trends in the 1980s and 1990s; governments' predilection for 'keeping unions in check' and creating practical obstacles to the development of collective bargaining; and the relatively new workers' knowledge of the stategy and tools of collective bargaining. In the long term, sustained stewardship training and general labour education will serve the workers and their unions well, according to Matanmi (2000: 99).

Another comparatively new pattern in emerging countries is industrial unionism, whereby workers in the same industry, irrespective of occupational or skill differentiation, belong to the same union. In South Africa, where industrial unionism is strongest, collective bargaining has undergone significant change in the past decade and a half. An adversarial, race-based dualistic system evolved following labour legislation in 1924 which led to trade union rights which excluded Africans. Only in 1980 were unions representing African workers legitimised. Inclusive bargaining councils were fostered through the Labour Relations Act in 1995. African unions grew to 3 million members in 2001, from less than 10 per cent of the formal sector workforce in the late 1970s. Union density in South Africa has declined to some 1.9 million in 2005. The largest unions are affiliated to union federations such as the Congress of South African Trade Unions (COSATU) and the National Council of Unions (NACTU).

The Labour Relations Act (1995) also established labour appeal courts, and the Commission for Conciliation, Mediation and Arbitration (CCMA). The CCMA handles both procedural and distributive or substantive justice in considering the fairness of a matter such as dismissal. The new Act sought to bring employment law in line with the constitution and ratified conventions of the International Labour Organisation. It aims to give effect to constitutional rights permitting employees to form unions, to strike for collective bargaining purposes, and the right to fair labour practices. Employers have the right to form and join employer organisations and the recourse to lockout for the purpose of collective bargaining. Strike action is protected only if a specified dispute procedure is followed.

While centralised industry level and decentralised enterprise or plant bargaining may occur, increased devolution and fragmentation of bargaining has occurred in the past nine years. The number of bargaining councils has declined to less than eighty as employers withdraw from them, favouring plant or enterprise bargaining and increased employment flexibility. This has occurred, for example, in the building and construction industries, as new forms of employment emphasising flexibility using independent sub-contractors, outsourcing, part-time and temporary work, and increased casualisation and informalisation of work. These practices are associated with a recent decline in private sector union density and some evidence of deterioration in employment standards in certain sectors (Horwitz *et al.* 2004). The Basic Conditions of Employment Act (1998), however, provides for establishing minimum standards of employment. These conditions cover areas from the designation of working hours to termination regulations and have been extended to farm and domestic workers. Work days lost through strike action have also declined since 1994. While under apartheid African unions fought for fair labour practices, worker rights, better pay and conditions of employment, they also were at the forefront of the struggle for political rights. Once political and labour rights complemented each other in the first democratic elections in 1994, this labour paradox was resolved. This resulted in an intense policy debate within the union movement as to its repositioning. The workplace as an arena for political struggle has largely been replaced with an emphasis on measures to try and preserve employment and HR issues such as training and development, and employment equity.

In South Africa, the Labour Relations Act (1995) seeks to promote employee participation in decision-making through workplace forums and employee consultation and joint decision-making on certain issues. It provides for simple procedures for the resolution of labour disputes through statutory conciliation and arbitration, and through independent alternative dispute resolution services. Amendments to the Act came into effect on 1 August 2002. New forms of dispute resolution were developed to include pre-dismissal arbitration and one-stop dispute resolution, known as Conciliation–Arbitration (CON–ARB) where if the former fails to settle a dispute, arbitration may occur immediately thereafter instead of the dispute being lodged again with a new date set down. Both unions and management have the power to request the CCMA to facilitate retrenchment negotiations to achieve constructive outcomes. There is a need to shift from a legacy of adversarial relationships to work place co-operation to compete successfully in the market place. There is evidence in some sectors, such as auto assembly, that this is understood by both parties. There is an increasing blurring of the distinction between industrial relations and HRM. The new agenda focuses beyond the traditional collective bargaining and adversarial dismissal disputes, to organisational transformation, performance improvement, human resource development, and employee benefits. Trade unions have become more willing to engage employers on these issues. Finding a productive balance between equity and workplace justice imperatives on the one hand, and HR and employment relations strategies enhancing competitiveness on the other, is a vital challenge for managers and unions.

In some countries the state views industrial relations as a vehicle for development priorities. In Botswana, for example, the National policy on Incomes, Employment, Prices and Profits guides salary structures in the government and private sectors. The policy is based on the objective of sustainable economic growth and economic diversification, international competitiveness, equitable income distribution and wage restraint aims contained in the National Development Plan (NDP). The NDP is produced every five years. Botswana's eighth plan covered 1997–2003 (NDP 8). There are various registered trade unions representing different industries in Botswana. These include the Botswana Federation of Trade Unions, Botswana Civil Service Association, Botswana Miners Union, Botswana Teachers Union, and Botswana Unified Local Government Service Associations. Organisations have collective agreements with trade unions or employee organisations, for example, on issues pertaining to working conditions, unfair dismissal, training, disciplinary action and pay. Employers are encouraged by employment policies to share work-related information to minimise conflicts and to facilitate collective bargaining. Employees are free to join trade unions and staff organisations/associations to protect and represent their interests at work. There have been conflicts between government and trade unions over issues relating to pay, resulting in strikes. In 2002 strike action was taken by teachers, as well as University of Botswana non-academic and academic staff and unified local government staff unions. This prompted government to appoint a commission to recommend an appropriate pay structure for public officers. Trade unions in Botswana are not yet as developed and well organised as those in other countries, and do not have a significant impact on the economy (Mpabanga 2004). The legislative framework designed to guide employment practices includes the Employment Act of 1982, The National Industrial Relations Code of Practice 1994, and the national Policy on Incomes Employment, Prices and Profits. Employers are also expected to conform to the National Policy on HIV/AIDS and Employment 2001, which is aimed at preventing and minimising the spread of HIV/AIDS in the workplace.

Public sector industrial relations

In Southern African countries the level of unionisation in the public sector is generally similar to that in the private sector. Some countries, such as Zambia, have experienced considerable privatisation, but the continuing fall in the size of the public sector does not seem to have affected the level of unionisation. Where trade unions are replaced by associations of civil servants (as in Zimbabwe, Botswana and Lesotho), the level of membership of such associations does not suggest a different level of unionisation (Kalula and Madhuku 1997). Southern African countries may be placed in two groups, in respect of public sector IR (Kalula and Madhuku 1997: 4–5):

- countries in which trade unions are allowed to operate freely in the public sector (in this group are South Africa, Namibia, Zambia, Mauritius and Malawi);
- countries that do not provide for the registration of recognised trade unions for government employees. (These include Zimbabwe, Botswana and Lesotho.) Government employees in this group are permitted to form workers' associations to represent their interests, but these associations are not as privileged as trade unions.

The trend in Southern Africa, however, is towards recognition of freedom of association of all workers, including those in the public sector. In Lesotho, the 1992 Labour code provided for free trade unions in the public service. Although this was recently changed by the Public Service Act (1995), it is instructive to note that the Societies Act 1996, specifically entrenched the right of public officers to form a staff association.

In all Southern African countries, there is a decline in unilateralism in the determination of terms and conditions of employment. Thus, in countries where the law does not provide for collective bargaining, either law or practice has entrenched some form of consultation between workers' bodies and government before the promulgation of terms and conditions of employment. In countries where collective bargaining is permitted by law, there is no clear trend towards either centralised or decentralised bargaining. The new Malawian Act, for instance, does not create any specific bargaining structure for the public service. South African legislation provides for establishment of different bargaining councils for different sectors in the public service, but also for a central Public Service Co-ordinating Bargaining Council dealing with certain uniform rules.

Zambian legislation has no specific structure for public service collective bargaining but the system of joint councils is based on sectorial bargaining. Similarly, in Namibia, the Namibian Act also does not have a specific structure for collective bargaining in the public sector, but it is clear that bargaining follows the level determined by the trade unions. In both countries a trade union with a majority of members in a unit or in a sector may engage the employer in collective bargaining. In Zambia, a trend towards a decentralised collective bargaining structure with some uniform broad rules for the entire public service, appears in certain aspects such as wages. Here, the Industrial Relations Act of 1993 (Amendment) provides for the formation of trade unions and prescribes conditions under which strikes may be called. Most unions in Zambia belong to one umbrella organisation, the Zambia Congress of Trade Unions (ZCTU). Contentious issues between unions and management usually centre on pay rates, cost of living adjustments (COLAs), health care, allowances (e.g. housing), layoff procedures, leave (e.g. sick leave and maternity leave), training and promotion, pension plans, and disciplinary cases (Muuka and Mwenda 2004).

The country has experienced high levels of unemployment and underemployment. Zambia has had relatively highly unionised IR, with union density averaging 56 per cent over the period 1995–2000. Total union membership has, however, dropped steadily – from a high of 289,322 unionised employees in 1995 to 234,522 in 1999, (ZCTU 1999). Job and union membership losses have affected the public sector, airlines, agriculture, banking, education and mining, etc. For the National Union of Public Service Workers, and Mineworkers Union of Zambia declining numbers have been largely due to the impact of SOE down-sizing as privatisation of those SOEs takes root. A serious factor has been the impact of HIV and AIDS in the public sector and also in others such as financial services, as well as the prolonged periods of drought. The decline in trade union membership can also be attributed to a lack of capacity by unions to organise in the new and increasingly hostile environment, particularly in the emerging private sector after privatisation.

Conclusion

Industrial relations in Africa have been subject to a multitude of influences. The first is the impact of structural adjustment programmes (SAPs), which most countries assessed here, with the exception of Libya and South Africa, have implemented, and World-Bank and IMF economic reform measures. The market-led reforms have had an effect on employment and industrial relations. Liberalised economies with privatisation and deregulatory measures have seen a drop in formal employment and a deterioration of labour standards. This is compounded by the fact that Africa receives less than one per cent of the world's foreign direct investment. While there is some evidence of a concomitant rise in industrial relations institutions such as collective bargaining and dispute resolution, as democratisation occurs, strong independent trade unions not linked to the state or employers, are rare. Positively, however, tripartite corporatist engagement is not uncommon, for example, in South Africa.

A second theme is that of HIV/AIDS, which especially in sub-Saharan Africa has a devastating impact on employment, employment and health care costs and decline in union membership. HIV/AIDS also has a deleterious effect on absenteeism, training, career and succession planning, with adverse effects on state and union negotiated medical schemes. A third theme is significant change in labour market policy and structures with both the state and employers in many countries either promoting or turning a blind eye to ineffective monitoring of legislative protection and collective agreements, as increased cost reduction and flexibility is sought, with a consequent deterioration in employment standards, social protection and rising informalisation and casualisation in labour markets. Examples include the decline of regional centralised bargaining structures in the building and construction industry in South Africa.

In a case study analysis of trade unions in the garment industries in Kenya, Lesotho, Swaziland and Malawi, Koen (2004) found that trade unions lacked strategic leadership, sound organisational practices, lack of capacity and regional co-ordination, sometimes resulting in significant power imbalances and dependency relationships with employers and the state. Tougher stances by employers in Kenya, for example, where a well-established tradition of industrial unionism has occurred have affected organisational efforts of the union, though this did not prevent spontaneous work stoppages by non-union members in January 2003. Union membership subsequently increased and recognition occurred with a two-year collective bargaining agreement. Driving the conduct of industrial relations and unionisation trends in these and other African countries, is a combination of macro-economic and trade policies using import and substitution, export processing zones, cheap labour and tax incentives to attract foreign direct investment, often from Asian countries like Taiwan. One of the consequences is the migration of clothing and garment manufacturing operations from one country to another. Attempts at militant union action and organisation have elicited harsh responses including factory closures and relocations. Conditions in factories organised by unions are exploitative often because of increasing pressures from the retail top-end of the supply chain in response to profit margin squeezes, low-cost products and stringent delivery times (Koen 2004: 56).

Bahadur (2004) notes a relationship between the African Growth and Opportunity Act (AGOA) and sweat-shop conditions. Much of this investment has been by Asian multi-nationals supplying retailers in other parts of Africa, and particularly by the United States. AGOA is a United States Act passed in 2000 offering preferential access for certain African exports. It reflects a philosophical shift in the US approach to Africa stemming from a policy of 'trade not aid' (Bahadur 2004: 39). At present thirty-seven sub-Saharan African countries qualify to export to the US under AGOA. One result is a switching of Malawian exports, previously destined predominantly for South Africa, to the USA. In a number of cases working conditions have deteriorated, for example, overtime increased to twenty-seven hours a week in Lesotho. In sub-Saharan Africa trade union rights have been repressed, labour laws are seldom enforced and there is high unemployment with the bargaining power of unions in this sector being compromised. In South Africa, over 20,000 retrenchments have occurred in the clothing industry, largely as a result of cheap imports from lower cost producers in Asia. A well-organised and soundly led union, the South African Clothing and Textile Workers Union (SACTWU) has struggled to fight this trend. One of its initiatives which has some employer support is a 'buy South Africa' campaign to try and preserve the region's jobs.

These industry examples reflect the increasingly precarious nature of employment and flexible labour markets in most African countries. Even in South Africa, arguably with a strongly protective Labour Relations Act (1995), institutionalised Labour Court, and statutory Conciliation Mediation and Arbitration Commission, as well as minimum standards legislation in the form of the Basic Conditions of Employment Act (1997) and arguably the strongest union movement on the continent, precarious, non-standard work has increased while formal work has declined. The combined effects of globalisation, trade policies, new technology, capital mobility new managerial practices, in some cases hostile labour market policies, and poorly implemented labour relations legislation, have served to place trade unions in Africa largely on the defensive. This even when ILO initiatives to establish dispute resolution machinery are occurring in several African countries. Kalula (2003) argues in this regard that labour laws in Southern Africa do not take into account the social realities of countries in the region, with their changing labour markets. He submits that labour law reflects Western models 'borrowing and bending' legal reforms seeking adherence to ILO standards, sometimes transplanting inappropriate legal precepts focusing on formal sector standard employment, ignoring the bigger reality of a dramatically increasing informal sector. He states that 'the vast majority are left out', arguing that 'labour law is a sharp instrument of social policy. Labour market regulation must strive to influence work beyond the formal sector narrowly defined. Mutual rights and obligations in the workplace remain important, but labour law must be part of an agenda for alleviating poverty' (Kalula 2003: 57).

In Africa, the industrial relations agenda will have to increasingly concern itself not only with managerial–working class relations, but with a growing and socially excluded underclass. Traditional trade union contests and power-conflict models may be inappropriate as are traditional distributive forms of collective bargaining based on an adversarial tradition. In Africa, union and employer strategies will need to increasingly focus on human resource development. Joint collaboration in the work place will be vital for effective competition in the market place.

References

Aryee, S. (2004) 'Human resource management in Ghana'. In Kamoche, K., Debrah, Y, Horwitz F.M. and Muuka, G. (Eds) *Managing Human Resources in Africa*, London: Routledge, pp. 128–130.

Bahadur, A. (2004) 'Taking the devil's rope – AGOA'. *South African Labour Bulletin*, 28 (1), pp. 39–42.

Beugré, C.D. (2004) 'Human resource management in Ivory Coast'. In Kamoche, K., Debrah, Y., Horwitz, F.M. and Muuka, G. (Eds) *Managing Human Resources in Africa*, London: Routledge, pp. 143–144.

Debrah, Y. (2004) 'Human resource management in Tanzania'. In Kamocke, K., Debrah, Y, Horwitz, F.M. and Muuka, G. (Eds) *Human Resource Management in Africa*, London: Routledge, pp. 80–82.

Fashoyin, T., Matanmi, S. and Tawase, A. (1994) 'Reform measures, employment and labour market processes in the Nigerian economy'. In Foshoyin (Ed.) *Economic Reform Policies and the Labour Market in Nigeria*, Lagos: Friedrich Ebert Foundation/Nigerian Industrial Relations Association, pp. 1–8.

Kalula, E. (2003) 'Labour laws need a dash of reality'. *South African Labour Bulletin*, 27(4), pp. 56–59.

Kamoche, K., Nyambegera, S. and Mulinge, M. (2004) 'Human resource management in Kenya'. In Kamoche, K., Debrah, Y., Horwitz, F.M., and Muuka, G. (Eds) *Managing Human Resources in Africa*, London: Routledge, p. 95.

Mekonnen, S. and Mamman, A. (2004) 'Human resource management in Ethiopia'. In Kamoche, K., Debrah, Y., Horwitz, F.M. and Muuka, G. (Eds) *Managing Human Resources in Africa*, London: Routledge, pp. 110–111.

Mpabanga, D. (2004) 'HRM in Botswana'. In Kamoche, K., Debrah, Y., Horwitz, F.M. and Muuka, G. (Eds) *Managing Human Resources in Africa*, London: Routledge, pp. 19–34.

Muhandu, V.H. (2000) 'Management in Zambia'. In Warner, M. (Ed.) *Management in Emerging Countries*, London: Thomson Learning, p. 239.

Muuka, G. and Mwenda, K. (2004) 'Human resource management in Zambia'. In Kamoche, K., Debrah, Y., Horwitz, F.M. and Muuka, G. (Eds) *Managing Human Resources in Africa*, London: Routledge, pp. 42–44.

Ramgutty-Wong, A. (2004) 'Human resource management in Mauritius'. In Kamoche, K., Debrah, Y., Horwitz, F.M., Muuka, G. (Eds) *Managing Human Resources in Africa*, London: Routledge, pp. 65–66.

Siddique, S.A. (1989) 'Industrial relations in Third World setting'. *Journal of Industrial Relations*, pp. 385–401.

Tamangani, Z. and Muranda, Z. (2000) 'Management in Zimbabwe'. In M. Warner (Ed.) *Management in Emerging Countries*, London: Thomson, pp. 245–246.

Theron, J. and Godfrey, S. (2000) 'Protecting workers on the periphery'. Development and Labour Law Monograph 1/2000, *Institute of Development and Labour Law*, University of Cape Town, pp. 1–51.

Verma, A., Kochan, T. and Wood, S. (2002) 'Union decline and prospects for revival'. *British Journal of Industrial Relations*, 40(3), pp. 373–384.

Yagoubi, M. (2004) 'Human resource management in Tunisia'. In Kamoche, K., Debrah, Y., Horwitz, F.M. and Muuka, G. (Eds) *Managing Human Resources in Africa*, London: Routledge, pp. 157–158.

Zambia Congress of Trade Unions (ZCTU) (1999) 'Survey on trade union membership and profile', Lusaka, Zambia.

Suggested key readings

Anstey, M. (2004) 'African Renaissance – implications for labour relations in South Africa'. *South African Journal of Labour Relations*, 28(1), p. 59.

Fashoyin, T. (2000) 'Management in Africa'. In Warner, M. (Ed.) *Management in Emerging Countries*, London: Thomson Learning, pp. 169–175.

Horwitz, F.M., Nkomo, S.M. and Rajah, M. (2004) 'Human resource management in South Africa'. In Kamocke, K., Debrah, Y., Horwitz, F.M. and Muuka, G. (Eds) *Managing Human Resources in Africa*, London: Routledge, pp. 1–18.

ILO 1997. World Labour Report 1997–8: 'Industrial relations democracy and social stability'. Geneva: ILO.

Jackson, T. (2002) 'Reforming human resource management in Africa, a cross-cultural perspective'. *The International Journal of Human Resource Management*, 13(7), p. 999.

Kamoche, K., Muuka, G., Horwitz, F.M. and Debrah, Y.A. (2004) *Managing Human Resources in Africa*, Routledge: London, p. xvi.

Kalula, E. and Madhuku, L. (1997) *Public Sector Labour relations in Southern Africa: Developments and Trends.* Institute of Development and Labour Law, University of Cape Town, pp. 4–7.

Koen, M. (2004) 'A tale of four unions: the state of clothing unions in four African countries'. *South African Labour Bulletin,* 28(1), pp. 53–56.

Matanmi, S. (2000) 'Industrial relations in emerging countries'. In Warner, M. (Ed.) *Management in Emerging Countries. International Encyclopedia of Business and Management.* Thomson Learning: London, pp. 95–104.

Nyambegera, S.M. (2002) 'Ethnicity and human resource management practice in sub-Saharan Africa'. *International Journal of Human Resource Management*, 13(7), pp. 1077–1090.

9 Industrial relations in India

VIDU BADIGANNAVAR

Introduction

There has been a growing interest among policy makers and analysts in the Indian industrial relations (IR) system since the early 1990s, primarily because of the new economic policy of liberalization, privatization and globalization adopted by the Indian Government since 1991 (Kuruvilla and Hiers 2000; Frenkel and Kuruvilla 2002; Bhagwati 2004; Papola 2004). It is argued that India has moved from an economic model of import substitution to export orientation and this transition in macro-economic policy has resulted in changes in the labour market policy in general and the industrial relations framework in particular. The economic reforms and the changes in industrial relations framework are an ongoing phenomenon and the cumulative effect of these changes is likely to have a substantive impact on the nature of ownership of public and private sector enterprises, corporate governance, labour laws and institutions, the nature and strength of trade unions, and the way in which firms manage their internal labour markets. This chapter examines some of the features of the post-reform Indian industrial relations system, the arguments of the advocates of reforms to the industrial relations system and, in the light of those arguments, reviews some of the evidence emerging in the Indian IR literature.

The IR policy debate in India

The underlying theoretical approach to the debate on industrial relations reforms in India is largely influenced by the institutional approach to labour–management relations (Kelly 2004). The primary focus of the institutional approach to the analysis of industrial relations is on the outcomes of collective bargaining and the policies of the employers, unions and the state (ibid.). According to the institutional analysis, the globalization of product, labour and capital markets have intensified competition for firms worldwide that during the 1980s operated in relatively 'protected markets' with high entry barriers for competition. However, the liberalization policies pursued by national governments through the General Agreement on Trade and Tariffs (GATTs treaty) which led to the setting up of the World Trade Organization (WTO) opened up markets for foreign goods. As a membership requirement of the WTO, national governments had to reduce their entry barriers for domestic and international competition. The intensified competition in turn provided a greater impetus and opportunity for capital to move across national boundaries in search of cheaper labour and infrastructure (Goldsmith 1995; Bhagwati 2004).

In the Indian context, the balance of payments crisis of 1991, when the government had to seek a loan from the International Monetary Fund to service its debts, served as an impetus to economic and labour market reforms. Over the past decade, the Indian economy as a whole and certain sectors such as the software industry in particular are doing well. NASSCOM – the regulatory agency for software and services industry – has urged organizations and corporate leaders to invest in their human resources, engage in long-term human resource planning, and more significantly, ensure lower unit labour costs through greater efficiency in order to thwart competition in the sector from China and Philippines (NASSCOM 2005).

As a result of globalization and increased capital mobility, it is argued that unions can no longer afford to engage in conflictual and adversarial industrial relations, nor can workers take improvements in their wages and conditions for granted. Union survival is now increasingly dependent on their ability to engage in co-operative industrial relations with employers with collective bargaining closely tied to the business goals of the enterprise (Haynes and Allen 2001). Such mutual co-operation is more likely to result in the financial success of the enterprise and thereby ensure better pay and conditions for the workers. Moreover, if workers perceive their union to be instrumental in delivering better employment conditions and providing them with an independent voice for employees, they are more likely to join the union and thereby improve the trade union membership strength (Ackers and Payne 1998; Ackers *et al.* 2004). At the macro-economic level, the State should create an 'investor friendly' market by unshackling the labour markets from institutional and legislative rigidities. This is likely to attract greater foreign direct investments which would in turn lead to employment creation and better pay and working conditions for labour (Kuruvilla and Hiers 2000).

It is argued that the competitive pressures and firm strategies impact heavily on the organization of work, employment relations, class structures and class-consciousness. Firms following the 'high road strategy' of competing on quality and innovation (rather than cost) are increasingly introducing 'high performance work practices' that encourage direct communication and worker participation in the organizations' decision-making processes and hence challenges the notion of representative participation through trade unions and works councils (ibid; Sprenger and van Klaveren 2004).

Some European evidence indicates that a substantial part of union membership in countries like the Netherlands, Germany and Denmark tend to perceive union structures as too bureaucratic, and want their union to be more of an 'activity' than an 'apparatus' (Bild *et al.* 1998; Hooiveld *et al.* 2002). Thus, it is argued that globalization and consequent changes to work organization have rendered traditional adversarial union approaches to collective bargaining redundant. In order to survive unions will have to go beyond job saving and wage bargaining and engage in joint problem solving with the employers to improve productivity and profits. This in turn requires union officials to learn new skills in co-operation and engagement with employers (Sprenger and van Klaveren 2004).

To what extent would this apply to the Indian context? Some analysts have argued that the trade union movement in India is very strong (Ramaswamy 1999). This strength comes not from high membership levels or mobilization capacity (which in fact is quite low as we shall see later) but rather from the political patronage that trade unions have enjoyed in the post-independence period and the affiliation of trade union federations to major political parties. For instance, the All India Trade Union Congress (AITUC) is affiliated to the Communist Party of India; the Centre of Indian Trade Unions (CITU), a breakaway faction of the AITUC, is affiliated to the Communist Party of India (Marxist); the Indian National Trade Union Congress (INTUC) is affiliated to the Congress Party and the Bhartiya Mazdoor Sangh (BMS) which is by far regarded as the largest trade union federation is affiliated to the Bhartiya Janata Party (BJP).

Since the early 1980s there has been a growth in the numbers of independent unions that are not affiliated to political parties or federations particularly in sectors such as textiles, engineering and local government. Some analysts have argued that the growth of such independent enterprise-level unions was a response to worker disenchantment with politically affiliated trade union federations with external leadership that is focused on party political interests, with highly centralized and bureaucratic structures (Ramaswamy 1997; Kannan 1999; Kuruvilla and Hiers 2000). Some anecdotal evidence also indicates that such enterprise-level unions have pursued more ambitious bargaining goals and delivered better bargaining outcomes to their membership compared to the unions affiliated to trade union federations (Ramaswamy 1997). More rigorous research with matched comparisons of unions and membership data is required to establish the effectiveness of independent and politically affiliated unions in India.

Historically, the active involvement of the trade union movement in the Indian independence struggle, earned it some public sympathy and in the post-independence era, trade unions were considered to be electoral assets due to the ability of their leadership to influence election outcomes by persuading their members to vote for particular parties and/or candidates to national or state legislature (Kuruvilla and Hiers 2000; Bhattacherjee 2002). Being perceived as an electoral asset has helped the labour movement to secure legislative protections that have rendered the labour market inflexible and unattractive to private domestic and international investments. Thus by implication, if India is to continue with the IMF recommended programme of liberalization it has to reform its labour laws and the state must withdraw its direct involvement in the market by privatizing the (inefficient) public sector. It is also argued that unions can no longer rely on political patronage but should engage in a meaningful dialogue with employers in delivering higher productivity and thereby protect the best interests of their members (Ramaswamy 1997, 1999; Bhattacherjee 2001).

This line of argument requires us to examine first, the extent to which the Indian institutional framework and in particular the labour laws and collective bargaining have indeed disabled employers from introducing the long-cherished flexible labour practices and, second, the extent to which employers in the neo-liberal era are willing to engage in a meaningful partnership with labour.

The institutional framework of collective bargaining and labour market flexibility

The Indian labour market

Before we examine the nature of the institutional framework for collective bargaining it would be useful to take a bird's eye view of the Indian labour market. In 1999–2000, the total workforce in India was 336.75 million of which only 27.96 million (i.e. 8.30 per cent) was employed in the 'organized' sector while the rest, 308.79 million (91.70 per cent), was employed in the 'unorganized' sector. Public sector accounted for 69.10 per cent of the total organized sector employment while the share of private sector was only about 30 per cent. Unemployment increased from 5.99 per cent in 1993–94 to 7.32 per cent in 1999–00 (source: *Economic and Political Weekly*, March 26, 2005).

The terms 'organized' and 'unorganized' sector do not indicate union membership status of employees (although unionized sector is a sub-sector of the organized sector) but rather the distinction indicates differences in firm size, regulation and remuneration (Kuruvilla and Hiers 2000: 21). The 'organized sector' consists of large and medium scale enterprises which fall within the ambit of labour laws and where workers enjoy better pay and job security. By contrast the 'unorganized sector' consists of small firms and the self-employed, where workers are usually not protected by national labour laws and they are employed on poor terms and conditions of employment. The second National Commission on Labour (1999–2002) appointed by the Government of India has defined the 'organized' sector as all firms employing twenty or more workers (Datt 2003).

Trade union coverage is largely restricted to the organized sector although more recently there have been some initiatives in organizing workers in the 'unorganized' sector. And within the organized sector, unions have a stronger presence in the manufacturing and the public sectors compared to the private service sector. According to the records of the Labour Bureau of the Government of India, in 1998 there were 61,199 registered trade unions which had increased to 65,286 unions by 2000. This indicates the extent to which the Indian trade union movement is fragmented. Only about 7,000 unions submitted their membership returns to the State Labour Commission in year 2000, which makes it difficult to estimate union density at national and sectoral levels (http://labourbureau.nic.in).

Union density estimates vary 'depending on the basis of calculation from 2.6 per cent of the non-agricultural workforce, to 38 per cent of wage and salary earners, to 75 per cent of the organized industrial workforce (large private and public sector firms)' (Frenkel and Kuruvilla 2002). Interestingly, trade union density in India in the organized sector increased marginally from 18.00 per cent in 1981 to 19.79 per cent in 1988 but later declined to 18.91 per cent by 1993 (ibid). The Labour Bureau of the Government of India also records 1,024 employers' unions in 1998 which declined to 770 unions in 2000. The main employer organization in India happens to be the Confederation of Indian Industry (CII) which actively lobbies the Government over economic and labour market reforms on behalf of its members.

Collective bargaining

Collective bargaining in India is deeply entrenched in the vast array of labour laws and institutions that regulate both procedural and substantive aspects of labour–management relations. Another feature of the Indian industrial relations system is the high levels of state intervention. This, it is argued, is a legacy of the British colonial past. During the colonial rule and particularly in the wake of the Second World War, the British government passed legislations to control industrial conflict and ensure uninterrupted supply of wartime production. In the post-independence period the Indian government retained these legislations to ensure a speedy economic recovery and to protect the interest of labour which was perceived to be weaker. Thus, the highly interventionist role of the state established by the colonial rulers continued in the post-independence period (Sen Gupta and Sett 2000: 145).

There are three important legislations that have played a crucial role in shaping the IR system in India. They are: the Trade Unions Act (1926), The Industrial Employment Standing Orders Act (IEA 1946) and the Industrial Disputes Act (IDA 1947). The Trade Unions Act provides for registration of unions but does not entitle the union to recognition by the employer for the purposes of collective bargaining. 'Labour' is on the concurrent list of the Indian Constitution which means both the State and Central Governments can legislate on this matter. Some state governments have passed laws that enable trade unions to gain recognition through secret ballots or majority membership verification by the appropriate local authority, which in most cases is the Labour Commission of the state government (Kuruvilla and Hiers 2000; Venkat Ratnam 2000). Registration of unions is fairly straightforward under the Trade Unions Act 1926. Any seven workers can come together and register a trade union. This rather lax criterion has resulted in multiplicity and fragmentation of trade unions. It is argued that labour law reforms should stipulate a minimum membership of say 10 per cent of the bargaining unit for a union to be eligible to register.

The IDA 1947 is the most important piece of legislation. It confers discretionary powers upon the State to intervene in any actual or potential industrial dispute. The state has powers to refer the dispute for conciliation or adjudication and may decide whether or not to implement the award of the Labour Courts and Industrial Tribunals (Sen Gupta and Sett 2000). In 1972 the IDA was amended which required employers to give a minimum of sixty days' notice to employees before any workplace closure. In 1982 the law was further amended to require employers to gain the approval of the state government before the closure (or retrenchment, or lay-off) of any establishment with 100 or more employees. The IDA also stipulates the level of compensation to be paid in such cases. It is argued that for populist reasons state governments seldom give permission for layoffs, retrenchments or closures of establishments. This creates artificial rigidity in the internal labour markets of the firms and, in tough market conditions, renders them financially non-viable (ibid.; Deshpande 2001).

Legislative provisions also regulate the level of wages to be paid to workers both in the organized and unorganized sectors. For instance, the Minimum Wages Act (1948) is a Central Act but implemented by state governments that set a 'floor' of wages to be paid to workers in different occupational categories. The state government can add to the list of occupational categories identified by the Centre. The minimum wages are revised periodically based on changes in the cost of living indices in the urban and rural labour markets. The trade unions can and do lobby the government to revise minimum wages. There are policies and laws that provide for additional payments besides minimum wages. For instance, state and central governments stipulate an 'industrial dearness allowance' which requires employers to pay an additional sum to workers for every point increase in the consumer price index. This, however, is based on estimates of how much the lowest paid workers would need to keep their salaries at par with the rising cost of living. The Payment of Bonus Act (1965) requires that employers with twenty or more employees must pay a minimum annual bonus to all workers. This minimum is stipulated at 8.33 per cent of the annual basic wage and dearness allowance. However, there is an upper limit of rupees 3,500 per month in wages for the calculation of the bonus (Kuruvilla and Hiers 2000).

The government also appoints tripartite committees for recommending wages for certain occupational categories. For public sector employees (which constitute the largest proportion of employees in the organized sector) the Central government and increasingly the state governments recommend long-term wage settlements. Although individual public sector enterprises do have the autonomy to negotiate locally with the trade unions, they are expected to conform within the guidelines provided by the Central government (Kuruvilla and Hiers 2000). These wage settlements have an impact on the private sector wages by setting a benchmark for union–management negotiations particularly in the organized sector. Once again it is argued that such interventionist policies of the state on wage determination create rigidities in the labour markets and are inimical to attracting private investment or employment creation.

Except in some industries such as insurance and banking, in most other industrial sectors, collective bargaining takes place at the enterprise and workplace levels. At the enterprise level an employer may be faced with multiple unions with varying demands for different bargaining units. However, since there is no provision in the Trade Unions Act 1926 for recognition of a union by employers but only certification/registration, an employer may or may not choose to negotiate with one or other of the union(s). A union's ability to engage in negotiations with an employer then rests in its ability to mobilize a majority membership and impose actual or potential economic costs on the employer or its ability to deliver a 'sweet heart' deal to the employers.

At workplace levels the Industrial Disputes Act 1947 provides for the setting up of 'works committees' by management in establishments with 100 or more employees. Works committees consists of equal numbers of employee and management representatives and are a means of direct communication between the employer and the workforce. In unionized firms, the union may nominate or appoint representatives to these committees. The primary function of these works committees is information sharing and reaching workplace-level agreements over issues such as productivity norms, shift patterns, overtime, maintaining workplace discipline, training, etc. Individual states such as Maharashtra have legislated to increase the scope of these works committees in order to promote a positive workplace industrial relations climate (Kuruvilla and Hiers 2000).

One might ask why the union or employee representatives should be asked to do the job of management through works committees such as enforcing discipline, controlling absenteeism or ensuring that productivity targets are met (Ramaswamy 1997). Evidence from the General Motors' Saturn Plant in the US indicates that such labour–management co-operation was detrimental to the interests of the union. Shop stewards who were appointed by management as 'team leaders' found that they could no longer represent the interests of their members and at the same time ensure management's productivity targets were met. The labour–management partnership at Saturn resulted in worker disenchantment with the trade union, resignations of shop stewards and calls from the rank-and-file to abandon this 'sweat heart' relationship with the management and revert back to adversarial industrial relations (Rubinstein 2001). Similarly, British evidence on labour–management partnership indicates that although partnership delivered substantial cost savings for management, it was associated with union membership loss, and erosion of shop steward structures (Badigannavar and Kelly 2004).

The Industrial Disputes Act 1947 also defines the procedures to be followed for dispute resolution. If the union and management are in dispute over a particular issue, the first stage is to refer the dispute to a conciliation board headed by a conciliation officer. These boards operate at district, regional and state levels, and a dispute may be referred incrementally to each of these levels depending upon the nature of the dispute. If the parties fail to resolve the dispute at the conciliatory stage it may be referred by the state government to the Labour Courts and later to the Industrial Tribunals. However, as mentioned earlier, the state has unprecedented powers under the Industrial Disputes Act in deciding whether or not to refer a dispute for adjudication and to implement the award of the courts and tribunals (Sen Gupta and Sett 2000). As such there is no specified time limit for the conciliatory boards or the courts to hear and settle a dispute and these processes can be expensive and time consuming.

Labour market flexibility

It is argued that the very nature of the industrial relations framework in India creates artificial inflexibilities in the labour market which is a disincentive to private investment and is not conducive to promote labour–management co-operation (Kuruvilla and Hiers 2000). Evidence, however, indicates that since the 1970s employers have rather successfully managed to circumvent these labour laws through various means such as subcontracting or outsourcing entire business operations, in some cases setting up their own outsourced companies, hiring workers through labour contractors and not employing them directly with the firm, or employing less than 100 workers to escape most of the statutory provisions that apply to establishments employing 100 or more workers. Some employers have even gone to the extent of forcing employees to work without any written records of wages or attendance while others shuffle their employees several times through different sister companies or terminate and rehire the same worker with a few days' or weeks' break between so that the workers can never complete the minimum days of employment contract with the same employer that will make them eligible for protection under labour laws. There is evidence of employers re-designating job titles of workers or changing their job descriptions to exclude them from the bargaining unit. For instance, telephone operators are re-designated as 'communications officers' and accounts clerks as 'payroll executives' (Mathur 1991, 1992; Sen Gupta and Sett 2000).

When employers wanted to close down an establishment with high levels of unionization or rigid wage structures they have resorted to the use of lockouts instead of 'closures' as the latter would require permission from the state authorities which is seldom given. There are instances where employers have deliberately defaulted in paying their electricity bills or paying their creditors or suppliers in order to declare the unit financially non-viable and further more have asked these creditors to file petitions in civil courts to close down the company under the Companies Act. Likewise employers have resorted to prolonged lockouts to force employees to accept stricter work norms or voluntary retirement on terms favourable to the employer. Employers prefer lockouts to closures because the former do not require permission from the state authorities and the employer is not liable to pay any compensation to the workers as would be required in formal closures (ibid: 149). One could argue that it is precisely for these reasons (non-compliance by employers) that labour laws should be amended or repealed. On the other hand, it could be argued that these laws provide for the basic protection and welfare of workers in a society where the state provides negligible social security, and non-compliance by employers who do not wish to recognize a trade union, or are unwilling to honour the basic worker rights of their employees, calls for a stricter enforcement of these laws and not their repeal (Papola 2004: 547).

Evidence also indicates a growing incidence of casualization of employment in the Indian labour markets in the post-reform period. A recent study of employment trends in fifteen states of India between 1983 and 2002 revealed that only about 13 to 14 per cent of employees nationally were employed in long-term, regular employment during the period. While the proportion of workers in casual employment, particularly in rural areas, increased from 31.5 per cent in 1983–84 to 35.4 per cent in 2001–02 (Bhaumik 2003), another study revealed the share of casual workers characterized by insecure employment and low wages had increased from 27 per cent in 1977–78 to 33 per cent in 1999–2000. More interestingly, an establishment-level study covering about 1,300 firms revealed that in larger firms employing more than 1,000 workers, an average of 48 per cent were casual compared with 24 per cent in firms employing fewer than 1,000 workers (Papola 2004; Deshpande *et al.* 2004; Datta 2001). Thus the argument that employers are unable to adjust their internal labour markets due to stringent labour laws or, that economic reforms coupled with weaker labour market regulation will create a higher number and better quality of jobs in the labour market seems to be questionable.

Patterns of industrial conflict in India

Advocates of the institutional perspective on industrial relations argue that in a globalized world with increased capital mobility unions should work in co-operation with employers to ensure profitability and this, in turn, would help the unions to protect and promote the best interests of their members. Mutual co-operation would lead to mutual gains (e.g. Ramaswamy 1999; Huzzard *et al.* 2004). Given the low union density in India, one could argue that employers have far lower economic risks of organized resistance and have no reason to be reluctant to engage in partnership with their unions (Martinez Lucio and Stuart 2004). The second National Commission for Labour appointed by the Government of India (1999–2002) has also urged unions to engage in partnership with employers (Datt 2003). Are employers in India willing to engage in co-operative rather than adversarial relations with labour?

The data in Table 9.1 indicates that during the 'reform' decade of 1991–2000 138.54 million man-days were lost due to employer lockouts compared to 91.60 million man-days lost due to worker strikes. The number of man-days lost per worker due to strikes in 1999 was only 9.7 compared to 76.2 man-days lost per worker due to employer lockouts, i.e. nearly eight times more man-days were lost per worker due to lockouts compared to those lost due to strike in that year alone. The Labour Bureau of the Government of India reports that during 2002 to 2003 the proportion of man-days lost due to strikes decreased by 66.83 per cent whereas the proportion of man-days lost due to lockouts during the same period increased by 59.86 per cent. In 2003 out of the 297 lockouts recorded, as many as 290 or 97.64 per cent of lockouts were 'pure lockouts', i.e. lockouts originating and terminating as lockouts. These were responsible for a time loss of 20.50 million man-days or 75.77 per cent of the total time loss caused by all lockouts in the country. These figures indicate an alarming rise in employer militancy during the period of economic reforms.

Table 9.1 Pattern of industrial disputes in India during 1991–2000

Year	Workers involved in (thousands)		Man-days lost in (millions)		Man-days lost per worker	
	Strikes	Lockouts	Strikes	Lockouts	Strikes	Lock-outs
1991	872	470	12.43	14.00	14.3	29.8
1992	767	485	15.13	16.13	19.7	33.3
1993	672	282	5.61	14.69	8.3	52.1
1994	626	220	6.55	14.33	10.6	65.1
1995	683	307	5.72	10.57	8.4	34.4
1996	609	331	7.82	12.47	12.8	37.8
1997	637	344	6.31	10.68	9.9	31.0
1998	801	488	9.35	12.71	11.7	26.0
1999[P]	1099	212	10.62	16.16	9.7	76.2
2000[P]	1044	374	11.96	16.80	11.5	44.9
1991–2000	7810	3513	91.60	138.54	11.7	39.4

P = provisional
Source: Ministry of Labour Annual Report (2001–2002), Government of India.

With respect to the causes of industrial disputes, the Labour Bureau reports that in 2003, 174 lockouts were due to worker 'indiscipline' and these alone accounted for 58.59 per cent of all lockouts. Lockouts over union's 'charter of demands' accounted for a time loss of 26.17 per cent while those due to 'wages, allowances and bonus' together resulted in a time loss of only 5.56 per cent of the total man-days lost. In contrast, 31.60 per cent of strikes were called over 'wages and allowances'. The manufacturing sector accounted for the highest proportion of industrial disputes (63.95 per cent) while agriculture and related services accounted for the lowest proportion of industrial disputes (9.67 per cent). In 2003, eighty-three 'major industrial disputes' were recorded (i.e. disputes which involve a time loss of 50,000 or more man-days). Of these only 3.61 per cent were recorded in the public sector, while 96.39 per cent were recorded in the private sector. This also indicates that the blame of 'inefficiency' and 'militancy' levelled against public sector workers and their unions is rather unsubstantiated.

The figures in Table 9.1 not only indicate a substantial rise in employer militancy in India during the period of economic reforms but also indicate that the 'individual intensity of lockouts was nearly 3.4 times as compared to strikes' (Datt 2003: 127). As reported earlier, employers prefer the use of lockouts compared to closures because they do not need prior permission for the former from the state authorities and they are not liable to pay compensation to workers. Moreover employers also use such militancy to force workers into accepting labour intensification, inferior pay deals 'voluntary retirement' (which is hardly voluntary) or simply to move production from a unionized plant with high wages to green-field non-union sites with low wages and poor conditions of work (Sen Gupta and Sett 2000; Shyam Sundar 2003). Evidence also indicates that employers may be victimizing workers and their representatives through disciplinary and dismissal procedures which is reflected in their frequent use of lockouts over the issue of workplace 'indiscipline'.

These findings do not inspire a lot of confidence in the intentions of employers to engage in partnership with their workers or unions. However, one might argue that the decline in the number and intensity of strikes indicates a greater appreciation of the changed reality of globalization and the need for co-operative industrial relations amongst Indian trade unions. Survey evidence lends some support to this assumption whereby unions have shown greater willingness to engage in communication and negotiation with employers, and this to some extent has helped them to improve their effectiveness perception among workers (Dhal and Srivastava 2003).

Industrial relations reforms in India

Both advocates and critics of labour market regulation in India are unanimous in calling for reforms to the industrial relations system (Ramaswamy 1999, Papola 2004; Datt 2003; Kuruvilla and Hiers 2000). The arguments for reform to the industrial relations system are based on the need to consolidate and simplify the vast array of labour legislation, particularly those covering the organized sector, improve the implementation and monitoring of this legislation, create new legislation to cover the vast majority of Indian workers (about 90 per cent) employed in the unorganized sector, facilitate union recognition and organization for workers in the unorganized sector and reduce state intervention in the industrial relations system by appointing an independent commission for regulating labour–management relations.

The Government of India appointed the second National Labour Commission (NCL) on 15 October 1999, first, to suggest rationalization of exiting laws relating to labour in the organized sector and second, to suggest an 'umbrella' legislation for ensuring minimum labour standards for workers in the unorganized sector. The Commission submitted its report to the Government on 1 June 2002 (Datt 2003: 109). The NCL seems to be strongly persuaded by the need for labour–management partnership. For instance, it argues that 'Attitudes of confrontation must give place to an attitude of genuine partnership. Organizations of workers as well as employers, and the State itself, should identify and create conditions on which the harmonious relations that we need can be created and maintained' (NCL 2002: 3).

The NCL maintains that any labour market reforms should necessarily take into account the fundamental rights enshrined in the Indian Constitution such as the rights to equality, freedom and against exploitation. In addition labour market reforms should also be consistent with the ILO conventions ratified by India such as: right to life, liberty and security, right against slavery and servitude, right to rest, leisure, holiday with pay, limitations to working hours and a standard of living adequate for the health and well-being.

Needless to say, it is imperative that the State as an employer in public sector undertakings should honour its commitments under the various labour laws and constitutional provisions thereby setting an example as a 'model employer' for the private sector. However, studies on agricultural labour (which according to the NCL 1999–2002 accounts to 110 million workers) have revealed that in some states the Government had set minimum wages for agricultural labour at a level below the official poverty line, thereby violating their constitutional right to a decent standard of life (Badigannavar 1998). There have been instances reported by trade unions such as the Hind Mazdoor Sabha (HMS) and the All India Trade Union Congress (AITUC) where contract labour working in public sector enterprises (hired through sub-contractors) was being paid wages below the official minimum wages. Non-payment of minimum wages under the Bonded Labour Abolition Act (1976) is deemed as slavery. This indeed is an ironical situation where, on one hand the state abolishes the practice of bonded labour and on the other fails to check such practices in its own enterprises.

In its spirit of labour–management partnership the NCL states 'The commitment of the workforce to quality and productivity must be high. This commitment and the new work culture can be created only when workers feel that they are receiving fair wages, a fair share of profits and incentives and the respect or consideration due to partners (NCL report 2002: 2)'. However, a study of sixteen large Indian firms cited by Datt (2003: 114–115) on managerial remuneration, corporate efficiency and employee wages indicates that between 1979–80 to 2000–1, employee wages in these firms lagged behind profits before depreciation, interest and tax, while managerial remuneration showed a much higher growth rate compared to employee wages, sales growth and profits. Interestingly, the study also finds that managerial compensation increased in these firms despite a significant decrease in return on capital employed and the return on equity. These findings provide little hope for the partnership aspirations of the NCL.

The NCL reinforces the need for employers to invest in multiple skills training and updating of skills to secure a functionally flexible and productive workforce. However, evidence indicates that even large firms employing over 1,000 workers, which one might expect to have the financial and technical resources to invest in skill training, rely excessively on numerical rather than functional flexibility through the use of contract and casual labour (Papola 2004: 546). Evidence from industrialized countries like Britain shows that, employers seldom invest in skill training of their workers beyond the immediate job requirements that would enhance their employability (Calveley *et al.* 2003; Adler 2004). To what extent, then, can workers in developing countries like India rely on employer goodwill to enhance their employability? In the following sub-sections we will review the recommendations of the NCL with respect to reforms to trade union recognition, collective bargaining, industrial disputes and labour market flexibility.

Trade union recognition

The NCL does make some significant recommendations with respect to recognition of trade unions for collective bargaining and union membership recruitment of the 'free riders', i.e. non-union workers in a unionised enterprise whose wages and conditions are covered by collective bargaining agreements. For instance, it suggests that a union with less than 10 per cent membership would have no collective or individual representational rights in an establishment. The negotiating agent should be selected on the basis of a check-off system (union membership dues deducted directly from workers' wages) and a union with 66 per cent membership should be recognized by the employer as the sole bargaining agent. If no union has 66 per cent membership, then unions with more than 25 per cent membership should be given proportional representation at the bargaining table. The Commission suggests that once the union is recognized as a bargaining agent, this recognition should be valid for four years, during which period no claim by any other union should be entertained.

With respect to 'free riders' the NCL recommends that

> a worker who is not a member of the trade union will have to pay an amount equal to the subscription rate of the negotiating agent or the highest rate of subscription of a union out of the negotiation college. The amounts collected on this account may be credited to a statutory welfare fund.

It is reasonable to expect that such provisions if incorporated by the Government in any future union recognition law would help the unions to recruit workers in establishments where they are recognized for collective bargaining. The NCL also makes a positive recommendation towards organizing workers in the unorganized sector of the economy. It suggests that the Trade Union Act should include a special provision for the registration of trade unions of unorganized workers, even if the union has less than 10 per cent membership, and even if an employer–employee relationship does not exist or is difficult to establish. However, over-reliance on statutory provisions is unlikely to help trade unions to improve their membership strength and mobilization capacity (Baccaro *et al.* 2003).

There is a greater need for unions in India to engage in rank-and-file organizing and recruit workers in the unorganized sector. Traditionally, unions have confined themselves to organizing and representing workers in the organized sector and they may lack the skills or resources required to mobilize workers in the unorganized sector and particularly those in the rural labour markets. However, they can overcome these limitations by forging alliances with non-governmental organizations (NGOs) and civil rights groups which have been working with the marginalized sections of the community both in the rural and urban areas for several decades. One such example of an NGO that has successfully organized women workers in India is the Self Employed Women's Association (SEWA) which has not only engaged in social advocacy for women's rights but has also facilitated the creation of economic opportunities through micro-savings and credit schemes, vocational training and self-employment programmes for nearly a quarter of a million women workers in rural India (Venkat Ratnam and Verma 2004).

Collective bargaining

With respect to collective bargaining, the NCL recognizes that there are well established industry-level bargaining arrangements in certain industrial sectors, such as banking and insurance, where it would like such practice to continue, but in other industries the Commission has expressed its preference for a decentralized enterprise-level bargaining in order to ensure efficient functioning of the establishment (NCL 2002: 42). Although the Commission appreciates the role of voluntary bipartite bargaining between unions and employers, it emphasizes the role of state as a partner in collective bargaining through conciliation, arbitration and adjudication where necessary. The Commission recommends a system of 'Lok Adalats' (people's courts) and Labour Relations Commissions at State and Central levels to administer and adjudicate over disputes covering employment relations, wages, social security, and welfare conditions. Some analysts have expressed greater confidence in one such independent Industrial Relations Commission (IRC) which would be a statutory body independent of the state executive and likely to be free from political influence and manipulation (Sen Gupta and Sett 2000: 152). The NCL also recommends that once a collective bargaining agreement has been reached between the parties such agreements should be binding on all workers in the establishment. However, as Datt (2003) argues, the NCL does not make it binding upon the management and there are several instances when the management violates such agreements. This issue needs further deliberation and revision in the NCL's recommendation.

Industrial disputes

With respect to industrial action – strikes and lockouts, the NCL observes that a stipulated period of notice (fourteen days) should be issued by the party. The union should take a strike action only if mandated by a majority of the workforce through a secret ballot while the employer can impose a lockout only after obtaining approval at the highest level of management except in cases of actual or grave apprehension of physical threat to the management or to the establishment. The NCL further recommends that any union that leads an illegal strike should be de-recognized and de-barred from registration or recognition for two or three years, while any worker who engages in illegal strike or work stoppage should lose three days wages for every illegal day of strike action. Likewise an employer that imposes an illegal lockout must pay three days wages per day of the lockout to workers.

However, Datt (2003: 126) argues that in its recommendations the NCL has not treated the actions of workers or union and that of the employer on an equal footing. An employer may impose a lockout on 'apprehensions of real or fancied physical threat to the management' (ibid), whereas the workers suffer a double jeopardy – they lose three days pay per day of strike deemed illegal and their union gets derecognized and debarred from registration and recognition. This potential discrimination is all the more worrying in the light of our earlier discussion about the rise in employer militancy and the greater adverse impact of lockouts on workers compared to strikes. In the essential services such as water supply, medical services, electricity and transport, the Commission recommends that a majority worker ballot (51 per cent) in favour of strike action should be treated as if the strike had taken place and the dispute must be referred to compulsory arbitration (NCL 2002: 40).

Labour market flexibility

The NCL has addressed the issue of labour market flexibility for firms with respect to down-sizing through lay-offs and retrenchments. The Commission recommends that 'prior permission (of state authorities) is not necessary in respect of lay off and retrenchment in an establishment of any employment size'. It is sufficient if workers are given two months' notice or pay in lieu of notice in case of retrenchment. The Commission recommends that the rate of compensation should be higher in a running and profitable organization (with 300 or more workers) compared with those that are closing down or continually incurring losses for at least three financial years. For instance, a loss-making firm should pay thirty days of wages per completed year of employment if the firm is being closed down and forty-five days of wages if the firm is shedding labour to become financially viable and continue trading. It also recommends that a profit-making firm should pay retrenchment compensation at the rate of sixty days of wages per completed year of service. Lower rates are recommended for firms employing less than 100 workers (NCL 2002: 44). However, some analysts have argued that the NCL is silent about retrenchment compensation rates for workers employed in firms with 100–300 workers and this potential legislative gap needs rethinking (Datt 2003: 128).

Conclusion

In this chapter we have examined the labour–management relations in India, particularly during the period of economic reforms (post-1991). The key criticisms of the Indian industrial relations systems are first, its deep entrenchment in a vast array of labour laws and institutions that govern labour–management relations and second, the high level of state intervention which has prevented the growth of a voluntary system of collective bargaining. It is argued that the current institutional framework of Indian industrial relations contributes to artificial rigidities and market imperfections that render the markets unattractive to private investments. Thus it is argued that the State should reform the industrial relations system to make it compatible with wider economic reforms. The advocates of reforms also argue that trade union militancy is inimical to commercial profitability of firms and economic development in general and, call for a genuine labour–management partnership which would result in mutual gains for the stakeholders.

Although one cannot deny the need for reforms to the Indian industrial relations system, the arguments of labour market rigidities and firms' inability to adjust their internal labour supply according to the demand for products or services is overstated. Evidence indicates that both large and small or medium-scale firms in various product market segments have been able to 'rationalize' their internal labour markets through various means such as outsourcing, subcontracting, use of voluntary retirement schemes, lockouts and firm closures. There is very little evidence to suggest that employers have invested in skill training and pursued the 'high road' of functional flexibility. Rather the evidence indicates greater employer reliance on numerical flexibility through casualization of employment. Not surprisingly, economic reforms have been associated with a rise in the number of insecure workforce employed in the unorganized sector.

The National Commission on Labour (1999–2002) appointed by the Government of India has made several valuable recommendations towards reforming the Indian industrial relations system. Particularly notable are its recommendations with respect to statutory recognition of unions as bargaining agents by employers and unionization of workers in the unorganized sector. However, there is a greater need for trade unions to go beyond their traditional strongholds of manufacturing and public sector enterprises in the organized sector and recruit and mobilize the large section of workers engaged in precarious forms of employment in the unorganized sector. The NCL's recommendations on establishing a Labour Relations Commission and an independent authority free from the state executive to ensure the implementation of labour laws is certainly a welcome suggestion. However, the NCL's recommendations with regards to penalties for illegal strikes and lockouts and the binding nature of collective agreements need further consideration.

With respect to labour–management partnership – which figures quite prominently in the recommendations of the NCL – the rise in employer militancy in India particularly since 1991 and, the growing disparity in managerial remuneration and workers' wages in relation to firm profits, offer limited hope for the development of meaningful labour–management co-operation. Where such co-operative arrangements may exist, a rigorous empirical assessment of the mechanisms and outcomes of partnership arrangements is required to better understand the factors that help to establish and sustain such co-operative relationships.

It is also argued that over-reliance of the Indian trade unions on political support has prevented them from engaging in rank-and-file organizing, which in turn has contributed to low levels of union density, lack of internal union democracy and worker disenchantment with unions and federations affiliated to political parties. This disenchantment may have contributed to the rise of independent establishment-level unions in India, particularly over the last two decades. However, to what extent such independent establishment-level unions have delivered better bargaining outcomes and a meaningful 'voice' to their members, compared to their politically affiliated counterparts, is a question that needs more systematic investigation. On the whole, a review of the Indian industrial relations system indicates a cautious programme of reform being introduced by the state to align the industrial relations system with the changes in the economy.

References

Ackers, P., Marchington, M., Wilkinson, A. and Dundon, T. (2004) 'Partnership and voice, with or without trade unions: changing UK management approaches to organisational participation', in Stuart, M. and Martinez Lucio, M. (eds) *Partnership and Modernisation in Employment Relations*, London and NY: Routledge.

Ackers, P. and Payne, J. (1998) 'British trade unions and social partnership: rhetoric, reality and strategy', *International Journal of Human Resource Management*, 9: 529–50.

Adler, P.S. (2004) 'Skill trends under capitalism and socialization of production' in Warhurst, C., Grugulis, I. and Keep, E. (eds) *The Skills that Matter*, Basingstoke, UK: Palgrave Macmillan.

Baccaro, L., Hamann, K. and Turner, L. (2003) 'The politics of labour movement revitalization: the need for a revitalized perspective', *European Journal of Industrial Relations*, 9(1): 119–133.

Badigannavar, V. and Kelly, J. (2004) 'Labour-management partnership in the UK public sector', in Kelly, J. and Willman, P. (eds) *Union Organization and Activity,* London: Routledge.

Badigannavar, V. (1998) 'Organising the agricultural labour: perceived challenges and possible responses', *Perspectives in Social Work*, 13(2): 20–23.

Bhattacherjee, D. (2001) 'The 'new left', globalization and trade unions in West Bengal: what is to be done?', *The Indian Journal of Labour Economics*, 44(3): 447–457.

Bhattacherjee, D. (2002) 'Organized labour and economic liberalization in India: past, present, future', in Jose, A.V. (ed.) *Organized Labour in the 21st Century*, Geneva: International Institute of Labour Studies.

Bhaumik, S. (2003) 'Casualisation of the workforce in India, 1983–2002', *The Indian Journal of Labour Economics*, 46(4): 907–926.

Bhagwati, J. (2004) 'Wages and labor standards at stake?', in Bhagwati, J., *In Defence of Globalization,* Oxford: Oxford University Press.

Bild, T., Brugiavini, A. and Calmfors, L. (1998) 'Do trade unions have a future? The case of Denmark', *Acta Sociologica*, 41: 195–207.

Calveley, M., Healy, G., Shelly, S., Stirling, J. and Wray, D. (2003) 'Union learning representatives – a force for renewal or 'partnership'?', paper at the 21st International Labour Process Conference, Bristol Business School, University of the West of England.

Datt, R. (2003) 'National Commission on Labour and Review of Labour Laws', *The Indian Journal of Labour Economics*, 46(1).

Datta, R. (2001) 'Economic reforms, redundancy and national renewal fund: human face or human mask?', *The Indian Journal of Labour Economics*, 44(4): 675–689.

Deshpande, L.K., Sharma, A.N., Karan, A.K. and Sarkar, S. (2004) *Liberalisation and Labour: Labour Flexibility in Indian Manufacturing*, New Delhi, Institute for Human Development.

Deshpande, L.K. (2001) 'Labour flexibility in India', *The Indian Journal of Labour Economics*, 44(3): 339–411.

Dhal, M. and Srivastava, K.B.L. (2003) 'Union effectiveness in changing industrial relations climate', *The Indian Journal of Labour Economics*, 46(4): 737–744.

Frenkel, S. and Kuruvilla, S. (2002) 'Logics of action, globalization, and the changing employment relations in China, India, Malaysia, and the Philippines', *Industrial and Labour Relations Review,* 55(3): 387–412.

Goldsmith, J. (1995) *The Response: GATT and Global Free Trade.* Macmillan UK.

Haynes, P. and Allen, M. (2001) 'Partnership as union strategy: a preliminary evaluation', *Employee Relations* 23(2): 164–87.

Hooiveld, J., Sprenger, W. and Van Rij, C. (2002) 'Twenty years after 2000', *Zeggenschap* 13(4): 32–36.

Huzzard, T., Gregory, D. and Scott, R. (2004) 'Strategic unionism and partnership: boxing or dancing?', paper at the 22nd International Labour Process Conference, University of Amsterdam, Netherlands.

Kannan, K.P. (1999) 'Changing economic structure and labour institutions in India: some reflections on emerging perspectives on organising the unorganised', *The Indian Journal of Labour Economics*, 42(4): 753–776.

Kelly, J. (2004) 'Social partnership agreements in Britain' in Stuart, M. and Martinez Lucio, M. (eds) *Partnership and Modernisation in Employment Relations*, London and NY: Routledge.

Kuruvilla, S., Das, S., Kwon, H. and Kwon, S. (2002) 'Trade union growth and decline in Asia', *British Journal of Industrial Relations*, 40(3): 431–461.

Kuruvilla, S. and Hiers, W. (2000) 'Globalization and industrial relations in India', Report for the International Labour Organization, Regional Office for Asia and the Pacific, Bangkok.

Martinez Lucio, M. and Stuart, M. (2004) 'Swimming against the tide: social partnership, mutual gains and the revival of tired HRM', *International Journal of Human Resource Management*, 15(2): 404–418.

Mathur, A.N. (1991) *Industrial Restructuring and Union Power*, New Delhi: ILO-ARTEP.

Mathur, A.N. (1992) 'Employment security and industrial restructuring in India', paper presented at the national seminar on Restructuring Indian Economy, Jan 17–18, Calcutta.

National Association of Software and Service Companies (NASSCOM) (2005) www.nasscom.org, accessed July 20, 2005.

National Commission on Labour (2002) Ministry of Labour, Government of India: www.labour.nic.in/lcomm2/nlc_report.html

Papola, T.S. (2004) 'Globalisation, employment and social protection: emerging perspectives for the Indian workers', *The Indian Journal of Labour Economics*, 47(3): 541–550.

Ramaswamy, E.A. (1997) *A Question of Balance: Labour, Management and Society,* Oxford: Oxford University Press.

Ramaswamy, E.A. (1999) 'Changing economic structures and future of trade unions', *The Indian Journal of Labour Economics*, 42(4): 785–792.

Rubinstein, S.A. (2001) 'A different kind of union: balancing co-management and representation', *Industrial Relations*, 40(2): 163–203.

Sen Gupta, A.K. and Sett, P.K. (2000) 'Industrial relations law, employment security and collective bargaining in India: myths, realities and hopes', *Industrial Relations Journal,* 31(2): 144–153.

Shyam Sundar, K.R. (2003) 'Industrial conflicts in India in the Reform Decade', *The Indian Journal of Labour Economics*, 46(4): 703–724.

Sprenger, W. and van Klaveren, M. (2004) 'Boxing and dancing: options in strategic choices for innovating trade unions', paper for the 22nd International Labour Process Conference, University of Amsterdam, Netherlands.

Venkat Ratnam, C.S. (2000) 'Competitive labour policies and labour laws in Indian states', *The Indian Journal of Labour Economics*, 43(4).

Venkat Ratnam, C.S. and Verma, A. (2004) 'Non-governmental organisations and trade unions: the case of India' in Verma, A. and Kochan, T.A. (eds) *Unions in the 21st Century*, Palgrave Macmillan.

Website of the Labour Bureau Government of India: http://labourbureau.nic.in

Website of the Confederation of Indian Industry: www.ciionline.org

Suggested key readings

Badigannavar, V. and Kelly, J. (2004) 'Labour-management partnership in the UK public sector' in Kelly, J. and Willman, P. (eds) *Union Organization and Activity,* London: Routledge.

Bhattacherjee, D. (2002) 'Organized labour and economic liberalization in India: past, present, future' in Jose, A.V. (ed.) *Organized Labour in the 21st Century*, Geneva: International Institute of Labour Studies.

Datt, R. (2003) 'National Commission on Labour and Review of Labour Laws', *The Indian Journal of Labour Economics*, 46(1).

Deshpande, L.K., Sharma, A.N., Karan, A.K., and Sarkar, S. (2004) *Liberalisation and Labour: Labour Flexibility in Indian Manufacturing*, New Delhi: Institute for Human Development.

Frenkel, S. and Kuruvilla, S. (2002) 'Logics of action, globalization, and the changing employment relations in China, India, Malaysia, and the Philippines', *Industrial and Labour Relations Review,* 55(3): 387–412.

Kuruvilla, S. and Hiers, W. (2000) *'Globalization and Industrial Relations in India'*, report for the International Labour Organization, Regional Office for Asia and the Pacific, Bangkok.

Papola, T.S. (2004) 'Globalisation, employment and social protection: emerging perspectives for the Indian workers', *The Indian Journal of Labour Economics*, 47(3): 541–550.

Ramaswamy, E.A. (1999) 'Changing economic structures and future of trade unions', *The Indian Journal of Labour Economics*, 42(4): 785–792.

Sen Gupta, A.K. and Sett, P.K. (2000) 'Industrial relations law, employment security and collective bargaining in India: myths, realities and hopes', *Industrial Relations Journal* 31(2): 144–153.

Venkat Ratnam, C.S. and Verma, A. (2004) 'Non-governmental organisations and trade unions: the case of India', in Verma, A. and Kochan, T.A. (eds) *Unions in the 21st Century*, UK: Palgrave Macmillan.

Part II

Contemporary developments in global industrial relations

10 International trends in unionization

CAROLA FREGE

Introduction

Despite structural shifts in the economy and in politics at both the international and national levels, trade unions retain important functions for capitalist economies as well as for political democracies. The ongoing crisis unions are facing all over the industrialized and developing world is an important issue. There is a growing concern that the labour movement may have reached a historical turning point. For those who believe that strong unions are essential characteristics of an efficient and fair market economy as well as of a healthy political democracy, these developments are worrying indeed. Union decline threatens not only the collective regulation of industrial relations (safeguarding better wages, working conditions and job security) but it also affects, if more indirectly, the quality of the broader civil society and political life by weakening one of its largest and most significant civil actors or, in the developing world, by not developing unions to support the growth of civil society (Kelly and Frege 2004: 1). In fact, unions may even be more necessary than ever before in playing a pivotal role in the growing resistance to corporate-led globalization (cf. Turner in Frege and Kelly 2004).

For some observers, the globalization of production, trade and investment is the driving force behind union decline. In recent years, the classic convergence theory originated by Kerr *et al.* (1960), has been revived and reworked into what is now frequently referred to as globalization theory, although there are several different accounts of the mechanisms that are supposed to produce similar economic structures and outcomes (cf. Weiss 2003). Technology, the internationalization of markets and market competition, and the erosion of collective institutions by opportunism have all been identified as possible forces for convergence across countries (Traxler *et al.* 2001: 287).

In particular, competitive pressures have significantly reduced employment levels in heavily unionized Western manufacturing industries as well as in some parts of the service sector during the past twenty years. The growing mobility of capital has greatly enhanced its bargaining power, weakening the scope for unions to extract concessions and demonstrate their effectiveness to workers not just in the West but also in developing countries. These same pressures have been reinforced by countries, anxious to retain national production sites and to attract foreign direct investment, and in the case of European countries, eager to comply with the disinflationary regime of monetary union. The logic of this form of globalization thesis is to predict a degree of convergence in the fate of union movements across the advanced capitalist as well as developing worlds. Since these movements everywhere are subject to increasingly similar economic and political pressures, albeit to somewhat varying degrees, then the associated phenomenon of union decline should be common, if not universal (Kelly and Frege 2004).

The alternative scenario is a continuing divergence of capitalist economies in the advanced as well as developing world. The 'new institutionalists' (e.g. Dore 1986; Hall and Soskice 2001; Hollingsworth and Boyer 1994; Weiss 2003) argue that markets and technologies are far from fully determining the structures and performance of capitalist economies and that national economic institutions can make a significant difference. The very idea of alternative and variation and choice implies that, to some extent at least, purposeful collective action – in one word: politics – can make a difference even and precisely for the nature of advanced capitalism (Crouch and Streeck 1997: 1). Thus, taken one step further, it can be argued that the strategies pursued by the major actors – employers, unions, and political parties – can also make a difference to economic and industrial relations outcomes. Actors' strategies are therefore embedded in specific national histories as well as in their current institutional structures. In recent years an increasing number of studies – of state economic policies and welfare programmes for example – have found less evidence of globalization-driven convergence and rather more of 'path dependent' divergence (Boix 1998; Hall and Soskice 2001; Swank 2002; Traxler *et al.* 2001). These studies have also highlighted the importance of actors' strategies within the different political economies. In particular, the highly influential work of Hall and Soskice (2001) has forcefully argued that employer strategies and national institutions vary significantly across countries thereby giving rise to different forms of capitalism and consequently of unions and their position in society. They distinguish between three forms of capitalism in the advanced industrialized world. These are characterized by different logics and forms of regulation: the liberal market economy (e.g. the US and UK) where the market obtains a dominant role of regulation, the co-ordinated economy (e.g. Sweden or Germany) where the market as well as society regulate industrial relations, and the Mediterranean economies (e.g. Italy and Spain) where politics or the state perform a major role in industrial relations. Transitional and developing economies, which are characterized by relatively unstable, not fully institutionalized industrial relations, were left out in their framework. However, one can discuss to what extent these countries will create their own distinctive systems or will develop along the lines of one of the three Western models. In sum, this theory argues that globalization does not necessarily produce convergence and that the national divergencies of capitalism and of industrial relations continue to exist.

This chapter will investigate the explanatory power of both theories, the convergence and the divergence thesis, for union decline. We focus on union membership trends as one major indicator of union strength or decline (others are bargaining coverage, see Chapter 12, and strike level, see Chapter 13). The present chapter starts by outlining the difficulties in defining and measuring union membership. We will then analyse the recent trends of unionization across the world, to what extent union decline is a universal phenomenon and its potential reasons. We can diagnose a trend of union membership decline in most countries, which on the surface may support the convergence thesis. However, more importantly as we argue, there is profound cross-country variation in the extent of decline, which is consistent with the logic of different national varieties of capitalism.

Methodology: union strength and union membership

Union density or unionization rate is a tool to measure union presence in society and is usually defined as the ratio of actual union membership to potential membership. There are various difficulties in measuring density levels across countries, which we will briefly outline. First, as Visser (2003) has pointed out, most discussions on densities are restricted to the OECD countries because union membership data on other regions of the world are hard to find. As far as we know, Visser's statistics (ibid.) are the first attempt to compare density levels across 103 countries, which together make up 2.5 billion of the three billion people, who according to the ILO (International Labour Organization), form the world's labour force (ILO 1998: 1). This chapter will therefore rely on his data set.

Second, cross-country comparisons of unionization rates are frequently difficult to perform. Membership data are based on self-reporting, either on the basis of reports of unions and/or their federations or from individual workers in the case of official labour force statistics or from enterprise surveys (Visser 2003: 375). Consequently, membership sources are often unreliable. For example, different countries may have different definitions of what constitutes a union (e.g. are all official unions registered?). Moreover, if the density data come from unions themselves as is usually the case (cf. www.eiro.eurofound.eu.int/tradeunion membership1993–2003) they may sometimes exaggerate their membership numbers for political reasons. In addition, unions frequently include in their statistics unemployed, retired, students and other non-active people. Different unions may also use different estimates of the potential membership and may use different definitions of the labour force and of eligible members. For example, eligibility of membership differs from country to country. In many countries senior civil servants and those working in basic public services such as police, military, teachers, etc. are not permitted to join a union. Taking these differences into account would make comparisons across countries extremely difficult. Moreover, as Visser (2003: 369) explains, potential membership can be differently defined, either as the non-agricultural labour force (which includes many categories of workers such as self-employed and unpaid family workers who do not belong to the traditional target population of unions), or as the formal sector of employment for wages and salaries, including agriculture. The latter definition provides a narrower concept of the potential membership, which makes density numbers slightly higher than the former definition. Visser (2003: 369) suggests that restricting the definition to people who work for wages and salaries, including agriculture, yields a potential membership closer to the target population as is prescribed in most legal statutes and union by-laws. On the other hand, it can be argued that wage and salary earners are no longer the only constituency of trade unions. The boundary between employment and self-employment is weakening in many countries (temporary work, freelancers, outsourcing etc.). According to the 'eiro' (European industrial relations observatory: 14) this has led to a growing interest in 'economically dependent workers' – workers who are potentially self-employed but depend on a single employer for their income. We agree with them and will therefore use the non-agricultural labour force as our definition of potential membership.

Finally, there are also problems about how to interpret the importance of union densities for a particular union. For example, small unions may be weak but if the membership is highly active they may be very effective in organizing work stoppages or strikes. Moreover, if an increasing percentage of union members are pensioners, as in the case of German unions, the pure membership numbers do not mirror unions' actual power on the labour market.

Given all these problems one may wonder about the benefits of comparing unionization rates. However, most scholars agree that union densities are nevertheless useful indicators of broader trends, in particular when compared over time. Moreover, a comparison of union densities on the basis of the two different definitions of potential membership (i.e. non-agricultural labour force and formal employment) showed both to be significantly correlated (Visser 2003: 372).

Data: International unionization rates

We present figures from Visser (2003) who calculated densities for two time periods, 1985 and 1997. As stated above, the Visser data set is the most comprehensible in terms of country coverage and is also the most standardized survey we are aware of. There are more recent membership figures available (e.g. eiro online or ILO) but these are unstandardized in terms of membership and of potential membership and are therefore difficult to compare cross-nationally. Moreover, the more recent membership figures of 'eiro' for European countries in 2003 confirm the trends presented in Visser's data set. We can therefore safely hypothesize that the broad picture of the mid-1980s and 1990s persists in the early 2000s.

Overall, the current total number of union members in the world can be estimated at around 320 million people: 91 million in China, 65 million in Russia, Ukraine and Belarus, 61 million in Europe (thirty-three countries) (excluding retired and unemployed, otherwise 74 million), 38 million in Asia (sixteen countries), 14 million in Africa (twenty-eight countries), 24 million in North America (Canada, US, Mexico) and 29 million in Central and Latin America (nineteen countries) (Visser 2003: 366). Visser estimated that the global union density is 23 per cent (excluding the world's labour force involved in agriculture) and also calculated regional densities. Average density rates are high in Russia (58 per cent) and China (42 per cent), medium in Europe (26 per cent) and in South America (25 per cent), and lower in Africa (16 per cent), North America (13 per cent) and Asia (10 per cent). These regional figures obviously do not take cross-country variations into account.

In the following six tables we present membership and density figures from Visser 2003 of selected countries in Western and Eastern Europe, North and South America, Oceania, Asia, as well as the Middle East and Africa. We thereby cover advanced industrialized countries (Western Europe, Israel, Turkey, North America, Oceania, Japan), transitional economies (Central Eastern Europe and Asia), as well as developing and poor countries (South America, Africa, Middle East). We have only selected countries, which possess data of the mid-1980s, and 1990s (e.g. most Middle Eastern countries are therefore missing). Since Chapters one to nine in this volume have widely discussed the industrial relations system and developments in these regions we will restrict ourselves to summarizing the basic developments of union densities in the advanced industrialized regions and in the transitional and developing economies. One should note that the ultimate country classifications are arbitrary and static and do not do justice to countries on the verge of developing to transitional or from transitional to advanced industrialized economies.

Advanced industrialized economies: North America, Oceania, Japan and Western Europe, Turkey and Israel

As is well known, the advanced industrialized countries with long-established industrial relations systems have experienced a continuing trend of union decline to varying degrees. The decline began in the latter years of the 1970s, generalized in the 1980s, and was more pronounced in the private sector of the economy. The United States was the first country to experience significant decline in union membership. In the 1950s US density was one-third of wage and salary earners in employment; in 1985 this proportion has been halved, and in 2000 it reached 13 per cent (Visser 2003: 381). Other Anglo-Saxon countries have followed the US trend but at a slower rate. Union density in Canada dropped from 34.6 per cent in 1985 to 30 per cent in 2000 (Visser 2003: 381). Similar developments occurred in Australia and New Zealand. Compared to the rest of the world, unions in the liberal market economies were the first to experience union decline in the industrialized world and subsequently experienced the longest density decline throughout the 1980s and 1990s. Well-known reasons are the decentralized industrial relations structure with non-existent employers' associations, decentralized wage bargaining, and unfavourable, often explicitly anti-union government policies and legislation.

In Europe, some countries managed to evade the downward trend during the 1980s, despite high unemployment (e.g. Britain, Belgium and Denmark), due to their union participation in the administration of unemployment insurance. During the 1990s virtually all European countries – especially Scandinavian ones – experienced stagnating or declining membership numbers (Visser 2004: 375). The aggregated union density in the European Union fell from 37.3 per cent in 1985 to 29.5 per cent in 1997. This trend is most visible in the large European countries (Britain, France, Germany, and to a lesser extent Italy) since unification in 1990. Since the mid-1980s density rates dropped by 34 per cent in Britain, 28 per cent in France, 27 per cent in Germany (since 1990) and 11 per cent in Italy. These figures can be compared to similar developments in other advanced

Table 10.1 Union membership and density in North America, Oceania and Japan

Country	Period t_1–t_2	Members t_1	Members t_2	Density t_1	Density t_2
Australia	1985–96	2793.0	2450.0	40.9	28.3
Canada	1985–98	3730.0	4010.0	30.2	26.9
New Zealand	1985–99	683.0	302.4	52.5	17.6
United States	1985–00	16996.1	16258.0	15.2	11.7
Japan	1985–00	12,417.5	11,539.0	22.8	17.8

Source: Visser 2003

Table 10.2 Union membership and density in selected countries of western Europe,
Turkey and Israel

Country	Period t_1–t_2	Members* t_1	Members t_2	Density t_1	Density** t_2
Austria	1985–99	1419.6	1209.3	46.3	33.4
Belgium	1985–95	1461.9	1611.1	49.0	51.0
Britain	1985–97	9738.9	7015.5	36.3	24.7
Denmark	1985–99	1726.5	1816.0	69.2	72.0
Finland	1985–98	1427.2	1443.7	66.6	73.2
France	1985–98	2443.0	2000.0	11.2	8.2
Germany W	1985–90	7892.8	8013.8	29.0	27.7
Germany	1991–98	11969.4	8326.9	32.7	21.7
Greece	1985–95	664.0	430.0	23.3	12.4
Iceland	1985–98	83.0	106.1	76.8	76.1
Italy***	1985–98	6125.5	5481.5	29.6	25.3
Luxembourg	1987–95	75.0	85.0	48.1	39.9
Norway	1985–97	1001.5	1103.7	53.0	51.2
Portugal	1986–95	1434.0	800.0	40.3	18.8
Spain	1985–97	672.4	1582.6	6.1	10.5
Sweden	1985–98	3247.9	3050.4	79.5	79.3
Switzerland	1985–99	808.9	729.6	25.4	18.9
EU 15	1985–97	40070.3	36869.7	29.3	22.8
Turkey	1987–99	1594.6	2988.0	16.3	21.7
Israel	1985–98	1850.0	450.0	99.1	18.9

* Without retired, unemployed and self-employed members (in the UK and Ireland a 10 per cent discount is applied)
** Unemployed members included in Sweden, Iceland, Denmark, Finland and Belgium (the five countries where the unemployed retain membership for insurance reasons)
*** Italian membership are based on the three main confederations excluding around 10–20 per cent members of non-affiliated unions
Source: Visser 2003

industrialized countries such as the US and Japan (25 per cent decline in each case), and around 10 per cent in Canada.

While some of the smaller European countries slightly increased membership in the early 1990s (such as in Finland, Sweden, Iceland, Belgium or Spain), this frequently only made up for earlier losses and the trend went into reverse in the late 1990s (eiro online trade union membership data for 1993–2003). All other smaller countries[1] experienced losses except Spain, which increased its membership between 1998 to 2003 by 0.8 per cent, and Luxembourg (plus 14.0 per cent).

In sum, Europe is an interesting case study since countries face to a certain extent similar socio-economic developments (as did the North American and Oceanian countries) which explain density decline, such as rising unemployment since the late 1970s, a shift towards the service sector, privatisation of the public services, increase in part-time and flexible work contracts, increase of female labour force, and increasing international competition (e.g. single market). On the other hand, national specific industrial relations institutions and practices are much more varied among European countries than in North America and Oceania and these differences explain the varying degrees of density decline. For example, one continues to find a North-South divide with higher levels of density in the Nordic countries than in Southern Europe, partly due to fewer divisions between competing union confederations and long-standing corporatist arrangements with employers and governments. In Southern Europe there is more competition between different union federations, more dependency on rival political parties and contingent government support, less stable collective bargaining arrangements, and, with the exception of Italy, a more limited and fragile form of union presence at the workplace (Visser 2003: 378).

Finally, we included Turkey (a potential candidate for European Union membership) and Israel since their economic and political situation (being the only two democracies in that region) is more similar to European than to Middle Eastern countries. The Turkish data suggest strong growth in the 1980s when union repression eased but show a slight decline in the 1990s. As Visser (2003: 389) states, more research is needed to explain this development. Israel also experienced membership losses, partly due to the changes in the National Health Insurance Law and the political defeat of the Labour Party in 1994 (Visser 2003: 389). Lastly, in Japan, which though an Asian country, belongs to the advanced industrialized economies, unions have continued to lose ground since the Second World War, when the then militant Japanese unions organized 55 per cent of the Japanese wage earners (Visser 2003: 384). One reason for the decline is that employment in the large companies, which personified the harmonious co-operative Japanese industrial relations model, has fallen sharply and companies outside this network are rarely targeted by enterprise unions (Chalmers 1989; Dore 2000).

Transitional and developing economies: Central Eastern Europe, South and South East Asia, Middle East, Africa and South America

Overall, although developing and transitional economies are socio-economically and politically very diverse they share some basic common features with regard to industrial relations. Western-style unions and industrial relations regulations are a relatively new phenomenon in these economies and unions encounter enduring difficulties in developing a forceful movement. If unions are not

Table 10.3 Union membership and density in selected countries of Central Eastern Europe

Country	Period t_1–t_2	Members t_1	Members t_2	Density t_1	Density t_2
Bulgaria	1991–95	2200.0	1500.0	62.0	37.7
Czech Rep.	1990–95	3820.0	1886.0	79.6	39.2
Estonia	1989–95	580.0	166.6	82.9	24.1
Hungary	1985–98	3000.0	1000.0	74.1	27.6
Poland	1989–99	6300.0	2700.0	47.1	18.5
Romania	1991–95	4000.0	3100.0	50.7	34.1
Russian Fed.	1985–98	70,000.0	40,000.0	91.4	58.2
Slovakia	1990–95	1920.0	1150.0	73.8	50.9
Ukraine	1985–96	26,000.0	21,850.0	100.0	99.3

Source: Visser 2003

repressed by authoritarian states, they are likely to become collaborators or extensions of political parties and perform a political role rather than a role as independent labour market actors (Ost and Crowley 2001 for Central Eastern Europe). In other words, in most countries industrial relations practices have not yet developed into institutional systems, which are quasi-independent from the political as well as economic sphere and thus are regulated by their own institutions and rules and without too much interference from the state. In these circumstances unions struggle to become independent actors. In addition, a fragile, corrupt or authoritarian state, a weak economy and rising international competition, the globalization of capital and product markets and the increasing interference of international bodies such as the WTO or IMF, make it difficult for developing and transitional economies to establish a pluralistic industrial relations system. This is ideally based on a power balance between the three actors, state, employers and unions. This provides a legal framework, which is

Table 10.4 Union membership and density in selected countries in South and South-east Asia

Country	Period t_1–t_2	Members t_1	Members t_2	Density t_1	Density t_2
China	1985–97	85,258.0	91,310.0	59.4	42.2
India	1980–91	5917.0	4256.0	6.6	2.8
Philippines	1985–96	2117.0	3587.0	18.4	21.7
Singapore	1985–98	201.1	272.8	17.0	15.4
South Korea	1985–99	1004.4	1481.0	8.5	7.8
Taiwan	1985–98	1549.0	3135.9	22.2	26.5
Thailand	1985–99	234.4	100.0	3.3	0.7

Source: Visser 2003

Table 10.5 Union membership and density in selected countries in the Middle East and Africa

Country	Period t_1–t_2	Members t_1	Members t_2	Density t_1	Density t_2
Egypt	1985–95	2720.0	3313.1	38.9	21.7
Syria	1985–96	437.3	644.9	20.7	21.1
Kenya	1985–95	700.0	500.0	41.9	18.3
South Africa	1985–98	1391.4	3202.0	15.5	21.2
Uganda	1989–95	101.5	62.6	7.8	3.8
Nigeria	1982–95	3000.0	3520.0	20.0	13.3
Zambia	1985–95	320.1	273.1	36.1	29.3

Source: Visser 2003

an executive (law enforcement) as well as a legitimate, uncontested role for unions representing workers' interests in the workplace and within society at large. The more likely scenario is, therefore, a quasi-dependency of industrial relations on the state, open or covert repression of unions, as well as strong pressure from employers to liberalize the labour market. The traditional Western-style industrial relations regulations such as collective bargaining, social partnership or co-determination exist, if at all, on a fragile basis. Collective bargaining is mostly decentralized if it happens at all. Corporatist arrangements, though popular, for example, in Central Eastern European countries, are mostly ineffective and often merely a political tool to get unions to agree to neo-liberal political reforms which are ultimately against the interests of the union constituency (Ost 2000).

In more detail, in the transitional former socialist economies of Central Eastern Europe conditions for unions have the additional problem of dealing with the

Table 10.6 Union membership and density in selected countries in South America

Country	Period t_1–t_2	Members t_1	Members t_2	Density t_1	Density t_2
Argentina	1986–95	3262.0	3200.0	48.7	25.4
Domin. Rep.	1989–95	360.0	450.1	18.9	17.6
Chile	1985–98	361.0	600.0	11.6	13.1
Columbia	1985–95	877.0	840.0	11.2	7.3
Cuba	1985–95	2892.8	2771.5	65.4	63.6
Guatemala	1985–94	65.2	88.6	7.7	4.8
Mexico	1991–97	7000.0	4000.0	31.0	13.9
Venezuela	1988–93	1700.0	1153.1	25.9	15.3

Source: Visser 2003
1. No data available for Norway.

legacy of the former socialist union movement (China is increasingly following their course). Unions are generally weak, not just because of the challenging economic conditions but also because of their historical legacies and current structural conditions. Since the former socialist unions were essentially bureaucratic arms of the Socialist Party State and mainly involved in the general welfare of the workforce but not in representing workers' interests regarding working conditions or pay, workers became disillusioned about the benefits of union membership after the collapse of the socialist regimes. This lack of trust among workers towards their collective representatives continued to challenge unions' efforts to regain legitimacy after the collapse of socialism, and made it difficult for unions to modernize (Frege 2000). Moreover, the transition to the market economy and sharply rising unemployment, increasing union rivalry, and non-supportive governments made it increasingly difficult for unions to keep their original high membership levels. In fact, countries which have been most successful in their transition to a free market economy, like Poland or Hungary, yield much lower membership levels than countries which took a slower route (e.g. Slovakia or Bulgaria) or are still socialist (e.g. Cuba).

In sum, the transition of unions from embedded political institutions of the old regime towards becoming independent actors that are instrumental in representing workers' economic and political interests in a marketizing and democratizing society has not to date proved successful.

It is slightly more complicated to analyse the union situation in Asia since it comprises very different economic and political developments in East Asian countries (South Korea, Hong Kong, Singapure and Taiwan), the 'Tigers' of South East Asia (Phillipines, Indonesia, Malaysia, Thailand and Vietnam) and China and the Indian subcontinent. However, despite this variation in the socio-economic environment of unions the union functioning in these countries shares many similarities. Industrial relations institutions are not strongly embedded in the political and economic culture, collective bargaining is decentralized if it exists at all, and most importantly, in many countries the state heavily controls industrial relations and, except in India (due to the legacy of the British colonial rulers), represses the union movement (Kuruvilla and Mundell 1999). A good example is South Korea where, despite the economic and democratic progress, industrial relations are still an unfriendly environment for unions, with many legal restrictions despite the fact that the union movement contributed significantly to the country's democratization (Song 2002).

Industrial relations and unions in the poorer or developing world are characterized by the dominance of the agricultural sector and small industrial sectors (such as textiles), which are exceedingly exposed to world market competition. In South America the union situation is generally characterized by the liberalization of the economy, the end of state-corporatist and populist models and concomitant forms of state–union relations, and the informalization of employment (Visser 2003: 394).

Typically, unions were state-sponsored and part of the bureaucratic–authoritarian regimes, and thus tied to government parties through clientelism. In some countries unions played an active role in overthrowing military regimes and in developing democracy (e.g. Brazilian unions in the 1980s). Finally, as Visser (2003: 391) suggests, it is hard to make general statements about developments in Africa. The economies are in decline because of or despite globalization and the opening of world trade. Civil war and ethnic conflicts provide unstable political regimes, which are not conducive for unions. Unsurprisingly, therefore, we observe in Africa the lowest unionization rates in the world.

Discussion

There are two main observations to be discussed. The data reveal a nearly universal trend of union membership decline during the 1980s and 1990s. At the same time, however, there is evidence of a continuing cross-country variation of union membership levels. Thus, although most countries experience declining numbers they do so in varying degrees. There is no convergence of membership levels, not even within the countries of the European Union, which increasingly share common political, legal and socio-economic developments. Now we will briefly review the main explanations for union density decline as well as for varying levels of union density.

How can we explain the universal pattern of decline in unionization?

Researchers have pointed to various factors. Metcalf (2005) for example argues that union growth or decline, is a function of five factors: the business cycle, workforce composition and the policies of the unions, the state and employer. Visser (1994) lists rising unemployment, inflation, decentralization of production and sectoral change, social attitudes and employer choice. These specific economic and labour market conditions have empirically proved to have a strong impact on membership numbers. A major underlying theme is the changing nature of capitalist production, thus the advent of so-called post-Fordism, second modernity or risk society (Beck 2000: 18). This is characterized by the structural decline of paid employment through the increased introduction of labour-saving technologies, individualization, globalization and gender revolution. These broad developments have implications on the socio-economic context that unions are working in, as well as on employer, state, union and worker strategies.

In particular, major themes in industrial relations in the last two decades were decentralization, flexible production and human resource management (Baglioni and Crouch 1990; Kochan *et al.* 1989; Piore and Sabel 1984). Under pressure from international markets, employers throughout the world became convinced that they had to find cheaper and more flexible solutions for industrial relations rather than uniform and centralized ones, that closer, more direct co-ordination with the market was needed and that customer service and quality were important competitive factors (Visser 1995: 65). At the same time, there is a sectoral employment change away from high-density industries and firms towards the service sector and white collar work – areas traditionally less attracted to unions. Highly skilled workers may be less inclined to commit to a union especially if they change jobs on a regular basis (thus individual labour market power and job mobility has a negative impact on workers' likelihood to unionize).

Related to this, the most important challenge for the labour movement throughout the world is usually seen to be internationalization or globalization. The increasing pressure of economic and political interdependence on a world scale has changed the rules of the game. In particular, the national models of industrial relations or the varieties of capitalism (Hall and Soskice 2001), which proved successful during the twentieth century, are now in a deep crisis. The nation state's role in a globalized market economy may be declining and this has dramatic implications not just for the industrial relations systems, which heavily rely on the state, like most countries in continental Europe, but also for the union movement as a whole. Despite the ideology of international worker solidarity, unions are by nature national entities and are organized within the national framework of industrial relations.

Furthermore, political scientists have pointed more specifically to changing politics, whereby political parties traditionally linked to the labour movement have started to loosen the links to the unions (such as the Labour Party in Britain or more recently the Social Democratic Party, SPD, in Germany). Moreover, various countries have experienced significant changes in government politics towards trade unions. In the West, the election of President Reagan in the US and Prime Minister Thatcher in Great Britain, for example, radically changed the role of the state in industrial relations. Mrs Thatcher began her policy of the 'rejection of compromise' (Crouch 1990), meaning that she intended to reduce the trade union to a mere interest group of minor importance. The emphasis of industrial relations shifted from the national to the company level, and from the political to the economic arena.

Finally, scholars have also pointed to sociological trends, such as the increased numbers of women and immigrants in the workforce, the individualization and higher education of workers as well as higher mobility endangering the classic blue collar working class communities with their traditionally strong union consciousness (Frege and Kelly 2004, chapter 2; Heery 2003). There is also a shift in public opinion and policy making questioning the necessity and power of the traditional collective labour market actors and emphasizing individual freedom in the labour market (Bacon and Storey 1993; Beck 2000; Dobbin and Sutton 1998).

In sum, there are major economic, political and societal factors, which help to explain the membership decline and crisis of most union movements across countries in the late twentieth and early twenty-first century.

What accounts for varying levels of union densities across countries?

The variation in union densities is usually attributed to the specific situation of trade unions in each country and the structural characteristics of national industrial relations systems such as government policies, labour laws and the economic conditions. For example, Clegg (1976: 27) has linked union density with collective bargaining coverage: 'Inter-country divergences are explained by variations in the extent and depth of collective bargaining and in support for union [membership] security, either directly from employers or through collective agreements'. Therefore, the greater the 'depth' of bargaining (in terms of the involvement of local union officers and shop stewards) and union support, then the higher the density, since members will be attracted if workplace benefits are secured and workplace services are provided. Bean and Holden (1992) found evidence for this thesis in a study of sixteen OECD countries. A positive association was found between union membership and the percentage of employees covered by collective agreements, together also with the degree of centralization of wage bargaining.

Another factor is whether unions are involved in administrating unemployment insurance schemes, which provides one of the strongest incentives for union membership. In countries like Sweden, Denmark, Finland or Belgium, the so-called 'Ghent' system of unemployment insurance is a system whereby unions control the unemployment insurance funds. Another example, in countries (such as Britain or the US) which have decentralized, company-level collective bargaining, the law usually requires that an entire workplace must be unionized to force the employer into collective bargaining. Such statutory requirements make organizing campaigns more difficult than in countries with centralized collective bargaining (e.g. in continental Europe) where organizing is not related to collective bargaining coverage since industry level bargaining agreements automatically cover all companies in one industry.

One may also point to a frequent argument that unified (or non-competitive) union organizations are associated with higher levels of unionization. Thus, the more integrated Scandinavian unions and national federations do better than Britain or the US where factionalism has predominated.

Moreover, the specifics of the national economies have an impact such as, for example, structural changes away from manufacturing towards a service economy. In countries, where the service sector dominates (such as in the US), membership organization is more difficult as white collar workers are more difficult to recruit. Moreover, the size of the public sector of a country is strongly and positively correlated to union density. Thus, the Nordic European countries profit from a relatively large public sector and this correlates with their high density figures.

Finally, union membership is not only shaped by different laws or structural conditions but also by differing strategies and roles of unions and of employers.

For example, union membership is heavily influenced by the identity or role unions are pursuing in a particular country.

Unions are generally defined as institutional, collective representatives of worker interests both within the labour market and in the wider society. They can, however, pursue different functions in different national and historical contexts and they display a multiplicity of organizational forms and ideological orientations (Hyman 2001: 1). Thus, unions may be seen as primary labour market actors engaged in collective bargaining over the terms and conditions of employment. This is the traditional union pattern in Anglo-Saxon countries. They may also be defined as social movements aiming at emancipating workers and improving their social status in society at large. In Europe, unions evolved before the advent of universal suffrage, and they played an important role in the struggle to extend democracy to the working class as well confronting employers in a frequently militant class struggle. In some developing and transitional economies such as in Asia or South America we can see similar developments of unions as democratizing agencies (e.g. Brazil or South Korea). Finally, unions can be seen as interest organizations, which put pressures on governments and political parties and are therefore components of the civil society engaging in the political order (Hyman 2001). German unions or the union movements of the Scandinavian countries are typical examples.

Related to their main functions or identities, unions have access to a variety of power resources. Overall, union strength depends on their economic (bargaining) and membership power (membership numbers, membership composition), their organizational vitality (internal democracy, efficient organization, centralized decision-making), and institutional power. The latter comprises legislation and coalition building with political, social and economic actors, in other words, unions relations to political parties, to other social movements and to business and employers' associations.

In some countries unions rely more on their institutional power provided by the state, such as favourable labour legislation, pro-union government policies or an institutionalized system of collective bargaining, which is legally supported by the state. In other countries, unions may focus more on their membership strength and economic rather than political power. Thus, unions, which are more political actors than labour market institutions, may have a different priority towards membership organizing than unions which very much rely on large membership numbers to boost their labour market strength. To give an example: union densities in Spain and the US are at similar levels; however, Spanish unions are much more embedded in the political governance of their country than in US unions and are therefore less dependent on membership levels than the US. A similar example is France, which yields notoriously low-density levels, but French unions remain influential. Since their union membership comprises highly active members and unions have a long-standing strong political status, their actual power is much higher than their union density would suggest. In other words, the importance of membership or unionization for union strength varies from country to country. One needs to take the specific position of unions in each country into account, with regard to political, economic and social conditions. In Visser's terms (2003: 367):

> Although union density captures some aspects of union bargaining power – it is probably more difficult to replace striking workers in the short run when most of the firm's or industry's workers are unionized – as a full measure of union strength it is inadequate. We cannot get the complete picture without studying labour and association laws, collective bargaining practices, organisational charters, public roles of labour … without understanding how workers are convinced to stay, pay, and, if needed, to act.

These comparative difficulties are not unique to density rates. In interpreting other indicators of union strength such as collective bargaining coverage (Chapter 12) or strikes (Chapter 13) we encounter similar difficulties since they are equally embedded in the specific conditions of unions in particular countries. However, it cannot be denied that union membership is ultimately one of the most basic power resources of all unions. Without enough members unions would not have economic or political clout or any state support.

Conclusions

To conclude, this chapter discussed broad trends in union membership levels across the world. There were two main findings. Union members are declining all over the world and the longitudinal data from the mid-1980s and mid-1990s suggest a continuing trend. Thus, at the beginning of the twenty-first century the worldwide union movement is, without doubt, in a severe crisis. On the surface this seems to support the globalization or convergence theory. However, the findings also suggest an enduring variation of density levels across countries. Some countries do better than others. Density levels did not converge and did not even fall by the same rate, as the convergence thesis would predict, and these findings therefore support the varieties of capitalism hypothesis. Density levels indicate the historical legacies of national union movements, their strategies as well as their national specific social, economic and political context. National unions react differently to common challenges of globalization, they rely on different resources and pursue different strategies of revitalization. The meaning of union density levels can therefore only be understood if one takes a country's specific industrial relations system and its political and economic environment into account.

Note

1 No data available for Norway.

References

Bacon, N. and Storey, J. (1993). 'Individualization of the Employment Relationship and the Implications for Trade Unions', *Employee Relations*, 15(1): 5–17.

Baglioni, G. and Crouch, C. (eds) (1990). *European Industrial Relations: The Challenge of Flexibility*. London: Sage.

Bean, R. and Holden, K. (1992). 'Cross-national differences in trade union membership in OECD countries'. *Industrial Relations Journal*, 23: 52–4.

Beck, U. (2000). *The Brave New World of Work*. London: Polity Press.

Boix, C. (1998). *Political Parties, Growth and Equality: Conservative and Social Democratic Economic Strategies in the World Economy*. New York: Cambridge University Press.

Chalmers, N. (1989*). Industrial Relations in Japan: The Peripheral Workforce*. London: Routledge.

Clegg, H.A. (1976). *Trade Unionism under Collective Bargaining: A Theory Based on Comparisons of Six Countries*. Oxford: Basil Blackwell.

Crouch, C. (1990). 'United Kingdom: the rejection of compromise', in Baglioni, G. and Crouch, C. (eds) (1990). *European Industrial Relations: The Challenge of Flexibility*. London: Sage, 326–355.

Crouch, C. and Streeck, W. (1997). 'Introduction: The Future of Capitalist Diversity', in C. Crouch and W. Streeck (eds), *Political Economy of Modern Capitalism: Mapping Convergence and Diversity*. London: Sage, 1–18.

Dobbin, F. and Sutton, F. (1998). 'The strength of the weak state: The rights revolution and the rise of human resources management divisions', *The American Journal of Sociology*, 104(2): 441–476.

Dore, R.P. (1986). *Flexible Rigidities*. Stanford, CA: University of California Press.

Dore, R.P. (2000*). Stock Market Capitalism, Welfare Capitalism*: *Japan, Germany vs the Anglo-Saxons*. Oxford: Oxford University Press.

Frege, C. (2000). 'The illusion of union management cooperation in postcommunist Central and Eastern Europe', *East European Politics and Society*, 14(3): 636–660.

Hall, P.A. and Soskice, D. (eds) (2001). *Varieties of Capitalism: The Institutional Foundations of Comparative Advantage*. Oxford: Oxford University Press.

Heery, E. (2003). 'Trade unions and industrial relations', in P. Ackers and A. Wilkinson (eds) *Understanding Work and Employment*. Oxford: Oxford University Press, 278–304.

Hollingsworth, J.R. and Boyer, R. (eds) (1997). *Contemporary Capitalism: The Embeddedness of Institutions*. Cambridge: Cambridge University Press.

Hyman, R. (2001). *Understanding European Trade Unionism: Between Market Class and Society*. London: Sage.

ILO (1998). *World Employment Report 1998–99. Employment in the Global Economy. How Training Matters*. Geneva: International Labour Office.

Kelly, J. and Frege, C. (2004). 'Conclusion: Varieties of unionism' in C. Frege and J. Kelly (eds) *Varieties of Unionism: Strategies for Union Revitalization in a Globalizing Economy*. Oxford: Oxford University Press.

Kerr, C., Dunlop, J.T., Harbison, F.H. and Myers, C.A. (1960). *Industrialism and Industrial Man: The Problems of Labor and Management in Economic Growth*. Cambridge: Harvard University Press.

Kochan, T., Katz, H.C., and McKersie, R.B. (1986). *The Transformation of American Industrial Relations*. New York: Basic Books.

Kuruvilla, S. and Mundell, B. (1999). *Colonialism, Nationalism, and the Institutionalization of Industrial Relations in the Third World*. JAI Press.

Metcalf, D. (2005). 'Trade union trends' in S. Fernie and D. Metcalf (eds) *British Trade Unions: Resurgence or Perdition?* London: Routledge.

Ost, D. (2000). 'Illusory corporatism in Eastern Europe: Neoliberal tripartism and postcommunist class identities'. *Politics & Society*, 28(4): 503–530.

Ost, D. and Crowley, St. (2001). 'Making sense of labor weakness in postcommunism', in St. Crowley, and D. Ost (eds) *Workers after Workers' States*. Boulder: Rowman & Littlefield, 219–234.

Piore, M. and Sabel, C. (1984). *The Second Industrial Divide*. New York: Basic Books.

Song, Ho Keun (2002). 'Labour unions in the Republic of Korea: Challenge and choice' in A. V. Jose (ed.) *Organized Labour in the 21st Century*. Geneva: International Institute for Labour Studies, 199–237.

Swank, D. (2002). *Global Capital, Political Institutions, and Policy Change in Developed Welfare States*. New York: Cambridge University Press.

Traxler, F., Blaschke, S. and Kittel, B. (eds) (2001). *National Labour Relations in Internationalized Markets*. Oxford: Oxford University Press.

Turner, L. (2004). 'Why revitalize? Labour's urgent mission in a contested global economy' in C. Frege and J. Kelly (eds) *Varieties of Unionism: Strategies for Union Revitalization in a Globalizing Economy*. Oxford: Oxford University Press.

Visser, J. (1994). 'European trade unions: The transition years', in R. Hyman and A. Ferner (eds) *New Frontiers in European Industrial Relations*. Oxford: Blackwell, 80–107.

Visser, J. (1995). 'Trade unions from a comparative perspective', in Joris van Ruysseveldt, Rien Huiskamp and Jacques van Hoof (eds) *Comparative Industrial and Employment Relations*. London: Sage, 37–67.

Visser, J. (2003). 'Unions and unionism around the world' in J. T. Addison and C. Schnabel (eds) *International Handbook of Trade Unions*. Cheltenham: Edward Elgar.

Weiss, L. (2003). 'Introduction: Bringing domestic institutions back in' in L. Weiss (ed.), *States in the Global Economy: Bringing Domestic Institutions Back In*. New York: Cambridge University Press, 1–33.

Suggested key readings

Addison, J. and C. Schnabel (2003). *International Handbook of Trade Unions*, Aldershot: Edward Elgar.

Brown, H.P. (1990). 'The counter-revolution of our time' in *Industrial Relations*, 29(1): 1–14.

Cornfield, D.B. and H.J. McCammon (eds) (2003). *Labor Revitalization: Global Perspectives and New Initiatives*. Greenwich: JAI Press.

European Journal of Industrial Relations, special issue on 'Union renewal strategies', Richard Hyman (guest-editor Carola Frege), 2003, 9(1).

Frege, C.M. and J. Kelly (eds) (2004). *Varieties of Unionism: Strategies for Union Revitalization in a Globalizing Economy*. Oxford: Oxford University Press.

Freeman, R. and J. Medoff (1984). *What do Unions do?* New York: Basic Books.

Kelly, J. (2003). *Union Renewal: Organising Around the World*. London: TUC.

Kelly, J. and Willman, P. (2004). *Union Organization and Activity*. London: Routledge.

Moody, K. (1997). *Workers in a Lean World: Unions in the International Economy*. New York: Verso.

Turner, L, Katz, H.C. and R.W. Hurd (eds) (2001). *Rekindling the Movement: Labor's Quest for Relevance in the 21st Century*. Ithaca: ILR/Cornell University Press.

Waddington, J. and Hoffmann, R. (2001). *Trade Unions in Europe*. Brussels: ETUI.

11 International labour standards

KEITH D. EWING

Introduction

International labour standards are designed to establish minimum terms for employment wherever workers are engaged. As such they serve several functions. The first is social in that international labour standards are designed to promote social justice and to protect workers from exploitation, reflecting the claim that 'labour is not a commodity' (O'Higgins 1997). The second is economic in that they are designed to ensure that international trade does not take place on the basis of low wage competition. And the third is legal in that they are designed to ensure respect for and protection of human rights, which are designed in turn to be universal and indivisible. Although the case for international labour standards is as old as the industrial revolution, it is a case that has been renewed and enhanced by globalisation, as corporations move freely throughout the world looking for cheaper sources of labour. In this chapter we examine the way in which international labour standards are made and supervised by the International Labour Organisation (ILO), and give an account of the international labour code. We also examine some of the emerging pressures – caused partly by globalisation – on the development and application of international labour standards, and examine the emergence of a range of different strategies adopted by governments, corporations and trade unions for the enforcement of these standards. The major problem, however, is that international labour standards are addressed mainly to governments, whereas the real wielders of power are often now transnational corporations over which national governments may have little control and over which international law has not yet developed effective forms of accountability.

The International Labour Organisation

The responsibility for establishing and creating international labour standards lies in the first instance with national governments, as well as trade unions and employers. It is, however, difficult to establish global standards in a vacuum, and it for this reason that the standards set by bodies such as the ILO are crucially important. The ILO organisation was founded in 1919 in the immediate aftermath of the First World War (Alcock 1971). The preamble to the ILO Constitution tells us something about its purpose, and something about its past. But we cannot overlook the significance of the Bolshevik Revolution which cast a shadow over Western Europe in the aftermath of the War (Ewing 1994). The shadow of the revolution is to be seen most clearly in the observations of George Barnes – a leading British trade unionist who had been involved in the drafting of the post-war treaty. According to Barnes, the ILO was 'an international Soviet of an evolutionary and constructive kind' (Barnes 1920: 16). For his part, Lenin is said to have been 'credited with the dictum that the workers must choose between Moscow and Geneva' (Phelan 1936: 184). But the shadow of revolution is not the only explanation, and certainly not the public explanation. The preamble to the Constitution reveals a concern to promote 'universal and lasting peace' which could be established 'only if it is based upon social justice'. Clearly this was not successful, though this was hardly the fault of the ILO the very survival of which during the 1930s was a remarkable achievement. But it would be a mistake to see the commitment to peace as the only rationale for the ILO: we ought not to overlook the extent to which government representatives were 'moved by sentiments of justice and humanity' or indeed the concern that 'the failure of any nation to adopt humane conditions of labour is an obstacle in the way of other nations which desire to improve the conditions in their own countries'.

ILO procedures

A crucial feature of the ILO is the principle of tripartism, whereby trade unions and employers' organisations participate with governments in the standard setting process. It has been said that:

> [the] system has now become familiar by long usage, but it must be remembered that it constituted at its inception an almost revolutionary novelty and an astonishing break with the traditions of official international conferences and the principle of State sovereignty on which their composition and procedure had been based.
>
> (Phelan 1936: 4)

Under the ILO Constitution, each member is entitled to send four representatives to the annual conference, one of whom is a representative of national trade unions, and the other a representative of employers. The non-governmental representatives must be chosen in consultation with trade union and employers' organisations respectively. A further nod in the direction of the independence of the non-governmental representatives is to be found in the provisions of the Constitution which provide that each representative is obliged to act as an individual. The freedom of trade unionists to support a line contrary to that of his or her government nevertheless is clearly easier for some than for others. The principle of tripartism is also to be found in the Governing Body which has a number of constitutional obligations. The Governing Body is an important body of fifty-six members, of whom twenty-eight are representatives of governments, and twenty-eight are representatives of employers and trade unions. In order to ensure that the major countries are represented on the Governing Body, ten of the twenty-eight government places are reserved for countries of chief industrial importance. Among its responsibilities are the setting of the agenda for the annual conference and the appointment of the Director-General of the ILO.

The ILO is best known for its work as a standard setting agency, and indeed this is its most important function. The standard setting role is performed by the making of conventions and recommendations. Although both types of instrument are made by the Conference, they have different legal consequences. Once brought into force, the former give rise to legally binding obligations on the part of those countries which ratify them. But there is no obligation on the part of any member of the ILO to ratify a convention, even though its government representatives may have supported it in the Conference. There is, however, a duty under the Constitution for every member of the ILO to bring a convention 'before the authority or authorities within whose competence the matter lies, for the enactment of legislation or other action' (article 19(5)), though the authorites are not required to enact such legislation. This must be done within twelve months of the making of the convention, and the member must then notify the Director-General of the steps that have been taken by the appropriate authority. The appropriate authority will usually be a national parliament, and problems arise in federal countries where the implementation of employment law may be a state or a provincial matter. In these cases the duty under article 19(5) is modified so that the convention must be brought to the attention of the appropriate federal, state or provincial authorities for the enactment of legislation. Here we have another novelty of the ILO machinery, in the sense that 'the work of the Conference was linked up with the national parliaments' (Phelan 1936: 5).

Supervision of standards

It is one thing to generate so many standards, and another thing to ensure that they are complied with. A country is bound only by those conventions it has ratified. In order to encourage compliance with ratified conventions, the ILO Constitution requires members to submit a report to the Governing Body 'on the measures which it has taken to give effect to the provisions of Conventions to which it is a party'. There are also powers to require the submission of reports periodically on non-ratified conventions. Since 1927 the task of examining these reports has been entrusted to a Committee of Experts which is a body of eminent jurists, now twenty in number. The committee examines the national submissions and produces an annual report which provides both an authoritative source of ILO jurisprudence as well as an indication of which countries are failing to comply with which obligations. The reports also indicate cases of progress, these being cases where the country in question has changed its law and practice to bring it into line with ILO requirements. But the procedure relies on publicity and encouragement: there is no sanction as such that may be visited upon a country because it is not complying with a particular convention.

Apart from the reporting procedure, there are other procedures under the Constitution for trade unions to make representations to the International Labour Office about non-observance of conventions by a member state (article 24), and for one member to make a complaint of non-observance against another (article 26). Details of these complaints are documented in the annual report of the Committee of Experts, and are sometimes the subject of examination by a tripartite committee appointed by the Governing Body. In the latter case the complaint may be referred to a Commission of Inquiry (and there have been eleven such commissions to date), with the outcome of which all members are bound. In 1996 a complaint was submitted under article 26 against the government of Myanmar concerning the non-observance of the Forced Labour Convention, 1930 (Convention 29). The Commission found 'ample evidence' that 'forced labour in Myanmar is a widespread practice, provided for by law, and carried on without any prospect of prevention or punishment of those who exact forced labour from the citizens of Myanmar'. The Government of Myanmar was therefore found to be in flagrant breach of Convention 29 (ILO 1998).

The International Labour Code

Since the first ILO Convention in 1919 there has been a great increase in the number of conventions and recommendations. There are now 185 conventions and 195 recommendations. The Constitution provides that in framing any convention or recommendation of general application, the Conference must have 'due regard to those countries in which climatic conditions, the imperfect development of industrial organisation, or other special circumstances make the industrial conditions substantially different' (article 19(3)). Instruments are thus to be made relevant for all member states – developed and developing countries alike. There is no point generating standards that are too low as to be irrelevant in the former countries or too high for the latter. One strategy is to be found in the Social Security (Minimum Standards) Convention, 1952 (102). Here members have a choice in the sense that in order to ratify it, they need only accept three of Parts II to X which cover a wide range of different social security benefits. Another is to be found in the Discrimination (Employment and Occupation) Convention, 1958 (111) whereby members undertake to promote by various means the elimination of discrimination on the ground of race, colour, sex, religion, political opinion, national extraction or social origin. Here there are no prescriptive rules that must be applied.

Basic human rights

The most important conventions cover a wide range of issues, with the most significant dealing with what is referred to (by the ILO) as human rights – freedom of association; freedom from forced labour; freedom from child labour; and freedom from discrimination. Freedom of association is one of the most important principles on which the ILO is constructed. It is one of a number of issues identified in the preamble to the constitution as being in need of urgent attention, and it is re-affirmed in the Declaration of Philadelphia by which the ILO was relaunched in 1944 (Alcock 1971). Quite apart from its role in helping to raise standards by collective bargaining, freedom of association is, of course, crucial to the very existence of the ILO in its present form. The ILO is based on the principle of tripartism, the very existence (and legitimacy) of which depends on a strong, vibrant (and representative) trade union movement in member states. But notwithstanding the commitment to freedom of association, it was not until 1948 that the first major freedom of association convention was made. The key freedom of association conventions are as follows:

- Freedom of Association and Protection of the Right to Organise Convention, 1948 (87). This provides that workers and employers 'without distinction whatsoever', have the right 'to establish and, subject only to the rules of the organisation concerned, to join organisations of their own choosing without prior authorisation' (article 2). It also provides that workers' and employers' associations 'shall have the right to draw up their own constitutions and rules, to elect their representatives in full freedom, to organise their administration and activities and to formulate their programmes' (article 3). It is this last provision which is the source of the right to strike as developed by the Committee of Experts, a right which has been very widely construed though there are a number of permissible limitations (Gernignon *et al.* 1998).
- Right to Organise and Collective Bargaining Convention, 1949 (98). This provides protection for workers against acts of anti union discrimination by employers (article 1) and seeks to protect workers' organisations from interference by employers, whether by financial or other means (article 2). It also imposes a duty on member states to promote the development of voluntary collective bargaining machinery, where necessary and in accordance with

national conditions (article 4). This last provision has been construed to mean that a trade union with majority support can be given exclusive bargaining rights, but that where there is no majority union, 'workers' organisations should nevertheless be able to conclude a collective agreement on behalf of their own members (Gernignon *et al.* 2000: 51).

So far as forced labour is concerned, this is covered by the Forced Labour Convention, 1930 (Convention 29), and the Abolition of Forced Labour Convention, 1957 (Convention 105). Under the former, ratifying States undertake to 'suppress the use of forced or compulsory labour in all its forms within the shortest possible period'. The latter deals with specific problems of forced labour as a form of punishment for political dissidents or as a means of labour discipline. The two core conventions dealing with child labour are the Minimum Age Convention, 1973 (Convention 138) which is set at fifteen for developed countries and fourteen for developing countries, though there are opportunities in the Convention to exclude certain categories of employment and to limit the scope of application of the Convention. The Worst Form of Child Labour Convention, 1999 (Convention 182) deals with specific abuses, such as slavery, prostitution, drug trafficking, and work which is harmful to health, safety or welfare. So far as discrimination is concerned, the main convention is Convention 111 to which reference has been made. But other important instruments include the Equal Remuneration Convention, 1951 (Convention 100) which recognises the principle of equal pay for work of equal value, long before it became a standard of the European Community.

The range of International Labour Standards

Although important – and of growing importance – the human rights conventions are only a small part of the international labour code. Other conventions and recommendations deal with a wide range of matters, some of which are of general application, some of which deal with particular categories of workers (such as women, migrant workers, older workers, or children), while others still deal with particular occupational groups (such as seafarers, fishermen, dockworkers, nurses, plantation workers, hotel and restaurant workers). A large bulk of the code deals with conditions of work, a generic term that shelters instruments dealing with wages, working time, and occupational health and safety. These require respectively:

- the creation of machinery for setting wages in industries where there is no collective bargaining and wages are exceptionally low (the Minimum Wage – Fixing Machinery Convention, 1930 (Convention 26);
- the establishing of an eight hour day (or a 48 hour week) (the Hours of Work (Industry) Convention, 1919 (Convention 1) and the Hours of Work (Commerce and Offices) Convention, 1930 (Convention 30);

- the formulation, implementation and periodic review of a coherent national policy on occupational health and safety (Occupational Safety and Health Convention, 1981) (Convention 155).

Other important instruments include the Workers with Family Responsibilities Convention, 1981 (Convention 156), the Termination of Employment Convention, 1982 (Convention 158), and the Part Time Work Convention, 1994 (Convention 175). But there has been some criticism of the standard setting process on the ground that there has been an over-production of standards, some of which are 'obsolescent, if not obsolete': they 'frequently remain open to ratification, and continue to bind those countries that have ratified them, even though the circumstances which gave rise to the need for ratification have long since passed' (Creighton 1995: 100). There was, however, an important revision of the maternity convention in 2000 (Maternity Protection Convention, 2000) (Convention 183), and in 2004 steps were in place to revise the maritime conventions which alone account for at least thirty-five of all ILO conventions. This will lead to a 'Seafarers' Bill of Rights', covering some 1.2 million maritime workers worldwide, and in the process consolidate sixty conventions and recommendations made over the last eighty years. But the other concern is that – with a number of notable exceptions – the standards produced in recent years sometimes appear to deal with peripheral issues. Although unquestionably important for the workers for whom they are designed to apply, they do not appear to have captured the full essence of the problems facing labour in the modern world. Four of the last eight conventions deal with technical issues in the maritime industry.

The ILO, The International Labour Code and globalisation

Although there are a large number of conventions and recommendations, a formal study of the legislation would give a very incomplete picture of their penetration and impact. There are in fact two problems by which the ILO has been beset. The first is political and the second is institutional. So far as the former is concerned, two related problems are the end of the Cold War on the one hand and globalisation on the other (Creighton 2004). The end of the Cold War means that the ILO is no longer required 'to play a key role as honest-broker between the ideological protagonists of East and West' (Creighton 1995: 96). The growth of globalisation and neo-classical economics – and with them privatisation and deregulation – have led many governments to question the value of labour standards generally. According to the Director-General of the ILO:

> Although globalisation obliges us to re-examine the basic concepts and values of standard setting and specify their meaning or relevance, it also instils, in an insidious and more radical way, doubts as to the pre-eminence of these values.
>
> (ILO 1997: 5)

One of the main features of globalisation has been the rise of the powerful transnational corporations (Hepple 1997: 2005), with which international labour standards are ill-suited to deal. This is because these standards are addressed to governments not corporations. Although there is an ILO Declaration of 1977 on Multinational Enterprises, international law has not yet found an effective way of holding transnational companies accountable to the obligations it imposes on states.

Problems with international labour standards

There are in fact a number of problems with the application of standards which diminishes to some extent the effort made to create them. The first problem is the problem of ratification. As pointed out, countries are bound by conventions only if they have ratified them. But although the ILO boasted some 7,317 ratifications in June 2005, this is in fact very low when compared to the number of potential ratifications. At the end of 2004 there were 185 conventions, though it is true that five had been withdrawn. Nevertheless this indicates a total of 32,040 possible ratifications, suggesting that the current level of ratification is only in the region of 22 per cent. So there is a chronic problem in terms of ratification levels. This is explained in part by chronic levels of ratification by some countries, and the chronic levels of low ratification of some conventions. Into the former camp belong countries such as the United States which has ratified only fourteen of the 185 conventions, and China which has ratified twenty-three. Into the latter camp fall no fewer than twenty-four instruments that have failed to secure even ten ratifications. Even the convention with the highest number of ratifications – Convention 29 (the Forced Labour Convention) – has only 163, which do not include China or the United States. It remains the case that the largest countries in the world have not ratified either Convention 87 or 98: this means that the majority of the world's workers labour in jurisdictions where the commitment to freedom of association does not extend to ratifying the core conventions of the ILO. But it is not only core Conventions where there is a problem of non-ratification. In June 2005 there were only six non core instruments that had attracted more than 100 ratifications.

Apart from the problem of ratification, a second problem is the problem of compliance. Under article 22 of the ILO Constitution, member states are expected to send regular reports to the Committee of Experts about their compliance with ratified conventions. Clearly it would overwhelm the Committee of Experts if it were to scrutinise all the 7,317 ratifications annually. As the Committee pointed out:

> At its first session in May 1927, the Committee was composed of eight members, and met for three days. It had to examine 180 reports on the application of ratified Conventions from 26 of the ILO's 55 member States.

The Conference had by then adopted 23 Conventions and 28 Recommendations, and the number of ratifications of Conventions was 229. The Committee's membership has now expanded to 20 members, and its annual meeting time to nearly three weeks. The Conference has adopted 184 Conventions and 192 Recommendations, and the number of ratifications has grown to 6,983 ratifications. There are in addition 1,980 declarations of application of Conventions to non-metropolitan territories. There are today 175 member States in the International Labour Organization.

(ILO 2004b: 10)

Yet although the Committee has adapted its working practices to enable it to examine different conventions on a cyclical rather than an annual basis, it is hampered by the fact that some countries fail to comply with reporting obligations and that other countries submit reports late. The point is made by the Committee in its 2002 report where it is said that:

A total of 2,313 reports were requested from governments on the application of Conventions ratified by member States (article 22 of the Constitution). At the end of the present session of the Committee, 1,512 of these reports had been received by the Office. This figure corresponds to 65.37 per cent of the reports requested, compared with 71 per cent last year.

(ILO 2004b: 86)

Some countries have not submitted any report on ratified conventions for a number of years.

The Declaration on fundamental principles and rights at work

These and other problems led to an important initiative in 1998 which was the adoption by the ILO of the Declaration on Fundamental Principles and Rights at Work. This reflects a need to concentrate on a few core themes and to ensure more widespread respect for certain core standards relating to freedom of association, the elimination of forced or compulsory labour, the effective abolition of child labour, and the elimination of discrimination in respect of employment and occupation. All member states of the ILO have signed the Declaration which boldly declares that all members 'even if they have not ratified the Convention in question, have an obligation arising from the very fact of membership in the Organisation, to respect, to promote and to realize, in good faith and in accordance with the Constitution, the principles concerning the fundamental rights which are the subject of those Conventions' dealing with the four areas referred to. The priority and commitment to these fundamental rights is reflected in the text of the Declaration. This makes clear that the ILO would make use of 'its constitutional, operational and budgetary resources' to attain these objectives, and that in doing so it would mobilise external resources and support, 'as well as by encouraging other international organisations with which the ILO has established relations'. Thus it was proposed that the ILO would offer technical support to promote the ratification and implementation of fundamental conventions, and to assist those members not in a position to ratify, at least to promote the principles embraced in these conventions.

An important feature of the Declaration is the follow up procedure which accompanies it. Each of the four principles is subject to a formal review on a four-year cycle. This is done by adapting the existing supervisory procedures and may require member states to submit reports about instruments they have not ratified, though concerns have been expressed that the Declaration represents a weakening rather than a strengthening of standards and their supervision (Alston 2004). The stated purpose is to identify areas where 'the assistance of the Organisation through its technical co-operation activities may prove useful to its Members to help them implement [the] fundamental principles and rights'. It is also expressly stated that the follow up procedure under the Declaration is not to be seen as an alternative to or as a challenge to the normal process of supervision and enforcement. At the time of writing, one cycle has been completed under the Declaration, and the reports make very grim reading. In 2002, for example, it was revealed that 'some 180 million children aged five to seventeen (or 73 per cent of all child labourers) are now believed to be engaged in the worst forms of child labour'. This is said to represent 'one child in every eight in the world' (ILO 2002: x). It was revealed in 2004 that '213 trade unionists were killed worldwide, some 1,000 were injured or subjected to violence, 2,562 were arrested and detained, and 89 were sentenced to prison terms'. This was said not to 'include many more who were dismissed or harassed on account of their membership of a trade union' (ILO 2004: 24). The murder of 184 trade unionists in Colombia alone in 2002 is said to threaten the 'very survival' of trade unions in that country (ILO 2004: 25).

International labour standards – Diversity in supervision

Although the procedures for the supervision and enforcement of international labour standards are weak, it would be a mistake to underestimate the influence and importance of the ILO as a source of international law and international practice. The influence of these standards can be seen first by virtue of the fact that they form the basis of the standards to be found in other international treaties. Both the International Covenant on Civil and Political Rights and the International Covenant on Economic, Social and Cultural Rights take ILO Convention 87 as their guide as setting a standard below which treaty obligations may not fall. Similarly, both the European Court of Human Rights and the European Court of Justice have shaped the European Convention on Human Rights and the European Community (EC) Treaty respectively to comply with the requirements of different ILO conventions. Moreover, it is possible that the importance of ILO conventions will be enhanced still further by the (as yet) non-binding European Union (EU) Charter of Fundamental Rights agreed at Nice in 2000. But apart from the influence of ILO conventions on other international treaties, the influence of international standards is to be seen in the initiatives taken by governments in their relations with each other, and in the attempts by international agencies and civil society to control the conduct of transnational corporations.

ILO standards and international trade

The contemporary impact of international labour standards is to be seen first in the area of international trade, where a number of bilateral trade agreements are being negotiated by the United States in particular with a view to 'liberalising' trade. During the 1990s there had been an active campaign by trade unionists and others to link tariff reform to compliance with international standards. One proposal was that there should be a social clause as part of the process of the World Trade Organisation (WTO), with elaborate procedures involving both the ILO and WTO in ensuring that members of the latter complied with labour standards as a condition of trade privileges (Chin 1998). Although widely supported, this is an initiative that has failed, opposed by governments in the developed and the developing world, with growing recognition that 'the mechanism of the WTO is particularly unsuitable for the enforcement of labour standards': Hepple 2002: 20. The first ministerial meeting of the WTO held in Singapore in 1996 'was reached with an understanding that there is no realistic hope of establishing a global social clause' (Gibbons 1998). Although those present renewed their 'commitment to the observance of internationally recognised core labour standards', they also expressed their belief that 'economic growth and development fostered by increased trade and further trade liberalisation contribute to the promotion of these standards'. The immediate effect was a revitalisation of international labour standards by the ILO, leading in turn to the Declaration on Fundamental Principles and Rights at Work 1998, discussed above. However, the linkage between trade and labour standards has not disappeared, and has resurfaced in a new form.

In the place of a global social clause there has emerged a series of bilateral trade agreements which include labour clauses, the most visible example of this being a number of free trade agreements which the United States has signed with countries such as Australia and Singapore. Take, for example, the US–Singapore agreement. By Chapter 17 the parties reaffirm their obligations as members of the ILO and the commitments which they made to the ILO's Declaration on Fundamental Principles and Rights at Work of 1998. In addition, each party to the agreement (in this case the USA and Singapore) undertakes to strive to ensure that these labour principles and other internationally recognised labour rights are protected by domestic labour law. Although the agreements do not expressly refer to ILO Convention 87 and 98, they apply specifically to internationally recognised labour rights, including 'the right of association', and 'the right to organise and bargain collectively'. The contradiction of these initiatives are not difficult to expose (O'Higgins 2004). The United States in particular has a poor record of ratification of core labour standards (not having ratified either conventions 87 or 98). It has also been found to be in breach of these conventions by the Freedom of Association Committee. This is because of a lack of adequate protection for workers against anti union conduct by employers during recognition campaigns, and because those involved in a lawful strike can be permanently replaced by other workers (Human Rights Watch 2000; Compa 2001).

ILO standards and global framework agreements

The use of international standards in trade agreements is an initiative designed – at least in principle – to ensure compliance by states. But ILO standards are used as a reference point in relation to other international agencies, and the standards which they develop (Gibbons 2005). The best example of this is the OECD which has revised guidelines for multinational enterprises, itself an important initiative in view of earlier comments about the ILO. These guidelines were adopted in 2000 and cover a wide range of issues from the environment and bribery to consumer interests and taxation. But they also deal with employment and industrial relations, with the preamble to the guidelines acknowledging the importance of the ILO Declaration of 1998 along with other instruments including the UN Declaration of Human Rights of 1948. Chapter IV of the Guidelines thus require enterprises should 'within the framework of applicable law, regulations and prevailing labour relations and employment practices':

- Respect the right to freedom of association
- Contribute to the effective abolition of child labour
- Contribute to the elimination of all forms of forced or compulsory labour
- Not discriminate against employees on the grounds specified in ILO Convention 111.

A 'strengthened implementation system' is designed to put 'the onus firmly on governments at the national level to make sure that companies observe the guidelines' (Trade Union Advisory Committee (TUAC) nd). Although there was some optimism that the new guidelines 'may be taken up as a tool to achieve change' (Murray 2001: 268), there is some concern that there is a lack of awareness about the procedure in some countries and that some governments (including the USA) are not fully meeting their obligations (TUAC 2004).

The other significant attempt to use ILO standards to guide the conduct of TNCs is by means of global framework agreements negotiated between global union federations and individual transnational corporations (Torres and Gunnes 2002). Most of these agreements have been negotiated with European multinationals, with US companies being some way off the pace. The first recorded example of such agreements is the agreement between Accor and the International Union of Foodworkers in 1994 (Wills 2002), and there are now over thirty such agreements to which global union federations are a party. The main point of these agreements is to commit the companies in question to core international labour standards throughout their global operations. This means a commitment to freedom of association, the abolition of child labour, the abolition of forced labour, and the elimination of discrimination. In some cases the commitments are embellished beyond the core ILO conventions. For example, the commitment to freedom of association sometimes includes a commitment to protect workers' representatives, often with an express reference to the Workers' Representatives Convention, 1971 (135). In other cases there is a commitment to a wider range of issues, and to fair labour standards on matters such as pay, working time and health and safety. But although this is an exciting and important development, we should not underestimate the difficulties which will be encountered in nurturing this embryo to maturity. Not least is the lack of support for the activity in international labour law which is still rooted in a model of national industrial relations regimes and fails adequately to deal with the global context within which that bargaining may take place. Several global union federations have been negotiated by European Works Councils, perhaps illustrating the value of a legal context for the further development of this action.

Conclusion

The growing movement for global framework agreements is only one example of initiatives 'emerging independently of the ILO' (ILO 2001: 62). These 'private initiatives in the social sphere' provide 'great potential' as a way of promoting ILO values, but they also raise 'complex issues' which need to be addressed. There is thought to be 'an obvious danger that private initatives will pick and choose from the ILO agenda, or that verification systems will be flawed' (ILO 2001: 62). The other danger is that the verification systems will lead to a dilution of standards by those without sufficient knowledge of ILO standards and the jurisprudence of the Committee of Experts. But given the scale of the problems facing workers throughout the world, it is inevitable and unavoidable that impatience with the ILO machinery will lead activists and others to find new ways to put pressure on governments and companies to ensure compliance with minimum standards (Ewing and Sibley 2000). The ILO leaves us in no doubt about the nature of these problems. In 2004 we are told that 'a number of vulnerable groups continue to have great difficulty in exercising their rights to associate nearly everywhere in the world, and that these basic rights continue to be denied in some countries' (ILO 2004a: 112). We are also told that 'abuses of fundamental rights persist in too many countries' (ILO 2004a: 113). The continuing murder of trade unionists in Colombia gives these sanitised statements a brutal reality. But as we reflect on the powerlessness of the ILO to deal with such abuse, we should also reflect that without the ILO it would be infinitely harder for those campaigning to hold governments and corporations to account.

References

Alcock, A. (1971) *History of the International Labour Organisation* (London).

Alston, P. (2004) "Core Labour Standards' and the transformation of the International Labour Regime' (2004) 15 *European Journal of International Law* 457.

Barnes, G. N. (1920) *The Industrial Section of the League of Nations* (Barnett House Papers No. 5, London).

Chin, D. (1998) *A Social Clause for Labour's Cause: Global Trade and Labour Standards* (Institute of Employment Rights, London).

Compa, L. (2001) 'Workers' freedom of association in the United States under International Human Rights Standards' (2001) 17 *International Journal of Comparative Labour Law and Industrial Relations* 289.

Creighton, W. B. (1995) 'The internationalisation of labour law', in R. Mitchell (ed.), *Redefining Labour Law* (Centre for Employment and Labour Relations Law, Melbourne, Vic).

Creighton, W. B. (2004) 'The future of labour law: is there a role for International Labour Standards?' in C. Barnard, S. Deakin and G. S. Morris, *The Future of Labour Law* (Hart Publishing, Oxford).

Ewing, K. D. (1994) *Britain and the ILO* (2nd ed., Institute of Employment Rights, London).

Ewing K. D. and Sibley, T. (2000) *International Trade Union Rights for the New Millennium* (Institute of Employment Rights/International Centre for Trade Union Rights, London).

Gernignon, B., Odero, A. and Guido, H. (1998) 'ILO Principles Concerning the Right to Strike' (1998) 137 *International Labour Review* 441.

Gernignon, B., Odero, A. and Guido, H. (2000) 'ILO principles concerning collective bargaining' (2000) 139 *International Labour Review* 33.

Gibbons, S. (1998) *International Labour Rights – New Methods of Enforcement* (Institute of Employment Rights, London).

Gibbons, S. (2005) *Decoding Some New Developments in Labour Standards Enforcement* (Institute of Employment Rights, London).

Hepple, B. A. (1997) 'New approaches to international labour regulation' (1997) 26 ILJ 353.

Hepple, B. A. (2002) *Labour Law, Inequality and Global Trade* (Hugo Sinzheimer Instituut, Amsterdam).

Hepple, B. A. (2005) *Labour Laws and Global Trade* (Hart Publishing, Oxford).

Human Rights Watch (2000) *Unfair Advantage: Workers' Freedom of Association in the United States under International Human Rights Standards* (HRW, Washington DC).

ILO (1997) ILO, *The ILO, Standard Setting and Globalisation. Report of the Director–General* (ILO, Geneva).

ILO (1998) ILO, *Report of the Commission of Inquiry Appointed Under Article 26 of the Constitution of the International Labour Organization to Examine the Observance by Myanmar of the Forced Labour Convention, 1930 (No. 29)* (ILO, Geneva).

ILO (2001) ILO, *Reducing the Decent Work Agenda – A Global Challenge Report of the Director – General* (ILO, Geneva).

ILO (2002) ILO, *A Future without Child Labour* (ILO, Geneva).

ILO (2004a) ILO, *Organising for Social Justice* (ILO, Geneva).

ILO (2004b) ILO, *Report of the Committee of Experts on the Application of Conventions and Recommendations*, Report III (Part 1A) (ILO, Geneva).

Murray, J. (2001) 'A new phase in the regulation of multinational enterprises: the role of the OECD' (2001) 30 ILJ 255.

O'Higgins, P. (1997) 'Labour is not a Commodity' – An Irish contribution to international labour law' (1997) 26 ILJ 225.

Phelan, E. J. (1936) E. J. Phelan, *Yes and Albert Thomas* (Cresset Press, London).

Torres, L. and Gunnes, S. (2002) *Global Framework Agreements: A New Tool for International Labour?* (Fafo, Oslo).

TUAC (nd) Trade Union Advisory Committee to the Organisation for Economic Co-operation and Development, *The OECD Guidelines on Multinationals* (TUAC, Paris).

TUAC (2004) Trade Union Advisory Committee to the Organisation for Economic Co-operation and Development, *TUAC Submission to the Annual Meeting of National Contact Points* (TUAC, Paris).

Wills, J. (2002) 'Bargaining for the Space to Organise in the Global Economy: A Review of the Accor – IUF Trade Union Rights Agreement' (2002) 9 *Review of International Political Economy* 675.

Suggested key readings

Alston, P. (2004) '"Core Labour Standards" and the transformation of the International Labour Regime' (2004) 15 *European Journal of International Law* 457.

Creighton, W. B. (2004) 'The future of labour law: is there a role for International Labour Standards?' in C. Barnard, S. Deakin and G. S. Morris, *The Future of Labour Law* (Hart Publishing, Oxford).

Ewing, K. D. (1994) *Britain and the ILO* (2nd ed., Institute of Employment Rights, London).

Gernignon, B., Odero, A. and Guido, H. (1998) 'ILO Principles Concerning the Right to Strike' (1998) 137 *International Labour Review* 441.

Gernignon, B., Odero, A. and Guido, H. (2000) 'ILO principles concerning collective bargaining' (2000) 139 *International Labour Review* 33.

Gibbons, S. (2005) *Decoding Some New Developments in Labour Standards Enforcement* (Institute of Employment Rights, London).

Hepple, B. A. (2005) *Labour Laws and Global Trade* (Hart Publishing, Oxford).

Human Rights Watch (2000) *Unfair Advantage: Workers' Freedom of Association in the United States under International Human Rights Standards* (HRW, Washington DC).

O'Higgins, P. (1997) '"Labour is not a Commodity" – An Irish contribution to international labour law' (1997) 26 ILJ 225.

O'Higgins, P. (2004) 'The end of labour law as we have known it?' in C. Barnard, S. Deakin and G. S. Morris, *The Future of Labour Law* (Hart Publishing, Oxford).

12 International collective bargaining

JACQUES ROJOT

Introduction

At first sight, international collective bargaining seems to be the natural next step after national level bargaining. Within most developed countries, historically, collective bargaining developed rapidly from local to national level. As the labour market moved from local to national, some degree of national level labour relations supplemented, and sometimes superseded, existing local labour relations. The case is well documented. In the case of the USA (Ulman 1955) the national union took over the local union, even though collective bargaining remained local, albeit under the auspices of the national union. It therefore appeared perfectly logical that the same process that had occurred within nations would take place internationally superseding the national one. As capital becomes more and more international and mobile, as financial markets globally never close, it seems only natural for organised labour to adjust and extend to the international scene. It also seems vital for labour to seek a new negotiating position *vis-à-vis* its traditional employer opponent when the latter is quickly achieving a global dimension under many guises – notably, but not exclusively in the shape of the multinational corporation (MNC). Indeed, it may sometimes appear to national labour movements to be a case of 'hanging together or hanging separately'. Nevertheless, in practice, things are far more complex and far from easy. While internationalisation of capital seems a natural desire for employers, it does not have the same appeal for labour (Lecher and Platzer 1988), especially in the case of collective bargaining. We shall review the various issues involved before gauging the few tangible results attained so far.

But first, we must give a usable definition of collective bargaining. It is not as easy as it appears (Rojot 2004). However, for the sake of efficiency we shall retain from a long and sometimes involved discussion of the idea that collective bargaining must occur between employers and bona fide unions, take place through bipartite discussions and negotiations between them, result in a written agreement regulating wages and conditions of work, as a significant tool of joint regulation, and that the parties have real power to apply the means and tools of co-operation and conflict, upon which bargaining ultimately rests. In other words, collective bargaining must not only exist in theory, in Labour Law Codes, but must also actually take place in practice, with significant degrees of freedom and means of reciprocal pressure granted to the parties. Without bargaining power, there is no collective bargaining.

We can see, then, that the international level raises obstacles much more formidable than those placed in the path of national level bargaining. Notably, the following issues cast doubts on its successful achievement. International solidarity of workers is much harder to achieve than national solidarity. There are differences in structure, status and power of the actors which make actual co-ordination of action difficult. National industrial relations systems remain very distinct; with divergent legal, technical and social contexts influencing labour relations issues. The lack of a framework or a forum for international labour relations, not only in legal but also in practical terms, as well as the unavailability of an international enforcement mechanism makes the enforceable settlement of disputes impossible to achieve. Also, the lack of representativeness and of the capacity to commit of both the international employers' organisations and international unions, at an international level, is a major issue. Finally, there is, at least for the employers side, a lack of positive incentives to engage in the process and to proceed to such activity because of the dangers that they may perceive to be inherent.

Also, from a more theoretical point of view, for a dynamic process such as bargaining to take place, one interested party must be willing to provide the initial impetus, be able to do so efficiently and meet with at least some degree of co-operation or some lack of opposition. Negotiation requires (at least) two parties. Therefore, in order to enter, or to agree to pursue international collective bargaining, management will have to find in it benefits that exceed its costs, or labour will have to demonstrate its ability to coerce and bring a reluctant management to the bargaining table by its own devices.

The actors of international collective bargaining

The first important issue to address is, therefore, who are going to be, or who could possibly be, the parties to international collective bargaining?

The employers' association side of the picture is relatively simple. Most international employers' associations, such as the international chamber of commerce, have no interest or mandate for being involved in labour issues. Many employers' trade organisations on an industry-wide basis share the same view to a greater or lesser extent. The main employers' organisations to be mentioned in the social and labour field are on a global horizontal level, the International Organisation of Employers (IOE) and at European level the UNICE, which carefully distinguish between social and labour and industrial relations issues as well as between social dialogue (of which they approve) and international collective bargaining (in which they decline to take part).

Created in 1920, the IOE represents the interests of business in the labour and social policy fields. It embraces 136 national employer organisations from 132 countries from all over the world. It promotes and defends the interests of employers in international forums, particularly in the International Labour Organisation (ILO), and ensures that international labour and social policy promote the viability of enterprises and creates an environment favourable to enterprise development and job creation.

At European level, the 'Union des Industries de la Communauté Européenne' (traditionally known under its acronym in French, UNICE) was founded in the wake of the creation of the European Economic Communities (the EEC, the forerunner of the European Union) in 1958. Its original mandate, still valid, included uniting the central national industrial federations to foster solidarity between them; encouraging a Europe-wide competitive industrial policy and acting as a spokes body to the European institutions. Its mission now includes the release of entrepreneurial energy, boosting innovation, unleashing the internal market, improving the functioning of the labour market, making environmental policy more effective and efficient, and fostering international trade investment.

Sectoral (trade) employers' organisations also exist at international European level but the extent to which they agree to deal with labour and social issues varies widely. Many only concern themselves with strictly economic problems. Of course, the employers' side is so constituted not only from associations, but also from the main new actors, multinational corporations.

The multinational corporation and organised labour

Multinational corporations are, of course not a new phenomenon. One can date the West Indies corporate ventures back to the sixteenth century. However, what is relatively new is their considerable impact on worldwide manufacturing and trade. Initially, when they were recognised as emergent major economic actors, the position of workers' organisations towards them was ambivalent and, sometimes somewhat reluctantly, they recognised that multinationals could have some positive aspects from the point of view of labour (Malles 1969). Soon, however, they were no longer bending over backward to recognise their positive aspects (Heise 1973) because they considered the threats that they posed towards their interests outweighed them. Those threats are well known and easy to list.

First, there is a general feeling of uneasiness in the face of the sheer size and power of large corporations. When a company's activities are spread over several countries, and sometimes several continents, this feeling is exacerbated. Local employment, wages and working conditions, decided from outside, are seen to be completely beyond the reach of the voice or actions of local workers' organisations. Global planning diktats issuing from far away headquarters or the fortunes of the entire multinational, depending on operations in other countries, can seal the fate of a local operation, whatever its own activities or performance.

Besides, indirect threats are felt more acutely. The one most often voiced is the power of the multinational to out-manoeuvre local and national unions, as well as any possible industrial action, by shifting production operations to other countries. This can be the the response to a strike, or even in the face of potential labour unrest or the presence of a strong and powerful union, where international management would probably transfer production facilities and channel new investment to other countries where the labour movement was weaker or less well organised. It is also argued that multinationals import their own, home country style industrial relations practices while disregarding custom or even labour law in the host country. This is felt particularly to be the case for union recognition, lay-offs and plant closures. Besides, the local and national unions of the host country feel that they can never reach and even less influence the real decision-making power when it is located outside of the country, while local management only applies to policies decided elsewhere, where the voice of the union and the employees cannot be heard. It is also felt that host country employment is reduced to assembly work, while research and high value jobs are reserved for the home country. Finally, the union is kept in the dark as to the global activities of the multinational and, at best, obtains fragmented information

Also, indirect threats linger. Multinationals are suspected of using internal transfer pricing between their units in different countries to make no profit appear where unions are strong and/or taxes high, in order to pay low wages and welfare benefits. They are also assumed to be able to put pressure on national governments that are anxious to obtain foreign direct investment, in order to get them to curb union power and activities.

International labour organisations

Unlike the multinational corporations, who emerged as a direct consequence of the internationalisation of industry and trade, the labour side has had to build its own international organisations from scratch. Of course, international worker organisations are also nothing new. 'Workers of the world unite!' is a battle cry dating back to the early nineteenth century. However, the First International Working Men's Association, created in 1864, was a political organisation devoted to ideological goals and not an organised labour movement per se. Its purpose was to achieve the overthrow of the capitalist system. Marx, who won, and Bakounin fought for its leadership with the global goals to promote the spread of communism or anarchy and to take over the government of the nations of the time. Its membership was much more extensive than simply workers and their representatives. Its objectives were thus much larger than the ones of a labour organisation devoted to the protection of the interests of its members within existing political systems, whose change would be at best a secondary objective.

Moves to establish an international union federation began to take place over the last quarter of the nineteenth century and the early part of the twentieth Century, but the establishment of a viable and durable movement was damaged by the two world wars, making enemies of workers and putting them on warring sides as well as creating ideological quarrels and subsequent splits between the socialist and communist-dominated factions of the labour movement. It was only after World War Two that a stable situation began to emerge, though established on the basis of history.

The forerunners of international labour organisations were the International Trade Secretariats (ITSs), created over the nineteenth century and existing to this day. They are 'vertical' organisations, aiming to gather internationally all worker members of a given trade. They are also known, some of them having changed their label recently, as global union federations (GUFs).

An individual union will usually belong to a national union centre in its country, which will then affiliate to a world body such as the ICFTU. The same individual union will also usually affiliate to a GUF relevant to the industry where it has members. Possibly unions with members in many different industries will belong to more than one GUF.

However, increasingly, the term 'Global Unions' is being used by the international labour movement for describing the major institutions of the international trade union movement sharing common objectives. This is all the more confusing as, together with the International Confederation of Free Trade Unions (ICFTU) and the Trade Union Advisory Committee to the OECD (TUAC), discussed below, ten 'Global Union Federations' call themselves 'global unions'. Thus GUF should not be confused with 'global unions' of which they are only a component, albeit a major one. ITF or GUF members of global unions are: Education International, International Federation of Building and Wood Workers, International Federation of Chemical, Energy, Mine and General Workers' Union, International Federation of Journalists, International Metalworkers' Federation, International Textile, Garment and Leather Workers' Federation, International Transport Workers' Federation, International Union of Food, Agricultural, Hotel, Restaurant, Catering, Tobacco and Allied Workers' Association, Public Services International and the Union Network International.

In parallel, 'horizontal' international organisations were created, aiming to gather under a common centre all workers of the world, by having as members national union federations, gathering to themselves all national industry and craft unions in each country, and not only single trade organisations. However, they were, and still are, ideologically divided and three of them exist side by side. The most important one is certainly the International Confederation of Free Trade Unions (ICFTU), which was set up in 1949, by a split from the WFTU (World Federation of Trade Unions) with the help of the then ITSs, now GUFs. It claims 234 affiliated organisations in 152 countries and territories on all five continents, with a membership of 148 million. It maintains close links with the European Trade Union Confederation (ETUC) (which includes all ICFTU European affiliates) and the Global Union Federations or ITSs, just discussed, which link together national unions from a particular trade or industry at international level.

The World Federation of Trade Unions (WFTU) was created in Paris on 3 October 1945. However, given that it included all unions of the Eastern Bloc as members, political tensions due to the Cold War led to the secession and establishment of the ICFTU. It lost many of its affiliates and much of its importance with the end of the Cold War and the fall of the communist 'people's republics' in Eastern Europe.

Finally, The World Confederation of Labour (WCL) is an international trade union confederation uniting 144 autonomous and democratic trade unions from 116 countries (October 2001) all over the world. Its head office is located in Brussels, Belgium, and it has over 26 million members, mainly from Third World countries. The last years have been marked by the affiliation of several African and Central and Eastern European organisations. The European organisations of the WCL, members or candidate members of the ETUC (European Trade Union Confederation), consult each other regularly. Originally referring to, and organised around, the Christian faith, the WCL now adopts an independent attitude towards governments, political parties, power blocs, religions and churches. A merger between the ICFTU and the WCL is increasingly discussed. It was notably an issue evoked at the last (December 2004) Congress of the ICTFU in Miyazaki, Japan, in terms of there being 'an overwhelming case'. The merger question, including an unaffiliated national unions centre (for those having left the WFTU), was hotly debated.

Both the WFTU and the WCL also contain within their internal structures 'horizontal' and 'vertical' structures. The horizontal structures are constituted of regional (in the sense of regions of the world) organisations (i.e. Latin America, Africa) and the vertical ones of sectoral international single trade organisations similar in structure to the ITF. However, both types of structure have different types of relationships with the world internationals to which they are linked. The matter is too complex to be dealt with in detail here. Let us simply note two points. On the one hand, the vertical structures of the WCL are internal divisions and they do not enjoy the independence of the ITSs or GUFs regarding the ICFTU, whose reciprocal relations are established by the Milano agreement. On the other, the ETUC (European Trade Union Congress), to be discussed below has affiliates belonging to both the ICFTU and the WCL, but is a member of neither.

To complete an already complex picture, it should be added that, the International Labour Organisation (ILO) being a tripartite organisation, includes unions as members on an equal footing with employers' organisations and national governments. However, it is an organisation of a totally different nature, with the status of an International Governmental Organisation, initially created in 1919 and, since the end of World War Two, linked to the United Nations. Also, it should be added that the Trade Union Advisory Committee (TUAC) enjoys a consultative status near the OECD, together with an employers' organisation (BIAC).

Finally, at European level, the European Trade Union Confederation (ETUC) was established in 1973 to provide a trade union counterbalance to the economic forces of European integration. At present, the ETUC has in its membership seventy-six National Trade Union Confederations from a total of thirty-four European countries, as well as eleven European industry federations, representing a total of 60 million members. Other trade union structures such as Eurocadres (the Council of European Professional and Managerial Staff) and EFREP/FERPA (European Federation of Retired and Elderly Persons) operate under the auspices of the ETUC. In addition, the ETUC co-ordinates the activities of the thirty-nine ITUCs (Interregional Trade Union Councils), which organise trade union co-operation at a cross-border level. The ETUC is recognised by the European Union, by the Council of Europe and by EFTA as the only representative cross-sectoral trade union organisation at European level.

International union action

Several paths are possible for international action by unions facing multinationals, including cross-national solidarity, consultative meetings, mutual help in training, sharing of information, sympathy strikes or other industrial action, co-ordinated strikes, co-ordinated bargaining, international collective bargaining and indirect pressure on national governments and/or international organisations to obtain . favourable to international labour interests. We shall focus here on collective bargaining but we shall also briefly mention other international developments in the labour relations field, such as occurrences of international industrial action, or other types of contact between international union bodies and multinational corporations apart from proper bargaining. Such occurrences are important for, on the one hand, other types of international activities while not constituting bargaining per se may constitute a beginning, a drive towards and/or help give rise to bargaining. On the other hand, as we shall acknowledge later, it is a mixture of actions other than bargaining that were the more successful, or least unsuccessful (at European Union level) in creating the European Works Councils.

International collective bargaining on a global scale

International collective bargaining has never really taken off at worldwide level. With the possible exception of the single case in 1967 of a United Auto Workers (UAW)–Chrysler collective agreement covering both the USA and Canada, under very specific conditions and limited to the two countries, it can persuasively be argued that no real 'collective agreement' properly speaking has ever yet been signed at an international level, involving reciprocal duties and commitments by the parties with an efficient means of enforcement. In a first wave of contacts and tentative agreements about twenty years ago, the most noticeable developments more or less remotely linked with bargaining on an international scale were among the following: activities preparatory to bargaining such as a tentative proposal to co-ordinate an international strike (ICF (then International Chemical Workers Federation)–St Gobain, 1969); attempts with international boycotts (ICEF (then International Chemical and Energy Workers Federation)/AKZO (the AKZO Multinational Corporation) and Coca-Cola/UITA (*Union internationale des travailleurs de l'alimentation, de l'agriculture, de l'hôtellerie–restauration, du tabac et des branches connexes*); agreements to hold periodical meetings regarding employment with several national unions from the countries over which a multinational corporation operates (BSN until 1980, AKZO until 1977); limited contacts between a company and an ITS (Brown-Boveri/IMF (International Metal Workers Federation) in 1970, Nestlé/UITA in 1972, CocaCola/UITA in 1980, EMF (European Metal Workers federation/Philips in 1973); more regular contacts between the same (Rothman/UITA, EMF/Continental).

Since then, little has taken place. The ICFTU, the WCL and to an even greater extent, the WFTU, are networks or forums for meetings and debating options. The International Trade Secretariats (ITSs) keep maintaining at the forefront of their action an effort to try to shape a credible opposition force to the multinational corporations. However, some of the world councils for multinational corporations, initiated in the automotive industry in the 1970s are still active, and some others have been created. They exist, for instance for companies such as Renault, Electrolux, IBM, Matsushita, SKF, although questions might be raised as to the level and extent of their influence, beyond the country of origin and some affiliates.

However, recently interesting innovative developments have involved contacts and agreements between various organisations, including but not limited to, multinational corporations and national unions: on the employer side sectoral groupings of employers have been involved, as well as ITS from the labour side. However, these contacts and agreements bear mostly upon part or all of a basic set of employees' fundamental social rights, as they are spelled out in convention numbers 29, 87, 98, 105, 100, 111 and 138 of the ILO, which, of course, have not been ratified by many countries within which multinational corporations operate, and also may well not be observed in practice in some of the countries where they have been ratified. One can, for instance, note several agreements: of 1994, on freedom of unionisation between Danone and the UITA; of 1997, on consultation on the social provisions accompanying restructuring and dismissals, between ACCOR and the UITA; of 1995, on freedom of unionisation, as well as, quite interestingly, in 1996, on a set of fundamental social rights between the International Federation of Football Associations and the ICFTU, the International Federation of Commercial, Clerical and Technical Employees (FIET) and the International Textile, Garment and Leather Workers' Federation (ITGLWF). To this should be added a declaration of principle from Euro Commerce and Euro Fiet against child labour. Nevertheless, these agreements while indicating a promising track for potential future developments, either remain at the level of a declaration of intentions or hit, as ever, the problems of representativeness of the parties (Euro Commerce) or of enforcement (FIFA). Besides, as before (Rojot 1976) their conclusion has rested on the employer's goodwill, prompted either by positive attitude towards organised labour (as it was in the case of Danone, which twenty-five years ago had already signed an agreement on the dissemination of information to unions in several European countries) or on purely circumstantial events (the widely broadcast TV documentaries showing child labour involved in making footballs for the FIFA agreement) and cannot be said really to have been imposed by the labour side.

Some cases of regulation of the activities of multinational corporations by nation states must also be noted, such as the regulation of bribes by national companies overseas by the US Government, and the requirement that overseas subcontracting by national companies follow minimum social guarantees by the Swedish government. An interesting instance of such a case is the co-ordination of national agreements between shipowners in several countries and the International Transport Workers Federation. This co-ordination at an international level of national agreements in several countries had for its goal the regulation of wages and working conditions of seamen to fight the practice of sub-standard conditions of employment on ships registered by nations under flags of convenience (Laffer 1977). Of course, in those cases, the situation is quite different from truly international collective bargaining. The scope is limited to national corporations headquartered in each of the countries concerned and it is the weight of the nation state that provides the means of enforcement. However, the direct power of a nation state is limited to its citizens and/or by its borders; the efforts of the US Senate notwithstanding.

It is hardly surprising that international collective bargaining did not take off in an environment where the parties were left to their own devices. It was facing formidable obstacles. Bargaining patterns vary between countries, as well labour law regarding negotiation. Also, the need for moving from a national to an international centre of decision-making raises difficult and crucial issues concerning distribution of power among the national and international unions, at all the relevant levels of authority. Also, ultimately, a labour movement rests upon working class solidarity. There are solid grounds to doubt the existence of such a solidarity at an international level, at least to the degree to which it would be efficient beyond lip service and token actions of support. Witness to that point are the lack of reactions, beyond weak protests and symbolic demonstrations, to production transfers and/or plant closures by multinational companies across borders. For instance, all rhetoric notwithstanding, the Renault plant in Vilvoorde is now closed and employees in the newly located Hoover plant did go to work, when those companies shifted production. Finally, more mundane issues, obvious and clearly visible but difficult to solve, such as differences in national cultures and languages, must be taken in account. It takes two parties to bargain, and international unions have never demonstrated bargaining power strong enough to compel reluctant multinational employers to sit at the negotiating table. The few instances of international agreements noted above, rested on management acceptance and goodwill.

Even though not pertaining to a process of collective bargaining properly speaking, it should also be mentioned that both the ILO and the OECD guidelines for multinational enterprises remain in existence (Blanpain and Engels 1998). However, both are still of a voluntary nature and have had quite a limited effect. No consequence seems to have followed the enactment of the ILO guidelines. The situation has been different for the OECD, under the skilled analysis and interpretation by the Trade Union Advisory Committee (TUAC) of the role of the Committee on International Investment and Multinational Enterprises. On the one hand, enforcement procedures of the guidelines were, and still are, non-existent. On the other hand, however, the practice of TUAC, institutionalised in the 1984 revision of the guidelines, to request 'clarification' of 'cases' raised by the behaviour of multinational corporations, or subsidiaries of multinational corporations, under the guidelines has doubtlessly exerted an influence in several instances, but not in all cases, by raising or threatening to raise unwelcome adverse publicity. For instance in the Badger, Hertz, Viggo, Batco and several other cases, a multinational corporation has adopted a behaviour conforming to the clarification requested and brought by the committee. However, in several other instances, such as the Hoover case, this did not occur. In fact, due to the inactivity of the 'national contact points' in some countries, most cases of investment/divestment do not even reach the committee (Blainpain and Engels 1998). We would therefore confirm here an earlier statement that the impact of the guidelines was net but limited (Rojot 1976), at the time, and it probably has markedly decreased since then.

International collective bargaining within the European Union

The EU environment offers an interesting case where a set of government intervention provisions aiming to favour EU-wide collective bargaining came to interact with the parties' strategies.

It has often been underlined that the objective of the EC Treaty of 1957 establishing the European Community was the establishment of a Common Market, i.e. an area in which 'economic' exchanges between member states are free. The vocation of the Community, at the outset, thus, was set in an economic union, with possible later political projections. However, there was no explicit recognition of the need for any European social policy. Better wages, working conditions, industrial relations were implicitly considered as quasi-automatically flowing from the benefits of improved competitiveness and growth in the EEC. In the famous words attributed to General de Gaulle, the day-to-day problems of supply were to automatically fall together, when the essentials were aligned.

A first stage in the building of a European social framework was the adoption by the European Council of several Directives (Blanpain and Engels 1998) in the social and labour policy field, during the 1970s. One should quote, for instance, the directives on collective redundancies (1975), transfers of enterprises (1977), insolvency of employers (1980), equality of remuneration (1975 and 1976), equality of treatment within social security systems (1978) and several other ones on health and safety. However, the impact of the directives remains limited. Indeed, they tend to bring about harmonisation in the different national laws but they only set objectives and leave the member states free to decide how to attain these objectives in their own respective ways through their own devices. Also, in January 1974, the commission had adopted its first programme of social action. Funds in order to ease the economic transformation were also established as well as observatory institutions such as CEDEFOP ('Cedefop' is the French acronym of the European Centre for the Development of Vocational Training (*Centre Européen pour le Développement de la Formation Professionnelle*) under which it is officially known) and the Dublin Foundation (European Foundation for the Improvement of Living and Working Conditions). It should be underlined, nevertheless, that the decision-making power remains in the hands of the Council of Ministers, for which the Commission prepares proposals.

Other significant changes were also noticeable later. For instance, the EEC Commission initiated, in 1985, a process of informal meetings between UNICE, CEEP and the ETUC which took place at the castle of Val Duchesse, after which name those meetings came to be known. They were designed to promote a Europe-wide dialogue between management and labour. They led, after a long and convoluted process, to the expression of joint opinions regarding policy to be followed in several areas, in particular regarding training, motivation, information and consultation relating to new technologies. However, the joint opinions have not had further impact at national level in the member States. Besides, the employers' side, opposed to anything even remotely linked to international collective bargaining, was careful not to let the dialogue expand into more substantial relationships. Consequently, despite a few provisions in favour of the promotion of European social dialogue, following a deliberate proactive policy of the Commission, one can feel that social and labour policy in general remained essentially a matter for the member states to regulate in accordance with national law up to about ten years ago.

Nevertheless, the past ten years have been characterised by some progress in the direction of a European social dialogue, which seems to be leading to significant changes in the building of a social and labour relations framework at the Community level, even if this also raises some new problems. The most significant steps in that process are probably marked by the adoption of three important European documents: the Single European Act, the European Charter of Fundamental Rights and the Social Protocol attached to the Maastricht Treaty. Finally, The Nice summit of 2000 declared the Charter of the Fundamental rights whose integration into the Treaties was to be re-examined in 2004 and finally adopt the statute of the Euro-company.

Among these steps, the provisions issuing from the Social Protocol must be outlined. They favour the principle of the development of collective agreements at the European level, and give new tools to management and labour to implement European collective contracts, since collective agreements (if both management and labour wish it) may be implemented by a Council decision, at the request of the Commission, which has been the case for instance under the shape of the Directive on Part Time work. The Protocol also places social dialogue between management and labour at the centre of the EC legislative process through Article 3 which states that the Commission must consult management and labour, when elaborating new legislative proposals in the social policy field. Moreover, in the consultation process, management and labour can forward to the Commission an opinion or, where appropriate, a recommendation. Finally, it is worth noting that the above consultation procedure, conducted by the Commission, might also lead to a collective agreement, at the request of labour and management, in application of Article 4, instead of a Council decision.

Consequently, it appears that some important changes have occurred over the past ten years in the building of European social dialogue. Of course, real dialogue rests on the will and power of the parties and the presence of that essential element has still to be evidenced. However, the institutional European framework has been put in place even if some technical questions and difficulties need to be answered before it can help Europe-wide social dialogue to emerge fully, when and if the parties are ready.

It first must be pointed out that industrial relations in the EU are still very much divided along national lines and that there are extremely strong differences between countries. For instance the scope of bargaining varies from plant level to national inter-industrial level, with all the possible intermediate variations (dominant sector level in France vs. regional level in Germany and plant level in the UK). The representation of employees at the workplace goes from elected to appointed, through unions only or by work councils or both (French *Comités d'Entreprise* vs German codetermination for instance). The structures of employers' associations and labour unions are very different; they can be unified or divided, craft-based or industry-based, with different jurisdictional lines and ideological standpoints (the chemical industry may or may not include the fragance industry, for instance, or unions may be split along ideological lines in the same industry, as is the case in France, Italy, Belgium, Spain and the Netherlands). Finally, the structure of collective bargaining in each country is different.

It should be added that there is very little automatic incentive towards unification of industrial relations. The rise of the national union historically occurred because it could provide local unions with a service that they needed and that they could not alone avail themselves of: namely a better control of labour in an expanding market. Employers associations followed. It is extremely questionable and even unlikely whether the international union can benefit from the same circumstances.

From European works councils to European international collective bargaining?

The more significant event in the area of European Social developments stems from a new directive. It should be recalled that, after an early debate, the international labour movement actors, reviewed above, aimed jointly at two goals: fully-fledged international collective bargaining, between international unions and MNCs, and the setting up of an international institutional mechanism for information and consultation of employees. They had roughly divided the tasks to achieve these respective goals between the ITS and the ICFTU. If direct attempts at both goals were unsuccessful, worldwide, after a long process, an institutional attempt to open a channel to the second goal at the level of the MNC still exists within the EU, which in turn can possibly open a way towards international European collective bargaining.

The Directive 94/45/EC, adopted on 22 September 1994 provides for the creation of a European Works Council (EWC) or alternatively a procedure for the provision of information, exchange of views and dialogue, in every Community-scale undertaking (i.e. multinational enterprise). It has a quite unique character, both by having allowed 'undertakings' submitted to escape its provisions by concluding voluntary agreements before its deadline for implementation was reached and by establishing 'fall-back' or subsidiary required provisions which are to apply failing an agreement to comply with the directive. Nevertheless, as befits a directive, it had to be implemented and transposed into national law in the member states, which allowed for differences.

Globally, the main effect of the directive is to provide for consultation between the management of an undertaking or group and the EWC. However, this concept is vague and subject to many interpretations. The definition retained is among the weakest possible: 'an exchange of views and the establishment of a dialogue between workers' representatives and central management or its representative or any other more appropriate level of management'.

Impact on European collective bargaining

Thus, the institutional dynamic on the part of the EU Commission has not been without results over time and significant steps have been achieved. However, one actor alone is not enough to bring about bargaining, particularly when it is not going to be one of the parties. In order to negotiate, as pointed out above, there has to be at least two willing partners.

In theory, one major consequence of the changes briefly reviewed which occurred over the past ten years is that technically international collective bargaining at the European level could theoretically be considered to have taken place or to be presently taking place, if only between the Special Negotiation Body of Employees representatives (SNB) provided for by the directive on EWC (in order to establish the procedure for consultation or an EWC, failing which the fall-back provisions are to apply), and MNC's management. However, the actual impact of the developments should be assessed in fact and not in theory alone.

It is clear that international collective bargaining at European level can be understood under different shapes and at different levels, as the definition of collective bargaining that was given in the introduction demonstrates. At least three models are conceivable: EU-wide global agreements between central social partners, such as UNICE, ETUC and CEEP (the Public Employers European Organisation); sectoral agreements covering only one industry, Europe wide, and company level agreements for multinationals within Europe, signed either with International Trade Secretariats (or global union federations) or an ad hoc representation of their unionised employees. The three possibilities need to be explored successively.

As far as the first level is concerned, the only possible framework for a global EU-wide agreement rests with the procedure established by the Maastricht agreement favouring the establishment of collective agreements at the European level, given the obstacles to international bargaining discussed above at the outset. Several have been passed to date, notably concerning parental leave and part-time work. However, for the enforcement of these agreements, the social partners at the European level have had to rely on the acceptance of the Commission to propose it to the Council, and for the latter to adopt it, as a Directive, under the usual majority rules. The other mode of application foreseen by the Maastricht protocol, in accordance with the procedures and practices in the member states, would be normal national level collective bargaining, whose scope, process and level vary tremendously among them. No obligation to see that this application is carried out weighs on the member states and the representative bodies having signed (UNICE, EURO-TUC and CEEP) have no power to see that it is either enforced or adopted in a national framework by their national constituents. There is no legal mechanism of enforcement of possible collective agreements at local level and there is presently no competence for the EU to establish one.

Clearly, the right to pass an agreement without any prerogative to see to its enforcement constitutes a very limited and restrictive version of collective bargaining. It is more a right of proposal (to the Council of Ministers of the EU) than anything else. Besides, neither of the Social Partners has any means of compulsion to bring about signatures. Thus we have also collective bargaining without bargaining power. As before, the conclusion of collective agreements rests alone on the goodwill of the management side. The institutional mechanism set up by the protocol is a step which offers tools, but their use is conditioned by the will of the potential parties. It has been recognised for long that UNICE, the managerial party concerned at this level, has steadfastly resisted European Bargaining, conceding only marginally and for avoidance of a worse issue, that is the enactment of compulsory directives and/or regulations by the Commission. This strategy is pursued openly.

At sectoral level, similar obstacles exist. There are no actors and/or forums for negotiating. Most sectoral employers' organisations consider themselves as economic or trade bodies, without competence in the social field, and the consultation between them and the labour organisations at that level by the EU administration reaches the same limits as the ones described above. In the same way, identical problems for enforcement and/or applicability of agreements are posed. The maritime sectoral agreement on the organisation of working time, signed on 30 September 1998 by the Federation of Transport Workers' Unions in the European Union and the European Community Shipowners' Association actually illustrates the similarity of the situations at both levels, rather than constituting a pioneering example for future examples of specific sectoral dialogue. It was reached under the threat of the Commission to issue a legislative proposal under its action programme and it is based on the Social Policy Agreement, relying on a EU Council decision for its implementation (EIRR 1988).

As the directive on EWCs made obvious, the level where developments around international collective bargaining were most likely to occur was the MNCs. Clearly, information and consultation might be considered as the forerunners of future negotiations, and the extent to which they bind management should be gauged. Even if the likelihood of EWCs concluding full-fledged agreements is generally considered as a very remote prospect, some authors see as a distinct possibility the appearance of virtual or arms' length collective bargaining (Marginson and Sisson 1998; Hermann and Jacobi 2000), through labour co-ordination. However, even this prospect is by no means certain for several reasons dealing notably with the actual structure of multinational enterprises as opposed to the concept of undertaking provided for in the directive, the mode of representation of employee representatives in the EWCs and the weak and unclear obligation that the directive puts upon management (Rojot *et al.* 2001).

Also, an argument has been often made in the literature dealing with the EWC (Marginson and Sisson 1998; Hermann and Jacobi 2000) that one of its main roles consists in providing employees' representatives, at the opportunity of meetings, with a free forum, financed by management. Union members and employee representatives across the MNC's operations would thus forge links between themselves, exchange information, get to know each other better, build relationships culminating in the establishment of a network. The result is assumed to become over time a common international bargaining strategy and a budding international organisation and therefore develop the groundwork for what is not yet but is becoming international industrial relations and collective bargaining. However, the reverse agreement is never made but can just as easily be credible: by bringing together union and employee representatives from different countries, cultures, political persuasions and ideologies, a very strong potential for conflict is created just as much for co-operation. Examples point towards such outcomes (Rojot *et al.* 2001).

Conclusion

It is clear that the high hopes for international collective bargaining held in the 1970s have not yet materialised. The obstacles alluded to in the introduction to this text have been demonstrated to be too formidable. In retrospect, it seems that for it to have a chance to appear it should happen in a region of the world where some degree of harmonisation of markets for all the factors of production would to some degree have occurred. This would in no way guarantee its development, but would set the minimum framework for its possible existence. This has not occurred in any region of the world except in the EU.

Therefore, the only potential opening for some degree of international collective bargaining seems to rest within the EU, where support for it is provided by the setting up by governments and the commission of elements of an institutional framework. Will it happen? The answer may again lie in the hands of the management of MNCs. A careful analysis of the past studies carried out on the subject (Gold and Hall 1992; Rojot 1976) again leaves little doubt, that, in the past, what has existed in terms of international information and consultation within MNCs, has been achieved on sufferance, and sometimes at the initiative of management. Whether the directive represents a real move towards a new EU level of productive and active information and consultation between MNCs' management and employees' representatives leading almost logically to some degree of collective bargaining or a cumbersome mechanism empty of meaning, rests again at the will of management.

So far, this concerns only a few cases among the ones evidenced by empirical studies (Rojot *et al.* 2001). However, it is not impossible for the environment to change. Strangely enough, European collective bargaining may come about in indirect ways. The voluntary proactive policy from the Commission to promote it for the past quarter century has met with very limited success, culminating in a directive that depends in a large measure on management goodwill. However, totally outside the social and labour field, momentous changes of an economic nature have taken place within the EU. The adoption of a European Central Bank and a single European Monetary Unit is an event without precedent. The move to a single currency and a single central bank will remove the use of all of monetary policy and most of fiscal policy tools from any participating country. In addition, it should be underlined that with the acceptance of the Pact of Stability by which the Governments entering the EMU have committed themselves to limit and reduce the public deficits, they have for almost all practical purposes additionally restricted themselves not to use actively any tool of budgetary policy. As we already pointed out, one of the major obstacles to European Collective Bargaining was the importance of the differences between the national systems of social security, working conditions, wage structure, financing of welfare systems etc. But, in the absence of the possibility of financing social costs and expenses by either devaluing the national currency, or increasing the national debt, or by taxation which would drive out investment, it is likely that market pressures will help to eradicate the relative differences among competitors, between nation states and regions within the EMU area. This, of course, is not likely to occur, at least in some member states, without major industrial conflict. Nevertheless, in that fashion, one of the major obstacles to European collective bargaining could be removed. Thus, paradoxically, international collective bargaining might be facilitated by flexibility and deregulation, where regulation has all but failed.

References

Blanpain, R. and Engels, C. (1998) 'European Labor Law' in R. Blanpain (ed.) *The International Encyclopedia for Labor Law and Industrial Relations*. Deventer: Kluwer.
European Industrial Relations Review (1998) No. 298.
Gold, M. and Hall, M. (1992) 'European level information and consultation in multinational companies: an evaluation of practice', *Dublin, European Foundation for the Improvement of Living and Working Conditions*.
Heise, P. A. (1973) 'The multinational corporation and industrial relations: the American approach compared with the European', *Relations Industrielles*, 28(1), January.
Hermann, W. and Jacobi, O. (2000) 'Ambassadors of the Civil Society: practice and future of the European Works Councils', in Hoffman, R., Jacobi, O., Keller, B. and Weiss, M. (eds) *Transnational Industrial Relations in Europe*. Dusseldorf: Edition der Hans Bockler Stiftung.
Laffer, K. (1977) 'Australian maritimes unions and the International Transport Workers Federation', *Journal of Industrial Relations*. (Australia), June.
Lecher, W. and Platzer H.-W, (1998) *European Union – European Industrial Relations?* London: Routledge.
Malles, P. (1971) 'The multinational corporation and industrial relations: the European approach', *Relations Industrielles*, 26(1), January.
Marginson, P. and Sisson, K. (1998) 'European collective bargaining: a virtual prospect?', *Journal of Common Market Studies*, 36(4), December.
Rojot, J. (1976) *International Collective Bargaining: An Analysis and Case-Study for Europe*. Deventer: Kluwer.
Rojot, J. (2004) 'The right to bargain collectively: an international perspective on its extent and relevance', *International Journal of Comparative Labour Law and Industrial Relations*. 20(4), Winter.
Rojot, J., Le Flanchec, A. and Voynnet-Fourboul, C. (2001) 'European collective bargaining, new prospects or much ado about little?', *International Journal of Comparative Labor Law and Indusrial Relations*. 17(3), Autumn.
Ulman, L. (1955) *The Rise of the National Trade Union*. Cambridge, Mass: Harvard University Press.

Suggested key readings

Blanpain, R. and Engels, C. (1998) 'European Labor Law' in R. Blanpain (ed.) *The International Encyclopedia for Labor Law and Industrial Relations*. Deventer: Kluwer.
Blanpain, R. and Windey, P. (1996) *European Works Councils*. Leuwen: Peeters.
European Foundation for the Improvement of Living and Working Conditions; Dublin, Several working papers and reports on European Works Councils: eiro@eurofound.ie
Lecher, W. and Platzer, H.-W. (1998) *European Union – European Industrial Relations?* London: Routledge.
Marginson, P. and Sisson, K. (1998), 'European collective bargaining: a virtual prospect?', *Journal of Common Market Studies*, 36(4), December.
Oeschlin, J.-J. (1998) 'International employers organizations', in R. Blanpain (ed.) *The International Encyclopedia for Labor Law and Industrial Relations*. Deventer: Kluwer.
Rojot, J. (2004) 'The right to bargain collectively: an international perspective on its extent and relevance', *International Journal of Comparative Labour Law and Industrial Relations*. 20(4), Winter.

Rojot, J., Le Flanchec, A. and Voynnet-Fourboul, C. (2001) 'European collective bargaining, new prospects or much ado about little?', *International Journal of Comparative Labor Law and Indusrial Relations*, 17(3), Autumn.

Windmuller, J. (1998) 'International trade unions', in R. Blanpain (ed.) *The International Encyclopedia for Labor Law and Industrial Relations*. Deventer: Kluwer.

13 Contemporary strike trends since 1980: peering through the wrong end of a telescope

JOSEPH WALLACE AND MICHELLE O'SULLIVAN[1]

Introduction

There has been limited interest among academics in strikes as a social and industrial phenomena in recent years. This has also been the case in the media, although the limited interest is punctuated with occasional headline status, as in the case of the fire-fighters' strike in the UK in 2002/2003, the lorry drivers' blockades in France in 2000 and the Volkswagen strike in Germany in 2004. Since the early 1980s there has been much greater focus in academic circles on new strategies for managing people and new forms of work organisation. This is true of both prescriptive texts and critical writings. The 1980s saw the birth of human resource management (HRM), which was managerialist in nature. Critical writers responded to that development by interrogating the logical consistency and empirical reality of that model. Subsequently, attention turned to the plethora of new forms of work organisation; Just in Time (JIT), World Class Manufacturing (WCM), Total Quality Management (TQM), High Performance Work Systems (HPWS) and Lean Production. In this rush to 'sell' or 'interrogate' these workplace-level developments, there was a noticeable lessening of attention on societal issues, in general, and industrial conflict in particular. This may be due, in part, to the fact that much analysis of the world of work has emanated from business schools and this tends to focus attention on organisational issues. However, this development may also be due to an underlying feeling that the strike problem had largely gone away or, at least, that the residual strike levels were insignificant. Indeed, just such a point has been argued by Hansen and Mather (1988: 27):

> the diminution of strike action in practice is accompanied by a new understanding that strikes themselves are inefficient and outdated means of bargaining. The strike threat is a crude weapon ill-suited to advanced societies in which workers have valuable skills to sell in an efficiently functioning labour market.

The degree of attention, which scholars had focused on conflict in the 1970s, may be absent today but conflict in general, and strikes in particular, continue to attract some interest. Two broad sets of articles have tended to appear in the literature. One set questions the extent of the decline in strikes (Aligisakis 1997; Gall 1999; Clarke *et al.* 1998), while the second questions the suitability of strike statistics as an indicator of levels of industrial conflict. Some articles in the first set raise concerns over the reliability of strike statistics and particularly the effect of changes to collection methods, which bias comparisons over time. It is suggested that in some countries there has been a systematic under-reporting of strikes and a consequent overstating of any decline. For example, Gall (1999) notes the exclusion of public sector strikes in Belgium, France, Greece (since 1993) and Portugal (since 1986). In these four countries, he argues, 'the impact of statistical exclusions is likely to be such that serious doubts must be raised about the validity of data used and the conclusions drawn from them' (Gall 1999: 371). Aligisakis (1997: 73) points to the 'wave of strikes' in France and Germany as indicative of counter currents within the general decline in strikes in Western Europe. Gall (1999) suggests that there was a greater diversity in strike trends, levels and trajectories than previously recognised. Within these articles the focus is generally on the exclusion of strikes in the public sector as there is general agreement that private sector strikes are on the decline. This mirrors the general decline in trade union density in the private sector (outside of Scandinavia) and the higher concentration of union members in the public sector.

The second approach questions the use of strike statistics as a useful measure of collective industrial conflict. Kelly and Nicholson (1980: 30) note 'the "iceberg tip" view of recorded strikes is correct insofar as this form of conflict is only part of a much larger picture …'. Blyton and Turnbull (2004: 328) reject Hanson and Mather's arguments noted earlier, and suggest that, 'if anything, the bases of conflicts have been heightened over the past two decades. What needs to be explained are the various manifestations of such conflicts, including non-strike forms of dissension'. Within this group there are two distinct trends. The first explore the existence of a displacement effect, which, at one level, can involve cut-price forms of industrial action such as a ban on overtime, work to rule, go-slows, etc., which official statistics fail to measure. It is also noted that collective forms of conflict may be displaced to the developing world. Arrighi (1990: 54) writes 'in the past the tensions of capitalism could be eased by expansion of the system into new regions and that capitalism now operates on a truly global scale'. In particular, the growth of strikes in South Korea has been cited as an example of this effect at work (cf. Cho 1985; Salamon 2000). The second trend points to the possible displacement of collective conflict with individual forms of conflict such as absenteeism, turnover and claims for bullying and harassment (cf. Edwards 1992; Wallace *et al.* 2004). Authors also point to management-initiated conflict such as speed-ups, stress at work and growing income inequality which is indicative of a heightened basis of conflict (Edwards 1992).

These points have a strong theoretical basis and undoubtedly strikes are an inadequate measure of the *level* of industrial conflict. However, the criticisms of the use of strike figures as a measure of *movements* in conflict only become relevant if strikes and other forms of conflict are negatively correlated. This does not appear to be the case and there are indications that there is a direct relationship between strikes and other forms of collective industrial action with high levels of strikes associated with high levels of non-strike action, and vice versa (cf. Stokke and Thörnqvist 2001; Clegg 1979). If this were the case, then a decline in strikes would likely be accompanied by a decline in other organised collective forms of conflict. This lack of availability of comparative data means that, whatever the limitations of strike statistics, they remain the one readily available source of data and their usage is almost inevitable in any comparative analysis of conflict levels. Their disadvantages are outweighed by the fact that they provide indices that can be readily compared across countries to provide a kind of 'league table'. This simplicity and ease of use, however, invites misuse and abuse of the indices and a clear understanding of the limitations of strike data is essential.

Measures of strike activity

There are four measures used to determine strike activity and it is generally advised that all four should be used. The four measures are:

- strike incidence (the number of strikes)
- strike breadth (the number of workers involved)
- strike duration (the length a strike lasts)
- working days lost.

Strike frequency has the greatest reliability problems due to two factors; the different criteria used by different countries for the inclusion of strikes and the likelihood that many smaller strikes, that meet the definition for inclusion, may not be counted. The second measure, *strike breadth*, measures the size of strikes and can indicate a degree of social mobilisation. The third index, *strike duration*, is seen as indicating the intransigence of disputes within a country. It can also reflect differing strike 'cultures' across countries, with French strikes having traditionally been short due to the absence of strike pay in trade unions and the fact that strikes can be demonstration strikes with a political purpose (cf. Wallace *et al.* 2004). The *working days lost (WDL)* index is derived by multiplying the number of workers involved by the strike duration. This is widely accepted to be the most reliable of the strike indices, because larger strikes tend to be counted due to their greater visibility and these account for the vast bulk of working days lost. By contrast, strike frequency is likely to be seriously compromised by a failure to count small strikes in some countries or at various time intervals. When comparing strikes across countries, working days lost per thousand employees is considered the most useful statistic as it standardises for employment levels, although not for unionisation rates. The latter is an important point as, although strikes can occur without unions, they are chiefly associated with unionisation.

An overview of problems in using strike statistics

While the attractiveness of strike statistics lies in their ability to generate ready and simple comparisons across countries, there are substantial limitations to any such comparisons (Shalev 1978). At a global level, there are so many methodological problems with the compilation and use of strike statistics that only an outline of the main exceptions and qualifications can be given. For example the following stand out:

- Data is frequently missing for years making consistent comparisons of countries across extended time periods difficult;
- Countries count different phenomena as strikes. In Hungary a two-hour sit-in counts as a strike but in others political strikes are not counted. This is a significant consideration, as political strikes tend to be large;
- As mentioned earlier, some countries exclude strike activity in the public sector;
- There are differing qualifications in terms of the size a strike must be in order to be counted. In most countries strikes lasting one day and involving a minimum number of working days lost (typically 10 or 100) are counted. Some countries only include strikes with a minimum number of workers involved. This is the case with the United States of America (USA) where only strikes involving at least 1,000 workers are included, while in Canada the qualifying size since 1984 is a strike involving 500 workers;
- There are differences between countries in the data collected. In some countries it appears that all or most strikes, which should be counted, are counted, while in other countries the data appears much less reliable or even haphazard (e.g. Cambodia);
- While the International Labour Organisation (ILO) categorises strike activity as including both strikes and lockouts, many countries only include strikes in their data.

Some changes are so major, such as those in the USA and Canada, as to have a significant effect on all strike statistics, including working days lost. In other instances, such as Denmark, the changes are relatively minor and more likely to affect the strike incidence than the working days lost figure. Readers interested in individual countries should look carefully at the effects of any changes on those countries. Table 13.1 summarises the major changes that have been made to strike statistics since the 1980s.

In undertaking a global analysis, the most crucial limitation is that for many countries data is missing for some years. The absence of data is potentially

Table 13.1 Major changes in strike statistics[2]

Canada	Beginning 1985, only includes stoppages involving 500 workers or more
Spain	Prior to 1985, excluded Catalunya; 1986–1990, excluded Basque country
UK	Revised classification applied since 1983
New Zealand	Prior to 1980, excluded political strikes. Prior to 1988, excluded public sector stoppages. Prior to 1989, included partial strikes with no work stoppages. From 2000, excludes work stoppages in which five workdays not worked.
Brazil	1989, new data series.
Hong Kong	Up to 1985, included stoppages involving fewer than 10 workers or lasting less than one day if 100 or more work days not worked
Denmark	Up to 1995, excluded disputes in which less than 100 work days not worked
Hungary	1991–1995, included work stoppages in which 800 hours or more not worked. Beginning 1986, included stoppages involving 10 workers or more.
Portugal	From 1986, new data series. Up to 1994, excluded Madeira and the Azores and enterprises employing fewer than 5 workers.

Data in the following years for the following countries is not strictly comparable with data in the years preceding them: Morocco (1998); Barbados (2001); Ecuador (1998); Guatemala (1996); Puerto Rico (1996); India (2000); Myanmar (1997); Pakistan (1994); Philippines (2001); France: (1994); Iceland (1997); Italy (1996); Norway (1995); Portugal (1997); Switzerland (1994); Sweden (1994); UK (1994)

Source: *ILO Yearbook of Labour Statistics*, various years

damaging to the working days lost figure, which we have noted is the most useful strike index. The absence of any data for some years may be due to only a small number of strikes occurring in the years for which data is missing. However, the alternative possibility exists that strike data may be unavailable for high strike prone years due to the social dislocation involved or the sheer embarrassment of national authorities at the high strike statistics. Which of these effects predominate can only be resolved in the context of local knowledge and cannot be discerned from the published ILO data. This means that a global perspective can only seek to answer broad questions in the first instance. We set out to examine global trends and to answer three broad questions:

- To what extent have strikes increased or decreased globally since 1980?
- Has there been a 'bottoming out' effect in the period 1991–2002? A bottoming out effect refers to any tendency there might be for any decline in strikes to lessen in the 1990s (cf. Gall 1999).
- To what extent is there evidence of a displacement of strikes to the developing world?

While a global analysis will lack the fine detail of an individual country or regional analysis, a global perspective has some compensating advantages. It is extremely unlikely that global trends will be systematically affected by undercounting of strikes and working days lost by comparison with a previous time period. Also, while at a global level it is not possible to have comparative data for all countries across time periods, data is available for a range of countries and, again, it is unlikely that the countries involved will be highly unrepresentative of global trends. We complement the global analysis by taking a closer look at developments in a number of selected regions. No general validity is claimed for this regional analysis as the countries have been selected to demonstrate some overall trends and countervailing developments. A selection of other countries might paint a somewhat different picture and more detailed analysis of individual countries would undoubtedly add many qualifications to the picture that emerges. In general, we have not sought to posit reasons for developments in countries/differing regions as we are of the view that this can only be done in an informed way by closer study of these regions. Due to space restrictions, at the global level we focus on two statistics – strike incidence (the number of strikes) and working days lost. While we recognise the limitations of the strike incidence index, we have used it to see if the trends are similar to, or different from, the more reliable working days lost figures.

Global strike trends

As indicated above, the major data problem at a global level is the fact that for many countries data is missing for various years. This means that if one were to test for every year since the 1980s it would be necessary either (a) to exclude a large number of countries or (b) to exclude years for a large number of countries. Excluding years for countries would raise the possibility that the excluded years were important and might have been missing due to the high incidence of strikes/working days lost in any year. Also it would make the resultant presentation of data difficult, as it would be necessary to record many qualifications. As we were interested to see whether strikes had declined since the early 1980s, a comparison is made between the years 1981–1985 and the years 1996–2000. Our approach brings into focus the movements over time. By focusing on two five-year time periods, we were able to reduce the number of countries that had to be excluded due to incomplete data. We also excluded countries that had major discontinuities in the collection of strike statistics in the time periods. Even using a restricted time period resulted in comparisons between forty-two countries on strike incidence and forty countries on working days lost. The analysis ending in 2000 minimised the number of countries that had not yet reported data but made the figures relatively up to date. We also compare the period 1991–1995 with the period 1996–2001 in order to test for a 'bottoming out' effect.

While the strike incidence may be suspect for comparison between countries, there is no reason to suspect that the collection and gathering of such data within countries has become any less reliable over time. Indeed it is clear from Table 13.1 that methodological changes would have increased the number of strikes counted in some countries. Thus it is a good indicator for making a time-based comparison to test for an increase or decrease in strikes. We use the raw working days lost figures rather than standardising for employment levels. This is justified as population and employment levels have generally risen since the early 1980s. Should there have been a fall in working days lost, this would only be accentuated by standardising for employment levels.

Global strikes: A comparison of 1981–1985 and 1996–2001

Figure 13.1 and Table 13.2 contain an analysis of the changes in the number of strikes in the time periods 1981–1985 and the period 1996–2000. Only eight of the countries displayed an increase between 1981–1985 and 1996–2000, while thirty-four countries registered a decline (Figure 13.1 and Table 13.2). Those countries registering a decline experienced a total fall of 63,765 in the number of strikes; an average of approximately 1,872 strikes per country. By comparison, the increase in strike numbers for the eight countries was far less at 5,183; an

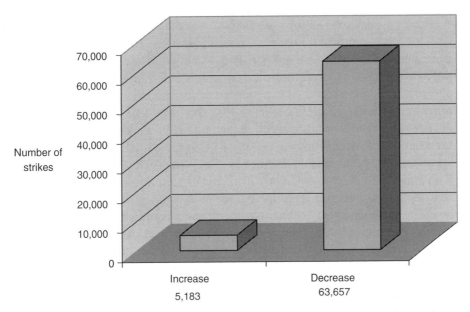

Figure 13.1 Total increase and decrease in the number of strikes and lockouts: time periods 1981–1985 and 1996–2000 compared*

Source: Derived from *ILO Yearbook of Labour Statistics*, various years
* Refers to the total increase in the number of strikes and lockouts in those countries experiencing an increase, and total decrease in the number of strikes and lockouts, in those countries experiencing a decrease

Table 13.2 Countries with an increase or decrease in the number of strikes and lockouts (number in parentheses): time periods 1981–1985 and 1996–2000 compared

Increase	Morocco (397); Mauritius (20); El Salvador (647); Netherlands Antilles (107); Denmark (3,959); Netherlands (6); Norway (34); Switzerland (13)
Decrease	Burundi (51); Guyana (1,735); Mexico (3,612); Panama (31); Peru (3,089); Puerto Rico (56); Trinidad and Tobago (28); Canada (2,133); USA (282); Bangladesh (368); Hong Kong (68); India (6,143); Israel (258); Japan (3,227); Republic of Korea (11); Malaysia (80); Pakistan (199); Philippines (834); Sri Lanka (326); Thailand (47); Austria (13); Cyprus (73); Spain (4,139); Finland (6,790); France (9,008); Iceland (21); Ireland (545); Italy (4,024); Portugal (1,415); San Marino (57); Sweden (524); UK (5,284); Australia (7,684); New Zealand (1,502)

Increase: 8 countries; Decrease: 34 countries

Source: Derived from *ILO Yearbook of Labour Statistics*, various years

average of almost 648 per country. These figures provide unambiguous evidence, within the countries examined, of a substantial decline in strikes since the early 1980s. Taking the forty-two countries as a representative of global developments, there appears to have been a dramatic global decline in strikes since 1980.

As data is available on an inconsistent basis for the number of strikes and working days lost, the countries in Figures 13.1 and 13.2 (and Tables 13.2 and 13.3) differ and, as such, the figures are not strictly comparable. However, even with a different group of countries the same pattern as in the strike incidence index is apparent. Only nine countries experienced an increase in working days lost, while thirty-one registered a decline (Figure 13.2 and Table 13.3). The magnitude of the decline was even more pronounced in the number of working days lost. Looking at the extent of the decline/increase in these groups, the total decline for the thirty-one countries was a massive decrease in excess of 467 million days by comparison with a minimal increase of slightly in excess of 13 million days lost in the remaining nine countries. Thus the reduction in working days lost, in those countries experiencing a decline, swamps by many orders of magnitude the much smaller increase in those countries where there has been a rise. The average reduction for the thirty-one countries was 15,080,929 while the average increase for the nine countries displaying a rise in working days lost was 1,472,477.

Strikes in the developing world[3]

Figure 13.1 and Table 13.2 show a decline in strikes across a large number of developing countries between the periods 1981–1985 and 1996–2000 as follows: Burundi (–51); Guyana (–1,735); Panama (31); Peru (–3,089), Puerto Rico (–56),

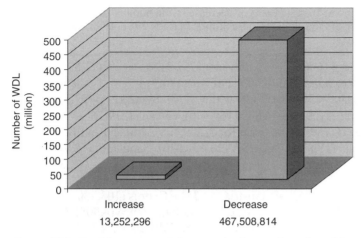

Figure 13.2 Total increase and decrease in the number of working days lost: time periods 1981–1985 and 1996–2000 compared*

Source: Derived from *ILO Yearbook of Labour Statistics*, various years
* Refers to the total increase in the number of working days lost, in those countries experiencing an increase, and total decrease in working days lost, in those countries experiencing a decrease

Trinidad and Tobago (–28), Bangladesh (–368), India (–6143), Korea (–11); Malaysia (–80); Pakistan (–199); Philippines (–834); Sri Lanka (–326) and Thailand (–47). These declines contrast with more modest growth in a small number of countries. These are Morocco (+397); Mauritius (+20); El Salvador (+647) and Netherlands Antilles (+107). Turning to the working days lost figures, there has been a substantial decline in working days lost in three of the countries for which consistent data is available: Peru (+10,750,250); India (+126,452,850); the Philippines (+5,115,883) and Korea (+5,914,320) (Figure 13.2 and Table 13.3). By contrast, the increases in two other developing countries, El Salvador (+792,317) and Panama (+1,886,184), are more modest. Obviously the small number of countries for comparison on the basis of working days lost makes this statistic insufficient to disprove a hypothesis of a displacement of strikes to developing countries.

There are wide disparities in the incidence of strikes between countries. While India had high, but falling, strike frequency levels in the 1990s; strike incidence in other countries was much lower. This is not always related to the size of the country, as demonstrated by China, where the number of strikes often falls below ten. Low strike incidence is often associated with the lack of opportunity to strike. Some countries make strikes virtually impossible due to legal or military constraints. Salamon (2000) notes the legal restraints placed on strikes in South-East Asian countries, that can extend to large swathes of the economy including transport, banking, tourism and export-oriented industries. In addition, Salamon (2000) explains that some fundamental aspects of the employment relationship, such as recruitment, promotion and dismissals, are excluded from collective

Table 13.3 Countries with an increase or decrease in the number of working days lost (number of days in parentheses): time periods 1981–1985 and 1996–2000 compared

Increase	Morocco (606,210), El Salvador (792,317), Panama (1,895,211), Israel (2,586,990), Republic of Korea (5,914,320), Thailand (283,446), Denmark (279,500), Norway (860,777), Switzerland (33,525)
Decrease	Mauritius (29,060), Chile (169,940), Guyana (219,762), Peru (10,750,250), Puerto Rico (299,408), Trinidad and Tobago (397,234), Canada (18,870,674), USA (26,491,240), Bangladesh (2,977,556), Hong Kong (33,947), India (126,452,850), Japan (1,840,233), Malaysia (61,446), Pakistan (1,540,356), Philippines (5,115,883), Sri Lanka (376,904), Austria (42,321), Cyprus (103,780), Spain (12,120,200), Finland (2,757,784), France (4,908,769), Germany (5,509,656), Ireland (1,452,290), Italy (187,942,800), Netherlands (335,862), Portugal (2,065,900), San Marino (12,737), Sweden (617,709), UK (44,309,000), Australia (7,566,100), New Zealand (2,137,163)

Increase: 9 countries; Decrease: 31 countries
Source: Derived from *ILO Yearbook of Labour Statistics*, various years

bargaining and therefore cannot be the subject of a dispute, and consequently, strike action. This is the case with Singapore and Malaysia. It should be noted that neither limitations are, of themselves, sufficient to explain fully the absence of strikes, as there are many societies which have tried such an approach without success. Such limitations on strike action may help to explain why South-East Asian countries make 'fairly extensive use of other forms of industrial action' such as sit-ins, hunger strikes and demonstrations (Salamon 2000: 449).

Strike trends in the developed world

An overview

The data in Figures 13.1 and 13.2 (and Tables 13.2 and 13.3) provide evidence for a remarkable decline in the number of strikes in a number of developed countries. This is particularly so in those countries that previously had high levels of strikes. Thus, Japan (–3227), Spain (–4139), Finland (–6790), France (–3185), Ireland (–545), Italy (–4024), Portugal (–1415), Sweden (–524), the UK (–5284), Australia (–7684) and New Zealand (–1502) all register a substantial decline in the number of strikes between the period 1981–1985 and the period 1996–2000. Focusing on working days lost shows large declines in the UK (–44,309,000), Australia (–7,566,100); New Zealand (–2,137,163), Spain (–12,120,200) and Japan (–1,840,233). One feature that stands out from the data is the widespread extent of the decline across countries with differing industrial relations systems. Countries which have had social partnership/neo-corporatist policies (Ireland,

Sweden and to an extent Italy) experienced a decline in the indices as have countries which have seen neo-liberal policies applied (Australia, New Zealand and the UK). This fact appears especially significant and is discussed further in our conclusion.

North and Central America

As the world's largest economy the strike experience of the USA is of special interest. Analysis of strike levels in the USA is complicated by the high criteria for including a strike in the statistics (involving 1,000 workers). However, this problem does not affect the internal USA strike trends. The decline in working days lost of 26,491,240 between the two periods 1981–1985 and 1996–2000 is indicative of a major reduction in the impact of strikes in that country. It is highly improbable that this decline could be counterbalanced by working days lost in strikes with fewer than 1,000 workers involved. Indeed the likelihood is that the decline in working days lost in large strikes will have been paralleled by a similar decline in smaller strikes.

Canada too experienced a decline in strike numbers and working days lost in the two periods. Thompson and Taras (2004) note that the largest five or six strikes account for 35 per cent of working days lost and that, in recent years, the average duration of strikes has been twelve to fifteeen days. They suggest that these characteristics may be accounted for by the presence of multi-national corporations and the fact that 'large unions can withstand long strikes at individual production units without the parent enterprises suffering major economic loss' (Thompson and Taras 2004: 106).

In Central America, Mexico experienced a reduction of 3,612 in the number of strikes between the two time periods. While data on working days lost in Mexico is unavailable for 1981, resulting in its exclusion from the examination, an analysis of the years 1982–1985 and 1996–2000 indicates a decrease in working days lost by almost 300,000 days. It is much more difficult to establish a pattern for working days lost for the late 1980s due to the existence of conflicting data.

The European Union and Norway[4]

As a major trading block, the strike levels within the European Union (EU) are of major interest and are considered to be one of the indicators of the health of EU social dialogue. Mirroring the global picture, there has been a substantial reduction in strike incidence and working days lost since the early 1980s within the EU. The European Industrial Relations Observatory (EIRO) (2003) notes that 'levels of industrial action throughout the EU are generally at a low level' and have fallen, not just since the early 1980s, but also in comparison to the second half of the 1980s. It concludes that the late 1990s and early 2000s have 'clearly been a period of relative industrial peace in many countries' (EIRO website 2003). While there has been a decline in strikes within the EU there have also been departures from the downward trend in some years, for example, both France and Germany experienced a strike wave in the mid 1990s (Aligisakis 1997), and Poland had a peak of 920 strikes in 1999.

France, Denmark, Spain, and Italy stand out as having relatively high absolute strike incidence over the years 1998–2001 while the UK, Portugal and Belgium come in a middle group (Table 13.4). These figures do not take account of country size; however, they do highlight some interesting features. EIRO (2003) points to the very different picture 'in the broadly comparable (in size terms) "big five" EU member states – France, Germany, Italy, Spain and the UK'. They note that France, Italy and especially Spain show considerably higher levels of industrial action than Germany. Perhaps the most noticeable feature of the table is the wide variation in the number of strikes across countries. Some countries, such as Austria, Luxembourg, Slovakia and Sweden, have a very low number of strikes, while others have large numbers. Thus political and social stability is consistent with wide variation in strike levels.

There is clear evidence of a decline in working days lost per 1,000 employees within the EU. Monger (2004) points to an overall decline of 25 per cent between the period 1993–1997 and the period 1998–2002. Looking at the composite working days lost per 1,000 employees, EIRO (2003) has divided the countries into three groups for the years 1998–2001 (Table 13.5). Denmark, Spain, Norway and Ireland are classified in the relatively high strike prone group with Austria, Germany, the Netherlands, Poland, Portugal, Slovakia, Sweden and the UK at the other end of the spectrum. Even such standardised figures can give a misleading picture. In particular, the ranking of a country over shorter periods of time is

Table 13.4 Total number of strikes in 17 EU countries and Norway, 1998–2001

Austria	2	Luxembourg	3
Belgium	759	Netherlands	85
Denmark	4,371	Norway	83
Finland	333	Poland	1,012
France	5,357	Portugal	677
Germany	9	Slovakia	0
Greece	53	Spain	2,813
Ireland	131	Sweden	45
Italy	3,503	UK	777

Note: For some years, data was unavailable for Greece, Slovakia and Portugal. For some countries, the data refers to a portion of a year.
Source: EIRO website 2003; Figure for Germany from Monger 2004

Table 13.5 Annual average working days lost (WDL) per 1,000 employees: EU countries and Norway, 1998–2001

Relatively high annual average WDL (over 70)	Denmark, Ireland, Norway, Spain
Moderate levels of annual average WDL (between 20–70)	Belgium, Finland, France, Greece, Hungary, Italy, Luxembourg
Relatively low levels of annual WDL (under 20)	Austria, Germany, the Netherlands, Poland, Portugal, Slovakia, Sweden, UK

Source: EIRO 2003

greatly affected by the time period chosen. Thus the high position of Denmark is due to the large number of working days lost in one strike in the private sector over a new collective agreement (EIRO 2003).[5]

Japan and Australia

An analysis of the data indicates that Japan experienced a decrease both in the number of strikes and working days lost in the periods 1981–1985 and 1996–2000 but, as mentioned earlier, strikes are but one face of conflict in the employment relationship. Thus, Kuwahara (2004: 292) notes that, in the case of Japan, 'one of the remarkable changes is that the weight of disputes is shifting from the collective to the individual. There have also been higher levels of labour turnover'. In Australia, there has been a massive decrease in working days lost but Lansbury and Wailes (2004) contend that this reduction cannot be attributed to the controversial 1996 Workplace Relations Act as the decline started prior to its introduction. Interesting to note, though, is Ellem's (2001) observation that there has been an increase in employer-initiated industrial action regarding the introduction of non-union agreements in the private sector.

Global strikes: A comparison of the periods 1991–1995 and 1996–2000

The above analysis indicates a major shift in strike patterns since the 1980s. Of particular interest is the extent to which this disjuncture continued in the 1990s or whether there is evidence of a bottoming out effect. In order to test this, we compare strike incidence and working days lost for the period 1991–1995 and the period 1996–2000 (Figures 13.3 and 13.4; Tables 13.6 and 13.7). For these time periods it was possible to compare data for the number of strikes in a total of forty-eight countries. This comparison shows that there was in fact a rise in strikes between the two time periods and not a decline. However, the picture is complicated by the inclusion of data for the Russian Federation in the comparison between the 1991–1995 and the 1996–2000 time periods. The Soviet Union was

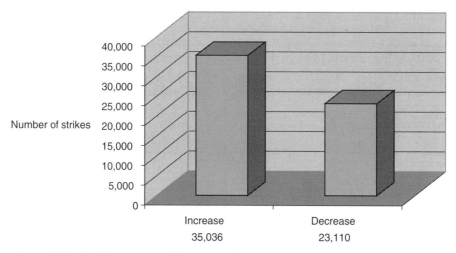

Figure 13.3 Total increase and decrease in strikes and lockouts: time periods 1991–1995 and 1996–2000 compared*

Source: Derived from *ILO Yearbook of Labour Statistics*, various years
* Refers to the total increase in the number of strikes and lockouts, in those countries experiencing an increase, and total decrease in strikes and lockouts, in those countries experiencing a decrease

not included in earlier (1981–1985 and 1996–2000) comparisons due to data issues and, in any event, their inclusion would not have made sense given the restrictions on strikes there during the Soviet period. Comparing the periods 1991–1995 and 1996–2000, there was a marked increase, rather than decrease, in the number of strikes. This increase is overwhelmingly accounted for by the Russian Federation (+26,886). This increase can be attributed to social and

Table 13.6 Countries with an increase or decrease in the number of strikes and lockouts (numbers in parentheses): time periods 1991–1995 and 1996–2000 compared

Increase	Egypt (15), Morocco (371), Mauritius (71), El Salvador (611), Panama (16), Trinidad and Tobago (33), Hong Kong (2), Sri Lanka (16), Belgium (499), Denmark (4,135), France (1,826), Isle of Man (1), Italy (495), Netherlands (5), Norway (41), Russian Federation (26,886), San-Marino (2), Switzerland (11)
Decrease	Tunisia (645), Chile (347), Mexico (478), Netherlands Antilles (52), Nicaragua (249), Peru (646), Puerto Rico (6), United States (30), Bangladesh (22), Cyprus (57), India (1575), Israel (93), Japan (476), Republic of Korea (82), Malaysia (38), Philippines (235), Thailand (22), Austria (10), Belarus (55), Finland (399), Iceland (14), Ireland (35), Poland (13,434), Portugal (267), Spain (2,300), Sweden (77), Turkey (496), United Kingdom (230), Australia (639), New Zealand (101)

Note: The figure for France is a cumulative total for localised and generalised strikes
Increase: 18 countries; Decrease: 30 countries
Source: Derived from *ILO Yearbook of Labour Statistics*, various years

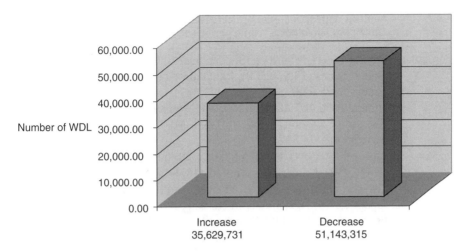

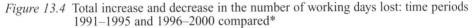

	Increase	Decrease
	35,629,731	51,143,315

Figure 13.4 Total increase and decrease in the number of working days lost: time periods 1991–1995 and 1996–2000 compared*

Note: The figure for France is a cumulative total for localised and generalised strikes

Source: Derived from *ILO Yearbook of Labour Statistics*, various years

* Refers to the total increase in the number of working days lost, in those countries experiencing an increase, and total decrease in working days lost, in those countries experiencing a decrease

political dislocation and not to a displacement effect – this is also true of the increase in El Salvador. Substantial increases have also occurred in three Western European countries, Denmark (+4,135), France (+1872) and Belgium (+499).

Turning to working days lost we find an overall decrease but this is much less marked than the decline from the earlier period (Figure 13.4 and Table 13.7). There was a decline of just over 51 million days lost by comparison with an increase of over 35 million days lost. Exclusion of the Russian Federation would only reduce this figure to in excess of 27 million days lost and this is much larger than countries experiencing an increase in days lost when comparing the periods 1981–1985 and 1996–2000. This is again indicative of a bottoming out effect at work, although the overall trend is still downwards.

Discussion and Conclusion

Overall, it is clear that there has been a major decline in the extent of strikes and their impact (as measured by working days lost) in the 1980s. This disjuncture in strike incidence and impact continued into the 1990s, with some evidence of a tapering off (or bottoming out) in the later period. The fact that there has been such a substantial decline at a global level suggests that national factors are insufficient to explain the trends. There may be a natural tendency, when examining the strike trends of a single country, to focus on developments internal

Table 13.7 Countries with an increase or decrease in the number of working days lost (numbers in parentheses): time periods 1991–1995 and 1996–2000 compared

Increase	Egypt (4,661), Mauritius (36,73), Puerto Rico (135,339), United States (13,570,500), Bangladesh (16,021), India (4,451,402), Israel (4,525,648), Sri Lanka (473,487), Denmark (3,048,200), Hungary (90,465), Ireland (46,141), Norway (797,340), Russian Federation (8,387,100), San-Marino (22,297), Switzerland (24,397)
Decrease	Morocco (18,988), Chile (967,247), El Salvador (937,217), Mexico (5,327,272), Netherlands Antilles (18,790), Nicaragua (924,283), Trinidad and Tobago (269,763), Cyprus (172,404), Hong Kong (14,932), Japan (229,613), Republic of Korea (1920,835), Malaysia (33,076), Philippines (1428,098), Thailand (81,447), Austria (72,834), Belarus (374,600), Finland (1417,085), France (1691,305), Iceland (168,723), Isle of Man (147), Italy (7,926,600), Netherlands (824,886), Poland (3750,100), Portugal (217,600), Spain (10,925,504), Sweden (753,771), Turkey (9,281,328), United Kingdom (70,000), Australia (1,128,200), New Zealand (196,667)

Increase: 15 countries; Decrease: 30 countries
Source: Derived from *ILO Yearbook of Labour Statistics*, various years

to that country. Credit is variously given to social partnership or government action to counter the power of unions. For instance, the reduction in strikes in the UK is frequently credited to the changes in collective labour law introduced under the Thatcher governments which have continued in place since then. However, Brown *et al.* (1997) have challenged this view, suggesting that the UK decline can only be understood as part of broader international developments. It is also useful to note that Ireland, which has a common legislative framework with the UK experienced major reductions in strike levels in the 1980s without any legislative changes affecting unions and those changes which were implemented in the 1990s have been much more modest than the UK changes (Wallace and O'Sullivan 2002).

The most obvious explanatory factor at a global level is the process of trade liberalisation which has been underway since the 1970s – the process of globalisation itself may be at the root of a decline in many countries. There are other potential causal variables, such as the decline of Keynesian economics. Keynesian demand management policies emphasised the need for governments to pursue policies to ensure full employment. These policies increased the power of labour and limited the impact of a reserve army of the unemployed. The rise of neo-classical economics following the first oil crisis in 1974, and the greater market discipline which this imposed, has arguably advantaged capital at the expense of labour. At a sub-global level, this change in the relative power balance has been accentuated by the rise of service-based economies with lower levels of unionisation and reduced potential for workers to display collective solidarity.

Indeed the processes of globalisation and the rise of service-based economies in the advanced economies may be inextricably linked. Thus globalisation gives employers greater options in dealing with their workers. Companies can promote competition between plants in differing countries. Companies that come under competitive pressure can relocate to Eastern Europe, China and developing countries.

Faced with such competitive pressures, workers there may see very limited prospects for successful strike action. There is considerable evidence from Western Europe that strikes are tending to involve large numbers, be relatively short and are frequently defensive in nature (Gall 1999; Aligisakis 1997). This is important because it clashes with the optimistic perspective of individual workers with strong market power position sketched by Hansen and Mather (1988). The picture that emerges from most of the industrial relations literature is one of working class movements in retreat and workers being negatively affected by the process of globalisation. Foroohar and Emerson (2004: 42) note that 'falling wages, reduced benefits and rising job insecurity seem to be increasingly entrenched features of the job scene across most of Western Europe, the United States and other parts of the developed world'. They see the new labour market as being shaped by growing global competition, and while noting emerging protests in Western Europe they suggest, 'protest won't turn the tanker of the global economy' (Foroohar and Emerson 2004: 42). Not only is that the case but the very process of globalisation floods the world with a massively increased labour supply, which decreases the possibility of protest and gives many alternatives to capital in dealing with organised labour. Thus, while there is a displacement effect at work, it is not one which sees strikes being displaced to developing countries but the power of organised labour being displaced in the developed world.

Notes

1 The authors wish to thank Emma Parkinson and Teresa Murray, research assistants in the University of Limerick, for their invaluable assistance with this chapter.
2 The *ILO Yearbook of Labour Statistics* provides no further detail on the nature of the changes. Thus, the meaning of some is not fully clear.
3 Some countries, classified here as developing, may have been so in the early 1980s but not currently. Thus, the use of the category, 'developing world', is an arbitrary one.
4 Because of its ready availability and greater number of country comparisons it allows, we use EIRO data for this section.
5 Looked at over the longer time period of the 1980s and 1990s and using a number of indices Aligisakis (1997) suggests the following four way classification:

   • countries with a very high propensity to strike: Greece, Italy, Spain
   • countries with a high propensity to strike: Iceland, Ireland, UK
   • countries with a low propensity to strike: Denmark, Finland, Sweden, Germany, Netherlands
   • countries with a very low propensity to strike: France, Portugal, Switzerland, Luxembourg.

References

Aligisakis, M. (1997) 'Labour Disputes in Western Europe: Typology and Tendencies', *International Labour Review*, 136, 1: 73–95.

Arrighi, G. (1990) 'Marxist Century, American Century: the Making and the Remaking of the World's Labour Movement', *New Left Review*, 179: 29–66.

Blyton, P and Turnbull, P. (2004) *The Dynamics of Employee Relations*. Basingstoke: Palgrave Macmillan, 3rd edition.

Brown, W., Deakin, S. and Ryan, P. (1997) 'The Effects of British Industrial Relations Legislation 1979–1997', *National Institute Economic Review*, 161: 69–83.

Cho, S.K. (1985) 'The Labour Process and Capital Mobility: the Limits of the New International Division of Labour', *Politics and Society*, 14: 185–222.

Clarke, O., Bamber, G.J. and Lansbury, R.D. (1998) 'Conclusions: Towards a Synthesis of International and Comparative Experience in Employment Relations' in Bamber, G.J. and Lansbury, R.D. (eds) *International and Comparative Employment Relations*. London: Sage Publications.

Clegg, H.A. (1979) *The Changing System of Industrial Relations in Great Britain*. Oxford: Blackwell.

Edwards, P.K. (1992) 'Industrial Conflict: Themes and Issues in Recent Research', *British Journal of Industrial Relations,* 30, 3: 361–404.

Ellem, B. (2001) 'Trade Unionism in 2000', *Journal of Industrial Relations*, 43, 2: 196–218.

European Industrial Relations Observatory (EIRO) (2003) *Developments in Industrial Action – 1998–2002*. Accessed at http://www.eiro.eurofound.ie/2003/03/update/tn0303104u.html

Foroohar, R. and Emerson, T. (2004) 'A Heavier Burden', *Newsweek,* August 23: 41–45.

Gall, G. (1999) 'A Review of Strike Activity in Western Europe at the End of the Second Millennium', *Employee Relations*, 21, 4: 357–377.

Hansen, C.G. and Mather, G. (1988) *Striking Out Strikes. Changing Employment Relations in the British Labour Market*. London: The Institute of Economic Affairs.

International Labour Organisation (ILO) (2003; 1996; 1989–90). *Yearbook of Labour Statistics*. Geneva: International Labour Office.

Kelly, J. and Nicholson, N. (1980) 'Strikes and other Forms of Industrial Action', *Industrial Relations Journal*, 11, 5: 20–31.

Kuwahara, Y. (2004) 'Employment Relations in Japan' in Bamber, G.J., Lansbury, R.D. and Wailes, N. (eds) *International and Comparative Employment Relations*. London: Sage Publications, 4th edition.

Lansbury, R.D. and Wailes, N. (2004) 'Employment Relations in Australia' in Bamber, G.J., Lansbury, R.D. and Wailes, N. (eds) *International and Comparative Employment Relations*. London: Sage Publications, 4th edition.

Monger, J. (2004) 'International Comparisons of Labour Disputes in 2002', *Labour Market Trends*, 112, 4: 145–152.

Salamon, M. (2000) *Industrial Relations Theory and Practice*. Essex: Pearson Education Limited, 4th edition.

Shalev, M. (1978) 'Lies, Damned Lies and Strike Statistics' in Crouch, C. and Pizzorno, A. (eds) *The Resurgence of Class Conflict in Western Europe Since 1968, Volume 1: National Studies*. London: Macmillan.

Stokke, T.A. and Thörnqvist, C. (2001) 'Strikes and Collective Bargaining in the Nordic Countries', *European Journal of Industrial Relations*, 7, 3: 245–267.

Thompson, M. and Taras, D.G. (2004) 'Employment Relations in Canada' in Bamber, G.J., Lansbury, R.D. and Wailes, N. (eds) *International and Comparative Employment Relations*. London: Sage Publications, 4th edition.

Wallace, J., Gunnigle, P. and McMahon, G. (2004) *Industrial Relations in Ireland*. Dublin: Gill and Macmillan, 3rd edition.

Wallace, J. and O'Sullivan, M. (2002) The Industrial Relations Act 1990: A Critical Review in D'Art, D. and Turner, T. (eds) *Irish Employment Relations in the New Economy*. Dublin: Blackhall Publishing.

Key readings

Bamber, G.J., Lansbury, R.D. and Wailes, N. (eds) (2004) *International and Comparative Employment Relations*. London: Sage Publications, 4th edition.

Bean, R. (1989) *Comparative Industrial Relations: an Introduction to Cross-national Perspectives*. London: Routledge.

Eaton, J. (2000) *Comparative Employment Relations. An Introduction*. MA, USA: Blackwell Publishers, Chapter 9.

Jackson, M.P. (1991) *An Introduction to Industrial Relations*. London: Routledge.

Salamon, M. (2000) *Industrial Relations Theory and Practice*. Essex: Pearson Education Limited, 4th edition.

Key websites

European Industrial Relations Observatory (EIRO) *www.eiro.eurofound.ie*
International Labour Organisation (ILO) *www.ilo.org*
Organisation for Economic Co-operation and Development (OECD) *www.oecd.org*

14 The juridification of industrial relations: the role of labour law in a globalised economy

ROGER BLANPAIN

Introduction

This chapter focuses on the importance of the law, especially of labour law, which regulates the individual and collective relations between employers, employees and between representatives of both sides of industry. Thus the role of the state and of regional and international organisations, which set the framework within which industrial relations evolve, is highlighted. In conceptualising the rules which the governmental authorities impose upon employees and employers, we include acts enacted by the legislature (parliament), of the government itself, of administrative authorities, social inspection, courts and the like. The basic question is: how far do these rules go and how much freedom is their left for the markets and for private actors? How far should these rules go?

The private actors, namely employees and employers, conclude individual agreements; employers and/or employers' associations and representatives of workers conclude collective labour agreements, setting wages and conditions at the level of the enterprise, of an industry sector, eventually the whole private economy of a given country or even at international or European level, e.g. global framework agreements or agreements establishing European Works Councils. Business and labour may, under certain conditions, engage in industrial conflict and strike or lock-out each other.

The law establishes expected standards for individual and collective behaviour on the labour markets and will monitor them. The state may enact rules concerning the conclusion of individual labour contracts, working time, pay, equal treatment and discrimination, sickness, leave, time off and vacation, termination of individual agreements, non-competition clauses and the like; equally concerning the recognition of trade unions, their legal status, trade union elections, information and consultation and other forms of workers' participation, collective bargaining (subjects, levels, binding effect), strikes and lock-outs. Administrative organs, like the American Labour Relations Board, may monitor some of these regulations, like the elections for majority unions. The ministry of Labour may organise conciliation and mediation services and engage in social inspection. Courts, including labour courts in some countries, or arbitrators may settle individual and/or collective disputes.

This not to say that employment regulation is the work of governments only. On the contrary, in many instances, business and labour do play an important role in setting the legal agenda and its outcome as far as labour law is concerned. A few examples illustrate this. The International Labour Organisation (ILO) is tripartite: composed of governments and representatives of employers' associations and trade unions. In the Organisation for Economic Co-operation and Development (OECD), the Trade Union Advisory Committee to the OECD (TUAC) and the Business and Industry Advisory Committee to the OECD (BIAC) give, on behalf of unions and employers, advice to governments; the same goes for the social partners at EU level. Also, in many states, there are national labour councils, economic and social bodies and the like advising parliament and government; while in other countries this is done on an informal, lobbying basis.

There is no doubt that there has to be a playing field and there have to be rules. The labour market can neither be a jungle nor a Wild West. There is a definite role for the public authorities; no one will question that. There is, however, a basic disagreement about how and how far government should intervene and how much freedom the social actors should enjoy. Some argue for more freedom; others are for more social dialogue and for more government intervention, still others for more protection of the employees. This is an ongoing debate, as much at international and regional as at state level. It is an ideological and a political discussion which is, however, very heavily influenced by the changes which take place on the labour markets that governments are supposed to regulate.

The globalised market economy

Indeed, there is no doubt that the global market economy has a profound impact on the way in which our labour markets function, as well as at international, regional as national levels (cf. Blanpain and Colucci 2004).

Firstly, the free market economy has been embraced globally, as evidenced by China and India opening their markets for free enterprise and for foreign investment. The free market economy equals competition: companies aim at the best product or service at the lowest price. This means that costs, including labour costs, have to go down. Head counts are daily routine, as well as ongoing restructuring. As productivity goes up, enterprises can do more with less people. Job security in the globalised economy is being continually challenged. Another challenge is that goods and also services can be provided by low wage countries. Indeed, information and communications technology (ICT) allows for white collar services to be performed off shore in other countries, allowing multi-nationals to operate at lower costs and on a twenty-four hour basis; as the European research team is followed up by the Indian team, by the Chinese team and the American team, each working consecutive hours, engaging in the same project on an ongoing basis.

Another aspect of globalisation is that many enterprises became regional or worldwide networks, having units, subsidiaries or other parts in various countries, in such a way that decision-making on important matters for those companies is centralised in headquarters, far away from the local plants, managers and employees. Indeed, decisions in most multi-national groups, especially regarding the kind of products they will make and/or services they will offer, regarding investment, location and relocation, having an important impact at national levels, and on employment, are taken in faraway headquarters.

To give one example: Ford Motor, Detroit (2004), decided that 3,000 workers in Genk, its plant in Belgium were to be dismissed. Local decision-makers, be they managers, trade unions or other representatives of workers, including politicians, had no impact, whatsoever, on that decision. They were passive spectators. The decision was made in a distant headquarters with limited input from host country stakeholders. On top of that, many local companies act as subcontractors to the big groups and are equally dependent on them.

Another aspect is that the manner in which companies are run is largely influenced by the way the involved managers view their enterprises: to whom do they consider themselves to be answerable to and what do they consider the key measure of success? Is it shareholders' value or stakeholders' value? Shareholders' value is well accepted in the Anglo Saxon culture. In cultures where shareholder value is the key driver of business operations, stock market performance is considered the key measure of success. Thus these firms often take a short-term view of the enterprise and companies constantly have to rationalise, right size, get labour costs down. Here huge pension funds, which invest worldwide, shopping for the best deal, play a very important role.

In contrast, this is not readily the case in other cultures, like the Japanese and also in the so-called Rhineland-continental European-model, especially in Germany and the Netherlands, where shareholders are stakeholders, like other groups, for example the employees. In the case of stakeholders' value, employees are the main stakeholders in Japan and of (almost) equal value compared to shareholders in the Rhineland model.

Many in continental Europe, academics, political leaders, trade unionists and others continue to contend that the stakeholder idea still holds its ground and that when managing a company, all involved have to take the interests of all groups, employees included, into account. There is, however, no doubt that the shareholders' idea is gaining ground, also in Europe and Japan, due to globalised pressure. Workers' interests become subordinate to those of the shareholders.

Our economies are indeed becoming more and more globalised (Kaufman 2004). The question, however, is: for whose benefit? In order to tackle the social problems, which may accompany globalisation, the International Labour Organisation established the World Commission on the Social Dimension of Globalisation. That commission had a look at the social impact of globalisation and developed a common agenda to make it work for all (ILO 2004). The commission's report acknowledges globalisation's potential for good – promoting open societies, open economies and a freer exchange of goods, knowledge and ideas. But the commission also found deep-seated and persistent imbalances in the current workings of the global economy that are 'ethically unacceptable and politically unsustainable'.

Indeed, in an opinion piece, Juan Somavia, Director-General, International Labour Office (Somavia 2004), underlines that 'the globalisation debate is at an impasse. Trade negotiations are stalled. Jobs are disappearing. Financial instability continues. Meanwhile, politically sensitive issues such as migration and outsourcing are high on people's concerns, but low on the global problem-solving agenda'. 'Since 1990', he indicates, 'global growth in gross domestic product has been slower than in previous decades. The gap between people's incomes in the richest and poorest countries has never been wider, having risen from 50 to 1 in the 1960s to more than 120 to 1 today. Globally, unemployment is at its highest level ever. More than one billion people are either unemployed, underemployed or the working poor. In addition, foreign aid is decreasing overall and is far below the long-standing target of 0.7 per cent of GDP – a shortfall of US$ 2.5 trillion over the past thirty years.

Clearly, globalisation's benefits are out of reach for far too many people. The global risks this poses are evident. We must take into account the need for security – whether that means the concerns of the poor, the anxieties of the middle-income workers or the uncertainties of business. There are no simple solutions to these problems, but the commission has proposed a commonsense agenda for action on a broad front: 'First, start at home. Second, make it fair. Balance patterns of investment. Third, make decent work a global goal. Fourth, rethink global governance'.

There is another trend, opposite to globalisation, namely localisation. Indeed, our economies become, at the same time, more and more local. As our societies are getting richer and people live longer, they are eager to be served. Personal services, like health, hospitalisation, care for the elderly and disabled, hairdressing, catering, education, hospitality in bars and restaurants, sports and local transport and other people oriented activities are in increasing demand. Contrary to the global economy, personalised services, which are not exported, but which stay local, employ more and more people. Employment in these sectors is, indeed, increasing expedientially. Moreover, there is hardly any growth in productivity in the personalised services. Indeed, someone pushing my wheelchair, when I will be 85 years of age, can only push one chair at a time. A hairdresser can only serve one client at a time. So, there are plenty of the jobs, at local level in the personalised sectors. Many of these jobs, like in health and education and so many others are subsidised by the tax payer. There is not enough tax money to meet adequately all the needs in education and health. The so-called 'white collar sector' regularly cries out for more staff, more nurses. Governments have to keep inflation and deficits under control. In the EU, member states are bound by the stability pact. Also here labour law has to adapt, help to keep the costs under control.

The more our economies are getting international, the more local communities become dependent on foreign decision-makers. Often all that local actors can do, is to see that the local market is attractive and investment-friendly, in order to seduce the foreign investor. The real decision-makers are international management, motivated by regional or worldwide strategies – a local unit being only one of the many flags of a multi-national group on the globe.

The lessons are straight forward: government has to see to it that national labour law and its application does not affect the competitiveness of enterprises and that the country remains attractive to foreign investment.

Enterprises, in their quest to be competitive, insist on internal and external flexibility, adapting working time to the needs of the company, remuneration to individual performance, ease with regard to hiring and firing, more possibilities for temporary agency work and the like. But also employees demand more flexibility, in order to better harmonise work and family life. In both, the global and the local economies, the real and important decision-makers are thus not located in the enterprises concerned. Neither is it the invisible hand of the market, although the market and competition have an important impact on what kind of decisions are made. Managers of the enterprises are less and less the real decision-makers, let alone the employees or their representatives. The same goes for the personalised sectors: 'flexibility and labour costs down' are the key messages.

The factors outlined above also lead to an evolution from hard law to soft law. This is amply illustrated by the increased use of soft law instruments, like guidelines, principles, voluntary codes of conduct and voluntary agreements (at EU level), which have only a moral effect, not a legally binding one. If the economy is international and labour law remains national, the balance of power changes dramatically in favour of international investment. In short, labour law, especially national labour law, has to and is becoming more flexible, more investment-friendly, more soft and less protective for the workers. Free enterprise and shareholder interests are gaining as a result of the (de)regulation of the markets.

National, regional and international labour law

The answer by labour law, challenging globalisation and centralised decision-making should be given at the same (global) level. If the European Union wants to confront foreign investment, which tends to play national systems off against each other, it should adopt European labour laws, setting minimum standards for those who want to invest in one of the twenty-five member states and have access to its 450 million inhabitants-customers. However, nothing is less true. Member states compete with each other for foreign investment, also on the basis of employment costs. Labour law, also in the EU, the most advanced regional organisation in the world, is still mainly national and is going to remain so. International and regional employment instruments are important, but they are only a framework, leaving the main competence to regulate at national level.

International Labour Law: the ILO

The International Labour Organisation is the UN specialised agency that seeks to promote social justice and internationally recognised human and labour rights (cf. Swepston 2004). It was founded in 1919 and is the only surviving major creation of the Treaty of Versailles which brought about the League of Nations and it became the first specialised agency of the UN in 1946. It provides technical assistance primarily in the fields of:

- vocational training and vocational rehabilitation
- employment policy
- labour administration
- labour law and industrial relations
- working conditions
- management development
- co-operatives
- social security
- labour statistics and occupational safety and health.

The ILO promotes the development of independent employers' and workers' organisations and provides training and advisory services to those organisations. Within the UN system, the ILO has a unique tripartite structure with workers and employers participating as equal partners with governments in the work of its governing organs.

Legislative acts: conventions and recommendations

The ILO formulates international labour standards in the form of conventions and recommendations setting minimum standards of basic labour rights: freedom of association, the right to organise, collective bargaining, abolition of forced labour, equality of opportunity and treatment, and other standards regulating conditions across the entire spectrum of work related issues. The ILO supervises the implementation of conventions and recommendations, and provides assistance to putting the findings into effect. Supervision is carried out mainly by two bodies, the Committee of Experts on the Application of Conventions and Recommendations and the Conference Committee on the Application of Standards. The Committee of Experts meets annually to examine reports received from governments and comments from workers' and employers' organisations. If the Committee of Experts notes problems in the application of ratified Conventions, it may respond in two ways. In most cases it makes Direct Requests, which are sent directly to governments in the countries concerned. For more serious or persistent problems, the Committee of Experts makes 'Observations,' which, in addition to being sent to governments, are published as part of the Committee's annual report to the International Labour Conference.[1] Between 1964 and 2003, the Committee noted nearly 2,400 cases in which governments took the measures requested of them to improve the application of Conventions – and these are simply the ones the office was able to document directly.

The Conference Committee on the Application of Conventions and Recommendations is the next level of supervision. It is a 'standing committee' of the International Labour Conference, and reflects the ILO's tripartite structure of governments and of workers' and employers' representatives. On the basis of the report of the Committee of Experts, the Conference Committee selects about 25 especially important or persistent cases and requests the governments concerned to appear before it and explain the reasons for the situations commented on by the Committee of Experts. At the end of each session, it reports to the full Conference on the problems governments are encountering in fulfilling their obligations under the ILO Constitution or in complying with conventions they have ratified. The Conference Committee's report is published in the 'Proceedings of the International Labour Conference' each year, along with a detailed report of the Conference's discussion.[2] In 2004, the Conference Committee examined, as an example, child labour in Indonesia, forced labour in Myanmar and Sudan, trade union rights in Colombia, Myanmar and Hong Kong, and child labour in Ukraine.

Globalisation and core labour standards: rights and principles

The ILO has a mandate to deal with the social challenges, brought about by globalisation. Here it seeks to provide a global answer, namely regarding (core) labour standards. All actors, international as well as national, seem to agree that (core) labour standards have to be respected both at international and at national levels. It is, indeed, self-evident that the full implementation of core labour standards constitutes a *conditio sine qua non* for economic globalisation to be successful. Here, one can ascertain the beginning of a (social) countervailing power. There is, indeed, no doubt that economic globalisation can only reap its total rewards and prosper if there are strong social systems, which provide excellent education, healthy collaborators and social peace.

In deciding on foreign direct investment (FDI) location decisions, multi-national enterprises look for skilled, competent and healthy workers, an appropriate infrastructure, and a developed consumers' market. The ILO (2003) rightly observes that:

> … negative effects of globalisation on certain groups of workers can arise from the absence or inadequate application of labour standards. When standards – national and international – are not applied, workers do not have the basic tools they need to defend themselves, and States do not have adequate tools to ensure the balanced distribution of the benefits of development. This is often the case for temporary workers, migrant workers and workers in some export processing zones, as well as in the informal economy. Women are particularly affected, as they comprise the majority of workers in these categories.

> An increasing amount of research shows that the failure to apply labour standards is damaging to national development. For example, forced or compulsory labour is a constraint on productivity gains and on economic growth, and questions the very value of labour as the basis for development. Child labour transmits and perpetuates inter-generational poverty; releasing children from work and providing them with adequate educational opportunities goes hand in hand with providing decent work for adults.

No doubt, there is a crucial role for all actors (both public and private) to promote and ensure that basic rights at work are effectively respected all over the world, without exception. Over the last decade, important areas of consensus have emerged concerning the social dimension of globalisation in the context of the ILO. Since the World Summit for Social Development in Copenhagen (March 1995), international consensus has been achieved on following categories of core labour standards:

(a) freedom of association and the right to collective bargaining
(b) the elimination of child labour
(c) the abolition of forced or compulsory labour
(d) the elimination of discrimination in occupation and employment.

This led to the adoption by the International Labour Conference in 1998 of the 'ILO Declaration on Fundamental Principles and Rights at Work' and its follow-up.

Regional labour law

The Council of Europe

The Council of Europe, founded in 1949, groups together forty-six countries, including twenty-one countries from Central and Eastern Europe. It has an application from one more country (Belarus) and has granted observer status to five more countries (the Holy See, the United States, Canada, Japan and Mexico). The Council was set up to:

- defend human rights, parliamentary democracy and the rule of law
- develop continent-wide agreements to standardise member countries' social and legal practices
- promote awareness of a European identity based on shared values and cutting across different cultures.

The main component parts of the Council of Europe are:

- the Committee of Ministers
- the Parliamentary Assembly
- the Congress of Local and Regional Authorities, composed of a Chamber of Local Authorities and a Chamber of Regions.

The protection of human rights is one of the Council of Europe's basic goals, to be achieved in four main areas:

(i)   effective supervision and protection of fundamental rights and freedoms
(ii) identifying new threats to human rights and human dignity
(iii) developing public awareness of the importance of human rights
(iv) promoting human rights education and professional training.

The Council's most significant achievement is the European Convention on Human Rights, which was adopted in 1950. It sets out a list of rights and freedoms which states are under an obligation to guarantee to everyone within their jurisdiction (among other things, the right to life, to protection against torture and inhuman treatment, to freedom and safety, to a fair trial, to respect for one's private and family life and correspondence, to freedom of expression (including freedom of the press), thought, conscience and religion). The convention establishes an international enforcement machinery, the European Court on Human Rights, whereby states and individuals, regardless of their nationality, may refer alleged violations by contracting states of the rights guaranteed in the convention to the judicial institutions in Strasbourg established by the convention. Its jurisdiction is compulsory for all contracting parties. It sits on a permanent basis and deals with all the preliminary stages of a case, as well as giving judgement on the merits.

The Council of Europe actively promotes social cohesion. Its main objectives are:

(i)   to guarantee an adequate level of social protection
(ii) to promote employment, vocational training and workers' rights
(iii) to provide protection for the most vulnerable groups of society
(iv) to promote equal opportunities
(v)   to combat exclusion and discrimination
(vi) to consolidate European co-operation on migration.

Social rights have played a prominent role in European development over the last century but despite progress in many areas not all Europeans enjoy them. The Council of Europe began work in 1999 on projects to find solutions to the many problems facing individual citizens when trying to claim rights to social protection, housing, health and education. The Council's legal instruments for the purpose include the European Social Charter and the European Code of Social Security. The European Social Charter guarantees a number of fundamental social rights. The European Code of Social Security and its Protocol guarantee minimum protection covering medical care, sickness, employment injury, maternity, among others. Some agreements facilitate international mobility for workers and their families, integration into host countries without loss of cultural identity, legal protection and welfare provisions. They are the conventions on Social Security, on Social and Medical Assistance and on the Legal Status of Migrant Workers.

The European Social Charter sets out rights and freedoms and the supervisory procedures guaranteeing their respect by the State Parties. All Europeans share these rights under the Charter and they affect every aspect of daily life, including housing, health, education, employment, social protection, personal travel and non-discrimination.

The European Committee of Social Rights (ECSR) checks whether member states have honoured their undertakings under the Charter. The State Parties report every year on their implementation of the Charter in law and in practice. The ECSR examines the reports, decides whether these procedures comply with the Charter and publishes its conclusions annually. If a state takes no action on a specific ECSR decision the Committee of Ministers addresses a recommendation to the state to change its laws or practices.

Complaints of violations of the Charter may be lodged with the European Committee of Social Rights under a protocol that came into force in 1998. The ECSR examines the complaint and declares it admissible if it meets the formal requirements. It then decides the case on its merits and reports its findings to the parties concerned and the Committee of Ministers which finally adopts a resolution.

The European Union

The idea of European integration was conceived to prevent the killing and destruction of World Wars I and II from ever happening again. It was first proposed by the French Foreign Minister Robert Schuman in a speech on 9 May 1950 (cf. Blanpain 2003; European Commission 2004).

The EU is, in fact, unique. Its member states have set up common institutions to which they delegate some of their sovereignty so that decisions on specific matters of joint interest can be made democratically at European level. This pooling of sovereignty is also called European integration.

Initially, the EU consisted of just six countries: Belgium, Germany, France, Italy, Luxembourg and the Netherlands. Denmark, Ireland and the United Kingdom joined in 1973, Greece in 1981, Spain and Portugal in 1986, Austria, Finland and Sweden in 1995. In 2004 the biggest ever enlargement took place with ten new countries joining.

In the early years, much of the co-operation between EU countries was about trade and the economy, but now the EU also deals with many other subjects of direct importance for our everyday life, such as citizens' rights; ensuring freedom, security and justice; job creation; regional development; environmental protection; making globalisation work for everyone.

The main EU institutions are:

- The European Parliament (elected by the peoples of the Member States)
- The Council of the European Union (representing the governments of the Member States)
- The European Commission (driving force and executive body)
- The Court of Justice (ensuring compliance with the law).

There are certainly clear European social ambitions and goals. They are laid down in Article 136 TEC as follows:

(i)   promotion of employment
(ii) improved living and working conditions
(iii) harmonisation while improvement is being maintained
(iv) proper social protection
(v)   dialogue between management and labour
(vi) the development of human resources
(vii) with a view to lasting employment and the combating of social exclusion.

This sounds great: the social sky seems the limit.

There are also fundamental social rights, formulated in the Treaty like equality and free movement of labour. Fundamental social rights are also promulgated in the Community Charter of Fundamental Social Rights of Workers (1989) and in the Charter of Fundamental Rights of the European Union (Nice Declaration – 7 December 2000).

These Charters are however only political declarations, although some of the rights they contain, may be legally binding, according to Article 6 of the TEU, be it only vertical (to be respected by the European institutions and the member states, when drafting or implementing legislation) and not horizontal between e.g. employers and employees (no dritt-wirkung). Moreover, the 'social goal' comes only second as far as objectives of the EU are concerned. Legally and politically, the European Monetary Union (EMU) with its goal of non-inflationary growth comes first. So, the social vision of Europe is at best second rate, as it is in the grip of the EMU and shareholders' value and not beefed up by enforceable fundamental social rights, which should also be horizontally binding.

Does the EU have sufficient competence to develop a fully-fledged European social policy? In answering this question, one needs to recall that the EU only has the competences, which are transferred by the member states to the EU and that these competences have to be exercised in the way indicated by the Treaty. On this point, the so-called European Social Model (EMS) is extremely weak. Indeed, social 'core' issues are *excluded* from the EU competence, namely: pay, the right of association, the right to strike and the right to impose lock-outs (Art. 137, 6 TEC).

For other important matters, *unanimity* in the Council is needed, namely for:

(i)   social security and social protection of workers
(ii) job security
(iii) representation and collective defence of interests, including co-determination (Art. 137, 3 TEC).

Unanimity between twenty-five member states is almost impossible. Even more, qualified majority voting for other matters like free movement of workers, equal treatment, health and safety and information and consultation has been made more difficult to achieve. So much so that the ESM, as far as competence is concerned, is almost non-existing. The catastrophe is that this will be a permanent feature as the Treaty can only be changed by way of unanimity, which will, as far as social policies are concerned, prove to be impossible. Obviously, there are other ways of convergence in the social field, like the so-called 'enhanced co-ordination strategy', used in the case of the employment guidelines, which lead to National Action Plans and to peer pressure for member states to conform to the guidelines. This strategy, which is important, could be used in other fields.

However, they do not prevent the EU being incompetent in enacting binding measures on core issues such as a European minimum wage, collective bargaining, social security, job security, collective bargaining and others, for which unanimity is required.

The conclusion is clear: the EU lacks the essential competences, which are needed to organise and establish a full-fledged ESM.

Notwithstanding its limited competence, over the years some important framework labour law steps have been taken, namely regarding:

(i)   free movement of workers
(ii)   individual employment contracts
(iii)   international private labour law
(iv)   child care and young people at work
(v)   equal treatment
(vi)   working time
(vii)   health and safety
(viii) restructuring of the enterprise
(ix)   workers' participation.

These labour framework steps have a prominent place in the case law of the Court of Justice as, over the years, hundreds of employment cases have been dealt with by the Court in a pro-European way. Indeed, the Court of Justice has been the guardian by excellence of the European ideals by fostering a Community based on law and especially by:

- making European law binding; making it stick, and effective
- furthering, expanding and broadening Community goals, and
- acting as a constitutional court in balancing the relationship between Community institutions at the one hand and between the Community and the Member States at the other hand.

The Court's decisions give a binding direct effect to Community provisions, where those provisions are clear, precise and unconditional. A case in point is Article 141 TEC on equal pay for work of equal value. In the Defrenne case (II) of 8 April 1976 (C-43/75, *ECR.*, 1976), the Court of Justice gave direct effect to Article 141 to be relied upon before national courts.

In the case of Maria Louisa Jiménez Melgar of 4 October 2001 (C-438/00), the Court judged that Article 10 of Council Directive 92/85/EEC[3] has direct effect and is to be interpreted to the effect that, in the absence of transposition measures taken by a member state within the period prescribed by that directive, it confers on individuals rights on which they may rely before a national court against the authorities of that state. It is clear that such decisions have a tremendous positive impact on the emancipation movement and the strife for equality between the sexes.

By imposing on the national legislators and the courts, there is an obligation to produce an effective outcome in cases involving community law. The rule of the Court is clear: when Community law is at stake, only 'full effectiveness' is sufficient.

Here labour law provides again many examples. In the case of *Sabine von Colson and Elisabeth Kaman* v. *Land Northrein-Westfalen* of 10 April 1984 (C-14/83), the facts showed clearly that a female candidate was not hired and that discrimination on the basis of gender was at hand. The German judge ruled that the German Arbeitsgericht in compensating the damage incurred by the victim, could only order reimbursement of the travel expenses incurred by the plaintiff when applying for the job, which was DM 7.20 or some € 4, the cost of the tram ticket.

The European Court did not agree with this and said that the 1976 Directive relating to access to employment, vocational training and promotion and working conditions leaves freedom to the member states to choose a sanction, but if the member states chooses compensation, then this must be effective, have a deterrent effect and in any event be adequate; in any case more than nominal, like the reimbursement of expenses.

The question was equally addressed in the very important case Marshall II (C-271/91) of 2 August 1993, concerning the amount of compensation recoverable by a victim of discrimination. At stake was the award of interest on compensation. The Court ruled that the interpretation of the 1976 Directive must be 'that reparation of damage sustained by a person as a result of discriminatory dismissal may not be limited to an upper limit fixed a priori and by the absence of interest intended to compensate for the loss sustained by the recipient of the compensation as a result of the effluxion of time until the capital sum awarded is actually paid'.

The effectiveness requirement self-evidently achieved its peak in the Francovich case of 9 November 1995 (C- 479/93). In that case, Italy had not implemented the Insolvency Directive of 20 October 1980, protecting the employees in case of insolvency of the employer. The Court accepted the principle of liability of the state. Indeed, the full effectiveness of Community law would be undermined and the rights deriving from it would be less safeguarded if individuals were unable to obtain reparation when their rights were undermined by the infringement of Community law imputable to a member state. It follows that Community law lays down the principle according to which the member states are obliged to compensate individuals for damage caused to them by infringements of Community law imputable to the member state.

These judgements undoubtedly represent important inroads on national sovereignty regarding legal procedure. Of similar importance is the judgement of the Court of Justice of 8 June 1994 (C-382/92 and 383/92) concerning the information and consultation right of workers under the Directives concerning collective redundancies (1975) and transfer of enterprises (1977). Since that judgement it is not any longer possible that there are no worker representatives in the case where a member state would not have an overall system of workers' representation. According to the Court of Justice – condemning the UK –

'employers face a statutory obligation to inform and consult with employees when they are planning collective redundancies, or if they transfer employees from one business to another'. This means that even non-unionised companies will have to establish machinery for consultation even if it does not already exist.

The second claim in that case was that the sanctions provided for in the national rules for failure to comply with the obligations to consult and inform were not a sufficient deterrent for the employers. The Court said that where a Community directive did not specifically provide any penalty for an infringement, or where it referred for that purpose to national laws, the obligations of the member states under the Rome Treaty were to require them to ensure infringements of EC law were penalised under conditions, both procedural and substantive, which were analogous to those applicable to infringements of national law of a similar nature and importance and which, in any event, made the penalty effective, proportionate and dissuasive.

Furthering and promoting the Community goals of integration is a second and very important role that the Court of Justice plays through a broad interpretation of Community Law leading to normative supra-nationalism. Once more many examples can be given to illustrate this point. Again Article 141 of the TEC comes into the picture, here regarding the notions direct and indirect discrimination, e.g. regarding female part-timers; in relation to the notion of pay, including contracted out pensions (remember the famous Barber case (C-262/99)), thus giving a broad interpretation to the fundamental human right of equality.

Regarding one of the pillars of the Common Market, free movement of workers, the court coined a community notion of the 'worker' (C-66/85) tabled the right for the worker to move freely from one member state to another looking for a job and to stay there a reasonable time without having a job, as was judged in the Antonissen case (C- 292/89); while interpreting restrictively the exceptions to the free movement of workers regarding employment in the public sector, by limiting them to jobs, which imply political or judicial power.

The role of the Court regarding Sports cannot be overestimated. In the world famous Bosman case (C-415/93) the Court ruled that a transfer fee at the end of the contract between a professional player and his club was contrary to the free movement of workers, while Article 39 TEC precludes the application of rules laid down by sporting associations under which, in matches in competition, which they organise, football clubs may field only a limited number of professional players, who are nationals of other member states (the so-called nationality clause).

Acting as a constitutional Court it has played an important role by, as indicated earlier, balancing the relationship between the Community Institutions, among themselves and the member states versus the EC. Also here, many examples in the area of labour law can be given.

First, regarding the legal basis under the EC rules concerning unanimity, qualified majority or simple majority. Here article 137 TEC comes into the picture and especially the notion of health and safety in relation to working time. The Court had an occasion to rule on this issue in the UK v. Council of the European Union case, in which the UK tried to obtain the annulment of the Directive on working time (1993). The UK contended that the directive was illegal, because it was based on Article 137 of the Treaty, which allows for qualified majority voting on the issue of health and safety. Article 137 has, according to the UK to be strictly interpreted and could thus not constitute an appropriate legal basis for a directive on working time. That directive should have been based on Articles of the Treaty, like 94 or 308, which, however, require unanimity in the Council of Ministers. The Court, however, ruled in favour of a broad interpretation. The Court said: '… where the principal aim of the measure in question is the protection of health and safety of workers, Article 137 must be used…' (C-84/94).

In the BECTU case (C-173/99), the issue of fundamental rights, here to annual leave, was addressed. The Advocate-General (8 February 2001) made a reference to the Nice Declaration. The facts were as follows. BECTU is a union in the broadcasting, film, theatre, cinema, and related sectors; it has about 30,000 members who are sound recordists, cameramen, special effects technicians, projectionists, editors, researchers, hairdressers, make-up artistes amongst others.

The British legislation which implements the European working time directive of 1993, provides that entitlement to leave is conditional upon the person concerned having been continuously employed for thirteen weeks by the same employer. Furthermore, it may not be replaced by a payment in lieu except where the employment is terminated.

The workers represented by BECTU are only employed on short-term contracts which are often less than thirteen weeks. As a result, they do not become entitled to the right to annual leave under British law.

According to the Advocate General, the right to paid annual leave is a fundamental social right; this is stated in various international instruments and is enshrined in the Charter of Fundamental Rights of the European Union of 7 December 2000. The Advocate General underlines that the purpose of the Charter, where its provisions allow, is a substantive point of reference for all those involved in the Community context.

More specifically, the Advocate-General declared:

> As early as 1948, the Universal Declaration of Human Rights recognised the right to rest, including reasonable limitations on working time and periodic holidays with pay (Article 24). Subsequently, both the European Social Charter approved in 1961 by the Council of Europe (Article 2(3)), and the United Nations Charter of 1966 on economic, social and cultural rights (Article 7(d)),

specifically upheld the right to paid leave as a manifestation of the right to fair and equitable working conditions.

In the Community context, it will be remembered that the Heads of State or Government enshrined that same right in paragraph 8 of the Community Charter of the Fundamental Social Rights of Workers adopted by the European Council in Strasbourg in 1989 which is referred to in the fourth recital in the preamble to the Working Time Directive itself.

The instruments to which I have so far referred collectively and in general terms are certainly distinct from each other in certain respects. As has been seen, their substantive content is not the same in all cases, nor is their legislative scope, since in some cases they are international conventions, in others solemn declarations; and of course the persons to whom they apply differ. However, it is significant that in all those instruments the right to a period of paid leave is unequivocally included among workers' fundamental rights.

Even more significant, it seems to me, is the fact that that right is now solemnly upheld in the Charter of Fundamental Rights of the European Union, published on 7 December 2000 by the European Parliament, the Council and the Commission after approval by the Heads of State and Government of the Member States, often on the basis of an express and specific mandate from the national parliaments. Article 31(2) of the Charter declares that: 'Every worker has the right to limitation of maximum working hours, to daily and weekly rest periods and to an annual period of paid leave. And that statement, as expressly declared by the Presidium of the Convention which drew up the Charter, is inspired precisely by Article 2 of the European Social Charter and by paragraph 8 of the Community Charter of Workers' Rights, and also took due account 'of Directive 93/104/EC concerning certain aspects of the organisation of working time'.

Admittedly, like some of the instruments cited above, the Charter of Fundamental Rights of the European Union has not been recognised as having genuine legislative scope in the strict sense. In other words, formally, it is not in itself binding. However, without wishing to participate here in the wide-ranging debate now going on as to the effects which, in other forms and by other means, the Charter may nevertheless produce, the fact remains that it includes statements which appear in large measure to reaffirm rights which are enshrined in other instruments. In its preamble, it is moreover stated that

> this Charter reaffirms, with due regard for the powers and tasks of the Community and the Union and the principle of subsidiarity, the rights as they result, in particular, from the constitutional traditions and international obligations common to the Member States, the Treaty on European Union, the Community Treaties, the European Convention for the Protection of Human Rights and Fundamental

Freedoms, the Social Charters adopted by the Community and by the Council of Europe and the case-law of the Court of Justice of the European Communities and of the European Court of Human Rights.

I think therefore that, in proceedings concerned with the nature and scope of a fundamental right, the relevant statements of the Charter cannot be ignored; in particular, we cannot ignore its clear purpose of serving, where its provisions so allow, as a substantive point of reference for all those involved – Member States, institutions, natural and legal persons – in the Community context. Accordingly, I consider that the Charter provides us with the most reliable and definitive confirmation of the fact that the right to paid annual leave constitutes a fundamental right.

The Advocate General added that the right to annual leave does not only concern the individual worker but corresponds to a general social interest for the health and safety of workers; therefore it is an automatic and unconditional right which does not fall within the derogations allowed for in the directive in other circumstances.

In other words, the Charter constitutes fundamental rights ... 'as they result from the constitutional traditions common to the Member States, as general principles of Community law' (Art. 6, 2 TEU). This is, of course, of the greatest importance. This opinion was confirmed by the Court (*ECR* 2001, 4881).

There is no doubt that the Court has played an enormous role in the elaboration, from fairly disparate European legislation, to a coherent legal body underpinning and guiding the European construction. May it continue.

The OECD

The OECD was set up under a Convention signed in Paris on 14 December 1960, which lists as the OECD's basic aims as contributing to economic development and trade expansion in the world economy, and achieving sustainable economic growth and employment as well as a rising standard of living in Member countries (cf. Tergeist and Blanpain 2004). There are currently thirty Members of the organisation: Australia, Austria, Belgium, Canada, the Czech Republic, Denmark, Finland, France, Germany, Greece, Hungary, Iceland, Ireland, Italy, Japan, Korea, Luxembourg, Mexico, the Netherlands, New Zealand, Norway, Poland, Portugal, Slovakia, Spain, Sweden, Switzerland, Turkey, the United Kingdom and the United States. The Commission of the European Communities also takes part in the OECD's work.

The principal political organs of the OECD are the Council, which consists of representatives of all Member States and usually meets once a year at ministerial level, and the Executive Committee, elected annually by the Council, which approves the annual programme of work and budget for the Committees. The Secretariat is led by a Secretary-General.

Only governments are members of OECD, unlike the ILO for example, which is tripartite and composed of governments, employers' and trade union organisations. However, business and union organisations have been granted consultative status and regularly participate in the work of Committees and working parties.

The Council has established around twenty-five committees that guide the work of the Secretariat and serve to facilitate the exchange of views and co-ordination of policies among countries within their fields of expertise. One of these is the Committee on International Investment and Multinational Enterprises (CIME).

The CIME interprets and implements the 1976/2000 Declaration and Decisions on International Investment and Multinational Enterprises.

The CIME was set up on 21 January 1975, particularly in order to negotiate and draft guidelines for Multi-national Enterprises and provide intergovernmental consultation procedures. After the adoption of the OECD Guidelines, the Committee was given the responsibility, *inter alia*, to regularly review their relevance and implementation, to respond to requests on specific or general Guidelines provisions, to exchange views on their role and functioning, and to organise appropriate promotional activities. Under its current mandate, it is charged with:

- developing and strengthening co-operation both among member countries and with non-members in the field of international investment and MNEs;
- serving as a policy forum to examine issues relating to globalisation, international investment and MNEs;
- promoting dialogue with the business community, trade unions and NGOs;
- holding exchanges of views on matters covered by the Guidelines, hearing reports from National Contact Points on the Guidelines' implementation and issuing clarifications of certain Guidelines provisions, when necessary.

The CIME is composed of representatives of Member Governments.

The OECD's advisory committees, representing both labour (TUAC) and the business community (BIAC), have been influential partners both in the design and the implementation of the Guidelines from the outset.

A number of NGOs have now joined forces and formed a clearinghouse called OECD Watch to help facilitate NGO activities around the OECD Guidelines and the work of CIME. The OECD Guidelines for Multi-national Enterprises (MNEs) were first promulgated in 1976. They responded to the advent of MNEs on the world scene in the 1960s, and to their growing economic influence which gave rise to concerns, especially among some governments and the international trade union movement. At the time, wide-ranging debates of a social, economic and political nature about the role of multi-national enterprises took place in the OECD as well as in other international organisations, like the UN and the ILO.

The Guidelines affirm that every country has the right to prescribe the conditions under which MNEs operate within its national jurisdiction, subject to international law and the international agreements to which it subscribes. They are not a substitute for national laws, to which MNEs are fully subject. They represent supplementary standards of behaviour of a non-legal character, particularly concerning the international operations of these enterprises. These are as follows:

1 *Freedom of association* (paras 1a and 7): Enterprises should respect the rights of their employees to be represented by trade unions and other *bona fide* organisations of employees (para. 1a); while employees are exercising a right to organise, not threaten to utilise a capacity to transfer the whole or part of an operating unit from the country concerned nor transfer employees from the enterprises' component entities in other countries in order to hinder the exercise of a right to organise (para. 7);

2 *Child labour* (para. 1b): Enterprises should contribute to the effective abolition of child labour and, in particular, not engage in the worst forms of child labour in their operations;

3 *Forced labour* (para. 1c): Enterprises should contribute to the elimination of all forms of forced or compulsory labour and, in particular, not engage in the use of such labour in their operations;

4 *Discrimination* (para. 1d): Enterprises should not discriminate against their employees with respect to employment or occupation on such grounds as race, colour, sex, religion, political opinion, national extraction, or social origin – unless selectivity concerning employee characteristics furthers established governmental policies which specifically promote greater equality of employment opportunity or relate to the inherent requirements of a job.

5 *Collective bargaining* (paras 1, 2, 8): Enterprises should respect the rights of their employees to engage in constructive negotiations with a view to reaching agreements on employment conditions (para. 1a); provide such facilities to representatives of the employees as may be necessary to assist in the development of effective collective agreements (para. 2a); provide to representatives of employees information which is needed for meaningful negotiations on conditions of employment (para. 2b); enable authorised representatives of their employees to conduct negotiations on collective bargaining or labour/management relations issues with representatives of management who are authorised to take decisions on the matters under negotiation (para. 8). In the context of *bona fide* negotiations with representatives of employees on conditions of employment, or while employees are exercising a right to organise, not threaten to transfer the whole or part of an operating unit from the country concerned nor transfer

employees from the enterprises' component entities in other countries in order to influence unfairly those negotiations or to hinder the right to organise (para. 7).

6 *Provision of information – consultation* (paras 2c and 3): Enterprises should provide representatives of employees where this accords with local law and practice, information which enables them to obtain a true and fair view of the performance of the entity or, where appropriate, the enterprise as a whole (para. 3); promote consultation and cooperation between employers and employees and their representatives on matters of mutual concern (para. 2c).

7 *Health and safety* (para.4b): Enterprises should take adequate steps to ensure occupational health and safety in their operations (para. 4b).

8 *Observance of employment standards* (para. 4): Enterprises should observe standards of employment and industrial relations not less favourable than those observed by comparable employers in the host country.

9 *Skills and training* (para. 5): Enterprises should to the greatest extent possible, utilise, train and prepare for upgrading members of the local labour force in cooperation with representatives of their employees and, where appropriate, the relevant governmental authorities.

10 *Reasonable notice and co-operation in case of major changes* (para. 6): Enterprises should, in considering major changes in business operations (in particular in the case of the closure of an entity involving collective dismissals), (i) provide reasonable notice of such changes to employee representatives and, where appropriate, to the relevant governmental authorities; and (ii) cooperate with the employee representatives and government authorities so as to mitigate to the maximum extent practicable adverse effects. In the light of the specific circumstances of each case, it would be appropriiate if management were able to give such notice prior to the final decision being taken.

11 *Access to decision makers* (para. 9): Enterprises should enable authorised representatives of their employees to negotiate with representatives of management who are authorised to take decisions on the matters under negotiation.

Since the Guidelines are drafted in fairly general terms, it has been necessary, on occasion, to clarify their purpose and intent. A follow-up procedure has been established for this purpose within the CIME. Most of the requests for clarification to date have referred to the Employment and Industrial Relations chapter of the Guidelines. They have been raised either by national delegations or by TUAC and have usually referred to some disputed behaviour of a particular enterprise.

NAFTA: The North American Agreement on Labour Cooperation (NAALC)

The NAALC, which is complementary to the North American Free Trade Agreement (NAFTA), concluded by Canada, Mexico and the United States (1993) may be seen as what is commonly called a 'social clause' in agreements to liberalise international trade: it deals with workers' rights, not for workers directly but in correlation with the establishment of the North American Free Trade Area (Preamble) (cf. Blanpain and Colucci 2004).

NAALC institutions are both international (the Council and Secretariat) and domestic National Administrative Offices (NAOs) in scope. Together, they provide an inter-governmental framework for the interaction of the full range of organisations and individuals involved in labour matters in the NAFTA countries: policy makers, administrators, employers, labour organisations, researchers and academics, legal practitioners, worker rights groups, and individuals.

The Commission for Labour Cooperation consists of a Ministerial Council and a Secretariat and is assisted by the NAO of each Party. The Commission is the institutional framework of the NAALC and the focal point of tri-national labour cooperation. If a matter related to occupational safety and health or other technical labour standards (NAALC's Labour Principles 4–11)[4] has not been resolved after ministerial consultations, any country may request the establishment of an independent Evaluation Committee of Experts (ECE). The ECE shall analyse, in the light of the objectives of the Agreement and in a non-

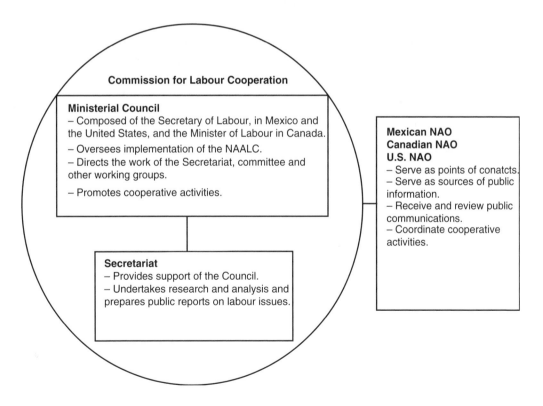

Figure 14.1 Structure of the Commission for Labour Cooperation

adversarial manner, patterns of practice by each country in the enforcement of these labour standards. The ECE will present a final report to the Council. ECEs may not be convened to examine matters that are deemed not trade-related, not covered by mutually recognised labour laws, or related to the NAALC's Labour Principles 1 to 3.[5]

If after consideration of a final ECE report a country believes that there is still a persistent pattern of failure by another country to effectively enforce its occupational safety and health, child labour, or minimum wage technical labour standards, it may request further consultation, and eventually, the establishment of an independent Arbitral Panel. Arbitral Panels consist of five members who examine effective enforcement of laws related to Labour Principles 5, 6 and 9. Based on the panel's final report and its recommendations, the disputing parties may agree on a mutually satisfactory action plan. Failure to implement the plan could result in fines or trade sanctions.

The substance of NAALC is tri-national and not supranational. Instead of yielding sovereignty over the content of their labour laws and standards, the NAFTA countries shaped the NAALC 'to open themselves up to trinational scrutiny of their enforcement regimes'.

However, that does not prevent relatively precise procedural standards being created by the Agreement itself governing the application of labour law in each of the three countries; these are requirements which each of the Parties must comply with in the operation of its administrative and judicial systems, though they are formulated by an external source. Moreover the Agreement provides for the intervention of independent third parties, evaluation committees of experts and Arbitral Panels to deal with various problems involving 'technical labour standards.' This adds another supranational aspect to an Agreement, which is in general still trinational in other respects.

The Parties indicated their desire to use cooperation and mutual consultation to ensure that the Agreement is given full effect.

Implementation of the NAALC rests with the Parties themselves. This applies to cooperative activities, cooperative consultations and evaluations, as well as the resolution of disputes.

The opportunity offered to members of the public, individuals or groups, whether union, employer or otherwise, to submit to the various NAOs for their consideration communications on questions dealing with labour legislation is thus a significant derogation from the otherwise public- or government-driven implementation of the Agreement. The detailed consideration of the processing of such public communications shows how important this window to the public is.

National labour law

Legal systems: convergence or divergence?

At present national labour law systems are extremely divergent. They differ so much from each other, that they are hardly comparable (cf. Blanpain 2004). Reasons for that divergence are self-evident. National systems are so much part of the overall culture of a given nation-country, of the existing power relations, which have evolved over more than 100 years, that they are bound to be different. Various values play, like individualism versus collectivism, affective versus neutral relationships, specific versus diffuse cultures, organisation of time and the like (Trompenaars 1997). So are the Italian, German and Japanese systems, to name a few countries, hardly comparable, since the underlying values in those cultures differ enormously.

Closer? The question is asked whether the globalisation at the one hand and the accomplishment of a real internal market (EU) at the other end will bring the different national systems of labour law and of industrial relations closer together, and eventually make them more harmonised or even uniform. One could indeed be of the opinion that the fact that our different national systems within that one large market will be confronted with the same challenges, such as ever-growing (international) economic competition, the continuous introduction of new technologies, with the new worker – more educated, more creative and more participatory (the knowledge worker) – with the same urbanisation of our societies, with similar environmental problems, will have a convergent influence. The fact is that similar problems tend to be solved by the same solutions. One could also advance the argument that the labour law rules of the game – like many other rules for that matter – should be the same in order so that fair competition between countries does not have an adverse effect.

The fact that it is easier to dismiss a worker in the UK than in the Netherlands disturbs the market. Investors may be attracted by cheaper conditions in those countries where there are the fewest 'social constraints'. Thus, in order to combat eventual competition falsification we need at least to harmonise or, if possible, make uniform labour law rules. It then becomes a duty for the (European) authorities to see to it that the rules of the game are the same for all or at least equivalent. A convergent movement, i.e. getting closer together, would first be brought about by the natural functioning of the invisible hand, the market, and subsequently through a pointed policy of the authorities.

Apart? One could also argue that the existent divergence between the national systems of labour law and of industrial relations will continue and even persist further and that governments should not intervene in that process, but let them take their natural (or national?) course. This attitude is based first in the enormous variety of solutions that currently characterise e.g. the labour law systems of the twenty-five Member States of the EU and which will probably persist.

Before answering the question 'divergence or convergence?', let us look into this diversity, which is greater than is usually realised. It is said, as indicated above, with reason that this diversity is not accidental, but rather the result of our own proper social, cultural, political, historical and societal developments, which must be respected in their individuality. Some examples may suffice to illustrate the point.

Formal or informal? A first distinction regarding labour between the states is undoubtedly the fact that some systems are very formal while others are very informal. One of the most formal systems of the EU countries is undoubtedly the German system, in which most matters are dealt with by law, in which judges intervene with authority and efficiency and where every German seems to be a born lawyer, believing in the rule of law and approaching societal problems from the legal angle. Workers' participation, to give one example, is meticulously detailed and the legal rules are lived up to in practice; in Germany a strike is not only legally but also *de facto* governed by the peace obligation between the social partners and so on. In other words, the German system is legally predictable and probably a little bit boring. In Belgium, on the other hand, one might say that law and strikes have almost nothing to do with each other. Strikes in Belgium are a matter of pure power relations in the field.

Germany is at one end of the spectrum, Italy is at the other: the formal elements in Italy are less important. Informality carries the day. Labour relations develop in relation to individual and collective emotions, which themselves are carried by the moods of the time, thus making Italy a paradise of immense creativity, and bringing a lot of – not always pleasant – surprises, such as was the case in the Coba wildcat strikes. It is only in Italy that the notion *stato di agitazione* as an element of industrial warfare is known.

Trade Unions: A second distinction can be found in the organisation of workers, more precisely the degree of unionisation, trade union structures and trade union ideology. The degree of unionisation differs enormously from country to country. Belgium and Denmark score rather high: some 50 per cent or more of workers are organised (there are no really controlled and certified figures available); France and Spain are at a much lower level with less than 10 per cent of the workforce organised. Lately, the number of trade union members has diminished dramatically in certain countries. In a space of ten years, the French unions lost 50 per cent of their membership. At present only 2 per cent of French young people between the ages of eighteen and twenty-four are members of a union. Other countries lie between the two extremes.

One can find the same diversity in the trade union structures: on the one hand, Germany has a streamlined trade union organisation per sector of industry, on the other, the UK still has craft unions, which are organised in certain sectors on the basis of craft or trade; then there are the demarcation lines between the trade unions themselves running along different patterns in the Member States, whereby, for example, workers organised by the French metal workers' union are members of the Belgian textile organisation.

The same is true for the trade union ideology: one distinguishes between unions from the North, which are more or less integrated in the neo-capitalist system, and the more contesting organisations from the South; while British unions are characterised by their adversarial approach with, as it is called, some touches of 'new realism' shown by certain organisations which are convinced that they can only adequately defend the interests of their members when they accept the reality of the market economy and the profit motive. Diametrically opposed to this is the still communist French *Confédération Générale du Travail*, which has the greatest number of members in France, and which for that reason was for a long time denied membership of the ETUC.

Employer associations: A third example of diversity can be found in the structure and the role of the employers' associations. Some organisations are more centralised than others, pursuant to the proper character of their own labour relations system. The *Deutsche Arbeitgebersbund* is more centralised in its organisation and decision-making structure than, say, the British Confederation of Industries. Another point: all employers' organisations self-evidently engage in wide-ranging political lobbying, giving advice to their members on tax and related matters, exports, etc. There is nevertheless an important difference depending on the question whether the employers' organisations also engage in collective bargaining and are parties to a collective agreement or not. Thus, we cite the Belgian Federation of Enterprises which has a clear profile as the employers' negotiator for the Belgian private sector as a whole. It is clear that the British organisation does not play such a role. This is again a very important point of diversity between the Member States regarding industrial relations.

Legal culture: Still another, and probably the most important distinction can be found in the difference in legal culture between the UK on the one hand and continental Europe (minus Scandinavia) on the other. It is indeed a fact that 'it is not in the tradition of Her Majesty's Government to regulate conditions of work by Acts of Parliament'. Working conditions in Great Britain are not regulated by Acts. This is a job for the social partners. And if the government feels that one of the partners has too much power, there may be legal intervention, such as Mrs Thatcher instigated, to curb trade union power and in so doing increase the power of the employers to make their points more easily accepted at the bargaining table, if there is bargaining at all. This could be looked upon as one pointed form of legal interventionism.

This characteristic of the British legal system is of the utmost importance for Community developments regarding labour law. Indeed, Mrs Thatcher was consistent with herself when she underlined in her famous speech in Bruges in 1988 that she was not going to accept labour law rules from Brussels, where she had prevented them successfully in London. That is why she refused to sign the Social Charter and why John Major did not accept the Maastricht Agreement on Social Policy. The European continent, on the other hand, is generally more legally interventionist: our labour law codes are more than full of texts, even in a period of so-called deregulation.

One should therefore not be surprised that Tony Blair, the flamboyant leader of 'New Labour' and who stands for 'a fair, but not a free deal', follows in the footsteps of Thatcher and Major and refutes European legislative initiatives.

Collective agreements: An equally striking difference concerns the legally binding effect of collective agreements. It is unthinkable for continental lawyers that a collective agreement in the UK is not legally binding and constitutes only a 'gentlemen's agreement', that it cannot lead to legal obligations because 'parties do not have the intention to create such obligations'. A collective agreement is only binding in law if the parties expressly declare this in their agreement. In continental Europe, on the contrary, there is, in accordance with the Roman adage *pacta sunt servanda*, a clear legal binding effect of the obligations created by the agreement.

Just as important is the possibility in certain Member States to give the collective agreement a general binding effect by which the normative part of the collective agreement, which is, say, concluded at sectoral level, becomes legally binding for all employers and all workers of that sector, whether they are members of the contracting parties or not. If the agreement is concluded at inter-industry level all employers and all workers of the private sector may fall within the scope of the legally binding agreement. Such a procedure by which agreements can be extended exists in Belgium, France, Germany and the Netherlands, to give a few examples.

The impact of this extension procedure on a national system of industrial relations is enormous. One example may suffice. In the UK where extension of agreements is not a given practice, Ford Motor Co. conducts negotiations with its employees on its own, without being for that matter a very active member of the employers' association. In Belgium, on the contrary, where extension of agreements is standard practice, Ford Motor Co. is a very active member of Agoria, the employers' organisation of the metal working trades. The reason is self-evident: Ford wants maximum influence over the outcome of the collective agreement that will be negotiated by Agoria, an agreement which Ford would be involved in, even if it were not a member of the organisation. In summary, the extension of agreements leads to stronger employers' associations and more centralised labour relations and therefore has a basic influence over labour law and industrial relations.

Income policies: The role of governments in industrial relations, particularly in the area of income policies, is another topical example. In certain Member States, governments play the role of third parties in the industrial relations scene, sometimes that of the most important actor, and do not hesitate to intervene in wage policies when it becomes necessary to protect the competitiveness of the undertakings. Over the last few years, such interventions have taken place in Belgium, France, Greece and Spain, not to mention other countries. In Germany, such an intervention is unheard of and almost constitutionally impossible.

In Germany, the holy principle of 'tariff' autonomy of the social partners prevails, meaning that the government cannot interfere directly in the setting of wages, as this belongs to the autonomy and prerogative of the social partners. The most the German government can do is bring the parties together within the framework of what is called 'concerted action' in order to give, on the basis of an experts' report on the economic situation in Germany, some guidelines concerning pay, which one hopes the social partners will respect. This situation in Germany is easily understandable when one realises that it is the outcome of a reaction against Nazi Germany, where a dictatorship controlled almost every aspect of life; in the Federal Republic the power of the government has been confined within the framework of a pluralistic democracy in favour of the social partners. This is just another large difference between the systems of the Member States.

Power relations: One could go on for ever citing examples regarding workers' participation, the way strikes are allowed and regulated and so on. Diversity is the general rule. In other words, there is no European system of industrial relations. The systems are mainly national and will remain so for a long time to come. Therefore one has to give a very nuanced answer to the question: convergence or divergence of labour law in Europe? First, it is clear that diversity will continue, not only because this lies in the nature of things: Germans are not Italians and vice versa and it is best that it stays this way. As important is the fact that the national systems constitute a delicate balance between social factors and actors, which has come about over the years and evolves in its own rhythm and tempo. Harmonisation over the boundaries jeopardises those balances and has a strong chance of being rejected.

This is certainly the case in relation to everything in labour relations to do with power, namely collective bargaining, workers' participation, strikes, lock-outs, etc. It is no accident that the European proposals concerning the workers' participation European Company Statute (SE) was on the table for more than thirty years before being adopted. These proposals encroach too much upon the existing balance of power. Moreover, collective labour relations are bedevilled by ideology and mask societal options: pro-market or pro-government intervention. Moreover, quite a number of voices quickly point out that our labour relations should become more decentralised and that problems regarding e.g. working time, except for very general framework (national or sectoral) agreements, must be dealt with at the level of the undertaking, thus taking into account that it is the enterprises that have to do battle on the markets and that the great diversity in goods and services prevalent today make simple, uniform formulae that are valid for all enterprises and situations totally inadequate.

Convergence of costs: On the other hand, it is likewise clear that the market comes into play and that it will push the national systems together from the point of view of cost, while a certain harmonisation 'while improvement is being maintained' (Article 136 EC Treaty) is also indicated. European measures, for that matter, can perfectly respect the diversity between the Member States. But here one should also be cautious. Lower unit labour costs and longer working hours may constitute, for example for Portugal, a winning card in the attraction of foreign investment and thus jobs, which would disappear if one started to equalise wages over the boundaries and make working time more uniform.

In a nutshell, one can say that there will be a convergence of systems and a certain harmonisation of labour law as far as the result and the cost of the systems are concerned: the market will come into play and lead, together with the common challenges that confront all Member States, to an unavoidable convergence which, supported by political and trade union pressure, will bring the systems closer to each other. This convergence will, however, go hand in hand with a continuous divergence as far as the content of labour relations and labour law is concerned: the way people are hired and fired, the way strikes are organised and so on. These will mainly be determined at a national level. Summing up: convergence of costs versus divergence of content. The danger is that convergence of costs goes together with an ongoing process of social dumping. There is asymmetry between an economic monetary Europe and a social Europe, which remains mainly national. Competing on labour costs in a free market without a social counter balance leads to social dumping and diminishing working conditions.

Facing the challenge of globalisation

Labour law has fundamentally changed. In their book on *International and Comparative Employment Relations* Bamber *et al.* (2004: 348–9) describe this development as follows.

> After World War II, many governments adopted a more active role in regard to employment relations. The roles undertaken by governments may be categorised in terms of five components: maintaining protective standards; establishing rules for the interaction between the parties; ensuring that the results of such interaction were consistent with the apparent needs of the economy; providing services for labour and management (e.g. advice, conciliation, arbitration and training); and as a major employer.

During the early post-war years of economic growth, all of these roles were extended. Protective legislation became more detailed, adding appreciably to unit labour costs. The volume of legislation concerned with the relations of the parties increased too, though less so than protective legislation and in different ways and times in different countries. Services to employers and workers expanded-notably in the field of work organisation and the quality of working life in the 1970s. In several countries, the conflict between collective bargaining outcomes and economic policies induced government intervention. There was widespread extension of the right of public-service workers to organise and to have forms of collective bargaining rights.

From the early 1980s there was a clear shift in such developments. Governments became cautious about extending protection, and some started to reduce protection-assessing whether the benefits justified the costs. France abolished the need for administrative authorisation for dismissals, and several countries relaxed rigid rules about working time and the rules about the employment of women on night work. There were some attempts to change employment relations rules through legislation. First, in Britain, Conservative governments sought, through a series of new laws, to reduce the volume of unofficial strikes and to strengthen the members' control of unions. The legislation helped change British employment relations: it made workers and their unions more hesitant about going on strike. Second, in France, the Auroux reforms of 1982 sought to establish more cooperative employment relations at the workplace. Although that legislation effected a number of changes, it did not transform French employment relations. A third case of change is Australia. From 1987, the several revisions of the Accord placed increasing emphasis on employment relations at the enterprise level, while the sweeping changes of the post-1996 conservative Coalition government's Workplace Relations Act further decentralised employment relations. Fourth, New Zealand until the 1980s had a century-old centralised arbitration system. However, vast changes to individual and enterprise bargaining were introduced by the Employment Contracts Act 1991. Although the subsequent Labour government has attempted to roll back many of these changes, employment relations in New Zealand remains fundamentally changed.

In their role as employers, governments had tended to follow practices equivalent to those of recognised 'good' private employers, but were subsequently faced with rapidly rising costs and restricted income. Hence, they found it necessary to cut their labour costs by reducing numbers and by limiting salary rises. Prime Minister Margaret Thatcher in Britain initiated the privatisation of publicly owned industries and enterprises, which took workers out of the public and into the private sector. A series of other countries followed this path, including Australia, even under a Labour government. A perceived need to restrain public-sector labour costs and the number of public employees continues to be widespread.

These changes seem, however, to be insufficient to face the challenges of globalisation and the information society.

In March 2003, the German Chancellor, Gerhard Schröder, outlined his reform plans, known as Agenda 2010, in four main areas: relaxing rules protecting workers from dismissal along with other labour market reforms; modernising the social welfare state; decreasing bureaucracy for small businesses and allowing crafts workers to launch new business ventures; and providing new low-interest loans to local authorities. The main employers' organisations saw these as key areas in which action is long overdue, and have offered broad support for the Chancellor's aims, albeit mixed with disappointment that they do not go far enough. However, trade unions rebuked Mr Schröder for his 'socially unbalanced' reform proposals.

According to a (2003) Report of the Employment Taskforce, *Jobs, Jobs, Jobs: Creating more employment in Europe,* chaired by Wim Kok, former Prime Minister of the Netherlands[6] underlines that '*labour markets must be made more flexible while providing workers with appropriate levels of security.* Flexibility is not just in the interest of employers; it also serves the interest of workers, helping them to combine work with care and education, for example, or to allow them to lead their preferred lifestyles. On the other hand, security does not just mean employment protection, but encompasses the capacity to remain and progress in work. Member States and social partners are advised to examine and, where necessary, adjust the level of flexibility provided under standard contracts, in order to ensure their attractiveness for employers and to provide for a sufficiently wide scope of contractual forms to enable employers and workers to adapt their working relationship to their respective needs and preferences. They are also advised to examine the degree of security in non-standard contracts'.

This message is, however, not necessarily universal.

In Japan, for example, the life time employment system still prevails as a fundamental characteristic of employment relations. As Araki (2002:18–20) notes:

> under a system of long-term employment relations where employment security is the general rule, the internal labour market plays a large role in the formation of the society's employment system. In the internal market, both the employer and the employee have an incentive to invest in firm specific skills and the long-term remuneration system, such as seniority based wages, develops. In the long-term employment system, workers accept flexible adjustments in their working conditions and internal transfers entailing change of workplace and job in exchange for employment security. Workers' concern is the terms and conditions in their particular company. Industrial-wide or national-level negotiation does not suit the real needs of either employers or workers under those circumstances. Unions at company level and collective bargaining within individual companies become a more efficient mechanism to meet the demands of the internal labour market. This is why enterprise

unionism is dominant in Japan. Accordingly, an employment system which incorporates employment security relies on internal, or qualitative, flexibility within the company, where terms and conditions of employment can be modified flexibly to fluctuating socio-economic conditions.

(cf. Hanami and Komiya 1998)

There is no doubt that this is not part of the social and cultural values of Japan, as Confucian ethics.

Moreover, the message that 'flexibility' is the way for more employment and prosperity is contested by many. They refer to countries like Denmark and Sweden, to give a few examples, where system of high protection and decent employment go hand in hand (Elliot 2004; TUC 2004).

Conclusion: looking for a balance

Labour law does not evolve in a vacuum. It is the result of an ongoing interaction between ideology and societal aspirations, culture and history of a given country, technological possibilities and economic necessities. Employment law is slowly adapting to the new realities of globalisation and ICT, trying to combine flexibility and security. Employability becomes more important than job security.

New balances are struck. The question is how to strike the right balance between what is economic necessarily, technologically possible and socially desirable, respecting self-evidently fundamental social rights. Only when that balance is found and respected will the economy flourish and people prosper.

The question is and remains: how to make all of us and not just a few gain from the benefits of globalisation? Whether that goal is a dream or not remains to be seen. Whatever the answer is, it is not forbidden to dream and sometimes dreams come true. Our job as labour lawyers has just begun.

Notes

1 Report III (Part 1A) at each session of the Conference – and published on-line within about two months after its adoption by the Committee.
2 Also available on ILOLEX.
3 On the introduction of measures to encourage improvements in the safety and health of pregnant workers and workers who have recently given birth or are breast-feeding.
4 4. Prohibition of forced labour. 5. Labour protections for children and young persons. 6. Minimum employment standards. 7. Elimination of employment discrimination. 8. Equal pay for women and men. 9. Prevention of occupational injuries and illnesses. 10. Compensation in cases of occupational injuries and illnesses. 11. Protection of migrant workers.
5 1. Freedom of association and protection of the right to organise. 2. The right to bargain collectively. 3. The right to strike.

6 November 2003, p. 7. See equally: the Report from the High Level group, chaired by Wim Kok, November 2004, under the title *Facing the Challenge. The Lisbon strategy for growth and employment*, p. 52
7 European Court Reports.

References

Araki, T. (2002) *Labor and Employment Law In Japan*. Tokyo: The Japan Institute of Labor.

Bamber, G. J., Lansbury, R.D. and Wailes, N. (2004) *International and Comparative Employment Relations: Globalisation and the Developed Market Economies, 4th edition*. London: Sage.

Blanpain, R. (ed.) (2004) *Comparative Labour Law and Industrial Relations in Industrialised Market Economies*. The Hague: Kluwer Law International.

Blanpain, R. (2006) *European Labour Law*, tenth revised edition. The Hague: Kluwer Law International.

Blanpain, R. and Colucci, M. (2004) 'The globalization of labour standards', *Bulletin of Comparative Labour Relations*, 52. The Hague: Kluwer Law International.

Elliot, L. (2004) 'Flexibility can tie you up in knots', *The Guardian*. March, 22.

European Commission (2004) *Employment in Europe 2004*, Brussels.

Kaufman, B. E. (2004) *The Global Evolution of Industrial Relations*, Geneva: ILO.

Kok, W. (2004) 'Facing the Challenge. The Lisbon strategy for growth and employment, November', Report from the High Level group, p. 52.

ILO (2004) *A Fair Globalization: Creating Opportunities for All,* Geneva: ILO.

ILO (2003) 'Activities on the social dimension of globalisation: synthesis report', (www.ilo.org).

Somavia, J. (2004) 'For too many, globalization isn't working', *The International Herald Tribune*, 27 February.

Swepston, L. (2004) 'The ILO standards and globalization' in R. Blanpain (ed.) 'Confronting Globalization', *Bulletin of Comparative Labour Relations*. nr. 55, Kluwer Law International, The Hague, 11–20.

Hanami, T. and Komiya, F. (1998) 'Japan' in R. Blanpain (ed.) *International Encyclopaedia of Labour Law and Industrial Relations*. The Hague: Kluwer Law International.

Tergeist, P. and Blanpain, R. (2004) 'The OECD guidelines for multinational enterprises' in R. Blanpain (ed.) *International Encyclopaedia for Labour Law and Industrial Relations*. The Hague: Kluwer Law International.

Trompenaars, F. (1997) 'Law across cultures: an overview' in R. Blanpain (ed.) *Law in Motion*. The Hague: Kluwer Law International: 27–46.

TUC (2004) 'Labour market flexibility: building a modern labour market, an interim report'. (available for download on: www.tuc.org.uk/economy/tuc-8926-f0.cfm).

Cases of the Court of Justice (EU)

Andrea Francovich v. *Italian Republic*, 19 November 1991, C- 479/93, *ECR.*, 1991, 5375.

Barber Douglas Harvey v. *Guardian Royal Exchange Assurance Group*, 17 May 1990, C-262/99, *ECR.*, 1990, 1889.

Commission of the European Union v. *United Kingdom of Great Britain and Northern Ireland*, 8 June 1994, C-382/92 and 383/92, *ECR.*, 1994, 2479.

Gabrielle Defrenne v. *Society Anonyme Belge de Navigation Aériennen Sabena*, 8 April 1976, C-43/75, *ECR*[7]., 1976, 455–483.

Miss Helen Marshall v. *Southampton and South West Hampshire Area Health Authority*, 2 August 1993, C-271/91, *ECR.*, 1993, 4367.

Lawrie-Blum tg. *Land Baden-Würtemberg*, 3 juli 1986, C-66/85, *ECR.*, 1986, 2121.
Maria Luisa Jiménez Melgar v. *Ayuntamiento de Los Barrios*, 4 October 2001, C-438/00,
    ECR., 2001, 6915.
Sabine von Colson and Elisabeth Kaman v. *Land Northrein–Westfalen*, 18 April 1984, C-
    14/83, *ECR.*, 1984, 1891.
The Queen v. *Immigration Appeal Tribunal*, ex parte Gustaff Desiderius Antonissen, 26
    February 1991, C- 292/89, *ECR.*, 1991, 745.
The Queen v. *Secretary of State for Trade and Industry*, ex parte Broadcasting, Entertainment,
    Cinematographic and Theatre Union (BECTU), Opinion of Advocate general Tizzano, 8
    February 2001, *ECR.*, 2001, 4881
The Queen v. *Secretary of State for Trade and Industry*, ex parte Broadcasting, Entertainment,
    Cinematographic and Theatre Union (BECTU), 26 June 2001, C173/99, *ECR.*, 2001,
    4881.
United Kingdom of Great Britain and Northern Ireland v. *Council of the European Union*, 12
    November 1996, C-84/94, *ECR.* 1996, 5755.
Union Royale Belge des Sociétés de Football Association ASBL and Others v. *Jean-Marc
    Bosman*, 15 December 1995, C-415/93, *ECR.*, 1995, 4921.

Suggested key readings

Blanpain, R. and Weiss M. (eds) (2003) *Changing Industrial Relations and Modernisation of
    Labour Law. Liber Amicorum in Honour of Professor Marco Biagi*. The Hague: Kluwer
    Law International.
Compa, L. (2003) 'Assessing assessments: a survey of efforts to measure countries'
    compliance with freedom of association standards', *Comparative Labor Law & Policy
    Journal*, 24(2), Winter: 283–320.
Compa, L. (2003) Diamond S. F. (eds) *Human Rights, Labor Rights and International Trade*,
    Philadelphia: University of Pennsylvania Press.
Flanagan, R. J. and Gould W. B. (eds) (2003) *International Labour Standards: Globalization,
    Trade and Public Policy*. Stanford University Press.
Hepple, B. (ed.) (2002) *Social and Labour Rights in a Global Context: International and
    Comparative Perspectives*. Cambridge University Press.
Hepple, B. (2004) *Labour Laws and Global Trade*, London: Hart Publishing.
ILO (2004) 'Report of the Director-General of the World Commission on the social dimension
    of globalization', *A Fair Globalization: The Role of the ILO*, 92nd Session, Geneva: ILO.
Neal, A. C. (2004) *The Changing Face of European Labour Law and Social Policy*, The
    Hague: Kluwer Law International.
Servais, J. M. (2001) 'Labour conflicts, courts and social policy: reflections based on ILO
    deliberations on decent work' in R. Blanpain (ed.) *Labour Law, Human Rights and Social
    Justice, Liber Amicorum Professor Ruth Ben Israel*, The Hague: Kluwer, 77–88.
Servais, J. M. (2005) 'International labour standards', *International Encyclopaedia of Labour
    Law and Industrial Relations*. The Hague: Kluwer Law International.

15 Multinationals, globalisation and industrial relations

WILLIAM N. COOKE

Introduction

Since 1980 there has been an extraordinary growth in corporate globalisation, marked by a greater than eight-fold increase in the number of multinationals and a nearly twelve-fold increase in foreign direct investment (UNCTAD 2004: Table B.3, 376). As of 2004, there were over 61,000 multinational companies (MNCs) that had ownership in over 900,000 foreign affiliated operations dispersed around the world. These foreign affiliates alone managed over US $31 trillion in assets, generated over US $17 trillion in sales, accounted for some 33 per cent of exports and 10 per cent of gross domestic product worldwide, and employed more than 54 million employees (UNCTAD 2004: 8–9). The ever-expanding transnational reach and influence of MNCs in the world economy raises a number of important industrial relations issues, especially against a backdrop in which union penetration has generally declined across most countries and stagnated in others over the last two decades (see Chapter 10).

In this final chapter we examine several fundamental IR issues not already covered in the preceding chapters. After laying out a highly simplified but fairly comprehensive and coherent framework to guide our analysis, we shall then examine the general business logic underlying foreign direct investment (FDI) decision-making by MNCs and recent trends and patterns in FDI. We will subsequently study the role of IR in MNC decision-making, including the diffusion of preferred IR practices abroad, MNC efforts at avoiding and marginalising unions, union resistance to the diffusion of MNC workplace strategies across foreign locations, and the influence of differences in IR systems on FDI decision-making. Lastly, in light of the increasing relative power of MNCs vis-à-vis organised labour resulting from globalisation, we will consider the prospects for transnational inter-union efforts to engage in collective bargaining with MNCs, the success of which hinges on unions' capacity to overcome substantial barriers to cross-border inter-union co-operation and co-ordination.

An analytical framework

Understanding the IR-related behaviour of management and organised labour underlying corporate globalisaton first requires understanding the primary objectives that motivate the parties' behaviour and second, requires identifying the salient factors that influence or constrain their behaviour as they act to achieve their respective objectives. We begin with two highly simplified theoretical assumptions about the objectives of the parties: namely, MNCs seek to optimise profits and unions seek to optimise gains to workers ranging from more narrowly focused 'bread-and-butter' gains for union members to more broadly conceived social and political gains for working class constituencies. The gains that either party can achieve are bounded, of course, by the constraints placed on organisations by the broader economic and socio-political environments within which they find themselves. The optimisation of gains from the employment relationship is determined in large part, furthermore, by the exercise of power by both labour and management. Within these constraints, it is assumed herein that the parties *seek to act* rationally in their efforts to optimise gains. That is, the parties are calculative in weighing the potential benefits and costs associated with the decisions they make towards optimising gains, but make those decisions with limited and imperfect information, uncertainty, and lack of perfect foresight, adjusting their decisions accordingly in response to unforeseen circumstances encountered, to trial-and-error outcomes, and to mistakes made.

With these assumptions about bounded optimising behaviour in mind, an analytical framework that guides our analysis of multinationals and IR issues in this chapter is shown in diagram in Figure 15.1. As illustrated, the business and configuration strategies pursued by MNCs are conditioned by the broader domestic and foreign economic and socio-political environmental contexts they face. Within these broader environmental contexts are a wide range of factors, including the home and alternative host country IR systems affecting the benefits and costs associated with alternative business and configuration strategies pursued by MNCs. Home country IR systems also affect the IR strategies pursued by parent companies across their home operations, which, in turn, influence the IR strategies pursued by MNCs across their foreign subsidiaries. The IR strategies pursued by MNCs across their foreign subsidiaries are also conditioned by host country IR systems. These host location IR strategies, in turn, may ultimately influence the domestic IR strategies pursued by parent companies in their home operations. In addition, union strategies can be expected to influence the IR strategies of MNCs, as well as be influenced by them. Acting independently, union strategies pursued in the home country operations of MNCs influence

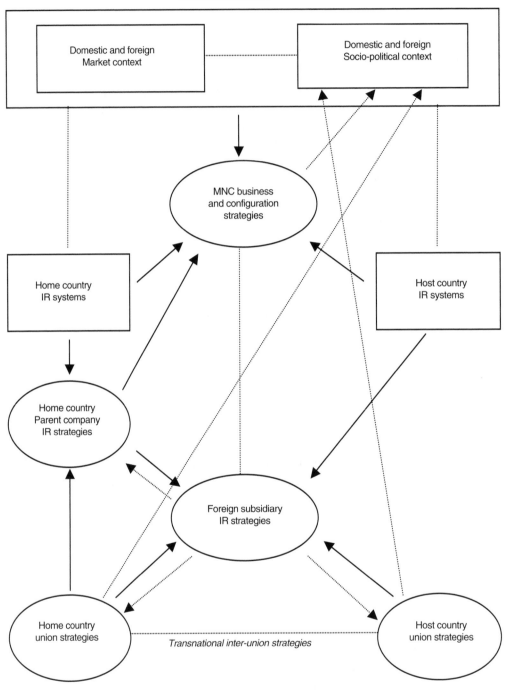

Figure 15.1 An analytical framework

domestic IR strategies, whereas union strategies pursued in host countries influence foreign subsidiary IR strategies. Acting in concert, the transnational inter-union strategies pursued by unions across borders will influence the IR strategies pursued by MNCs across both their foreign subsidiaries and operations in their home country. Lastly, both unions and MNCs will attempt to influence the socio-political context in ways favourable to each as they pursue their respective objectives.

MNC business and configuration strategies

In their persistent quest to optimise profitability, MNCs face complex choices about their global market positioning strategies. Central to these choices are decisions about the emphasis placed on cost leadership, differentiation by quality and innovation, and on the scope of products produced and services offered (Porter 1985, 1991). Also central to market positioning strategies are the offensive-defensive emphases pursued, which include the relative emphases placed on protecting and/or expanding existing markets, and developing new markets (Miles and Snow 1978; Porter 1985: Ch. 14). Linked to MNC market-positioning choices are decisions about the optimal configuration of operations.

The fundamental configuration options before MNCs include so-called 'external' market transactions (exportation, importation, subcontracting, licensing and franchising), so-called 'internal' market transactions (investment in home operations and FDI), and hybrid arrangements that combine both internal and external market transactions (joint ventures and alliances). Towards optimising profitability, MNCs are driven to choose that combination of internal and external market transactions that align best with their market positioning strategies. By including FDI as part of their broader configuration strategies (an act that defines a company as a 'multinational' company), companies have concluded that their global market positioning strategies can best be pursued through internal control of some cross-border transactions. Such FDI may better serve MNCs in penetrating foreign markets (known as 'market-seeking' FDI), reducing costs (known as 'efficiency-seeking' FDI), or in extracting natural resources (known as 'resource-seeking' FDI) or any combination thereof.

By engaging in FDI, companies perceive that they enjoy some inherent firm-specific ownership advantage(s) over firms operating in other countries that can be exploited. Ownership advantage may be derived, for example, from economies of scale, ready access to investment capital, and special competencies in marketing, research and development (R&D), logistics, design, or, as discussed later, in IR (Hymer 1976; Buckley and Casson 1976). Given ownership advantages, decisions about where and how much to invest across alternative locations are, additionally, a matter of comparative location advantages (Dunning 1993). Those foreign locations, that is, that offer greater market opportunity for

MNCs to penetrate or to defend against competitors or lower operational costs attract greater FDI (Hennart and Park 1994; Casson and Buckley 1998). MNCs whose market positioning strategies are based primarily on product innovation and expanding existing or developing new markets (and thus engage in market-seeking FDI) will be influenced more by a location's market opportunity advantages than its operational cost advantages. MNCs whose market positioning strategies are based primarily on cost leadership and protecting existing markets (and thus engage in efficiency-seeking FDI) will be influenced more by a location's operational cost advantages than its market opportunity advantages.

Among environmental factors affecting these market opportunities and relative costs across alternative host locations are differences in: (1) market size, wealth, and growth; (2) proximity between parent headquarters, subsidiaries, customers, and suppliers; (3) the availability and access to capital, R&D, and natural resources; (4) transportation, telecommunications, and utility infrastructures; (5) currency valuations and fluctuations; (6) labour skills and compensation costs; (7) government policies on taxation, incentives and disincentives to investment, tariffs, and related trade barriers; and (8) political or social stability. Additionally, of primary importance to the analysis in this chapter are differences in IR systems. Before examining the role of these differences in IR systems on MNC investment decision-making and the diffusion of IR ownership advantages abroad, it is instructive to examine the trends and patterns in MNC investment abroad.

Trends and patterns in MNC investment abroad

Although we have witnessed extraordinary growth in FDI, as well as the rapid spread of MNCs and their affiliated operations around the globe over the last two decades, observable trends and patterns of FDI reveal that it remains highly concentrated: by country of origin, by host region and a small number of economies within regions, by sector, and by a relatively small number of large MNCs. With respect to outward FDI, MNCs from just four countries (the US, UK, France, and Germany) accounted for 54 per cent of the ownership of FDI stock accumulated worldwide by 2003 (UNCTAD 2004: Table B4, 382–386). MNCs from just ten economies (upon adding the Netherlands, Switzerland, Hong Kong, Japan, Canada, and Italy) accounted for a full 75 per cent of the ownership of FDI stock worldwide by 2003. In addition to a heavy concentration of FDI made by MNCs from a handful of economies, the distribution of that FDI across foreign locations is, likewise, highly concentrated. First, as reported in Table 15.1, the spread of inward FDI is highly concentrated by host region and in a few economies within those host regions. Across developed countries, five host countries were the recipients of more than two-thirds of all FDI stock accumulated by 2003, with the US being the largest recipient, followed by the UK, Germany, France, and the Netherlands.

Table 15.1 FDI inward stock by host region and largest host economies, 1980–2003 ($US billions)

Region/Economy	1980	1990	2000	2003
World	693	1,948	5,952	7,982
Developed Countries	391	1,400	4,012	5,702
France	26	87	260	434
Germany	37	120	471	545
Netherlands	19	69	241	336
UK	63	204	439	672
US	83	395	1,214	1,554
Developing Economies	301	548	1,940	2,280
Africa	32	51	141	167
Angola	1	1	8	17
Egypt	2	11	20	21
Nigeria	2	8	20	24
S. Africa	17	9	43	30
Tunisia	3	8	12	17
Asia and Pacific	220	380	1,287	1,465
China	1	21	348	501
Hong Kong, China	178	202	455	375
Singapore	6	30	112	147
Latin America and Caribbean	50	117	512	648
Bermuda	5	14	56	81
Brazil	17	37	103	128
Chile	1	10	45	47
Mexico	8	22	97	166
Central and Eastern Europe	—	3	138	263
Czech Republic	—	1	22	41
Hungary	—	1	23	43
Poland	—	—	34	52
Russian Federation	—	—	25	53

Source: UNCTAD, *World Investment Report 2004*, Annex Table B.3, pp. 376–81.

Across developing economies in the Asia and Pacific region, just three economies were recipients of 70 per cent of all FDI stock accumulated in that region as of 2003; with China being the largest recipient, followed by Hong Kong (China), and Singapore the distant third-ranked recipient. Similarly, across Latin America and the Caribbean, just four countries accounted for nearly two-thirds of all FDI stock accumulated in that region in 2003; with Mexico being the largest recipient, followed by Brazil, Bermuda, and Chile. Likewise, across the transition

Table 15.2 Distribution of outward FDI stock between developed countries and developing/transition economies, 1980–2003 (US$ billions)

	Total stock				*Change in stock*		
	1980	1990	2000	2003	1980–1990	1990–2000	2000–2003
Developed countries	391	1,400	4,012	5,702	1,009	4,140	1,690
Total %	56	72	66	69	80	63	78
Developing/transition economies	302	548	2,078	2,543	248	1,528	2,543
Total %	44	28	34	31	20	37	22

Source: UNCTAD, *World Investment Report 2004*, Annex Table B.4, pp. 382–86

economies of Central and Eastern Europe, four economies accounted for some 72 per cent of all stock accumulated in that region; with the Russian Federation accumulating the largest stock, followed by Poland, Hungary, and the Czech Republic. Lastly, as of 2003, five countries accounted for 63 per cent of all FDI stock accumulated across the entire continent of Africa; with South Africa the largest recipient, followed by Nigeria, Egypt, Tunisia, and Angola.

Second, although the flow of FDI going to developed countries relative to developing and transition economies over the last two decades has fluctuated, the largest proportion of FDI continues to flow into highly developed countries. As reported in Table 15.2, roughly 56 per cent of total inward FDI in 1980 was located in developed countries. The proportion going to developed countries rose to 72 per cent by 1990, dropped to 66 per cent by 2000, and rose again to 69 per cent by 2003. Over the 1980–1990 period, MNCs clearly favoured investment in developed countries, with 80 per cent of stock accumulated during that period going to developed countries and only 20 per cent going to developing economies. In contrast, over the 1990–2000 period there was a marked shift in investment patterns, whereby 37 per cent of all stock accumulated during that period went to developing and transition economies. Over the last few years, however, the pattern of investment has mirrored more closely the trend during the 1980s in that only 22 per cent of the total stock accumulated over the 2001–2003 period went to developing and transition economies.

We have seen, furthermore, an increasing concentration of FDI in services and away from manufacturing. In 1990, 47 per cent of all outward FDI stock was held in service industries, 44 per cent held in manufacturing, and 9 per cent held in primary sector industries (e.g. mining, petroleum, and agriculture). As of 2002, approximately 66 per cent of all outward FDI stock was held in services, 28 per cent held in manufacturing, and 4 per cent held in the primary sector (UNTCAD: Table A.I.19, 303). Lastly, we find that a relatively small number of MNCs account for a highly disproportionate share of FDI. For instance, the top 100 non-financial MNCs, which accounted for less than 0.2 per cent of some 61,000

MNCs, accounted for roughly 12 per cent of total worldwide foreign assets in 2002 (UNCTAD: Table A.I.3, 276–278).

In addition to being highly concentrated, FDI reflects a reshuffling of assets primarily through merger and acquisition (M&A). Indeed, over the 1999–2003 period, the value of FDI through M&As equalled 75 per cent of total outward FDI flows.[1] The reshuffling of assets, furthermore, reflects shifts in total investment away from the domestic operations toward the foreign operations of MNCs. Such a pattern is evident, for instance, across US-owned MNCs over the last decade. Between 1989 and 2001, the total domestic assets of these US MNCs increased 100 per cent, whereas the total foreign assets increased by roughly 450 per cent. The result of this shifting emphasis toward investment in foreign affiliates increased the ratio of foreign assets to total MNC parent assets from 27 per cent in 1989 to 42 per cent in 2001.[2]

The role of industrial relations in MNC decision-making

We examine next the role of IR considerations in the strategic decision-making of MNCs. Assuming that MNCs seek to act rationally (however bounded) in their pursuit to optimise profits, the choices they make in configuring and managing their global operations will be influenced by any IR ownership advantages they enjoy and IR system location advantages (or disadvantages) associated with selected host country locations. To sort through this kind of decision-making, we first develop the logic behind exploiting any IR ownership advantages abroad and review the relevant evidence. Subsequently, we examine the salient IR system factors that influence MNC decisions of where and how much to invest abroad and then synthesise the relevant evidence about such choices.

Exploiting IR advantages abroad

As discussed earlier, MNCs can be expected to attempt to exploit abroad any perceived ownership advantages they can, including competitive IR advantages. Hence, MNCs enjoying IR ownership advantages have incentive to diffuse these advantages abroad. MNCs not enjoying IR ownership advantages (either because they have not been able to develop any special IR competencies or because they view IR strategies as relatively inconsequential to achieving their broader business strategies) have no incentive to diffuse any given IR policies or practices to their foreign subsidiaries. These MNCs, therefore, will simply allow host location managers to decide on IR strategies pursued.

Among those MNCs enjoying IR ownership advantages, any decisions to diffuse these advantages abroad are, nonetheless, conditioned by the ease with which they can realise the same ownership advantages abroad. As briefly described below by a number of researchers, MNCs face local isomorphic pressures to adapt embedded localised workplace strategies and practices in their foreign subsidiaries (Ferner and Quintanilla 1998). MNCs wanting to diffuse preferred (and presumably superior) IR strategies or selected core best practices abroad, therefore, may encounter costly workplace constraints in foreign locations, which impede the diffusion of IR ownership advantages abroad. The greater the extent to which workplace norms, customary practices, and institutional arrangements differ between the country-of-origin and host country locations in which IR ownership advantages would be diffused by the parent, the more difficult or costly will be such diffusion (Kostova 1999).

Whether or not MNCs will seek to diffuse IR ownership advantages abroad depends on cost–benefit calculations (however imperfect) of the perceived net gain achievable by any efforts at diffusion. In weighing the potential benefits, parent company executives must first judge the degree to which their preferred IR strategy or core best practices are truly superior to the IR strategies and practices that would otherwise be pursued at the local level by alternative host locations. In short, how much would performance improve if IR ownership advantages were transferred? Second, the parent organisation would need to take into account the added benefit derived from having uniform IR practices and processes across its subsidiaries for purposes of organisational control and co-ordination of integrated operations (Kobrin 1991; Rosenzweig and Singh 1991).

In weighing the potential costs associated with diffusing preferred IR strategies or core practices, MNCs would need to assess the capacity and receptivity of local managers and workers to the organisational changes that would be required to successfully diffuse IR ownership advantages. In making their assessments of the capacity for change, MNCs need to estimate the costs associated with moulding foreign workplaces to fit the preferred IR strategy or practices. Here, MNCs would estimate, for example, the costs associated with investments in recruitment, selection, re-orientation, training, development, and the re-design of work. In making their assessments of host location receptivity to change, MNCs would also estimate the costs associated with obtaining the necessary buy-in from local managers and workers. Such costs could include, for example, financial and career opportunity incentives, as well as threatened or actual divestment options.

Upon conducting these kinds of cost–benefit efficiency analyses as they would apply to any given foreign subsidiary, as well as to prospective foreign locations, MNCs would rationally only pursue diffusing their IR ownership advantages to select foreign locations where the perceived benefits would outweigh the perceived costs. Indeed, given limited resources, MNCs will be inclined to diffuse IR ownership advantages where the net benefit is greatest. Consequently, everything else being the same, MNCs will invest more in those existing subsidiaries or prospective locations in which they can enjoy the greatest net benefit from diffusing any IR ownership advantages.

Unfortunately, data are not available to provide the reader with an accurate profile of MNC efforts and success at diffusing preferred IR strategies or practices abroad. However, based on numerous studies of such diffusion, it appears that the extent of diffusion varies widely along a continuum, ranging from nearly full diffusion of preferred IR practices at one end to virtually no diffusion at the other end. Some Japanese MNCs, for example, have been insistent on replicating home-based IR strategies across their foreign subsidiaries, believing that their IR strategies offer superior advantage over those of their competitors anywhere in the world (Bird *et al.* 1998). The diffusion of these preferred IR strategies has often been marked by intensive efforts to mould foreign workplaces to fit their preferred strategies through extensive recruitment and selection activities and substantial reorientation and training for both workers and managers in foreign operations.

At the other end of the continuum, some MNCs have decided, apparently, that the costs outweigh the benefits of diffusing preferred IR practices abroad. For example, Brewster and Tregaskis (2003) found in their study of MNCs with operations in several European countries that the use of contingent employment practices (e.g. the hiring of part-time, temporary, and fixed-term contract employees) paralleled the usage common to host countries and sectors within countries. The authors conclude that the institutional and cultural antecedents of host locations have dominant effects on the extent to which MNCs can diffuse preferred IR practices, at least with regard to the diffusion of contingent employment practices. Other case studies have shown, likewise, that some MNCs have all but abandoned efforts to diffuse preferred IR practices abroad after encountering strong resistance in host locations (Kenney and Tanaka 2003).

Between the extremes of this continuum, other MNCs (and perhaps most MNCs) have both adopted some IR practices more in common with host country locations than those deployed in their home-based operations and diffused other IR practices core to their preferred IR strategies but ones often modified to varying degrees to accommodate local subsidiary differences in workplace cultures, norms, customary practices, and institutional arrangements (e.g. see Florida and Kenney 1991; Doeringer *et al.* 1998; Purcell *et al.* 1999; Martin *et al.* 2003; Edwards *et al.* 2005). In their study of a UK-US-owned pharmaceutical MNC with subsidiaries in the UK, US, Spain, and Germany, Edwards *et al.* (2005) describe both the isomorphic pressures from the corporate centre to diffuse preferred IR practices (e.g. variable pay linked to performance and job grading) and local isomorphic pressures constraining headquarters' freedom to diffuse such practices. The authors found a sufficient degree of 'malleability' across all subsidiaries (regardless of host country) that allowed the MNC to find alternative ways to diffuse its preferred IR policies across locations, albeit modified in specific practice to accommodate local host differences and preferences.

Central to the present analysis are the important roles of union representation and collective bargaining with respect to both IR strategies pursued by MNCs and host location resistance to the diffusion of IR practices. Here, a number of recent studies indicate that (1) many if not most MNCs have attempted to avoid union representation and collective bargaining when the costs of avoidance have not been perceived as too high and (2) MNCs have often encountered varying degrees of resistance from unionised locations to MNC efforts at diffusing preferred IR practices abroad.

For example, Florida and Kenney (1991) found in their study of Japanese automobile assemblers and parts subsidiaries that Japanese MNCs vigorously avoided union representation in the United States. The primary exception to pursuing union avoidance strategies were found in just three joint ventures undertaken with US automobile producers and in one case in which Ford Motor Company was a partial owner. In these cases, Japanese MNCs did not seriously challenge union representation by the United Automobile Workers and collective bargaining agreements were negotiated wherein the MNCs were able to diffuse preferred IR practices and production systems, albeit modified to varying degrees. One of the core components of the Japanese IR model that was not widely diffused to US automotive plants, however, was an individualised pay system based on merit and seniority. Demanding more uniform wages based on job duties and classifications, US workers and unions greatly resisted or rejected the individualised pay schemes preferred by Japanese MNCs. Even in non-union subsidiaries, Japanese MNCs did not attempt to force preferred pay schemes on their American workforces, fearing that such action would trigger union-organising drives.

In their study of Japanese subsidiaries in Australia, Purcell et al. (1999) found that in over 80 per cent of the manufacturing sites MNCs recognised unions. In sharp contrast, only in about 3 per cent of finance and tourism subsidiaries did MNCs recognise unions. As summarised by the authors and consistent with Florida and Kenney's (1991) findings, Japanese MNCs did not strongly resist union representation when it appeared that the costs outweighed the benefits in doing so, but otherwise aggressively resisted union representation. In an apparent attempt, nonetheless, to marginalise unions, roughly three out of four of the unionised subsidiaries established non-union channels of joint consultation through the creation of employee representation committees. Purcell et al. also report that in contrast to the IR strategies deployed in their Japanese home sites, only about one-third of the Australian-based subsidiaries paid bonuses to all of their employees.

Kenney and Tanaka's (2003) assessment of the failed efforts of Japanese MNCs to diffuse preferred IR practices deployed in their television assembly operations in Japan to their transplant sister operations in the US, demonstrates, furthermore, how deeply embedded workplace cultures and traditions in host locations can impede the diffusion of even highly preferred IR strategies abroad. They found, in particular, that the Fordist tradition of hierarchical job protection and seniority rights governing job assignment were so strongly engrained in both organised labour and local US management that it proved virtually impossible for Japanese MNCs to transfer their preferred 'learning bureaucracies' to their US subsidiaries. Similarly, as a result of deep-rooted labour-management traditions, GM encountered strong resistance from the Canadian Auto Workers to the diffusion of GM's IR work organisation strategy embodied in its North American standardisation of production system in truck assembly (Huxley 2003). As a result of this resistance, GM was unable to deploy its preferred formalised team-based system in its Oshawa, Canadian truck operations. Lacking the same deep-rooted labour-management traditions, the unionised workforce in its greenfield plant in Silao, Mexico, readily adopted GM's preferred IR practices, including its formalised team-based system.

Other studies have also shown that union avoidance plays an important role in the global IR strategies of many MNCs. Sometimes these efforts reflect a benign opportunism whereby MNCs merely take full advantage of relatively low union penetration levels in host countries. For example, in their study of greenfield investments in the UK, Guest and Hoque (1996) found that foreign-owned subsidiaries recognised unions at about the same relatively low rate associated with similarly situated domestic UK companies (at roughly 20 per cent). For other MNCs, union avoidance reflects a more calculated, orchestrated effort at avoiding unions in their non-union subsidiaries and at reducing union representation across their foreign operations by shifting investment away from organised sites to unorganised sites. In their study of German-owned subsidiaries in the UK, Beaumont et al. (1990) found that German MNCs were markedly resistant to recognising unions in their UK operations. Similarly, Cooke (2001b), found that European and Japanese MNCs investing in the US have recently and widely adopted the well-known union avoidance and deunionisation culture of the American IR system, having sharply reduced union penetration across their foreign-owned subsidiaries from nearly 30 per cent in 1980 to below 15 per cent by 1998. This reduction in coverage is the result of MNCs closing and reducing employment in sites represented by unions, while expanding employment in non-union sites and otherwise avoiding union representation in sites opened or acquired.

Even in highly unionised Ireland where US-owned MNCs have invested heavily, US multinationals have largely avoided recognising unions in their subsidiaries (Gunnigle et al. 2002). In their study of two large US-owned pharmaceutical companies in Ireland, Gunnigle et al. (2004), furthermore, report that even US MNCs with a long tradition of voluntary union recognition have recently pursued double-breasted IR strategies by which the companies have avoided union recognition in their newest sites. Perhaps the most concerted documented union avoidance strategy pursued by MNCs is that of the McDonald's Corporation across European countries. As detailed by Royle and Towers (2003), taking full advantage of the nature of its largely contingent workforce, McDonald's has been able successfully to diffuse its anti-union American tradition across most of its sites in Europe. Consequently, in spite of fairly strong traditions and government policies of supporting extensive employee interest representation via unions and works councils, the vast majority of McDonald's fast-food outlets in Europe have remained union-free.

Influence of IR systems on FDI decisions

As discussed earlier, in deciding where and how much to invest across alternative foreign host locations, MNC executives will rationally invest more in countries that offer the greatest location advantages in terms of market opportunities and lower operational costs as both influence the gains achievable by exploiting existing ownership advantages abroad. Given that IR considerations are more a matter of controlling operational costs than increasing market opportunities, MNCs pursuing cost leadership market positioning strategies and engaging in efficiency-seeking FDI can be expected to invest more (less) in countries whose IR systems yield lower (higher) net unit labour costs; again, all else being equal. Differences in net unit labour costs are a function of differences in compensation, skills, government workplace policies and regulations, collective bargaining contexts, and other workplace cultural factors. These factors not only affect net unit labour costs directly but also indirectly to the extent that they constrain or increase the costs to diffusing IR ownership advantages abroad.

In comparison to operating non-union sites, the potential added unit labour costs of union representation and collective bargaining are incurred as a result of organised labour's efforts to optimise gains for workers, which generally includes some trade-off between achieving equity as perceived by unions and achieving efficiency as perceived by management. Included among the potential added costs in unionised workplaces are those associated with more restrictive workplace practices, higher wages and benefits, transaction costs incurred through negotiations and contract administration, and wider divisions between labour and management (as manifested, for example, by work stoppages). As discussed in the previous section, moreover, there is reason to believe that MNCs have been more likely to encounter location-specific resistance (at least more effective resistance) to the diffusion of preferred IR practices in unionised sites than in non-union sites.

Hence, unless MNCs perceive that union representation and collective bargaining yield added value that at least equalises net unit labour costs between comparable union and non-union operations, MNCs will pursue FDI strategies designed to minimise exposure to unions and collective bargaining. The evidence is highly consistent with the proposition that most MNCs view union representation and collective bargaining as costly and act accordingly in making FDI decisions about where and how much to invest across alternative host locations. In particular, Cooke (1997, 2001a, 2001b) and Cooke and Noble (1998) have estimated the effects of national union penetration rates and centralised collective bargaining structures on the distribution of FDI, controlling for a wide range of market, socio-political, and other IR system factors (including differences in hourly compensation costs, education levels, and government workplace policies regarding layoffs and works councils). The evidence shows that the greater the union penetration in a country, the lesser the investment. FDI is reduced further in countries characterised by negotiation structures that are centralised beyond company-wide levels and in which there is extensive union contract coverage.[3] The estimated effects of union penetration and centralised bargaining structures, moreover, are found to be quite sizeable. Cooke (2001a) also finds that MNCs invest less in countries in which lost days of work due to work stoppages are greater. The effect of these union representation and collective bargaining factors on the distribution of FDI generally apply, moreover, to MNCs based in all highly developed countries (i.e. not just US-owned MNCs, which are usually characterised as being highly antiunion).

In summary, the evidence presented indicates that it is common practice for MNCs to pursue union avoidance strategies. First, MNCs invest less in countries in which the likelihood of being organised by unions or brought under collective bargaining agreements is higher. Second, where MNCs invest, they pursue IR strategies abroad that are designed to minimise the likelihood that their foreign locations will come under collective bargaining agreements. The outcome of these union avoidance strategies, furthermore, increases the prospects that MNCs can effectively pit unions across borders against each other by either shifting or threatening to shift investment to union or non-union operations. That is, through calculated 'coercive comparisons' made across their internationally integrated unionised and non-union operations, MNCs are better able to extract concessions from unions as each vies for scarce capital investment or limited production (Streeck 1992; Martines Lucio and Weston 1994; Marginson and Sisson 2002). One can reasonably conclude, therefore, that against a backdrop of extraordinary growth in corporate globalisation and generally declining or otherwise stagnating union membership worldwide, the evidence presented herein of union avoidance and marginalisation is bound to have shifted the balance of power in favour of MNCs. In the next section, we address the response of unions across borders to this growing challenge.

Transnational inter-union strategies

In response to the growing power of MNCs, national unions and global union federations have stepped-up their broader social, political, legal, and grassroots movement agendas designed to enhance union countervailing power (e.g. see the analyses made along these lines in the *World Labour Report* 1997: Chapter 2; Wells 1998; Waterman 1999; Nissen 1999; Gordon 2000). On the other hand, although unions have long engaged in cross-border consultation and have occasionally co-ordinated international corporate campaigns in response to global

IR strategies pursued by MNCs (e.g. Juravich and Bronfenbrenner 2003), unions have yet to mount sufficient transnational leverage to negotiate effectively with MNCs over the central global issue of FDI and movement-of-work decisions (and the negative consequences of these decisions on workers and unions). Although there appears to be a growing interest among union leaders across borders in forging more effective and enduring alliances for the purpose of engaging in transnational-level negotiations with MNCs, unions (with few and even then, limited exceptions) have not likewise reconfigured their collective bargaining structures beyond national boundaries.

As addressed by Ulman (1975) and Taira (1980–81) and more recently by a number of authors, differences in union contexts across countries make transnational co-ordination of collective bargaining problematic (e.g. Hyman 1999; Nissen 1999; Gordon and Turner 2000; Gennard and Ramsay 2003). In particular, unions have evolved quite differently with respect to strategic orientations and identities. Organisational priorities, structures, governance and control, policies, and customs across unions are, therefore, often markedly different, even within the same country, sector, or industry. Given these differences and the political, democratic nature of independent unions – unions, moreover, typically have deep-rooted desires for maintaining autonomy and national identity. Differences in national IR systems and social welfare policies further complicate how bargaining priorities would be set across borders and how collective bargaining would be conducted. A further barrier to forging partnerships is the substantial transaction cost that would be incurred, including that associated with overcoming language barriers. Cross-border partnerships, that is, would require unions to reallocate or increase their already limited budgets and devote key personnel to developing and co-ordinating transnational activities.

One need only look to the exceptional opportunity available to unions in Europe via the European Works Council Directive to appreciate the size of the challenge faced by unions in taking even initial steps toward forming transnational partnerships. Although some unions have apparently begun to form networks among themselves for the purpose of co-ordinated bargaining across borders, it does not appear that unions have yet to exploit the full opportunities available through the Directive (EIRR 2001b). Even within a legally mandated forum that by design brings together employees (typically union representatives) representing various locations of the same MNCs across European borders, few unions appear to have used this unique opportunity to overcome transnational barriers (including, in some cases, substantial distrust) and, in turn, to build even minimal alliances (Martin and Ross 2000; Beaupain et al. 2003).

Unions, nonetheless, have formed and participated in a wide range of global trade union federations (historically called 'international trade union secretariats') and other international associations. These international organisations have largely focused their attention on the pursuit of broader social and political agendas aimed at improving employment and workplace conditions, and protecting freedom of association and collective bargaining rights (Windmuller 2000; EIRR 2000; EIRR 2001a). Although some global union federations have formed various 'world company councils' around major MNCs, these councils have yet, with few exceptions it appears, evolved into inter-union partnerships expressly formed for the purpose of transnational collective bargaining with MNCs. Instead they have limited themselves to sharing of information, consultation, and modest tactical and financial support for each other's struggles (Gollbach and Schulten 2000; Marginson and Sisson 2002; EIRR 2001c).

Among the more concerted emerging efforts at forming partnerships are those being pursued by graphical worker unions in Europe and by the Union International Network (UNI) formed in 2000 by the merger of several former international trade secretariats (to which the graphical unions now belong). As described by Gennard and Ramsay (2003) and Gennard and Newsome (2005), graphical unions in Europe have been pursuing an ambitious transnational co-ordination strategy. Their efforts are based first on collecting, sharing, and analysing data across the various unionised locations of given MNCs and second on developing a long-term bargaining strategy under which unions pursue common demands across the various subsidiaries of MNCs. UNI, likewise, was formed for the expressed purpose of engaging MNCs and their unions in transnational negotiations. Although analyses of UNI's early success or lack of it are not available, its very creation marks an exceptional recognition by its roughly 1,000 member unions of the need and potential value of developing inter-union partnerships for the purpose of transnational collective bargaining with MNCs (*Financial Times* 2001, Ng 2001).

The generally limited forms of inter-union consultation and co-ordination around collective bargaining with MNCs described would not appear to constitute inter-union partnerships that can mount sufficient and sustainable resistance in the face of corporate globalisation and strategies pursued by MNCs to avoid or weaken unions. Hence, it would appear that most unions to date have concluded that the barriers are all but insurmountable or have otherwise concluded that the likely gain in relative power from forging such partnerships does not justify the costs incurred in restructuring themselves and collective bargaining beyond local or national boundaries. However, given the generally long-term decline in union penetration worldwide, on the one hand, and burgeoning corporate globalisation, on the other hand, the balance of power between labour and management continues to shift to the advantage of MNCs. Without some significant change in union strategies across borders, therefore, organised labour's power to improve the terms and conditions of employment across MNCs will likely erode further.

Based on his modelling of the exercise of power within the general context of a prisoner's dilemma game, Cooke (2005) addresses the essential conditions and incentives that unions across borders would need to satisfy to forge sustainable partnerships. Central among a number of practical, strategic-level implications, unions would first need to reach agreements among themselves whereby each national or local union would achieve greater gain through the aggregated relative power of the inter-union partnership than each would achieve by continuing to act primarily on its own. Because MNCs continue to restructure themselves as a result of mergers and acquisitions and through expansions and contractions of given operations, any given union partner at any given time, of course, will also face the potential displacement of its membership. As noted earlier, MNCs will also attempt to pit unions in one country against unions in other countries. Consequently, viewing each other as 'competitors' for investment and jobs, unions would need to develop strategies ensuring that no one partner would unduly gain at the expense of another and that any loss to a partner would be less than it would otherwise incur without the partnership. Moreover, the primary focus of collective bargaining strategies would be on minimising the ability of firms to pit unions across borders as competitors for investment and jobs.

In addition, inter-union partnerships would need to structure themselves and collective bargaining in ways that minimise any intervention in or disruption to existing national/local union organisational structures and decision-making; and in so doing, accommodate partners in the light of the substantial barriers described earlier. Whether or not unions across borders can ultimately satisfy the necessary conditions warranting such inter-union co-operation is a question yet to be answered. If the exceptional efforts, for example, by the graphical worker unions in Europe and UNI to forge such partnerships prove successful, other unions across borders may well follow suit.

Conclusions

Cast in a fairly comprehensive, albeit simplified analytical framework (depicted in Figure 15.1), we have examined several key and interrelated dimensions of the role of IR in the context of corporate globalisation. We began by addressing the logic of MNC business and configuration strategies as MNCs attempt to optimise profitability via how they position themselves in a global marketplace. Taking into account ownership advantages that can be exploited abroad and differences in location advantages across alternative host countries, MNCs decide where and how much to invest abroad. As reviewed, we have witnessed an extraordinary growth and spread of MNCs and FDI over the last two decades. This has occurred primarily through the acquisition of and merger with foreign-owned companies, resulting in an increasing shift in MNC investment away from domestic to foreign operations. An examination of FDI trends and patterns indicates, furthermore, that FDI remains highly concentrated. Most FDI is made by a very small proportion of today's more than 61,000 MNCs, who are headquartered in a mere handful of highly developed countries, who continue to concentrate the bulk of their FDI across a mere handful of highly developed countries, and who invest most of the remaining FDI across a relatively small number of developing economies.

Wherever MNCs invest, they must decide on the optimal IR strategies to pursue. For those MNCs enjoying IR ownership advantages in their home operations, headquarter executives will decide on which, if any, preferred IR policies and practices to diffuse abroad. Facing isomorphic pressures from host locations to adopt local workplace norms, customary practices, and institutional arrangements, decisions by parent company executives to diffuse IR practices abroad depend on cost–benefit calculations of the perceived net gain achievable by any efforts at diffusion. Here, executives would first weigh the potential operational gains that would be derived in fully diffusing their preferred IR strategies or core best practices abroad, as well as any gains from added organisational control and co-ordination of integrated operations by having uniform IR practices across their global networks of operations. Against these perceived potential benefits, executives would weigh the potential costs associated with diffusing preferred IR practices given both the capacity and receptivity of foreign subsidiaries. The evidence shows that the extent of diffusion falls along a continuum ranging from little or no diffusion to fairly extensive diffusion. It appears, nonetheless, that most MNCs seeking to diffuse preferred IR practices have created hybrid strategies in which IR practices common to host locations are deployed alongside preferred core practices diffused from the home office (ones often modified to some degree to better accommodate the foreign locale).

Central to any assessment of the IR strategies of MNCs are the roles of union representation and collective bargaining, which come into play both in the decisions MNCs make about where and how much to invest across alternative host locations, as well as in their decisions about the diffusion of preferred IR practices. With respect to the diffusion of IR strategies abroad, the evidence indicates that it is common practice among MNCs to avoid union representation and collective bargaining across their subsidiaries, except where the costs of avoidance are perceived as too high. The evidence also shows that MNCs shift production from unionised to non-union operations, in part one can reasonably presume, to reduce union leverage. Where they remain organised, MNCs often (but not always) encounter stiff resistance from unions to the diffusion of preferred IR practices seen by them as inconsistent with the optimisation of gains for their members. In turn, MNCs often engage in coercive comparisons by exercising the threat of divestment and movement of work to achieve concessions. With respect to MNC decisions about where and how much to invest abroad in the first place, the evidence shows that (everything else being the same) MNCs invest less in countries with higher union penetration rates and where collective bargaining is more centralised.

Finally, we examined the extent to which unions across borders have forged transnational inter-union partnerships for the purpose of collective bargaining with MNCs over FDI and movement-of-work decision-making. With few exceptions, unions have yet to forge alliances or partnerships along these lines but instead have engaged in fairly limited forms of information sharing and transnational consultation. As discussed, unions face numerous barriers to developing cross-border partnerships, the most challenging of which requires workable strategies on how equitably to share the potential gains and suffer the potential losses associated with MNC decisions regarding FDI and the movement of work in an ever-increasingly competitive and uncertain global marketplace.

In closing, IR issues and union-management relations are important in any assessment of multinationals and globalisation. Given the continued growth and spread of FDI, the steady shift in investment by MNCs away from home operations to foreign operations, the persistent changes in MNC business and configuration strategies in response to intense global competition, and the consequent organisational disruptions resulting from mergers and acquisitions activity that underpins most FDI, the potential for substantial displacement of workers at home and abroad cannot be dismissed. Against this backdrop of flux and unprecedented expansion of MNC operations that easily permeate borders, few unions have yet effectively to bridge the borders that separate them. Given the general decline in their leverage to optimise gains for workers in the face of corporate globalisation, however, the time may indeed soon come whereby transnational inter-union partnerships directly engage MNCs in negotiations over FDI and the movement of work across borders.

Notes

1 Data drawn from UNTCAD, 2004. Specifically, the ratio of the value of M&As (Annex Table B.7, p.411) is divided by the value of FDI outflows (Annex Table B.2, p. 372).
2 1989 data are taken from *US Direct Investment Abroad*, 1989: Table II.A.2, p. 43. 2001 data taken from Mataloni, 2003: Table 12.2 and Table 13.
3 This union contract coverage is the product of highly centralised negotiations between unions and employer federations. By law, government policy, or accepted practice, these agreements are 'extended' to employers on an industry-, occupation-, or country-wide basis. Based on the latest published estimates available (*World Labour Report 1997–98*: Table 3.2, p. 248), the following contract coverage rates are reported for the mid-1990s: Denmark (55%), France (90%), Germany (90%), Ireland (90%), the Netherlands (80%), Norway (66%), Spain (82%), and Sweden (85%).

References

Beaumont, P., Cressey, P., and Jakobsen, P. (1990) 'Some key industrial features of West German subsidiaries in Britain', *Employee Relations*, 12(6): 3–8.
Beaupain, T., Jefferys, S. and Annand, R. (2003) 'Early days: Belgian and UK experiences of European works councils' in W. Cooke (ed.) *Multinational Companies and Global Human Resource Strategies*. Westport, CT: Quorum Books: 329–346.

Bird, A., Taylor, S. and Beechler, S. (1998) 'A typology of international human resource management in Japanese multinational corporations: organisational implications', *Human Resource Management*, 37(2): 159–72.

Brewster, C. and Tregaskis, O. (2003) 'Convergence or divergence of contingent employment practices? Evidence of the role of MNCs in Europe', in W. Cooke (ed.) *Multinational Companies and Global Human Resource Strategies*, Westport, CT: Quorum Books: 143–65.

Buckley, P. J. and Casson, M. C. (1976) *The Future of the Multinational Enterprise*, London: Macmillan.

Casson, M. C. and Buckley, P. J. (1998) 'Models of the multinational enterprise', *Journal of International Business Studies*, 29(1): 21–44.

Cooke, W. N. (2005) 'Exercising power in a prisoner's dilemma: transnational collective bargaining in an era of corporate globalisation?', *Industrial Relations Journal*, 36(4): 283–302.

— (1997) 'The influence of industrial relations factors on US foreign direct investment abroad', *Industrial and Labour Relations Review*, 50(1): 3–17.

— (2001a) 'The effects of labour costs and workplace constraints on foreign direct investment among highly industrialised countries', *International Journal of Human Resource Management*, 12(5): 697–716.

— (2001b) 'Union avoidance and foreign direct investment in the USA', *Employee Relations Journal*, 23(6): 558–80.

Cooke, W. N. and Noble, D. (1998) 'Industrial relations systems and US foreign direct investment abroad,' *British Journal of Industrial Relations*, 36(4): 581–609.

Doeringer, P. B., Evans-Klock, C. and Terkla, D. G. (1998) 'Hybrids or hodgepodges? Workplace practices of Japanese and domestic startups in the United States', *Industrial and Labour Relations Review*, 51(2):171–86.

Dunning, J. H. (1993) *Multinational Enterprises and the Global Economy*, New York: Addison-Wesley.

Edwards, T., Collier, X., Orits, L., Rees, C. and Wortmann, M. (2005) 'How important are national industrial relations systems in shaping restructuring in multinational companies?', *European Journal of industrial Relations* (in press).

EIRR (2000) 'International trade secretariats in focus – part one', *European Industrial Relations Review*, 318 (July): 29–32.

EIRR (2001a) 'ITSs in focus – part two', *European Industrial Relations Review*, 324 (January): 26–9.

EIRR (2001b) 'EWCs taking on a bargaining role?', *European Industrial Relations Review*, 322 (September): 24–7.

EIRR (2001c) 'International trade secretariats in focus – part three', *European Industrial Relations Review*, 327 (April): 31–6.

EIRR (2002) 'Global agreements spread', *European Industrial Relations Review*, 341 (June): 29–32.

Ferner, A. and Quintanilla, J. (1998) 'Multinationals, national business systems and HRM: the enduring influence of national identity or a process of Anglo-Saxonisation', *International Journal of Human Resource Management*, 9(4): 710–31.

Financial Times (2001) 'More jobs are on the line', September 19: IX.

Florida, R. and Kenney, M. (1991) 'Organisation vs. culture: Japanese automotive transplants in the US', *Industrial Relations Journal*, 22: 181–96.

Gennard, J. and Newsome, K. (2005) 'Barriers to cross-border trade union cooperation in Europe: The case of the graphical workers', *Industrial Relations Journal*, 36(1): 38–58.

Gennard, J. and Ramsay, H. (2003) 'Strategic international labourism: MNCs and labour in the graphical sector' in W. Cooke (ed.) *Multinational Companies and Global Human Resource Strategies*, Westport, CT: Quorum Books: 269–92.

Gollbach, J. and Schulten, T. (2000) 'Cross-Border collective bargaining networks in Europe', *European Journal of Industrial Relations*, 6(2): 161–79.

Gordon, M. (2000) 'The International Confederation of Free Trade Unions: bread, freedom, and peace' in M. Gordon and L. Turner (eds) *Transnational Cooperation among Labour Unions*, Ithaca, NY: Cornell University Press: 81–101.

Gordon, M. and Turner, L. (2000) 'Making transnational collaboration work' in M. Gordon and L. Turner (eds) *Transnational Cooperation among Labour Unions*, Ithaca, NY: Cornell University Press: 256–61.

Guest, D. and Hoque, K. (1996) 'National ownership and HR practices in UK greenfield sites', *Human Resource Management Journal*, 6(4): 50–74.

Gunnigle, P., O'Sullivan, M. and Kinsella, M. (2002) 'Organised labour in the new economy: trade unions and public policy in the Republic of Ireland' in D. D'Art and T. Turner (eds) *Irish Employment Relations in the New Economy,* Dublin: Blackhall Press.

Gunnigle, P., Collings, D. G., and Morley, M. (2004) 'Hosting the multinational: exploring the dynamics of industrial relations in US multinational subsidiaries in Ireland'. Paper presented at *Multinationals and the International Diffusion of Organisational Forms and Practices: Convergence and Diversity within the Global Economy*, IESE Business School and DeMontfort University, Barcelona, Spain, July, 2004.

Hennart, J. F. and Park, Y. R. (1994) 'Location, governance, and strategic determinants of Japanese manufacturing investment in the United States', *Strategic Management Journal*, 15: 419–36.

Huxley, C. (2003) 'Local union responses to continental standardisation of production and work in GM's North American truck assembly plants' in W. Cooke (ed.) *Multinational Companies and Global Human Resource Strategies*, Westport, CT: Quorum Books: 223–47.

Hyman, R. (1999) 'Five alternative scenarios for West European unionism' in R. Munck and P. Waterman (eds) *Labour Worldwide in the Era of Globalisation*, New York: St. Martin's Press: 121–30.

Hymer, S. (1976) *The International Operations of National Firms*, Cambridge, Mass: MIT Press.

Juravich, T. and Bronfenbrenner, K. (2003) 'Out of the ashes: the steelworkers' global campaign at Bridgestone/Firestone' in W. Cooke (ed.) *Multinational Companies and Global Human Resource Strategies*, Westport, CT: Quorum Books: 249–68.

Kenney, M. and Tanaka, S. (2003) 'Transferring the learning factory to America? The Japanese television assembly transplants' in W. Cooke (ed.) *Multinational Companies and Global Human Resource Strategies*, Westport, CT: Quorum Books: 123–42.

Korbin, S. J. (1991) 'An empirical analysis of the determinants of global integration', *Strategic Management Journal*, 12(5): 17–31.

Kostova, T. (1999) 'Transnational transfer of strategic organisational practices: a contextual perspective', *Academy of Management Review*, 24(2): 308–24.

Marginson, P. and Sisson, K. (2002) 'European dimensions to collective bargaining: new symmetries within an asymmetric process?' *Industrial Relations Journal*, 33(4): 332–50.

Martin, A. and Ross, G. (2000) 'European integration and the Europeanisation of labour' in M. Gordon and L. Turner (eds), *Transnational Cooperation among Labour Unions*, Ithaca, NY: Cornell University Press: 120–49.

Martin, G., Beaumont, P. and Pate, J. (2003) 'A process model of strategic HRM/LR change in MNCs: The case of AT&T and NCR in the UK' in W. Cooke (ed.), *Multinational Companies and Global Human Resource Strategies*, Westport, CT: Quorum Books: 101–22.

Martines Lucio, M. and Weston, S. (1994) 'New management practices in a multinational corporation: the restructuring of worker representation and rights?' *Industrial Relations Journal*, 25: 110–21.

Mataloni, R. J. (2003) 'US multinational company operations in 2001', *Survey of Current Business*, November, pp. 85–105.

Miles, R. E. and Snow, C. C. (1978) *Organisational Strategy, Structure, and Process*, New York: McGraw-Hill.

Ng, C. (2001) 'Improving labour standards in a globalising world: trade unions' aspirations and responses', *Philippine Journal of Labour and Industrial Relations*, 21(1 and 2): 105–21.

Nissen, B. (1999) 'Alliances across borders: US labour in the era of globalisation', *Working USA*, (May/June): 43–55.

Porter, M. E. (1985) *Competitive Advantage: Creating and Sustaining Superior Performance*, New York: Free Press.

Porter, M. E. (1991) 'Towards a dynamic theory of strategy', *Strategic Management Journal*, 12: 95–117.

Purcell, W., Nicholas, S., Merrett, D. and Whitwell, G. (1999) 'The transfer of human resource and management practice by Japanese multinationals to Australia: do industry, size and experience matter?', *The International Journal of Human Resource Management*, 10(1): 72–88.

Rosenzweig, P. M. and Singh, J. V. (1991) 'Organizational environments and the multinational enterprise', *Academy of Management Review*, 16: 340–61.

Royle, T. and Towers, B. (2003) 'Regulating employee interest representation: the case of McDonald's in the European Union' in W. Cooke (ed.) *Multinational Companies and Global Human Resource Strategies*, Westport, CT: Quorum Books: 347–68.

Streeck, W. (1992) 'National diversity, regime competition and institutional deadlock: problems in forming a European industrial relations system', *Journal of Public Policy*, 12(4): 301–30.

Taira, K. (1980–81) 'Labour and business in a new international economic order: will workers of the world unite?' *Hokudai Economic Papers*, 10: 68–87.

Ulman, L. (1975) 'Multinational unionism: incentives, barriers, and alternatives', *Industrial Relations*, 14(1): 1–31.

UNTCAD (2004) *World Investment Report 2004*, New York: United Nations.

US Direct Investment Abroad (1989) US Department of Commerce, Bureau of Economic Analysis, Washington D.C.

Waterman, P. (1999) 'The new social unionism: a new union model for a new world order' in R. Munck and P. Waterman (eds) *Labour Worldwide in the Era of Globalisation*, New York: St. Martin's Press: 247–64.

Wells, D. (1998) 'Building transnational coordinative unionism' in H. Juares Nunes and S. Babson, *Confronting Change: Auto Labour and Lean Production in North America*, Puebla, Mexico: Benemerita Univeridad Autonoma de Puebla: 487–505.

Windmuller, J. (2000) 'The international trade secretariats' in M. Gordon and L. Turner (eds) *Transnational Cooperation among Labour Unions*, Ithaca, NY: Cornell University Press: 102–19.

World Labour Report (1997–98) Geneva: International Labour Office.

Suggested key readings

Bird, A., Taylor, S. and Beechler, S. (1998) 'A typology of international human resource management in Japanese multinational corporations: organisational implications', *Human Resource Management*, 37(2): 159–72.

Cooke, W. N. (2005) 'Exercising power in a prisoner's dilemma: transnational collective bargaining in an era of corporate globalisation?' *Industrial Relations Journal,* 36(4): 283–302.

Cooke, W. N. (2003) (ed.) *Multinational Companies and Global Human Resource Strategies*, Westport, CT: Quorum Books.

Cooke, W. N. and Noble, D. (1998) 'Industrial relations systems and US foreign direct investment abroad', *British Journal of Industrial Relations*, 36(4): 581–609.

Dunning, J. H. (1993) *Multinational Enterprises and the Global Economy*, New York: Addison-Wesley.

Ferner, A and Quintanilla, J. (1998) 'Multinationals, national business systems and HRM: the enduring influence of national identity or a process of Anglo-Saxonisation', *International Journal of Human Resource Management*, 9(4): 710–31.

Gennard, J. and Newsome, K. (2005) 'Barriers to cross-border trade union cooperation in Europe: the case of the graphical workers', *Industrial Relations Journal*, 36(1): 38–58.

Gordon, M. and Turner, L. (eds) (2000) *Transnational Cooperation among Labour Unions*, Ithaca, NY: Cornell University Press.

Marginson, P. and Sisson, K. (2002) 'European dimensions to collective bargaining: new symmetries within an asymmetric process?' *Industrial Relations Journal*, 33(4): 332–50.

Porter, M. E. (1991) 'Towards a dynamic theory of strategy', *Strategic Management Journal*, 12: 95–117.

Index